RACE, CLASS, AND NATIONALISM IN THE TWENTY-FIRST-CENTURY CARIBBEAN

RACE, CLASS, AND NATIONALISM IN THE TWENTY-FIRST-CENTURY CARIBBEAN

EDITED BY
SCOTT TIMCKE
AND SHELENE GOMES

THE UNIVERSITY OF
GEORGIA PRESS
ATHENS

Portions of this work appeared previously, in somewhat different form: chapter 8 as "Sociolinguistic Indexicalities in Ethnic Diversity: Perceptions of Ethnicity and Language in Suriname," by Gerald Stell, in *New West Indian Guide / Nieuwe West-Indische Gids* 92, nos. 1–2 (2018): 35–61, reprinted courtesy of the author under creative commons license CC BY 4.0 DEED (https://creativecommons.org/licenses/by/4.0/); chapter 11 as "Caribbean Exceptions: The Problem of Race and Nation in Dominican Studies," by Brendan Jamal Thornton and Diego I. Ubiera, in *Latin American Research Review* 54, no. 2 (2019): 413–28, doi:10.25222/larr.346, reprinted under creative commons license CC BY 4.0 DEED (https://creativecommons.org/licenses/by/4.0/); chapter 13 as "Social Structure and Institutional Incongruity: The Background of Guyana's 2020 Elections Impasse," by Duane Edwards, in *Journal of Eastern Caribbean Studies* 45, no. 3 (2020): 33–59; and chapter 16 as "A Caribbean Perspective on China–Caribbean Relations: Global IR, Dependency and the Postcolonial Condition," © Ruben Gonzalez-Vicente and Annita Montout 2021 taken from Third World Quarterly © 2021, Vol 42 (2), © 2021 Global South Ltd © 2020, reprinted by permission of the publisher, Taylor & Francis Ltd., http://www.tandfonline.com, on behalf of the 2021 Global South Ltd.

© 2024 by the University of Georgia Press
Athens, Georgia 30602
www.ugapress.org
All rights reserved
Set in 10.25/13.5 Minion 3 Regular by Kaelin Chappell Broaddus

Most University of Georgia Press titles are available from popular e-book vendors.

Printed digitally

Library of Congress Cataloging-in-Publication Data
Names: Timcke, Scott, editor. | Gomes, Shelene, editor.
Title: Race, class, and nationalism in the twenty-first-century Caribbean / edited by Scott Timcke and Shelene Gomes.
Description: Athens : The University of Georgia Press, [2024] | Includes bibliographical references and index.
Identifiers: LCCN 2024013182 | ISBN 9780820366364 (hardback) | ISBN 9780820367026 (paperback) | ISBN 9780820367033 (epub) | ISBN 9780820367040 (pdf)
Subjects: LCSH: Caribbean Area—Social conditions—1945- | Caribbean Area—Race relations. | Social classes—Caribbean Area. | Nationalism—Caribbean Area.
Classification: LCC HN192.5 .R325 2024 | DDC 306.09729—dc23/eng/20240708
LC record available at https://lccn.loc.gov/2024013182

CONTENTS

CHAPTER 1. The Fundamentals Have Not Changed: A Critical Introduction to the Caribbean | SCOTT TIMCKE   1

PART ONE. Formations and Formulations

CHAPTER 2. The Shifting Construction of Difference Making in Trinidad | DYLAN KERRIGAN   27

CHAPTER 3. Leeward Islander Regionalism in Antigua and Barbuda | STANLEY H. GRIFFIN   54

PART TWO. History and Activism

CHAPTER 4. Garifuna Deportees and Land Defense in the Bay of Trujillo | JUAN VICENTE IBORRA MALLENT AND KIMBERLY PALMER   79

CHAPTER 5. Labors of Love: Returnee Women's Care-Motivated Migration | SHELENE GOMES, ANTONIA MUNGAL, AND MARIA THÉRÈSE GOMES   100

CHAPTER 6. The Politics of Civic Ascription and Self-Fashioning in Contemporary Cuba | JULIO CÉSAR GUANCHE AND MAIKEL PONS-GIRALT   120

CHAPTER 7. Masculinism and Gendered Power Relations in the Caribbean Left | AMÍLCAR PETER SANATAN   143

PART THREE. Domination and Expression

CHAPTER 8. Perceptions of Ethnicity and Language Use in Suriname | GERALD STELL   161

CHAPTER 9. Thinking beyond the Coloniality of Power with Patrick Chamoiseau | SAVRINA CHINIEN   181

CHAPTER 10. Cultivating Black Authenticity in Jamaican Popular Music |
NADIA WHITEMAN-CHARLES   201

CHAPTER 11. The Problem of Race and Nation in Dominican Studies |
BRENDAN JAMAL THORNTON AND DIEGO I. UBIERA   227

CHAPTER 12. Moving beyond Narrow Nationalist Historiography |
JEROME TEELUCKSINGH   251

PART FOUR. Local Politics and International Pressures

CHAPTER 13. The Background of Guyana's 2020 Election Impasse |
DUANE EDWARDS   269

CHAPTER 14. Global Capitalism and Regime Volatility in Suriname |
JACK MENKE   296

CHAPTER 15. Antisystem Politics in the Postcolonial Predicament |
SCOTT TIMCKE   314

CHAPTER 16. China and the Caribbean beyond South-South Relations |
RUBEN GONZALEZ-VICENTE AND ANNITA MONTOUTE   341

Acknowledgments   361

Contributors   363

Index   367

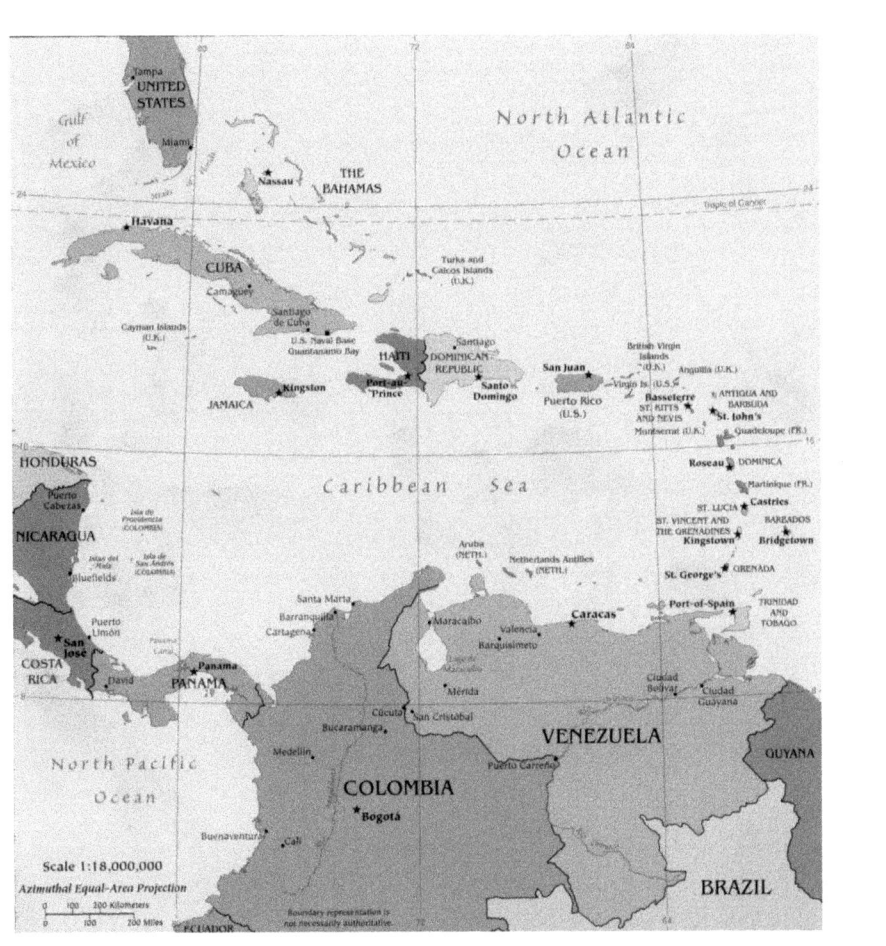

Map of the twenty-first-century Caribbean

RACE, CLASS, AND NATIONALISM IN THE TWENTY-FIRST-CENTURY CARIBBEAN

CHAPTER 1

The Fundamentals Have Not Changed
A Critical Introduction to the Caribbean

SCOTT TIMCKE

All the transformative thinkers from the Caribbean spoke with such incisiveness and urgency. And many were placed under house arrest, exiled, or murdered. Frantz Fanon, Walter Rodney, Claudia Jones, Jacqueline Creft, and C. L. R. James are well known, but there are many more. And the list grows longer year by year. When it is convenient, the nationalists who have ascended to power ritualistically invoke these names but not their convictions. Reduced to intellectual iconography, the rich analysis of such thinkers lies outside centers of power. Instead, those who now rule license programs of elite enrichment and the looting of the state, the harms of which are compounded by an eager collaboration with local and global capital. This project is supported through the embracing of a value system that accepts a repressive racialized class structure, using it to shore up minority-class rule. As to be expected, this exploitation is denied by those who occupy the commanding heights of the Caribbean political economy.

Given its history of violent antagonisms, the Caribbean has been an extraordinary site for the development of a considerable span of ideologies and regimes, ranging from Trujillo and Duvalier to Manley and Castro. As "power here is more naked than in any other part of the world," to employ a line from James's *The Black Jacobins*, it has also thoroughly tested concepts, theory, and analysis like few other places. More than equal to this task was James's method of revisiting the totality of social life. This approach involves more than a standpoint or history from below; it includes an analysis of high politics and crises in the ruling class, of revolutionary and reactionary politics. And as James demonstrates, the West Indian plantation system existed to produce sugar. The depravities of that system came about because of the demand for forced labor; racism "justified" the violence and abjection used to keep the enslaved working.[1]

This line of analysis with its attention to political economy was strengthened and deployed by the New World Group in the 1960s.[2] It also found expression in entities like the New Jewel Movement in Grenada, the Working People's Alliance in Guyana, and other popular street movements that conceptualized decolonization as necessarily exploring the dialectics of race and class. Yet this historical sociological framework has since been replaced with narrow cultural and ethnically based nationalisms, as Anton Allahar has described.[3] Such a turn correlates with the arrival of neoliberalism in the region. In the 1980s the rule of the market was strengthened, with a corresponding decline in the status of radical thought, observable in the marginalization and purging of radicals from institutions of governance and scholarship. What arose was a powerful political motivation as Caribbean states sought to legitimate the polity by providing the proverbial "peace, order, and good government." But as Selwyn Ryan writes, this led to the deterioration of social cohesion.[4]

Like Lothrop Stoddard, who could only see "race" as the sole axis of politics in the region, contemporary nationalists have recast nineteenth- and twentieth-century Caribbean history as primarily a conflict between white supremacy and Black nationalism, with the former seeking to enforce minority rule and the latter looking to incorporate Blacks as full members of the polity through enfranchisement and subsequently designing means for upward social mobility. But at times this produced, as Shona Jackson argues, a flat understanding of the Caribbean that overlooks centuries of Indigenous genocide, creolization, exploitation, and culture contact.[5]

The inversion of the Stoddard thesis can also be seen in the present moment where in the Caribbean demands to remove statues depicting colonizers and slave owners have gained considerable traction. But there is also a refusal to broach the issues of higher marginal taxes, examine the role of Caribbean tax havens in maintaining the global racial wealth gap, pursue aggressive mobilization for wealth redistribution, or establish more worker cooperative enterprises of major industries. For these nationalist elements, even suggesting that the multiracial Caribbean elite consciously perpetuates whiteness is deemed blasphemy. Through this partiality, nationalists are actively implementing many of the mechanisms that Michel-Rolph Trouillot identified, where dishonest misrepresentation and repeated inaccuracies come to be accepted as fact.[6] So it is very much worth repeating James's remarks in the appendix to the 1963 edition of *The Black Jacobins*: "In 1963 the old colonial system is not what it was in 1863; in 1863 it was not what it had been in 1763 or 1663." But "the fundamentals," he writes, "have not changed."[7] Nationalism thrives by silencing these fundamentals. Accordingly, from my perspective, the goal here is not to engage in an either/or debate on race and class. Others have cleared that area well.[8] Rather, it is to form an understanding of how and why they both matter to comprehend the contemporary Caribbean. Along with other concepts, they are necessary to develop the kinds of nuanced histories James produced.

Historical moments are complex and cannot be explained by any simple correlation between race, nationalism, and ideology. Nor can programmatic agendas be solely explained by referring to the objective membership of a class that presupposes a fully formed consciousness. Similarly, racial identities are not "false consciousness" imposed onto subordinate classes; they are projects that have been made and remade by the working class and petty bourgeoisie themselves. Nevertheless, the sociological task is to analyze the material factors that give rise to these subjective experiences, not to cynically use them to rule and perpetuate capitalist exploitation. Despite the legion of books on nationalism in the Caribbean, few have attempted to look at it as a political invention that does not, and cannot, serve the interests of all—how essentialist, reductive, overdetermining nationalism is a political and conceptual confusion that forever stalls the project of universal human emancipation.

This collection focuses on the political dynamics of race, class, and nationalism in the contemporary Caribbean. In their collective expression, the curated chapters help trace these processes through the contours of a broader political, economic, and social geography. Notions of racial identity have changed over time, but this series of reformations is not independent of class rule or nationalism either. The contributors examine these dynamics through the lens of several case studies focused on the development of political organizations, hardships, and ideology to map some of the main social relations in the Caribbean in the early twenty-first century while also exploring why unsatisfactory explanations for race, class, and nationalism have increased in prominence. Put differently, to take the radical debate forward they have sought to concentrate on what is essentially the project of self-determination outside of capitalism while also examining how elites enamored with nationalism undermine that struggle. The critique in this book is less about chastising nationalists, or any other ideological grouping that may wield power. Rather, the goal is to undertake a collective political analysis driven by a positive commitment to liberation in all its forms.

Presently there is much debate about whether racialized experience is produced by fungibility, disposability, precarity, stigma, abjection, functional inequality, or station within a sociopolitical order. As conceptualization varies across different bodies of academic literature, there is utility in setting out some of the primary terms in this collection. Shaped by the work of Frantz Fanon, Achille Mbembe argues that race "is more a mechanism of attribution than of self-designation."[9] This is not to deny that people can find affirmation in ascribed racial identities. Indeed, Aimé Césaire is well known for sustained difficult reflection on this matter. The tension between ascription and affirmation can be empirically shown in language use about racial positioning, as a few of the chapters discuss. Still, as a malleable fiction, ideas and expression of race constantly shift with the politics of the time, also like the contributors note. In line with the full implications of the social construction of identity, it is useful to look at the totality of historically situated social relations, rather than just the intersections of partial discrete elements. Beyond a narrow vision of politics wherein persons are overdetermined by civic ascriptions or affirmation, our point here is that identities are synthetic products used to justify burdens and deprivations or rewards and abundances.

At the same time, there are ways in which race is currently connected to projects that stem from natal politics. The racial essentialism of Caribbean nationalisms enrolls a politics of authenticity where certain kinds of ideas, tastes, and experiences are deemed "Black," for instance. Regardless of whether there is a strong or weak ideological commitment to viewing race as an essentialist category, this comprehension has an irrecoverable fault as it plots no pathway to make race a negligible element in life chances. Additionally, these perspectives suggest that "mere facticity" anchors one's political agenda—that points of origin are points of destination. This natal politics is at right angles to what scholars know about how material culture is shaped by history.

Whereas these two points concern the connection between the philosophy of the person and political agendas, our third point is empirical. Great caution should be taken when encountering monocausal explanations of racial outcomes. Especially in Guyana, Suriname, and Trinidad, where there are cleavages between Afro- and Indo-Caribbean people, politics is organized in such a way that political institutions—when occupied—often perpetuate racial clientelism. As such, once one recognizes that conceptualizations of race necessarily alternate between rigidity and flexibility to serve as a rationalization for dynamic mechanisms of domination, then the apparent inconsistencies in the politics of racial brokerage can be more easily explained. In short, race matters because class matters.

Key Issues in the Critical Analysis of the Contemporary Caribbean

Arguably, one of the most significant changes in the past twenty years in the Caribbean has been—due largely to trade liberalization—a shift away from traditional agricultural commodity exports like bananas in Saint Lucia and other Windward Island producers. The sugar industry also collapsed in Saint Kitts and Nevis, Guyana, Puerto Rico, and Trinidad and Tobago, among other places. While there have been some efforts toward agricultural diversification, almost all of these countries have become overwhelmingly dependent on service-based industries like tourism. But as Kamala Kempadoo's extensive studies of the social changes brought about by the rise of the service sector show, Caribbean political economy typically "rests upon sexual energies" that take advantage of preexisting "fluid types of transactional sexual relations." As a result, "Caribbean colonial and postcolonial states are increasingly incorporating sexuality into their national strategies for competing in the globalized economy."[10] Effectively, Caribbean states leverage the bodies of their citizens to take earnings from tourists.

Concurrently, as the persistent undercollection of taxes and redistribution efforts show, Caribbean states lack effectiveness. For example, Antigua and Barbuda has no income taxes; unsurprisingly, it is also the fifteenth most unequal country in the world. These developments are supplemented by various citizenship by investment programs that hinge on low tax regimes and the general hardening of social boundaries through gated communities, exclusive invite-only events, and other "pay to play" transactions for social encounters. The looping effect is that states are less willing or able to provide basic services. Even capitalists and upper-middle-class professionals feel the strain. Factors like these drive external migratory flows. For those that remain, the fear of crime cultivates calls for "strong men" to provide social and economic security for those families whose mild gains following independence are ever more threatened by precarity. These realities are causally connected with interpersonal violence in poor communities as gangs seek to provide the security the state often cannot.

Other demographic factors sit side by side with class decomposition. For example, from the 1970s the ethnic composition of Suriname's population changed significantly. Most striking was the growth of people who identify as Maroon. Following a gold mining boom that employs Maroon workers, this sector has moved to the center of the country's politics, greatly shifting electoral dynamics. Nearby Guyana is on the precipice of upheaval. Already sugar, rice, gold, shrimp, timber, and bauxite make up 90 percent of its exports and nearly 60 percent of the country's GDP, but in the past few years significant quantities of oil have been discovered in the Suriname-Guyana basin. There is hope that oil will act as a catalyst for Guyana's development. Given the country's governance structures, however, it is more likely that existing patterns of extraction, exploitation, and rent seeking will exacerbate social inequality and other social ills. Already, the quality of governance in Guyana is hindered by protracted conflict between indigenous Amerindians and Indo- and Afro-Guyanese. Meanwhile, Guyanese political factions compete for the short-term spoils from the very oil policies that will likely leave their offices submerged by rising sea levels.

Undoubtedly the climate emergency will bring great ecological and economic losses to the region. Right now, the Cayman Islands is undertaking climate risk assessments to mitigate these crises. But these plans can be juxtaposed against reports that "Cayman's per capita emissions are some of the highest in the world and significantly higher than the rest of this region."[11] In Martinique a chronically high unemployment rate has led to a significant demographic change. By some estimates a full one-third of the population has moved to metropolitan France. Those remaining contend with exposure to and ecological disaster borne from chlordecone toxicity. Like in Guadeloupe, local crops are contaminated; to wit, "epidemiological studies have revealed that there are effects during critical windows of exposure ... and possibly long-term effects such as cancer with side effects for pregnancy and infant development."[12]

Other countries in the region are experimenting with debt-restructuring instruments, such as Belize receiving debt relief on USD $5.3 billion provided it funds a USD $23 million environmental trust and otherwise invests in marine conservation of barrier reefs.[13] With memories of colonial drainage and reparations in mind—but not explicitly stated—the Caribbean Development Bank advocates for rich countries to finance climate adaption measures in small island developing states.[14] As countries like these are especially prone to coastal flooding, Mia Mottley in Barbados suggests a 1 percent tax on high emitters to offset the losses to GDP due to the climate emergency. It remains to be seen if Mottley's ideas excuse high emitters like Trinidad and Tobago.

Nationalists are quick to point to the imperial and neocolonial activities of the United States, France, the United Kingdom, and Canada and these countries' long-standing connection to enslavement, racism, and modes of domination. At the same time, nationalists eagerly seek to do business with these markets. While notwithstanding the rhetoric of integration based on a "common civilization," intra-Caribbean trade is negligible. Attempts at regional integration through the formation of a customs union—a project underway since the mid-1980s—have mostly been a process of market building through lowering barriers, but there has also been considerable skepticism that outright rejects the transfer of power from countries to regional regulatory bodies. For example, local economic elites have frequently used ties with their local political class to retain protectionist measures for their existing local market share. On the relationships to importers and exporters more broadly, Caribbean nationalists are especially silent on the human rights abuses in China, hesitant to ask questions about whether the abuses of Uyghurs constitute enslavement. When pressed, nationalists invoke pragmatism. Reality imposes hard choices, they say. But rarely does the hard choice place limits on the self-interest of the most powerful groups in Caribbean societies.

Yet not all developments are bad. The expansion of educational infrastructure has been one notable success. Trinidad and Tobago, riding an economic boom in the first decade of the 2000s was able to invest in higher education in an unparalleled way for an Anglophone Caribbean country. The student population grew as the government introduced the Government Assistance for Tuition Expenses (GATE) program. Unfortunately, the neoliberal underpinnings of the higher education market and elusive goal of "attaining first-world status" designed an education system with severe shortcomings. Still, this project achieved one of the highest levels of tertiary education achievement in the Caribbean. In another development the Cuban public health care system invests in research and development to maintain good accessible medical facilities.

Finally, one notable change is the calls for reparations that acknowledge the long-term impacts of colonialism on the region. This is an admirable development that unfortunately coincides with the systemic devaluation of the Caribbean heritage sector. In Jamaica, for instance, the 1987 Jamaica National Heritage Trust (JNHT) Act and subsequent amendments lack the institutional and governmental backing to implement and operationalize its main objectives of researching and preserving Jamaican culture and heritage.[15] It is quite ironic that an increased interest in the modern-day ramifications of the colonial past occurs in a political climate that is simultaneously disinterested in the historical processes that justify reparative action. This leaves us asking, "After reparations, what then?"

National Expressions of Neoliberalism

Responding to the rise of postwar social democracies, late twentieth-century capitalists instituted a revanche of the market. As the impact of this revanche spans the totality of social life, it is hard to isolate discrete elements, but there are some common features like using deregulated market coordination aided by novel applications of communications and computation to primarily address social problems, most often through the sphere of financial exchange. Given how centrally money mediates social relations, the result is "the commodification and commercialization of everything," as David Harvey calls it.[16] The universalization of the market and its accumulative impulse mean that the pursuit of value has colonized the whole world, creating a "unified field for global capitalism."[17] As Norman Girvan anticipated, in this unified field the preferred monetary policy permitted the mobility of capital helping multinational corporations do business on their terms, making and taking profits across state jurisdictions, seeking to shape the outline of the state to their benefit.[18] Certainly, capital fights states when they seek to limit the influence of capital or bend to popular calls for social protections from the market. But capital also needs states to perpetuate a regime of accumulation, protect private property and profits, and curtail workers' power. Girvan's view that the Anglo-Caribbean is "in-dependence" partly due to the limited project of national elites aligns with my view that nationalists are useful compradors who have furthered the ends of neoliberalism, deeming it an acceptable system of political management provided that some cultural realms are left relatively untouched.[19]

While there is no master transition to neoliberalism—for it was polycentric and a series of conjunctural conditions are always at play—technical assistance programs shifted to favor greater fiscal restraint, trade liberalization, and privatization. Within the Western Hemisphere, Pinochet's government in Chile was a laissez-faire laboratory for the "shock doctrine" of neoliberal policy prescriptions.[20] In the short term Chile's initial growth and low inflation were contrasted with significant crises in neighboring Argentina, Brazil, and Peru. Regionally, there was a collapse of confidence in Latin American populists like Peron, Allende, and Alan Garcia in the 1980s. As Robert Kaufman and Barbara Stallings wrote specifically about these governments, "The economic and political limitations of populist policy cycles" led to "very high levels of inflation, stagnation of growth and exports, capital flight, and political polarization."[21]

The change in material conditions was reinforced by a significant change in the way of governing. In the 1980s neoliberal reasoning provided a commensurate intellectual framework for justifying tight fiscal and monetary policies.[22] Constraining and undermining the public sector became prescriptive de jure for the vanguard championing of market rule, although uneven and conditioned by local circumstances. At the same time the Reagan administration altered relationships with the Third World (as the Global South was then called) through low-intensity conflicts.[23] These "small wars" were arming insurgents to destabilize governments that resisted the "Washington Consensus."[24] The "lawfare" of neoliberalization found local elites in the periphery, then sought to interpolate them to act as agents.

Following the 2008 Great Recession there was a resurgence in academic studies predicated on the critique of mature neoliberal capitalist political economy. But while this critical wave was global in nature—meaning it spanned hemispheres and was not confined to metropoles—and while it very much sharpened the hereunto diluted Marxist arguments that could be found in orthodox studies of globalization and neoliberal development—two mainstay topics in Caribbean studies—the impact of this intellectual turn remains somewhat absent when one scans the academic work produced in the region. Certainly, there are anticapitalist studies done by Caribbeanists—many of whom are in active conversation with the currents of their chosen disciplines; Carole Boyce Davies's *Left of Karl Marx*, Peter Hudson's *Bankers and Empire*, and Jeb Sprague's *Globalizing the Caribbean* are cases in point.[25] But throughout the 2010s, at a time when it was near impossible to attend a conference where Marxist analysis was not in the foreground, there was considerably less attention to matters of the critique of political economy in the region.

Unfortunately, this inattention came at precisely the time when northern scholars were attempting to critically reevaluate capitalism's origin myths, many of which were formed by neglecting the role of the region. Tellingly, as Hudson writes about the scholarship associated with the "New History of Capitalism," this reevaluation skirts over the contributions made by Caribbean intellectuals like James and Eric Williams.[26] At best, Caribbeanists are in the footnotes. (European scholars would be greatly mistaken if they think they are spared censure here.) But even if Caribbeanists believed that the revival of the Marxist critique of capitalism was weak on issues of race, they have also shown little inclination to join the renewed interest in the work of Cedric Robinson around racial capitalism, as extended by scholars like Robin Kelley, Ruth Wilson Gilmore, and Tithi Bhattacharya, among others.[27]

During modernity the Caribbean was a key site for revolutionary activity and the development of robust revolutionary thought. Yet, much like other parts of the globe, the onset of capitalist realism in the late twentieth century saw the near total evaporation of explicit radical politics. Guided by the adage that some influence is better than none, oftentimes activists in the region made pacts with parties, governments, and markets to try to advance a progressive agenda on poverty alleviation, gender equity, and sexual rights. While there have been notable successes, the general reluctance by this establishment to act on the climate emergency shows the limitations of this approach. Accordingly, there is much need for strategies to rebuild radical organizational capacities to make oppositional politics a viable alternative for social progress.

Antidemocratic Bureaucratic Structures

Like other countries, Caribbean states cause deep moral injuries. For example, one feature of these governments is how frequently they waste people's time. People wait in line at the hospital. They wait in line at the clinic. They wait in line at the courts. Regardless of intention, typically portions of the work of administrating social insurance programs falls onto individual applicants. Guided by the larger project of making "responsible subjects," programs nominally meant to help the poor are time consuming and mentally taxing. With a levy of paperwork mediating the relationship between the state and citizens, nearly every encounter becomes a source of aggravation. Accessing social services is stressful enough, yet the constant anxiety of administrative burdens denies basic citizenship rights to people who do not have the time, cannot afford the time, do not have the free time to request assistance. But which people have the funds to commission lawyers and accountants to work on their behalf? Then consider how the state is dictating a particular presentation of the self as a precondition for accessing human rights when public buildings bar entry to those without "dignified clothing." At a visceral level, inequalities like these encapsulate one reason why public confidence in governments is low.

It is not too much to describe the excessively rigid hierarchical administrative structures that traverse the Caribbean as antidemocratic. As Mindie Lazarus-Black's research shows, "rites of domination" are aplenty in citizens' day-to-day encounters with states.[28] These rites limit citizens from meaningfully contributing to shared governance issues; they are dissatisfied with tepid consultation exercises and symbolic endorsements of foregone decisions. This practice has severe consequences that limit participatory and egalitarian governance. Yet when citizen groups make efforts to redress routines, they are met with a timbre of systematic indifference and hostility. Such is to be expected when officials mistake gatekeeping for accountability.

On matters of governance, appeals to existing "policy and procedure" promote an uncritical, reactionary organizational culture that is more interested in doing things "the right way" than doing "good things." There are two well-documented by-products of proceduralism. The first is estrangement that arises as persons discover that they cannot advance a project of good things because ultimately excessive policy and procedures nominally intended to ensure fairness practically hamper its timely achievement. The second by-product is what political scientists call "rule by law, not of law." That is, the excessive procedures provide many opportunities for people to unjustly exercise power over others and pursue vendettas. These and other outdated and ill-suited procedures for running institutions lead to considerable loss of productivity, energy, and spirit.

Within the Caribbean, the quest to insulate the policy formation process from democratic oversight—across all levels of government—is at the heart of neoliberal accumulation. The consequence has been a decline of social wages. But not all lament this development. Every regime has a discourse constructed that can justify it; every regime has a constituency, even neoliberalism. And de-democratization is not an announced project; no one admits that they intend to exclude, to stigmatize. Yet these are the outcomes. And they more than suit some.

Decolonization and the Political Class

Many Caribbean societies have a freedom myth that allows the local ruling class to mask themselves by using the language of social progressivism. Having co-opted the language of the Left, nationalists fought incredibly hard for cultural citizenship. But there are limits to this exercise. It is striking that there is absolutely no serious effort to deny legal citizenship to corporations. And they also tend to ignore the terrible working conditions of "free labor" in their own societies. Despite the radical visions by the labor and independence movements, postindependence rulers and societies have made little progress in ending the harms from capitalism. Rather, they have thwarted egalitarian movements to preserve the hierarchy they sit atop. In doing so they misappropriate political capital that others have earned.

Historiography and revolutionary strategy are two distinct but co-constructive issues. The main motif of the Caribbean-based historiography in the initial postindependence period was recovery. Conditioned by nation-building exercises, there was much "retrieval," oftentimes focusing on the "contributions" of the various particular groups in segmented and segregated societies. The histories produced gave attention to demographics, family structure and kinship, culture, and the other building blocks of Caribbean life. Another dominant genre was how the enslaved defended their humanity, a theme that could also be seen in popular culture, like Bob Marley's *Songs of Freedom*. Yet much of this lay, popular, and scholarly work failed to fully bring forth postindependence alternatives to the tropes within European nationalist histories that were predominantly shaped by the imperial rule and colonial experiences. With a broader orthodox fashion of modernization and technical assistance, ideas of progress and development fitted hand in glove with teleologies of the past.

The traditions of inquiry produced in the 1980s in the Anglo-Caribbean did not generate an archive and analysis that took seriously the gendered components of social relations. In being insufficiently attentive to the setting and situation, the historiography was unnecessarily partial. Second, revolutionary politics was similarly inattentive to gender oppression; thus those projects were less emancipatory than they claimed. From a certain altitude, the subsequent historiography of the revolutionary moment, itself being a product of that moment, could not detect how revolutionaries overlooked gender, and thus they were not well positioned to see the deficiencies in that strategy. The result is, as Girvan wrote in 2012, that "political decolonisation of Caribbean countries is incomplete; indeed it has come to a virtual standstill."[29]

The by-product of a concerted effect by Catherine Hall, Nicholas Draper, and many others to make it a public matter is a resurgent interest in decolonization in the Anglo-Northern academy. Like the earlier work of Eric Williams, this project is necessary because a good portion of British people do not quite see linkages between enslavement and the historical foundations of their lives. Given how little substantive attention there has been to Caribbean scholarship that dealt with many of these questions fifty years prior, unsurprisingly Anglo-Northern scholars are still trying to figure out the vectors, venues, and variety of stances on what racial liberation means. Many are still trying to make sense of projects within this movement that point differently to diverging goals of nonracialism, primordialism, a multicultural West, or de-Westernization. From many Anglo-Northern scholars, they are only starting to recognize distinctions between different (and contesting) ideological blocs within the decolonization discourse.

Watching from the Caribbean, much of the discourse around decolonization is often a self-congratulatory Western exercise in self-criticism. This is because much of this wave of theorization lacks awareness of interwar Pan-African thought and South Atlantic critiques of capitalist expansion. Certainly, there are theorists who do address this error, and so rightly there is growing awareness of the role of colonization in shaping the modern nation-state and contemporary international system, but it is unreasonable for these few theorists to do the work. Reflecting on the spirit of the interwar years, James said, "There were never all told more than a dozen of us, who banded ourselves together in 1935 to propagate and organize for the emancipation of Africa. For years, we seemed, to the official and the learned world, to be at best, political illiterates."[30]

Through asking about the processes that deemed James ignorant, and which powers forgot them, there is more value in asking which perspectives are currently deemed "politically illiterate," even while international affairs may be proving the very value in their insights.

Economies of Experience; Experience of Economies

The long-standing critique of the industrialization of culture is near absent in the Caribbean. Rather, states lean into the commodification of experiences and events. Festivals can create meaningful human experiences and be key points in the making of global culture. But they are not autonomous; rather, they magnify preexisting social, economic, and cultural politics. For example, while ranging in scale and visibility, many Caribbean countries have sought to convert their cultural practices into events, like Carnival in Trinidad or Crop Over in Barbados. Certainly this is the most recent iteration of a process that began with the international expositions in the nineteenth century by world powers but intensified during the twentieth century. Caribbean festivals compete with other smaller, niche mega events for attention and commerce. The sense of urgency and poor contracting processes create opportunities for scandal, allegations of bribery, and a set of grievances of local talent if they are excluded from the lineup, even if they do not have the drawing power of other artists.

Civic life and leisure are strongly influenced by the rhythms and expectations of these events, which become celebration of identity and the nation. They are welcome opportunities for distraction and creative expression. And while the commodification is the most apparent, some groups invest these festivals with meaningful political statements about an alternative modernity. Due to the public visibility, these events shape economies and provide moorings for diasporic communities to return for the renewal of their identity.

Scholars are also attracted to this commercialism, but they can be uncritically caught up in the symbolism and public enthusiasm.

The promotional machinery of marketing Caribbean festivals aims to promote Caribbean identity as well as assert the virtues of Caribbean capitalist modernity. While these spectacles of accumulation might not be capitalized to the same extent as mega events in the Global North, festivals in the Caribbean themselves are venues for the struggle over public investment. There is staging to promote economic interests and some urban revitalization, although at a smaller scale; along with tourists, some who come to consume the local bodies on display, well-off members of diasporic communities return and spend foreign currency to stimulate local economies. Also it is a common belief that cash injections help local firms survive in lean seasons, although the evidence is inconclusive on this "trickle-down effect," especially when it comes to everyday infrastructure, the creation of more affordable housing, or increased wages. Festivals and fetes are institutions that promote intense spectacle for all, speculative investment for a few, and survivalism for the remaining many.

One aspect of festivals is a self-conscious international public relations exercise. Festivals offer opportunities for Caribbean societies, typically neglected and marginalized, to showcase entrepreneurial spirit and organizational competence, which among other similar factors is used as a social proof of a society capable of protecting investments. The aim of this national image is to use the cultural realm to help integrate Caribbean economies in the global circuits of financialization, real estate markets, and tourism. In stating these intentions so starkly we do not wish to detract from or diminish extra-economic impulses that orbit matters of recognition and respect—the positive assertion that cultural practices and rituals have meaning and depth on par with practices and rituals that occur in the primary nodes of global society.

These elements of preservation and enterprise, nationalism and internationalism display accommodationist attitudes to capitalism, the symbolic registries of which are informed by the experience of labor migration control regimes. Festivals in the Caribbean seek to present this experience, either in names, costumes, or characters. Coming in the wake of decolonization, as Arif Dirlik notes, these "festivals of modernity" provide avenues for "restor[ing] the voices of the colonized, and open[ing] the way to recognition of the spatial and temporal co-presence of those whom a Eurocentric modernization discourse had relegated to invisibility and backwardness."[31] For Caribbean societies, the aggressive pursuit of festivals and fetes is meant to signal their inclusion as sites of meaning in global capitalist modernity, if not as full peers, then at least as sites of specialized spectacle that can be experienced.

Given their economic importance and symbolic value, festivals preemptively become objects of protection. Citizens may consent to higher levels of security and surveillance. Then there are reports of potential terror attacks, as in Trinidad and Tobago's 2018 Carnival. In this case local media made little to no mention of direct U.S. military guidance of operation.[32] Local forces can act, but they are supported by foreign actors. This gives another dimension to the military aspects of imperialism discussed in this introduction. Meanwhile, terror threats provide rationales for increased security and acquisition of high-tech surveillance tools without much parliamentary oversight. Once built and deployed, this military security apparatus becomes ready at hand for the state should it need to exercise coercion. In Jamaica, for example, after decades of use, the normalization of states of exception shows the limits of substantive democracy. These festivals are linked to the weakening of democratic governance that is being experienced in the twenty-first century.

The Status of Inquiry

The academic study of development has taken off, not just because of the implicit social mandate for the societies that universities serve, but also because of professional windfalls that can come through prestigious associations with international development organizations, business organizations, governments, and other entities that work within the paradigm of national development exercises. But much of this scholarship, even when it appears progressive in intent, tends to downplay the negative or contradictory features of capitalism. This is especially true when it comes to matters related to injustice and inequality. This can leave little room to consider how states, for instance, use urban development corporations to clear slums and displace poor citizens or how state security forces abuse their authority when given a social license to criminalize poverty.[33]

Granted, trenchant activist criticisms of Caribbean governments, societies, and markets can—and do—find places in noncritical university syllabi. But their sampling is mostly there to bolster claims about the comprehensiveness of the course. In practice the critical material is often taught without sufficient rigor or explanatory depth to be persuadable. Through poor and narrow instruction of critical materials, the point is to inoculate students against anticapitalist thought that questions hegemonic values. Under the guise of due professional diligence, the desired conclusion is that radicals and activists have nothing socially relevant to say to the current moment.

Should the strategy of containing criticism need supplementation, there is the tactic of co-opting critical scholars. In this way the targeted institutions can claim they are better advancing their mission through course-correction exercises. As the lines between governors and academic critics grow thin and porous, those that thrive are those best able to show restraint with their criticisms. They are deemed savvy for preserving their social capital for crucial moments, moments only ever known in hindsight. This book, whose contributors take a largely critical view of the nexus of race, class, and nationalism, is no exception to this wider dynamic.

In recent years, senior academic administrators in Anglo-Caribbean university systems have publicly acknowledged that there is an endemic problem with faculty members publishing material in vanity presses and with other predatory publishing practices.[34] Aside from the many obvious problems, when faculty use their positions of institutional authority to cowrite with their postgraduate students in these kinds of venues, they jeopardize their charges' academic job prospects in the global academic labor market. The role of patronage to professional and academic success compounds these issues. Especially in a small region, strong interpersonal ties and other relational mechanisms like supplication greatly factor into hiring decisions and grant dispersion. Additionally, there is a kind of expectation from abroad about what kinds of research are expected from the Caribbean. So emerging scholars in the region feel pressures to cater to the demands of the purchasers in the global knowledge economy. Effectively, the things that need to be written cannot be written. That is, the social conditions of academic production and its sanctioning components have created an archive that does not even attempt to describe to the way Caribbean polities are ruled.

Another downside of interpersonal transactions shaping scholarship is that grudges and grievances have an outsized influence in the shaping of research agendas. Even academic publishers are shaped by relational networks, making the critique about old school ties and gatekeeping more acute. At the level of symbolic mannerism too, there is a deep investment to preserve colonial honorifics, the trapping of rank used to trump the merit of reasoning among equals. Altogether this conduct veils a complex machination of exploitation, oppression, and alienation.

Returning to the point about anticapitalist thought, neoliberal postcolonial identarian theorists suggest that there are limitations to the critique of political economy and associated analysis of imperialism. They indict Marxism as Eurocentric and attempt to relitigate the stale, mistaken (and truth be told terribly boring) debate about economic determinism of capitalism and racial obliviousness.[35] These kinds of theorists think that suggesting there are additions to the critical project, like sensitivity to issues of hybridized self-fashioning, civic ascription, and gendered differences, by itself renders Marxism obsolete. But without the Marxist critique of political economy, what remains are studies of history that are not historical—studies of material culture that are not materialist. Political struggles waged through identity may well be struggles for dignity and justice. But unless matters of class and anti-imperialism are primary pillars too, then the struggle for emancipation will forever be partial.

Perhaps to put the matter differently, the main issue is not the nationalists' disdain for Marxism but that they offer no serious critiques of Marxism. The problem is that they are lazy toward ideas they do not like. Furthermore, nationalists perpetuate the mistaken idea that some spaces are drivers of theory, while others are relegated to mere sites of application. There is no need to undertake a roll call of scholars' names to know that Caribbean people have also been drivers of Marxist theorizing, whether about the region, from the region, or about other places. Still, mistakes betray mystification. The point is that nationalists prefer that there is no critique of the political economic system itself; only critiques aimed at refining efficacy of prior routines and aspirations are permissible. Again: the problem can never be the core aspirations themselves, only execution.

Aside from a few notable exceptions, it is for this reason that a good portion of the "ordinary research" produced in the region can be fairly characterized as naive empiricism. If literature reviews are merely pro forma assembly of factoids and recycled cultural intuitions, then they lack scholarly attempts to clarify what is at stake and why. It is worth asking how social science and critique can be advanced if there is no theoretical grounding in a large body of literature that has an epistemological project. In our view the abandonment of Marxism in the region led to the near abandonment of well-specified, overarching theoretical frameworks. The result is naive empiricism anchored in personal intuitions and folk theories.

A better method would be for scholarship to build principles that flow from overarching theoretical frameworks, an intellectual project shared about a community of practitioners that do not see themselves as rivals or competitors but as fellow journeymen who are refining their craft on the most important projects they can find. Historical materialism offers this approach. Aside from guiding research efforts making this labor economical through motivating certain foci, a large overarching theoretical framework helps develop criteria for clear predictions; they set expectations for under what conditions a finding may be valid and how it might integrate into the existing body of research, in turn setting up criteria for scrutiny, replication, and confirmation.

Certainly, methodological improvements are much needed and the quality of data could be better. But the critique is more fundamental. It is whether there is a cohesive conceptual framework that guides what methodologies to use and what kinds of data are worth collecting. This is about ranked priorities given finite resources. And so pet folk theories just will not do.

The Project of This Book

These arguments are likely to be a surprise to many politicians, pundits, and professors in the Caribbean. These kinds of readers may balk at a conclusion that is contrary to the very mythos that is intended to sustain their polities. It might even be seen as somewhat disrespectful to three generations of activists and public servants who have sought to plant, tender, and reap the very freedom that allowed these chapters to be written. But we urge caution about the seductions of these so-called self-evident conceptions of freedom, as well as those who claim to safeguard it from persons characterized as rebellious upstarts. Attaining freedom is not a one-off event. Indeed, it is better to think of democracy as an ever-present and ongoing process, the quality of which can wane if it is neglected or deprioritized.

In compiling the chapters in this book we had several central organizing questions in mind. Foremost among these was: what are the present historical-material factors that shape the expression of nationalist sentiments in the region? Related questions involve the economic, political, and social stakes over which nationalism competes. In a related fashion, what might an approach that centers class relations reveal about the conceptualization of local struggles, as well as how these struggles intermesh with the tendencies introduced by neoliberal democracy and its justification of elite enrichment? Furthermore, what does the tacit acceptance of social inequalities tell us about the agenda of the current class that holds the bulk of political power? And finally, if this class is silent on class, are they stewards worthy of entrusting matters involving reparations and the associated fiscal components of decolonization? Might their failure to confront imperialism disqualify them as a class capable of governing in the interests of Caribbean people? Any one of the chapters that follow does not offer definitive answers to the questions raised by this introduction. Nor would it be fair to presume that they could, given the nature and expression of the social questions that span the region. But taken collectively, they highlight several important issues that we believe are useful in orienting how scholars might approach economies of experiences and the experiences of economy that produce inequalities and injustices.

In keeping with the range of issues described above, we have organized chapters into four broad thematic areas: (1) formation and formulations; (2) history and activism; (3) domination and expression; and (4) material and international pressures. In the first section, Dylan Kerrigan expands on the formation of (post)colonial state violence by addressing the interplay between the accumulation of capital and shifting constructions of difference. He pays particular attention to the motion of capital on the island of Trinidad, using a social history of the Port of Spain suburb Woodbrook to trace the transformations in race, class, and nationalism as the macrosocial structure of the island shifted between the nineteenth and early twenty-first centuries.

Stanley Griffin builds on these themes by discussing the heterogeneous ways in which race, class, and nationalism are formulated in different places in the Caribbean. He underscores how the circumstantial realities of each colonial society dictated how these three issues were co-articulated. For example, with no need for documentation, or even at times the requisite boat fare, Leeward Islanders moved at will between islands, forging familial and commercial relationships as well as influencing island politics. While the legacy of shared resources and institutions are still present today within the lived experiences of Leeward Islanders, regionalism remains an inconspicuous characteristic of the various ideas around race, class, and nationalism. In short, this triad is differently articulated relative to other larger territories of the former British West Indies, ones that often receive the lion's share of attention in academic studies.

Turning to issues at the nexus of history and activism and speaking to the themes of the commodification of land, property rights, and displacement, Juan Vicente Iborra Mallent and Kimberly Palmer's chapter is a case study of young Garifuna deportees organizing for the recovery of ancestral lands in the Bay of Trujillo, Honduras. They argue that the dispossession of Garifuna from their ancestral territories is caused by—and consistent with—wider imperatives of global neoliberalism. They use ethnographic data to further clarify the linkages between Canada's support of the Honduran coup d'état in 2009, Canadian real estate investment, illegal land sales in the Bay of Trujillo, and forced migration.

Caribbean women have historically done productive and reproductive work that has been undervalued economically and socially for the state, family, and community. Exploring these intersections, Shelene Gomes, Antonia Mungal, and Maria Thérèse Gomes discuss how migrant women in the Caribbean diaspora continue to fulfill these responsibilities transnationally, with distance complicating how these duties are conducted. This leads to conflicting obligations for women, some of whom feel compelled to return to their countries of origin to provide proximate care for aging relatives. What is striking in the testimony of these women is how the capitalist logic of work and the cultural logic of kinship are operationalized in women's descriptions of their decisions. The result is that unwaged caregiving is presented as an expression of love for aging relatives, one to be done without complaint.

On the topic of the tug between the past and the present, taking the 2021 protests in Cuba, Julio César Guanche and Maikel Pons Giralt use this moment to compare older and newer conceptions of race relations in the country. These discourses represent not only different ideological commitments, values, and styles of reasonings, they say, but also efforts to revisit the kinds of social pacts that were struck during the twentieth century.

Amílcar Sanatan ends this section by discussing the gendered historiography of "revolutionary tales" by focusing on the conceptualization of the politics of the Grenada Revolution. As he writes, the decline of the Grenada Revolution marks a wider decline of political projects for revolutionary change in the Caribbean Left. Still, the kinds of historiography of the revolution can be one means of assessing the status of the Caribbean Left.

How we talk about these items matters a great deal. The third section of the book turns to expression and domination. Gerald Stell looks at perceptions of ethnicity and language use in Suriname. As he discusses, ethnicity and language have often been studied together on account of their strong mutual links. "Hard" ethnic boundaries are manifested by the continued use of heritage languages, while dynamics of intergroup assimilation reduce linguistic distinctions. Savrina Chinien examines how writers like Patrick Chamoiseau in the Franco-Caribbean have been caught up in cultural imperialism via the French language. For Chamoiseau, even after Martinique became an overseas department of France in 1946, the coloniality of power still subsisted as matrix morphed into a metropolitan and even a global coloniality. Chinien mediates on Chamoiseau's dictate about writing "in a dominated country," probing for the opportunities and limitations of whether rejecting Eurocentric value systems is enough to bring radical politics to the region.

Similar issues are covered in the two chapters by Nadia Whiteman-Charles and by Brendan Jamal Thornton and Diego I. Ubiera, in their discussions about presumption around race and nationalism in Jamaica and the Dominican Republic, respectively. Drawing on ethnographic data, Whiteman-Charles looks into the politics of distinction wherein the outside musical styles of reggae and dancehall came to be treated as emblematic of the authentic Jamaican national identity, whereas rock music, which is coded as "foreign" and "white," is thus inappropriate for the local soundscape. This is a shame, she concludes, as such nationalistic fetishizing misses the history of how productive borrowing between these styles made them what they are. In a rewarding chapter about the ethics of transposing categories, Thornton and Ubiera look at how conceptual conventions formed in northern academies have come to shape the field of "Dominican" studies in ways that can be estranged from lay conceptions that circulate in the country. Quite rightly, they argue that better analysis could be produced if more attention were given to existing homegrown scholarship.

Jerome Teelucksingh asks readers to reflect on what it means when everyday historical narratives privilege the contributions and struggles of Afro-Caribbean persons. Despite the significant Indo-Caribbean population and other ethnic minorities like persons of Jewish, Syrian, Chinese, Lebanese, and Portuguese descent in the Anglo-Caribbean, efforts to produce synthetic social histories have at times been met with ridicule or deliberately misconstrued as solely invested in promoting ethnic particularity; racial flattening and exclusion occurs to the detriment of the minorities who have also been subject to the same logic of oppression that stems from racial capitalism. Teelucksingh attributes this friction to intraclass contests as the Caribbean class structure, or more precisely its self-comprehension, evolved in the latter part of the twentieth century.

The final section looks at local politics and international pressures. A set of chapters by Duane Edwards and Jack Menke looks at the elections in the region in 2020. Edwards provides a materialist account of the stakes in Guyana's 2020 elections as new oil discoveries came to shape who got to direct the expected spoils. He discusses how the institutional arrangement in Guyana, as well as the social structure in the country, create lines of division that make race a salient political category. Menke addresses the evolution of Suriname's political democracy from 1949 to 2020 across seventeen elections and two military regimes. His main argument is that despite the relatively peaceful transition from mono-ethnic to multiethnic mobilization and populism, the structural foundations of the political economy did not change.

In the next chapter, Scott Timcke contrasts the phenomenon of antisystem politics in Jamaica and Trinidad and Tobago with their respective postcolonial predicaments. Through focusing on how permutations of electoral systems and creditor-debtor relations shape the character of popularist responses to rising social inequality, he undertakes a comparative analysis of contemporary popular politics in these countries. While both were subject to enslavement and British colonialism, their political economies were dissimilar especially in the latter half of the twentieth century, in turn giving rise to different kinds of popularist movements. In the final chapter, Ruben Gonzalez-Vicente and Annita Montoute study the People's Republic of China's political economic footprint in the Caribbean. They use concepts and categories of radical Caribbean social theory and apply them to the study of China's contemporary relations with the Caribbean community, drawing broader implications for the Belt and Road Initiative as the Caribbean fits into China's global vision.

This introduction has sought to undertake a theoretical reflection on some of the macrosociological issues that are shaping the Caribbean. The aim is to chip away at the language of postcolonial neoliberal democracies to look more closely at the reactionary core, to revisit the storied (if entirely fictional) histories that were (and are being) naturalized throughout the region about the character of mature postindependence societies, which by and large have absorbed the logic of capitalism, rendering the accrual of wealth by the few a desirable social and political goal. In totality our project seeks to make a case for a revived critique of political economy in the Caribbean, as we believe this perspective has the explanatory range to comprehend the deep politics around race, class, and nationalism. By necessity such an exercise requires multidisciplinary efforts of documentation and standpoints of criticism, hence the variety of people, places, and philosophies covered in the coming chapters. This critique is not motivated by malice or the desire to find reasons to chide those with authority. The critique is driven by the awareness that the lives of people, our lives and the lives of our loved ones in our communities, are at stake. Getting the right answer matters.

It should be evident by now that my view leans toward encouraging Caribbean societies to pursue anticapitalist, postconsumerist, deep decarbonization paths of political development that aspire to the rational management of social goods led by the working class. For unless its political class is forced to engage in debates about social justice and experiments with different visions of the fundamental political-economic order, the region will remain a "second home" for the dominate transnational capitalist ruling class, as is most of the Anglo-Caribbean now. Mia Mottley is making great strides on the global stage with the Bridgetown Initiative. This is a worthy project, although what comes next is implementing a revolutionary political project predicated on the immanent critique of global systems of accumulation, dispossession, and domination. Anything less is insufficient to meet our moment with the multiple overlapping crises all of us confront.

Scott Timcke
Christ Church, Barbados
February 2022

NOTES

1. C. L. R. James, *The Black Jacobins* (New York: Vintage, 1989), quotation on 408. Also see Barbara Fields, "Slavery, Race and Ideology in the United States of America," *New Left Review*, May/June 1990.

2. Scott Timcke, "Revisiting the Plantation Society: The New World Group and the Critique of Capitalism," *Historical Materialism* 32, nos. 2/3 (2023).

3. Anton Allahar, "Situating Ethnic Nationalism in the Caribbean," in *Ethnicity, Class, and Nationalism: Caribbean and Extra-Caribbean Dimensions*, ed. Anton Allahar and Shona N. Jackson (Oxford: Lexington Books, 2005).

4. Selwyn Ryan, "The Clash of Cultures in Post Creole Trinidad and Tobago," *Caribbean Dialogue* 3, no. 2 (1997): 7–28.

5. Shona Jackson, *Creole Indigeneity: Between Myth and Nation in the Caribbean* (Minneapolis: University of Minnesota Press, 2012).

6. Michel-Rolph Trouillot, *Silencing the Past: Power and the Production of History* (Boston: Beacon, 1995).

7. James, *Black Jacobins*, 406.

8. Charles Mills, *Radical Theory, Caribbean Reality* (Kingston: University of the West Indies Press, 2010).

9. Achille Mbembe, *Critique of Black Reason*, trans. Laurent Dubois (Durham, N.C.: Duke University Press, 2017).

10. Kamala Kempadoo, *Sexing the Caribbean: Gender, Race, and Sexual Labor* (New York: Routledge, 2004), 2, 3.

11. Cayman News, "Cayman's Climate Change Risk to Be Assessed," *Cayman News*, November 3, 2021, https://caymannewsservice.com/2021/11/caymans-climate-change-risk-to-be-assessed/.

12. Luc Multigner, Philippe Kadhel, Florence Rouget, Pascal Blanchet, and Sylvaine Cordier, "Chlordecone Exposure and Adverse Effects in French West Indies Populations," *Environmental Science and Pollution Research International* 23 (2016): 7.

13. Marc Jones, "Analysis: Belize Offers Ocean 'Blue' Print with Debt-for-Reef Swap," Reuters, November 5, 2021, https://www.reuters.com/business/cop/belize-offers-ocean-blue-print-with-debt-for-reef-swap-2021-11-05/.

14. Caribbean Development Bank, press release, "CDB Calls upon Developed Countries to Allocate 2% of SDR for Adaptation Investment in SIDS," November 8, 2021, https://www.caribank.org/newsroom/news-and-events/cdb-calls-upon-developed-countries-allocate-2-sdr-adaptation-investment-sids.

15. Stanley H. Griffin and Scott Timcke, "Re-framing Archival Thought in Jamaica and South Africa: Challenging Racist Structures, Generating New Narratives," *Archives and Records* (2021), DOI: 10.1080/23257962.2021.2002137.

16. David Harvey, *Rebel Cities: From the Right to the City to the Urban Revolution* (London: Verso, 2012), 109.

17. William Robinson, "Global Capitalism Theory and the Emergence of Transnational Elites," *Critical Sociology* 38, no. 3 (May 2012): 353.

18. Norman Girvan, "One Thing Led to Another," 2007, https://sta.uwi.edu/uwitoday/pdfs/A%202007%20essay%20by%20the%20late%20Norman%20Girvan.pdf.

19. Norman Girvan, "50 Years of In-Dependence," in *Jamaica: Reflections*, talk deliv-

ered at SALISES 50–50 Conference, Kingston, August 22, 2012, https://www.alai.info/wp-content/uploads/2012/08/girvan-jamaica-in-dependence.pdf.

20. Naomi Klein, *The Shock Doctrine* (Toronto: Knopf, 2007).

21. Robert Kaufman and Barbara Stallings, "The Political Economy of Latin American Populism," in *The Macroeconomics of Populism in Latin America*, ed. Rudiger Dornbusch and Sebastian Edwards (Chicago: University of Chicago Press, 1991), 15.

22. Jamie Peck, *Constructions of Neoliberal Reason* (Oxford: Oxford University Press, 2010).

23. For a Caribbean appraisal of U.S. imperial policy from the vantage point of the Caribbean, see Michael Manley, *Jamaica: Struggle in the Periphery* (London: Third World Media, 1982).

24. See Vijay Prashad, *Washington Bullets: A History of the CIA, Coups, and Assassinations* (New York: Monthly Review Press, 2020).

25. Peter James Hudson, *Bankers and Empire: How Wall Street Colonized the Caribbean* (Chicago: University of Chicago Press, 2017); Carole Boyce Davies, *Left of Karl Marx: The Political Life of Black Communist Claudia Jones* (Durham, N.C.: Duke University Press, 2008); Jeb Sprague, *Globalizing the Caribbean: Political Economy, Social Change, and the Transnational Capitalist Class* (Philadelphia: Temple University Press, 2019).

26. Peter Hudson, "The Racist Dawn of Capitalism," *Boston Review*, March 14, 2016, https://bostonreview.net/books-ideas/peter-james-hudson-slavery-capitalism; Scott Timcke, *Capital, State, Empire* (London: University of Westminster Press, 2017).

27. C. J. Robinson, *Black Marxism: The Making of the Black Radical Tradition* (Chapel Hill: University of North Carolina Press, 1983).

28. Mindie Lazarus-Black, "The Rites of Domination: Practice, Process, and Structure in Lower Courts," *American Ethnologist* 24, no. 3 (August 1997): 628–51.

29. Norman Girvan, "Colonialism and Neo-colonialism in the Caribbean: An Overview," paper prepared for IV International Seminar Africa, the Caribbean and Latin America, Saint Vincent and the Grenadines, November 24–26, 2012, https://www.alainet.org/images/Girvan_St-Vincent_paper.pdf.

30. C. L. R. James, "Tomorrow and Today: A Vision," *New World Journal*, n.d., https://newworldjournal.org/british-guyana/tomorrow-and-today-a-vision/.

31. Arif Dirlik, "Spectres of the Third World: Global Modernity and the End of the Three Worlds," *Third World Quarterly* 25, no. 1 (2004): 131–48.

32. Ryan Browne and Barbara Starr, "U.S. Military Helps Thwart Trinidad Carnival Terror Attack," CNN, February 9, 2018, https://edition.cnn.com/2018/02/09/politics/trinidad-carnival-terror-attack-thwarted/index.html.

33. David Dodman, "Developers in the Public Interest? The Role of Urban Development Corporations in the Anglophone Caribbean," *Geographical Journal* 174 (2008): 30–44; Alana D. Osbourne, "Touring Trench Town: Commodifying Urban Poverty and Violence in Kingston, Jamaica" (PhD thesis, University of Amsterdam, 2018), https://pure.uva.nl/ws/files/29425142/Thesis.pdf.

34. Clive Landis, "Predatory Publishing: Time to Grasp This Nettle," lecture, UWI, Saint Augustine, October 4, 2017, https://sta.uwi.edu/news/ecalendar/event.asp?id=3030.

35. Kevin Anderson, *Marx at the Margins: On Nationalism, Ethnicity, and Non-Western Societies* (Chicago: University of Chicago Press, 2010).

PART ONE
FORMATIONS AND FORMULATIONS

CHAPTER 2

The Shifting Construction of Difference Making in Trinidad

DYLAN KERRIGAN

Using the social historiography of Woodbrook, a suburb of Port of Spain, Trinidad, this chapter demonstrates how the shifting construction of difference making in Trinidad is linked to the vested interests of capital accumulation and the securing of state power. These forms of difference making include the production of racial hierarchy, the generative contradiction of cultural assimilation and cultural resistance (i.e., Creole nationalism),[1] the role of Afro-Saxon "organic intellectuals," and today, the means by which the original colonial logic and binary of divide and conquer intersects with contemporary class politics to exacerbate social stratification, economic division, state violence, and, in terms of social development and the nation, a hegemonic neocolonial politics of the continued exclusion and othering of the "masses" from the "people."

To provide the narrative structure, the first six sections offer a chronological account of Woodbrook's emergence and its development from 1780 to the present. The final two sections of the chapter then consider the central outcomes of this 225-year process of change in the context of the decline of middle-class respectability, the erosion of the Afro-Saxon class that drove independence, and the end of creolist national power. In particular, the chapter considers how the decline of Woodbrook and its transformation signify the disarticulation of the Creole nationalist mode of power toward satisfying the demands of transnational neoliberal capital and the collapse of nationalist social cohesion this change engendered.

The Early Woodbrook, Pre-1780s to 1900s

The land on which Woodbrook developed comes from the incorporation of three sugar estates at the end of the 1700s. The location of Woodbrook Estate was a muddy mangrove that today is the western edge of modern Woodbrook.[2] By the early nineteenth century Woodbrook Estate was a productive 367.5-acre sugarcane plantation within one mile of the town of Port of Spain.

Following emancipation and the emergence of the indentureship system, between 1843 and the mid-1890s, mostly East Indian indentured workers labored on the sugar plantation alongside some Afro laborers, including migrants from Barbados. In terms of residents, East Indians were joined by Afro-Creoles, some of working-class means and others of a higher economic status who worked for the colonial government and could now be found on the edges of the estate, which now extended into the town of Port of Spain and provided less crowded housing opportunities. By January 12, 1895, the *Port of Spain Gazette* was able to speak of "Woodbrook Village," a "curious conglomeration of dwellings some of which are well built and comfortable enough, whilst others are mere huts."

Having bought the estate in 1899 for £50,000, in 1909, under financial pressure, the Siegert family, of Angostura fame, put Woodbrook Estate up for sale. At the time of purchase by the Port of Spain Town Board in 1911, Woodbrook was transforming to become a suburb. The sugar factory was gone and the cane fields replaced by lots for rent to a burgeoning colored middle class who saw the area as respectable and desirable. As the politics of the economy shifted from slavery to post-emancipation and forward into the twentieth century, the racial hierarchies of pre-emancipation began to shift in the post-emancipation era as colored and Black social mobility became somewhat more entrenched with professional jobs.

Pre- and Post-emancipation Racial Hierarchy

As a residential suburb of Port of Spain, Woodbrook was first home to low-income renters of various ethnic persuasions at the end of the Victorian era. Yet as the economy of Trinidad changed rapidly over the next twenty years, so too did the class composition of Woodbrook. Most important, the local Creole elite and merchant class moved in. One factor in this class transformation of the area was a policy by the town board to replace lower-income dwellers with higher wage earners who could pay higher land taxes. This was achieved by twenty-five-year leaseholds and putting a "minimum value requirement" on the houses built in Woodbrook. This figure was far larger than what most working-class tenants could pay.[3] More generally, the imposition of tariffs and taxes like these is often a mechanism in the process of gentrification for class formation.

Another spur in the changes Woodbrook experienced during the opening decades of the twentieth century was connected to the island's position in global commodity chains—specifically, the profits the cocoa industry accrued through well-positioned social groups like French Creoles in industrial production of chocolate in Britain. This industry emerged through the mobilization of technology, investment, and "taste patterns," and Trinidad with its high quality and abundant crops of cocoa was incorporated into this industry through what David Harvey has called "the capitalistic logic of searching for 'spatio temporal fixes.'"[4] According to Frances Bekele, Trinidad's cocoa industry experienced a "tremendous boom" with 1866–1920 described as the "golden years of cocoa in Trinidad."[5] The "boom" experienced in the cocoa industry was the increased capital now moving into the hands of the French Creole class. This drove their structural and ideological incorporation into the political class of the bourgeois British plantocracy on the island.[6] For the field workers and laborers the "boom" was a period of pauperization that forced many into chronic indebtedness.[7]

By 1884 cocoa production had taken the place of sugar as "the leading agricultural commodity and became the economic barometer of the country."[8] Cocoa profits remade the local society. The French Creole class, who had during almost a century of British colonial rule been part of the sociocultural elite before the British forced them out of the sugar economy and into relatively hard financial times, was now well placed to partake in the politics and culture of Western bourgeois capitalism. Cocoa turned around French Creole economic fortunes, and the profits also enlarged a Creole middle class of phenotypically distinct persons from Black to colored (referring primarily to Black and white admixtures) to white to mixed, with numeric ascendance among the lighter-skinned groups. The color gradient and racism of colonialism, with its distinctions in landownership and educational opportunities, produced economic differentiation across the non-British elite that further entrenched economic stratification as capitalism advanced. Over a short time many of the newly wealthy middle class, alongside the families of the local Creole elite group, increasingly grew into the suburb of Woodbrook, displacing many of the lower economic residents. Concurrently the character and feel of the suburb shifted, as wrought-iron railings were added to the property lines and houses were electrified.

By 1920 Woodbrook had a symbolic register in Trinidad's development as a capitalist society. Put differently, it reflected the "reorientation of territorial politics towards the requirements of the capitalistic logic" that Harvey raises.[9] While remnants of the aspirant lower class remained—Eric Williams wrote that his family was constantly vulnerable to the "ordeal of removal" for late rent payments—Woodbrook's residents were mostly colored professionals who worked in government, law, the growing education system, and almost all the other sectors of colonial society. These groups were "working for colonial authorities."[10]

Leveraging their wealth from cocoa, the elite French Creole class would soon move on to the affluent districts of St. Clair and Maraval. Yet rich or poor, Woodbrook people were now assimilating to British bourgeois values and the internalized code of conduct required for upward class mobility. But they were also starting a process of transculturation with their neighbors and cultures. Woodbrook was now mixed racially and ethnically, and it denoted an emergent new middle-class value structure. In a sense it represented the new people—"Trinidadians"—or at least what they would come to aspire to.

Creole Nationalism and an Afro-Saxon Elite

For a capitalist economic system to function, it requires an elite. In Trinidad this class was shaped by and tied to the assimilation of metropolitan class interests flanked by "British values" reproduced through the education system, Anglicanization, and local forms of government.[11] Moreover, Afro-Saxons would evolve out of, and maintain close ties with, a plantocracy (French and Spanish) who controlled sugar cultivation in the first half of the nineteenth century, was supplanted by foreign capitalists (the British), and later switched its investments to the cocoa economy in the 1880s.[12] Gradually an increasingly local elite (Creole-French, colored and Afro) diversified its interests and entrenched itself in moneylending, commerce, and light industry as well as the professions. By 1920 the economic characteristics of this "national bourgeoisie" were tightly linked to the circulation of foreign capital through trade and British values, and the Creole elite had long "since healed the differences between themselves and the foreign capitalists"—for which can be read the British upper class.[13]

According to Kelvin Singh, in the early decades of the twentieth century the island's colonial and Creole elite was composed of three interlocking groups. It is from the bourgeois interests of these three groups that the Afro-Saxon elite developed:

> the administrative elite (the governor, the colonial secretary, the attorney-general, the Commandant General of local military forces and the Chief of the Constabulary, the chief justice, and their immediate subordinates in their respective areas of jurisdiction, all subject to the ultimate authority of the governor within the colony, and the final authority of the Colonial Office in Britain); the commercial elite (essentially the import/export merchants, financiers and shipping agents); and the plantocratic elite (owners or managers of large family estates or company estates) [French Creoles]. These three interlocking elites, joined after 1920 by a mineral-exporting elite (directors and managers of oil companies), dominated both the political and economic systems and enjoyed the highest social status by virtue of their economic and political power, as well as by virtue of their race.[14]

The collusion and interests of this early elite—a class for itself—are best seen in their varied opposition to the organized and volatile working-class movements that emerged in the 1920s and 1930s, their mechanisms of control such as pauperization, and their unwillingness to redress the violent symbolic and real legacies of colonialism.[15] Another mechanism was the deployment of "divide and conquer" politics.[16] This politics normalized class divisions, furthered subdivision, and endured through the activities of various "organic intellectuals" like Arthur Cipriani and Eric Williams (both former residents of St. Clair and Woodbrook) by influencing and organizing the consciousness of the local population.[17] Arguably Afro-Saxons can then be read as aspirant compradors whose attitudes developed in the various spheres of colonialism and emerged from the dialectic of local "automatic solidarity" and cultural assimilation as global flows of capital accumulation remade the island's social structure.[18] The social category "Trinidadian" in the opposition between capital and labor served bourgeois class interests. As the category "Trinidadian" self-consciously refashioned the spontaneous philosophy of contemporary Trinidad society, it reproduced a new and capitalist worldview in the lives of locals.[19] Its formation and acceptance are perhaps a glimpse into the motion and logic of capital itself. In Gramscian terms the emergent strata of local middle-class consciousness identifiable in 1920s Woodbrook demonstrated early signs of becoming the postcolonial elite and, in this context, elements in a Gramscian historical bloc and an "alliance of forces" that extended into the 1990s before decline and disarticulation.[20] These Afro-Saxons represented the group who would eventually organize Trinidadian politics and nationalist identity, first on a path to self-government, then independence, and finally usher in the neocolonial relations within late twentieth-century global capitalism.

What comes next is the formation and subsequent transformation of a local economic class grouping in twentieth-century Woodbrook that extended the legacies of colonial inequality. The ideas of this new nascent elite class and economic grouping went on to become dominant and pervasive throughout Trinidad society—essentially the "moment" of a "historical bloc" with its synthesis of economic, political, intellectual, and moral ideas. To illuminate this last point, I suggest Capt. Andrew Arthur Cipriani and Eric Williams (two persons tied to Woodbrook) as Afro-Saxon organic intellectuals linked to the dominant class and the local consolidation of the capitalist mode of production in the early part of the twentieth century.

Woodbrook in the Interwar Years

Cipriani is remembered mostly as the long-serving mayor of Port of Spain and for establishing the Trinidad Labour Party. Testament to his impact on Trinidad is a statue of him in Port of Spain's Independence Square. He was born in Trinidad in 1878 to white Corsican parents who arrived in Trinidad in the mid-nineteenth century to invest in cocoa and commerce. Nationalist narratives relay that from a young age Cipriani served his country on various fronts like politics, agriculture, and commerce, and by improving the working and living conditions of the poor.[21] At the outbreak of World War I, Cipriani advocated that a regiment of West Indian soldiers join the war effort. While there was some pushback, by 1915 West Indian troops were sent abroad.[22] The accounts of Cipriani's military career, including his concerns for the welfare of the soldiers under his command when they encountered racism, are glowing. Some go as far as to state that Cipriani was idolized by his men.[23] On returning to Trinidad in 1919 Cipriani was elected president of the Soldiers and Sailors Union, leveraging that position to become president of the Trinidad Workingmen's Association (TWA), the most important working-class organization of the time. In 1921 he was elected to a seat on the city council of Port of Spain. He served as mayor of Port of Spain from 1929 until 1940, an unbroken eight terms. By agitating for enfranchisement, self-rule, and local representation, he "represented in practice what many other French Creoles merely preached."[24]

Clearly, Cipriani was pulled in multiple directions. Yet his willingness to serve the British Empire complicates nationalist narratives, or otherwise at least implies a kind of continuity and coloniality between selected aspects of colonial and postcolonial ruling ideology.

Following the mythologizing around independence, Cipriani's politics were domesticated as he was posed as a benevolent force on the path to self-government.[25] It is less interesting to delve into the rights and wrongs of such interpretations, but there is much to be gained from using this nationalist domestication to understand the historical formation of global capitalism and its entrenchment in former colonies. This is because it is useful to look for certain events, conduits, and persons who can help illustrate the development of the political economy of modern capitalism in Trinidad, matters of complicity, and how hegemony is created.

The demobilization in 1919 of Black soldiers who had served in the British West Indies Regiment can be used as a significant marker in Trinidad social history.[26] From here on out a "Trinidadian" capitalist-class society began to emerge to "fight with" and "fight against" foreign capitalists. Concurrently, working-class groups and the labor movement built themselves into formidable political blocs.[27] Some of these changing certainties include the discovery of large quantities of oil for commercial export in 1910 (with the economic and strategic importance this brought), the increase in unemployment as the price of cocoa slumped, the end of indentureship in 1917, and the growth in popularity of a working-class consciousness.

Significantly, the war had temporarily diverted attention away from a popular working-class consciousness emerging out of the increasing urban tension developing between a growing Black and colored urban laboring class movement and the white colonial ruling class. Tensions rose primarily due to the harsh and deteriorating living conditions the urban poor faced in overcrowded barracks rooms and on the streets of Port of Spain.[28] The war had also brought further distress for the poor with consumer price increases, low wages, and unemployment. The Colonial Office calculated that in 1914–19 prices in Trinidad had risen by 145 percent.[29] As demobilized Black soldiers were refused the same level of material compensation as their white counterparts, economic inequality and white racial superiority added another layer of militancy to relations between the metropolitan ruling class and the masses. Tough economic times, which left many of the soldiers unemployed, made the social situation even more volatile. Singh (1994) suggests that the Black and colored Creole civilians of higher economic standing identified nationalistically with the unfair treatment meted out to the soldiers and suggested political ways for such inequality to be tackled. Within weeks, Black soldiers and seamen had organized into the Returned Soldiers and Sailors Council.

This council garnered great working-class support and sympathy across ethnic groups, with rural Indian workers and local dockworkers supporting their cause. These links led to a more general working-class unrest spanning the end of 1919 into 1920.[30] Clearly, the terms of the parties involved in the growing tension could be identified by phenotype—the authorities were white, those experiencing economic discrimination Black and Brown. Race tension across this white/colored binary was acute. The local Argos newspaper and the Garveyism of the era further stoked the ideology of race politics in the island and increased the threat felt by the local white community. Within two months of the soldiers' return, events exploded in Trinidad.[31] At the end of July 1919, Black civilians and soldiers attacked white sailors on shore leave from the HMS *Dartmouth*.[32] The police, composed mostly of Afro-Barbadians with English senior officers (who represented foreign interests, not home rule), came out in force to stem the violence.[33] They were met with flying bottles and stones. The unrest simmered and continued into the next week, and the white elite soon became increasingly nervous about the racial tone and frustration of the mob going as far as to fire off a petition to the Colonial office demanding a white garrison on the island and the right to arm the colony's white men.[34] The Council of Returned Soldiers and Sailors held its first public meeting at the height of this tension and drew a large, emotionally charged audience. Under the threat of violence, the president of the council, Algernon Burkett, a prominent Afro-Trinidadian, articulated demands for small allotments and a small monetary grant. In this largely divisive atmosphere, of locals against colonials, Cipriani, a white member of the French Creole elite, intervened.

Cipriani returned to Trinidad from the front a month after the social unrest began. He was informed of the local tensions and, in a move that many say began his path toward political leadership, took on the plight of the soldiers and sailors. It was not unfamiliar ground for him. While stationed in Italy Cipriani had lobbied the white commanding officer in charge of the West Indian Regiment about the ill treatment many Black soldiers experienced.[35] Now in Trinidad he used this as evidence to support his "organic" sincerity of purpose for equal treatment for all soldiers who fought in the war. Over the following months Cipriani, with great oratory skill, criticized the militant and aggressive turn of earlier events. He appealed to the valor and sacrifice undertaken by the soldiers and sailors. He put down the white civilian head of the Discharged Soldiers Central Authority for not being a soldier and thereby not qualified to deal with the business of soldiers. All in all Cipriani aided the creation of solidarity within the soldier fraternity. Strategically, he convinced soldiers to withhold the exercise of force as supposedly this would lead to exacting more concessions from the colonial government. A firm believer in British cultural superiority, Cipriani shepherded working-class colonial subjects to British bourgeois forms of political resolution.

Around three months later the governor-general came to a decision on the matter. No Trinidadian soldiers would be entitled to what the imperial government gave British soldiers. However, they would be given a small financial reward and training in a profession to establish themselves. What not to miss in this story of Cipriani is how he and other members of his local bourgeois strata failed to gain the concessions they had promised the Black soldiers and sailors—equal treatment for all soldiers who fought in the war—but also how Cipriani and his emergent capitalist class did gain some concessions from London that advanced the accumulation of capital: (1) concession from the local government on a small financial reward, (2) diffusion of the initial agitation, (3) the general support and unity of working-class Blacks and Indians across the island, and (4) the culture of proletarization engendered among the poor.

At the time Cipriani also joined the TWA to fight for the labor demands of the Creole masses. The deteriorating economic conditions, in particular inflation and lack of jobs, and the working-class consciousness and unrest they fed further paved the way for the TWA to become "a vibrant body offering leadership to the whole of the working class."[36] From 1919 until the middle of the following year, labor politics and organization on the island developed rapidly as modern capitalist social relations began to replace colonialism. As dockworkers, Black slum dwellers, Indian wholesalers, and "lower ranking civil servants and shop assistants, mostly black or of mixed ancestry," forged cross-cultural solidarity in the name of their class interests, working-class consciousness grew. This soon turned into a transethnic working-class movement as porters, carpenters, grass cutters, scavengers, and then East Indian plantation workers joined together.[37] This movement was best symbolized in the 1921 waterfront strikes for increased wages, overtime pay, and an eight-hour workday, which escalated into colony-wide labor unrest. The unrest was only halted, and the white elite eventually reassured, with the arrival of the HMS *Calcutta* and its British troops, who put down the labor unrest with mass arrests of the leaders of the strikes and repression. Nonetheless, working-class networks and organization had been established.

In 1923, cementing an embryonic national alliance between white and colored Creole liberals and the Black and colored laboring class, Cipriani was voted leader of the TWA, now the single representative organization of Trinidad's workers and soon to be the main vehicle for left-wing ideology in the

Caribbean.[38] Under Cipriani's leadership the TWA developed close links with the British Labour Party (BLP) and formed links with like-minded organizations in the Caribbean, bringing the class politics of capitalism firmly into life on the island. Constitutional reform was also on the table at the beginning of the 1920s, and the TWA, representing the urban workers, in conjunction with members of the colored and Black middle classes, led the reform campaign's struggle for adult franchise. The campaign led to the Wood Commission, a colonial commission sent from London in 1922 to make recommendations on constitutional reform. The head of the Royal Commission of Enquiry and Parliamentary Under-Secretary of State for the Colonies, Maj. E. F. L. Wood, full of ethnocentric assumptions and racism, recommended partial franchise, something that would not change until 1946—another example of a Cipriani promise unfulfilled and a linkage between the French Creole class and the metropolitan center.

In the best organizational traditions of Gramsci's "organic intellectual," Cipriani provides an illustration of the process by which the strata of a colonial organic intellectual functioned. Cipriani was elected to the new legislative council of the 1920s, and his articulation of reforms both for workers and the constitution connected the Creole working class with the emerging Creole middle class or "transitional class" that Woodbrook symbolized. In his realization that the fate of the workers depended on compromise with the government, he set both local groups against the colonial elite. His election brought the masses into direct contact with Western administrators and the colonial political elite. It also united locals in a multiethnic form that would later define the nationalist movements and political interests of "Trinidadians" and have implications for the extension of the historical bloc into the future.[39]

Cipriani fought for legislation to protect trade unions. In 1932 he was successful in getting a trade union ordinance enacted by the British government. Previously trade unions in Trinidad were permitted but lacked fundamental rights like the right to peaceful picketing and immunity from actions in law. As Susan Craig has outlined, based on evidence from "confidential notes of meetings between British Colonial officials," on closer inspection this British acquiescence to Cipriani's demands for such trade unions, and this ordinance in particular, can be interpreted as the strategy of the British government in response to the upheavals and a change in the mode of control of the imperialist system. These new trade unions were permitted so long as "they would be guided by the British into constitutional channels. In the opinion of the Secretary of State for the Colonies after the island-wide strikes in Trinidad and Tobago of 1937, trade unions were to be the future instrument for disciplining and controlling the militancy of colonial workers. To this end, a whole machinery for regulating labour disputes was established."[40]

The period between 1919 and 1937 in Trinidad was a new stage in the economic development of the island. This can be seen in the conflict between the organized workers' union and the local middle classes allied to the capital interest of the colonial administration, including some residents of Woodbrook.[41] The actions of Cipriani as an organic intellectual, tied in the final instance to the latter group, managed to channel both race and class tensions into a capitalist accommodation that promised much for protonationalist formation but continued to represent the racist hierarchy of groups sown by colonialism.[42] Under Cipriani's leadership, the TWA failed to provide substantive lasting benefits to the working class other than position it in the institutional and ideological framework of a capitalist society.[43] Yes, after the limited franchise of 1925, workers had three representatives on the island's legislative council, but the workers had no real share in the government of the colony. Furthermore, Cipriani focused on legislative changes that either culminated in dead ends or were sufficiently stalled to undercut the momentum of working-class politics. In other ways his failures were equally co-optive. For example, early in his political career Cipriani affiliated with the BLP and saw himself as a socialist in that tradition; he was fond of saying that what was good for the British Labour Party was good enough for him.[44] While he might have had good faith intentions, he failed to comprehend the relationship between race and class, between colony and metropole. As such his faith in the BLP, a white colonial entity that came to power in Britain in 1929, was misplaced. The BLP in policing the racial boundaries of colonialism and capitalism failed to change colonial policy along the lines of its pledges and programs. Indeed, the Labour colonial secretary explicitly rejected constitutional change for Trinidad on the grounds that the colony was not ready for further self-government. The racism of international capitalism is clear. Working-class rights and self-government were only permissible in white-majority nations.[45] While later lamenting this development, Cipriani never retracted his support for the BLP, illustrating how in the colonies, no matter one's allegiance to the colony and its masses, local cross-class and race solidarity could be trumped by loyalty to capitalist formations, or put another way, to white bourgeois class interests.

Woodbrook on the Path to Independence

In the 1940s and 1950s, with its "first-world" amenities—paved streets, street lighting, piped water, sewerage, and underground storm drainage—Woodbrook attracted aspirant new residents. Although he had resided there previously as a child, Eric Williams was one of these new residents. Williams had been recently removed from a position with the Anglo-American Caribbean Commission and soon, in 1962, would become the first prime minister of an independent Trinidad and Tobago. According to one source, Williams told colleagues that his move to Woodbrook would make him "a part of the people and less apart from them."[46] As part of this strategy, he soon began to hold many of his early cottage meetings at the Little Carib Theatre. Here Williams and his colleagues, which included a few young and dynamic East Indians or Indo-Saxons, articulated their cross-ethnic solidarity and desire to "create and lead a nationalist movement in Trinidad and Tobago based on disciplined, nationalist, party politics."[47]

By now the residential makeup of Woodbrook represented the culmination of a process begun after emancipation. Mostly as beneficiaries of limited educational opportunities for locals, a lower middle class had developed into a concrete middle-class stratum. This class was active in local society, culture, and politics and included many leading doctors, teachers, lawyers, pharmacists, and journalists. This is not to deny confrontations and agitations with other class groups in Trinidad. There were, most specifically with the working-class masses, both prior to and after the election. However, by the mid-1960s it was the new Trinidadians, a class of people symbolized in the middle class of Woodbrook and their creolized Afro-Saxon values, who would seize control and steer the destiny of the island.

The emerging Creolist national sentiment and an invigorated sense of cultural selfhood was an outcome of a people interpenetrated by a plethora of new and old ideas, unforeseen constellations and mixtures. This contradiction is a theme similarly portrayed in the poetry of Derek Walcott, who also moved to Woodbrook at the same time and put on many works at the Little Carib Theatre. One motif of Walcott's work was to suggest an ability in these new postcolonial Afro-Saxons to straddle more than one tradition, to take the public world of the colony and mix it with private cultural memories—creolize it, if you will.

Writing of this period, some scholars propose that "race . . . had begun to play a lesser role, and education and employment status emerged as the major determinants of social class by the post war period."[48] Certainly race was a factor, but one of declining significance. Writing in the early 1970s, Camejo observed, "While race is probably no longer the overt factor in social and economic stratification a form of discrimination still exists, [which] is based on social class and is termed 'market discrimination.'"[49] Building from his point, as a multiracial class had achieved hegemony, so status had come to shape access to opportunities in intraclass contests. For example, educational ties and residence became considerations in job qualification. These, I suggest, were an indicator of the type of ideas a person had assimilated (preferably Afro-Saxon middle- or upper-class British ones), ideas objectified in the "best schools." It is not by accident that many of these schools were in or adjacent to Woodbrook.[50]

While not the only marker, school ties are emblematic of the role of cliques in settling socioeconomic questions around allocations, rewards, and distributions. Cliques can involve cultural traits too, like religion, language, and dress. These differences between cliques may be less pronounced than others. Whatever the case, the existence of such cliques within one neighborhood lends itself to the ability for individuals to learn much about different cultural traditions in day-to-day interaction with neighbors. It can also explain the way in which Trinidadian multiculturalism was co-opted by the class interests of Afro-Saxon ideology to generate class cohesion at a time of rapid social change.

In this analysis there emerges "a single combination of ideas," which scholars might call the ideology of self-government. Eric Williams represents a lightning rod who took these ideas and made them "dominant and pervasive throughout society," leading to stage five of Gramsci's historical bloc, "the moment of historical bloc with its synthesis of economic, political, intellectual, and moral ideas," something I suggest can be symbolized in independence.[51]

Woodbrook in the first half of the twentieth century was perhaps as stratified and conservative as Trinidad ever got. Ahye describes it as "the most conservative and consciously British community" in colonized Trinidad and Tobago. Yet it was an integral part of the culturally rich western side of Port of Spain. Here in large measure may be traced the origins of the steelpan. The Ellie Mannette and the Invaders steel band was itself based in Woodbrook and supported by Beryl McBurnie, Trinidad's most famous cultural activist. Here the cultural traditions of Europe, Africa, China, and India creatively collided. It should be noted that in the Trinidadian space as a whole, class distinctions are quite fluid. West Port of Spain was no exception, where elite and poor communities—the barrack yards—were found close to each other.[52] In short, Woodbrook transformed into a center of theater arts, Carnival arts and action, and music. It was now a self-confident Creole middle-class area and a central driver of nationalist culture and politics.

George Bailey, considered Trinidad Carnival's greatest bandleader, was born in 1935 in Woodbrook. He produced his first Carnival band at the young age of twenty-one. His bands are remembered for how they changed popular opinion of Africa, history, and the Carnival arts, an observation in line with the growing self-confidence characteristic of the time.[53] Previously in the Carnivals of the nineteenth and early twentieth century, Africa was only ever represented in tribal and savage Carnival imagery. By contrast, "in only his second year as a bandleader and designer," Bailey "presented Back to Africa, perhaps the most celebrated band in the history of modern Carnival, winning the 1957 band of the year award. With this single presentation, Bailey changed popular perceptions of Africa, history, and Carnival itself.... It was a watershed moment, both for Carnival and for Trinidad society."[54]

Along with Harold Saldenah, Cito Velasquez, and Beryl McBurnie, among others, Bailey's generation transformed Carnival from a perceived street festival to a "theatre of the streets" and stage of artistic expression. Each Carnival artist, and there were many in this loose movement, possessed the skill and imagination to elevate what was once seen as a lower-class diversion into a nationalist movement.

The talent of this generation of Carnival designers coincided with the ascent of nationalist sentiments and movement looking for traditions and symbols. This was not lost on Williams and the newly emerged Trinidadian people he wanted to symbolize. Carnival was a mechanism of nation building, set to serve the interests of the local ruling class while also acting as an experimental force of self-definition for this community.[55] Eric Williams appropriated the reinvention of Carnival as a government-endorsed symbol of a newly emergent nation. In doing so the nationalists took a "vulgar" celebration of the lower-class masses and recast it as a "demonstration of the genius of the people." Green and Scher go on to note that such a move was a central pillar in establishing the legitimacy of the People's National Movement (PNM) to first agitate and then rule as the representative of "the people."[56] In using the part to represent the whole, much like their Western counterparts, the Afro-Saxon political class treated their interests as the interests of an entire nation.

One place to "see" the construction of one class's interests as "the national interest" in action is in Williams's speeches at Woodford Square. Known as Trinidad's first university, the "University of Woodford Square" emerged in 1955 as Williams and his colleagues sought a way to produce an informed citizenry, politically conscious and conversant with a local account of history.[57] What started out at the Trinidad Public Library as several well-received speeches on the social and political history of the West Indies grew after June 21, 1955, when

Williams was dismissed from the Anglo-American Caribbean Commission.[58] The same day he went to the square and delivered a fifty-one-page lecture documenting his relationship with the commission and the reasons for his removal. Ryan, citing Williams himself, claims there were some ten thousand people in Woodford Square to hear this lecture.[59] While this is likely apocryphal, the sentiment is one of solidarity, of a fight against the "Imperialist enemy." From stories, at the end of the lecture the square roared its approval, and thus the "people's parliament" was born. Over the coming years Williams gained a public constituency to which he imparted his sense of national pride. The titles of his lectures give some indication of the topics and themes: "The Educational Problems of the Caribbean in Historical Perspective"; "John Locke"; "Lands, Peoples, Problems"; "Massa Day Done"; "The British West Indian Federation"; and "The Democratic Tradition in Western Civilisation and Its Relevance for the West Indies." As George Lamming argued,

> William's [sic] lectures: turned history, the history of the Caribbean into gossip so that the story of a people's predicament seemed no longer the infinite barren tract of documents, dates and texts. Everything became news: slavery, colonialisation, the forgivable deception of metropolitan rule, the sad and inevitable unawareness of native production. His lectures always retained the character of whisper which everyone was allowed to hear, a rumour which experience had established as truth.[60]

As it is mythologized, the working class were proud to have an intellectual among them. As Williams stressed national pride and confidence, a bond was forged. On the road to independence this bond was central to the success of the PNM party attaining power in democratic elections. It allowed politics to shift from a terrain of class conflict with its trade unions and the existing political organizations to a terrain of "national unity" with its combination of economic, political, intellectual, and moral ideas.

Most commentators agree that at Woodford Square Williams won the support of the working class and the urban poor. It was here that the most "politically informed and sophisticated citizenry in the Anglophone Caribbean" of the 1950s was forged.[61] Williams's rhetoric was both radical and empowering. He gave the island a sense of self-confidence in determining its own destiny. He decried the imperial powers of first Britain and then the United States. He argued for a clean slate, a local foundation for the new Trinidad and Tobago he envisioned. And he rallied the masses in the same vein, achieving a consensus that swept his party to election victory again in 1961. His mandate was now large enough and he pushed for independence immediately, first as a member state in a new Federation of the West Indies, and when that failed, the independence of Trinidad and Tobago alone. On August 31, 1962, Trinidad and Tobago was declared an independent country.

While Williams advanced popular education and literacy, with the cumulative effect of raising general educational levels and the resulting expansion of the middle class, his governance was not as radical as his rhetoric. Shortly after independence he made his peace with U.S. imperialism, siding against the masses.[62] Apologists like Oxaal call Williams a "tragic statesman," implying that Williams's hand was forced as preexisting "industrialisation by invitation" development policy forged a complete reliance on foreign capital, technology, expertise, manufacturing industries, and personnel.[63] But regardless of personal intent or lament, the government of Trinidad and Tobago cooperated with the imperatives of Euro-American capitalist hegemony. As Ryan observes: "Williams' constitutional proposals were a model of moderation. What was striking about them were the enormous concessions which were made to the vested interests ... which on the surface, Williams appeared to be attacking."[64] As such, Williams can be viewed as an agent of mystification obscuring his compromised intent and the institutional framework of capitalism his government supported.

Like Cipriani, Williams was "organizing" the "masses" and leading them. He believed his intellect and lower-class origins meant he could lead the country to independence and freedom from colonial control. He was an Afro-Saxon, shaped by Woodbrook and then well versed in British forms of government and debate. Indeed, he had somewhat made peace with capitalism. Williams was a bourgeois "organic intellectual," and though he believed himself to be and installed himself as the sole "professor" who could lead and free his "people," he was organizing them for an international system of global capitalist relations and neocolonial economic inequality.

The Punishment of Capital Accumulation

Woodbrook occupies a real and imagined place in Trinbagonian politics. Through the cultivation of certain habits, dispositions, and sensibilities, an Afro-Saxon middle class came to effectively "inherit" control of the state, thereafter steering it toward the interests of capital. In doing so, whether they would admit it or not—whether they realized it fully or not—they weakened working-class politics by downplaying real and meaningful class antagonisms. These decisions still have cascading consequences in the twenty-first century, some of which I will address in a moment. Anticipating some of these issues,

C. L. R. James, Williams's mentor and ultimately most disappointed critic, described Williams as an Afro-Saxon of the highest grade. Yes, through independence he enabled the moment of historical bloc with its synthesis of economic, political, intellectual, and moral ideas. Still, and for all the nationalist mythology, Williams was a bourgeoisie politician, albeit an exceptional one. This meant there were limits to understanding the brewing social grievances of unemployed Black youth that would later take the form of Black Power riots in the 1970s and is still a sociological social problem today.[65] To the extent that riots can communicate a message—as it became clear, Williams was no socialist, and his state was an "active collaborator" with foreign and local capital interests[66]—these protests targeted nationalism, arguing that it was not as revolutionary as it seemed. As Sankeralli remarks, "Nationalism degenerated into a new bourgeois Eurocentrism" and "an even more vicious colonial bureaucratic power structure was imposed."[67] The relations of domination and subordination in colonialism became the relations of domination and subordination in capitalism. Nationalism mystified and narrowed the possibilities of what independence meant. Independence became dependency.

The dominant economic activity in Trinidad for most of the twentieth century was the production and export of oil. The oil sector was—and still is on some levels—an economic enclave, operated mainly by foreign corporations with capital-intensive operations, employing relatively few workers at high wages. Since independence the main bridge between the oil sector and the rest of the economy has been taxes on oil company exports. In 1973–74, due to the quadrupling of international oil prices, Trinidad experienced a decade of prosperity when government revenues exploded, recalled locally as the "oil boom."[68] Initially, expenditures were restrained, and a substantial proportion of the oil windfall was saved. After a year or so, as international reserves soared, government expenditure picked up—the "boom" was underway—and a classic "Dutch disease" experience shortly followed.

In 1982 global oil prices collapsed, causing the local economy to enter a recession. During the booming 1970s, however, the large middle class had grown accustomed to a Western lifestyle, and for political expediency the necessary adjustment measures were delayed. Consequently, the country's social ecology experienced the consequences and punishment of massive external debt, rising unemployment, high inflation, falling real estate prices, crashing personal income, sharp income disparity, and burgeoning fiscal and current account deficits. In a short time Trinidad and Tobago ran through its large stock of foreign exchange reserves accumulated during the oil boom. Serious adjustment only began around the mid-1980s with the tightening of import and exchange controls and devaluation in 1985. In search of a solution to their economic problems and in common with many other postcolonial societies, the government was pushed into a formal program of structural adjustment in collaboration with the International Monetary Fund and the World Bank. Under the terms of the agreement, the government was required to implement several policies that were designed to shift resources from consumption to investment and to alter the balance in favor of private sector and export sector growth in a process Harvey might call a transnational consolidation of class power, and one I call neocolonialism.

In terms of popular culture, following the oil boom years of the early 1970s, Trinidad's consumption of media, consumer goods, and professional styles became decidedly North American.[69] From music and dress to sports and TV, the language, style, and frame of reference of a majority of the urban population exhibited North American cultural influence. As a result of IMF and World Bank–directed structural adjustment requirements, and then a distinct upsurge in the development of the local energy scene, by the late 1990s the economic situation in Trinidad generally can be described as one of neoliberal consolidation. Cronyism of the state and private sector cliques established by Afro-Saxon politicians and capitalists in the mid-twentieth century absorbed or funneled out of the country much of the new investment and offered little economic benefit to the wider society.[70] Less than a decade after gaining independence, 80 percent of manufacturing investment was still foreign, the banking and insurance industries were under 100 percent foreign ownership, and almost 50 percent of construction revenue went to foreign firms. The revenues taken out of the country during this early postindependence era speaks to empirical continuities between colonialism and postcolonialism.

The petroleum sector was revived and became the liquid natural gas sector, as Trinidad and Tobago emerged from economic woes as a small but significant player on the global energy scene. In fact, over this period the twin-island republic moved from a moderate oil-based economy to a globally important natural gas–based one that accounted for a large percentage of all U.S. liquid natural gas imports. As economic enclaves reaped the capital benefits of this situation, the wider social terrain began to experience an intensification of already present forms of structural violence and aggressive class politics.[71]

The Decline of Woodbrook

At a 2010 town meeting Woodbrook residents met with their member of Parliament, the mayor, and the director of town planning. Nearly every voice that spoke focused on the negative impact of the rapid commercialization of the suburb and its bar culture. The complaints seemed deep and heartfelt. People described their neighborhood as "under siege."[72] They spoke of blocked driveways, constant parking problems, and an influx of commercial users who were destroying residential communities. Some residents spoke about how they were forced to go by relatives on weekends to get away from "the unruly behavior of intoxicated fools," while another mentioned the disgusting actions of bar patrons who urinated in the front entrances of residents' homes. All in all, residents resented the commercial changes the neighborhood had suffered and that such changes were far beyond their control. Yet a feature of the neighborhood "under assault" and the sense of siege narratives some residents spoke about seemed to be class-specific rather than aimed at the commercialization taking place. This kind of stereotyping was visible when residents of Woodbrook in the meeting implied that lower-income people from outside of Woodbrook were dangerous and untrustworthy.

This narrative of poor versus rich is a glimpse into how residential patterns had been laid down historically. Perceptions of violence and threat in Woodbrook began to flatten Euro-American racial hierarchies and overlook local forms of interethnic and multicultural solidarity to become class-specific experiences, reflecting the legacy of population patterns since 1797. The binary was no longer strictly between Black and white or East Indian and African or foreigner and local—if it ever were that simple—but instead those with wealth and those without.

It can be suggested that this historical disconnect and obfuscation about the consequences of colonialism link the constant motion behind the accumulation of capital to the shifting production of difference making as a mechanism of neocolonial control. Why, for example, and as Thomas and Clarke note, does class drop out of the scholarship of the Caribbean, and culture become dominant? One answer they offer is that in focusing on culture—retentions, syncretisms, and difference—culturalist analysis focuses in on the connections of transplanted populations to their "roots" and ignores questions of the state, alternative ways to constitute political economy, and is less likely to question the political economy of international capitalism itself. Hence, residents of Woodbrook do not blame the commercialization of the neighborhood and the impetus for capital accumulation for their sense of siege but rather concentrate on the character of poor people. The cultured poor that once produced the symbols of a new nation as seen in Carnival, steelpan and calypso in the pre- and postindependence periods, are now the economic poor and untrustworthy—another example of the shifting production of difference making. Many current efforts to "invest in" Woodbrook take the form of gated communities, designed to cater to fly-in-fly-out oil executives. This increasing privatization of public space impacts a visual representation of difference making about who can afford to belong. It is fueled by fears of crime and the way the rich seek to remove themselves from the criminogenic environments they created.[73]

Between 1990 and the present, crime and violence in Trinidad and Tobago increased rapidly. From 1999 to 2007 the murder rate "rose precipitously, from fewer than 100 murders per year—in a country of around 1.4 million people—to 395. Since then, it has stubbornly remained above 400, even exceeding 500 in some years."[74] In 2023, the second bloodiest year in Trinidadian history, there were 575 murder victims; in 2022 there were a record 605 murders for the year. To a point, in a country of this size the violence has touched everyone, from the states of emergency and curfews, to the violence moving out of areas where it was previously most concentrated, such as the low-income locations and communities of Beetham, Laventille, and Morvant, to areas like Woodbrook with its popular bars and hangout spots. Since February 2023, five people have been shot dead on the popular strip of bars in Woodbrook. The police station that was moved out of the neighborhood in the 1980s was reopened in the late 1990s as robberies and assaults in the area increased. Another temporary police post was constructed in Adam Smith Square in the heart of Woodbrook in 2023.[75]

This same period, the 1990s to the present, might also be described as the decline of Woodbrook from the community its residents had once felt it to be during earlier times. Empty residential homes where previous owners had migrated or passed away were snapped up as commercial properties. In their development, planning laws were often not properly followed. Revitalization efforts such as One Woodbrook Place (three large, high-cost, high-rent apartment blocks on the western edge of Woodbrook) came to symbolize a degeneration of community for the capital accumulation of local and foreign elites. These high-rise and high-rent apartment complexes are mostly occupied by members of the emergent class of transnational capitalists and those who manage their globalized enterprises—a "Manhattanization" of the area, if you will. This demonstrates the precise "instrument effects" of neoliberal transformation with a focus on the emplaced signifiers of modes of governance, and Woodbrook's transformation from Creole nationalism to forms consistent with the demands of neoliberal transnational capitalism that have come to define Trinidad and Tobago in the twenty-first century. This combination of commercial development with residential zones, the development of Miami-type skyscrapers like One Woodbrook Place, and local capital flight heading west and east, to Goodwood Park, Westmoorings, Bayshore, Fairways, Glencoe, Valsayn, or out of the country, suggests that what Woodbrook once was has gone away. The decline of Woodbrook and its transformation also signify the decline and disarticulation of the Creole nationalist mode of power. The decline was accompanied by the physical shift in the community to Westmoorings and "the West," which is the current residential community of the new transnational class and the new signifier of the transnational mode of power. The Creole middle class has been dispersed to newly formed communities that signify their loss of power, most importantly to newly developed gated communities like Trincity.

A final question to consider in this social history of Woodbrook and the shifting construction of difference making is to think about where the Afro-Saxons and their Creolist mode of power went. The children and grandchildren of the original Afro-Saxons went abroad to Canada, the United States, and the United Kingdom to acquire education, work, reside, and attain citizenship. Some returned after successful careers abroad. Many never returned to live. Perhaps this was the culmination of their class project, arrival, and continuance in the metropole?

An extension of this reality is that because hegemony requires constant adjustments, culture changed. Afro-Saxons no longer provided the organic intellectuals needed to connect national independence with neoliberal capitalism. A new transnational class project took over this role.

In their respective ways Cipriani and Williams were organic intellectuals pulled in multiple directions. The social mode of production they experienced meant, concurrently, that they were resistant to the colonial enterprise yet enjoyed the benefits of economic differentiation and their middle-class status, and through education they possessed bourgeois class interests and aspirations. This in general terms is a metaphor for the culture of the Afro-Saxon architects of Trinbagonian nationalism—and why in race and class terms the Creolist mode of power failed the nation.

Conclusion

This historiography of Woodbrook has two central lessons for the reader. The first covers the displacement of the symbolic architecture (literally) of middle-class respectability, manifest in growing disrepair of iconographic houses of the community of Woodbrook and their transformation to accommodate the growing centrality of commerce and entertainment and of forms of "Manhattanization" associated with transnational neoliberal capital. The second lesson concerns how the Creole nationalism central to the golden era of cultural and social production in Woodbrook from the 1950s to the 1970s transformed to be consistent with the demands of neoliberal transnational capitalism and how the decline of Woodbrook and its transformation signify the disarticulation of the Creole nationalist mode of power.

Yet the historical narrative stressed by many contemporary local political leaders, academics, and historians conjures a triumphant picture of the nation's development, with the overthrow of Crown Colony rule, the growth of a nationalist movement and self-government, independence, and finally self-determination. But this Creole nationalist account has difficulties explaining economic inequality, entrenched class interests, and a political class removed from the lay citizenry—a present situation remarkably similar to the colonial conditions of a hundred years ago.

In this chapter I have described how the relationship between the shifting construction of difference making in Trinidad is related to the logic of capital accumulation, be it the transition of colonialism to capitalism, the emergence of capital dependency, or the punishment of neoliberal capitalism. The forms of difference making as I have shown include the production of racial hierarchy, the generative contradiction of cultural assimilation and cultural resistance, the role of Afro-Saxon "organic intellectuals," and today, how the original colonial logic and binary of divide and conquer intersects with contemporary class politics to exacerbate social stratification, economic division, state power, and, in terms of social development, the nation, and politics, the continued exclusion of the "masses" from the "people."

To make this case I provided a social history of the urban district of Woodbrook, Port of Spain, across three main eras: nineteenth-century Trinidad, independence-era Trinidad, and contemporary Trinidad. This historiographical focus captured the changing social ecology of the community of Woodbrook, which came to signify middle-class Creole nationalist formation and its rise to governance in Trinidad and Tobago, and also the subsequent decline of this Creole nationalist mode of power in the face of neoliberal transnational capitalism.

This analysis helps us understand how intersections of race, class, and nationalism shifted over those periods—in particular, how the transformations experienced by the community reflect fundamental changes occurring in the processes and practices of global capital. While I added more nuance and qualifiers as the chapter developed, looking at the transformations in ideas around race, class, and nationalism helps encapsulate a larger point about how macrosociological shifts are predicated on changes in global political economy, items that can be detected in civic ascription and subjective comprehension. In particular, the chapter has documented the transformations experienced in the community of Woodbrook that reflect the fundamental changes occurring in the processes and practices of global capital.

NOTES

1. Fragano S. Ledgister, *Only West Indians: Creole Nationalism in the British West Indies* (Trenton, N.J.: Africa World Press, 2010).
2. Carlton Robert Ottley, *The Story of Port of Spain: Capital of Trinidad, West Indies: From the Earliest Times to the Present Day* (Trinidad: Harran Educational Publishers, 1962), 11–12.
3. Michael Anthony, *The Making of Port of Spain, 1757–1939* (n.p.: Key Caribbean, 1978), 105.
4. David Harvey, *A Brief History of Neoliberalism* (Oxford: Oxford University Press, 2005), 43.
5. Frances Bekele, "The History of Cocoa Production in Trinidad and Tobago," Cocoa Research Unit, University of West Indies, Saint Augustine, 2004.
6. "The term 'French Creole' is by no means restricted to persons of purely French parentage born in the West Indies. It also included the free people of colour, the children of the French planters of the early times with their African slaves, and later, their mulatto, quadroon and octaroon mistresses. Some of these children were recognised by their fathers and legitimized and freed, receiving educations at French universities and inheriting land and property. Several families settled in the south of Trinidad, many in Port of Spain, their children becoming in turn the doctors, lawyers and school masters in the latter part of the nineteenth century. They were, however, a minority, almost a curiosity in the social structure of the colonial society. Nothing remains of the Frenchness of Trinidad's French Creoles, except some family names. As a recognisable group with distinct traditions, language, customs or outward appearance they have vanished completely. But they gave, in their decline, to the country personages like Poleska de Boissiere, Jose Dessources, Captain A. A. Cipriani and Dr. Eric Williams, Trinidad and Tobago's first Prime Minister." *Newsday*, Millennium Special (2000), 10.
7. "Cheating of illiterate people, indebtedness at high rates of interest, lower prices for the smallholder whose was mortgaged to the local shop, reduced access to further credit, all led, for countless people, to the loss of their holdings, either to the estates or to the shops, which were often one and the same. Every report on the cocoa industry in Trinidad documents this merciless usury with painful frankness." Susan Craig, *Smiles and Blood: The Ruling Class Response to the Workers' Rebellion of 1937 in Trinidad and Tobago* (London: New Beacon, 1988), 15–17.
8. Bekele, "History of Cocoa Production."
9. Harvey, *Brief History of Neoliberalism*, 44.
10. Eric Williams cited in Selwyn Ryan and Eric Williams, *The Myth and the Man* (Kingston: University of the West Indies Press, 2009), 16; "The Civil Services are over ninety per cent coloured; newspaper reporting, elementary education and some sec-

ondary, all routine and a large part of the executive work of the majority of the business houses (except a few from which they are jealousy excluded) all are done by coloured men." C. L. R. James, *The Life of Captain Cipriani: An Account of British Government in the West Indies* (Nelson, U.K.: Coulton, 1932), 13.

11. C. L. R. James, *Beyond a Boundary* (New York: Pantheon, 1963), 71; Carl Campbell, *The Young Colonials: A Social History of Education in Trinidad and Tobago, 1834–1939* (Kingston: University of the West Indies Press, 1996), 167; Trevor Sudama, "Class, Race, and the State in Trinidad and Tobago," *Latin American Perspectives* 10, no. 4 (1983): 75–96.

12. Kim Johnson, "Crime and Decolonization in Trinidad" (PhD diss., University of the West Indies, 1981), 61.

13. Sebastian Raphael, "The Political Economy of Capitalism of Trinidad and Tobago: An Overview," *Tribune: A Journal of Socialist Thought* 1, no. 1 (1981), 41–55, quotation on 47.

14. Kelvin Singh, *Race and Class Struggles in a Colonial State: Trinidad, 1917–1945* (Calgary: University of Calgary Press, 1994), xx.

15. Raphael, *Political Economy of Capitalism*, 47.

16. Eric Williams, *Documents of West Indian History* (Port of Spain: PNM, 1963), 87; James, *Beyond a Boundary*, 58.

17. Antonio Gramsci, *Selections from the Prison Notebooks of Antonio Gramsci*, trans. Q. Hoare and G. Smith (London: Lawrence & Wishart, 1971), 5.

18. Lloyd Best, "Race, Class and Ethnicity: A Caribbean Interpretation," lecture delivered at the Third Annual Jagan Lecture, York University, March 2, 2001. To paraphrase, he asked, what is the response of people who have been transplanted from many different places and forced to wear the straitjacket of slavery, indenture, and colonialism? One of Best's suggestions was that persons in such a situation must make home and community anew in a form of "automatic solidarity."

19. Gramsci, *Selections from the Prison Notebooks*, 323.

20. "Structures and superstructures form a 'historical bloc.' That is to say the complex, contradictory and discordant ensemble of the superstructures is the reflection of the ensemble of the social relations of production." Gramsci, *Selections from the Prison Notebooks*, 366.

21. Williams, *Documents of West Indian History*; James, *Life of Captain Cipriani*.

22. Paget Henry and Paul Buhle, *C. L. R. James's Caribbean* (Durham, N.C.: Duke University Press, 1992), 267, 268.

23. James, *Life of Captain Cipriani*; Williams, *Documents of West Indian History*; Singh, *Race and Class Struggles*.

24. Ivar Oxaal, *Black Intellectuals Come to Power: The Rise of Creole Nationalism in Trinidad and Tobago* (Cambridge, Mass.: Schenkman, 1968), 54.

25. Oxaal, 54.

26. Bridget Brereton, *A History of Modern Trinidad, 1783–1962* (London: Heinemann, 1981), 157.

27. Jerome Teelucksingh, *Labour and the Decolonization Struggle in Trinidad and Tobago* (New York: Palgrave Macmillan, 2015).

28. Williams, *Documents of West Indian History*, 230.

29. Brereton, *History of Modern Trinidad*, 157.

30. By "working-class support" I include those in waged labor as well as the poor and

dispossessed. This would include slum dwellers, dockworkers, former cocoa and sugar workers, oil workers—essentially the proletariat working force who were disconnected from the means of production and were forced to sell their labor to survive and ensure the viability of the system of capital accumulation.

31. The events mirrored similar racial clashes taking place in British ports like London and Liverpool where white soldiers (and sometimes British white women) returned to find their jobs at the ports had gone to Black men.

32. Brereton, *History of Modern Trinidad*, 161.

33. Craig, *Smiles and Blood*, 24.

34. Singh, *Race and Class Struggles*.

35. James, *Life of Captain Cipriani*.

36. Brereton, *History of Modern Trinidad*, 160.

37. Singh, *Race and Class Struggles*, 27.

38. The 1930s were a time of rebellions and upheaval against colonial authority and exploitation throughout the Caribbean. Some claim the TWA connected across all British Caribbean colonies and played a leading role in the industrial agitation.

39. Oxaal, *Black Intellectuals Come to Power*, 54.

40. Craig, *Smiles and Blood*, 418, 386.

41. William Fred Santiago-Valles, "Memories of the Future: Maroon Intellectuals from the Caribbean and the Sources of Their Communication Strategies, 1925–1940" (PhD diss., Simon Fraser University, 1997), 333.

42. As Lears noted, "The idea of historical bloc departs significantly from notions of class embedded in the Marxist tradition: it promotes analysis of social formations that cut across categories of ownership and nonownership and that are bound by religious or other ideological ties as well as those of economic interest." T. J. Lears, "The Concept of Cultural Hegemony: Problems and Possibilities," *American Historical Review* 90, no. 3 (1985): 571.

43. Daphne Phillips, "Class Formation and Ethnicity in Trinidad" (PhD diss., University of the West Indies, 1984), 128.

44. Oxaal, *Black Intellectuals Come to Power*, 54.

45. Anton Allahar, *Ethnicity, Class, and Nationalism: Caribbean and Extra-Caribbean Dimensions* (Oxford: Lexington Books, 2005), 123.

46. Williams cited in Ryan and Williams, *The Myth and the Man*, 74.

47. Kirk Meighoo, "Ethnic Mobilisation vs. Ethnic Politics: Understanding Ethnicity in Trinidad and Tobago Politics," *Commonwealth and Comparative Politics* 46 (2008): 115.

48. R. Briggs and D. Conway, "The Evolution of Urban Ecological Structure: Theory and a Case Study, Port of Spain, Trinidad," *Social Science Quarterly* 55 (1975): 871–88.

49. Acton Camejo, "Racial Discrimination in Employment in the Private Sector in Trinidad and Tobago: A Study of the Business Elite and the Social Structure," *Social and Economic Studies* 20, no. 3 (1978): 294–317.

50. Campbell, *Young Colonials*, 1996.

51. Gramsci, *Selections from the Prison Notebooks*, 406.

52. Burton Sankeralli, "What in Dreams We Do—the Times of Beryl McBurnie" (2001), 1–2. Copy of manuscript in author's possession.

53. Dylan Kerrigan, "Creatures of the Mas," *Caribbean Beat*, January/February 2004, http: https://www.caribbean-beat.com/issue-71/creatures-mas.

54. Dylan Kerrigan and Nicholas Laughlin, "Artists of the Streets," *Caribbean Beat*, January/February 2003, http: https://www.caribbean-beat.com/issue-65/artists-streets.

55. Oxaal, *Black Intellectuals Come to Power*, 148.

56. Garth L. Green and Philip W. Scher, eds., *Trinidad Carnival: The Cultural Politics of a Transnational Festival* (Bloomington: Indiana University Press, 2007), 19, 3–4.

57. Colin Palmer, *Eric Williams and the Making of the Modern Caribbean* (Chapel Hill: University of North Carolina Press, 2006), 9.

58. Brereton, *History of Modern Trinidad*, 233–34.

59. Ryan and Williams, *The Myth and the Man*, 75.

60. Lamming quoted in Ryan and Williams, *The Myth and the Man*, 54.

61. Palmer, *Eric Williams*, 285.

62. "But Williams had eventually made his peace with imperialism—a restless, irritable peace to be sure, but a peace. Williams the tragic statesman: the soul of the angry petit bourgeois intellectual in the black hide of the opportunistic colonial politician." Oxaal, *Black Intellectuals Come to Power*, 60.

63. Oxaal, *Black Intellectuals Come to Power*, 60.

64. Ryan, Eric Williams.

65. For European and U.S. readers, the label "Black Power" is easily associated with the civil rights movements in the United States. However, while certain ideas were transferred from Canada and the United States to Trinidad and the wider Caribbean at this time—and there were certainly protagonists who sought to stress the "Blackness" of the participants—such a limited perspective would be incorrect. "'Blackness' was essentially viewed in the movement's rhetoric and ideology as a socio-economic condition ... very far indeed from advocating ... ethnic exclusiveness, at the expense of class solidarity." Oxaal, *Black Intellectuals Come to Power*, 41.

66. Oxaal, *Black Intellectuals Come to Power*; Phillips, *Class Formation*, 141–58. Williams was far more interested in industrialization, and the form of industrialization he chose replicated the structure of Euro-American society. It was an Afro-Saxon stance many feel betrayed the cultural substance of the people whom his "charismatic authority" carried to independence. This is most obviously seen in the dominant Western capitalist values that came to permeate the middle class, and the entrenchment of foreign capital in manufacturing, the media, and business.

67. Sankeralli, "What in Dreams We Do," 5.

68. "The quadrupling of oil prices in 1973 revived the economy and created a 9.6-percent real annual growth rate from 1974 to 1979. Trinidadians and Tobagonians, nicknamed the 'Arabs of the Caribbean,' were known throughout the region in the 1970s for the Carnival of consumption that they participated in with their instant oil wealth. The downturn in oil prices in 1982, however, plummeted the economy into a deep depression in 1983 from which the country had not emerged by 1987. Negative growth peaked in 1984, when the economy contracted by nearly 11 percent." S. W. Meditz and D. M. Hanratty, *Caribbean Islands: A Country Study* (Washington, D.C.: Federal Research Division, Library of Congress, 1987).

69. Daniel Miller, *Modernity, an Ethnographic Approach: Dualism and Mass Consumption in Trinidad* (Oxford: Berg, 1997).

70. James Ferguson, "Seeing Like an Oil Company: Space, Security, and Global Capital," *American Anthropologist* 107, no. 3 (2005): 378.

71. In the first quarter of 2004 Trinidad and Tobago accounted for 80 percent of all U.S. LNG imports.

72. The comments and quotations in this paragraph were recorded by the author at the 2010 meeting.

73. Dylan Kerrigan, "'Who Ent Dead, Badly Wounded': The Everyday Life of Pretty and Grotesque Bodies in Urban Trinidad," *International Journal of Cultural Studies* 21, no. 3 (2018): 257–76.

74. Adam Baird, Matthew Louis Bishop, and Dylan Kerrigan, "'Breaking Bad'? Gangs, Masculinities, and Murder in Trinidad," *International Feminist Journal of Politics* (2021): 632–57, quotations on 633.

75. Joshua Seemungal, "Residents Worry over Increase in Violent Crimes on Ariapita Avenue," *Guardian*, January 8, 2024, https://www.guardian.co.tt/news/residents-worry-over-increase-in-violent-crimes-on-ariapita-avenue-6.2.1893361.7c17e1e806.

CHAPTER 3

Leeward Islander Regionalism in Antigua and Barbuda

STANLEY H. GRIFFIN

The ways in which race, class, and nationalism are formulated in the Caribbean are heterogeneous because the circumstantial realities of each colonial society dictated how these three issues were articulated. Moreover, where several islands constituted one legal society, this triad is further complicated by the dynamics and politics of regionalism. The islands of Saint Christopher (hereafter Saint Kitts), Nevis, Antigua, Barbuda, Anguilla, Montserrat, and the Virgin Islands are closer than geography and recent political divisions suggest. Since 1671, when the British commenced colonialism in the Caribbean, these territories formed part of a federal colonial governance structure, a single multi-island colony. Thus, the experiences of the larger British Caribbean colonies—like Jamaica, Barbados, and Trinidad and Tobago—do not adequately represent the realities of the smaller regional colonies, like the Windward Islands and Leeward Islands.

Through focusing on the twin-island state of Antigua and Barbuda, this chapter explores the ways in which independent states treated insular constructs of race, class, and nationalism at the expense of frameworks like cooperative regionalism, which highlights how the triad was differently articulated relative to the other larger territories of the British West Indies. In essence, this regionalism is interwoven in the politics and construction of collective identity and economic activities, perpetuated via shared common services, and imbedded in cultural practices as well as amorous and familial ties.

Race, Class, and Regionalism

Much of the historical discourse on the Eastern Caribbean, and in particular Antigua, focuses on the slavery experience, plantation life, and the emancipation years (wherein emancipation ended in 1834 and went into effect immediately, without an apprenticeship period as in other parts of the British Empire).[1] This history has impacted the racial composition of the population of Antigua and the subregion. Undoubtedly, these island societies were stratified by race, that is, the legislated differentials in phenotypes, and class, that is, one's occupational and gender roles as well as familial positioning in the island society. These social orderings were further complicated by the freedoms to move from island to island within the colony. Thus, issues of race and class are still part of both insular and subregional societal narratives. However, unlike other Caribbean territories, these had subregional manifestations and implications and were discussed by class rather than color. The labor movement, for example, was typically made up of not only Blacks but the working poor in general (of several phenotypes). Migratory waves, as in the one to the Dominican Republic from the 1880s to the 1930s, included several phenotypes from several islands, yet all were described as persons from working poor communities.

The question of race is nevertheless inherent to the discourse on nationalism and cultural identities. Stuart Hall posits that race is a floating signifier within the constructs of identities. Race, like identities, is a social and political construct and is based on and subjected to the politics of the society. He states, "The reason why [race] matters is not because what's in our genes, it's because of what is in our history. It's because Black people [for example] have been in a certain position in society in history over a long period of time that these are the conditions they're in and that's what they're fighting against.... The term Black is referring to this long history of political and historical oppression."[2]

Race is therefore part of the historical narrative and informs the individual and collective lived experiences. Frantz Fanon maintains that race was also a tool used to stratify and divide the colonized society. The language and culture of the colonizer was used to dehumanize the colonized and their cultural expressions.[3] Rex Nettleford posits further that race influences the discourse on cultural identities. One's cultural positioning is determined by the racial stratifications and politics within society. The racial strand of identity is further complicated where racial-phenotype mixtures, such as coloreds or mulattos, have evolved. The cultural stereotypes that have been linked with geographic locations: Blackness—African, whiteness—European, Indian—India, Chinese—China, Syrians—Lebanon, and so on—are hard to separate in the racial combinations that have emerged from miscegenation. To be, for example, Antiguan, Kittian, Leeward Islander, or "from the Eastern Caribbean" is to be a racial and cultural product of the phenotypes and cultures of several geographies, movements, and generations.[4] Moreover, Howard Johnson and Karl Watson maintain that the articulation of racial politics was dependent on the roles of all races within the society. There could be no master without enslaved, no hierarchy of whiteness without the subjugation of Blackness.[5] Consequently, Stuart Hall is right in his assertion that "race works like a language," a pair of lenses for the reading of society.[6] An understanding of race is to further grasp the tenets of a society: its identities, its expressions, and its meanings. Race, class, and nationalism in the Eastern Caribbean, as illustrated via the Antiguan context, are further convoluted by the cultural, geographic, historical, and socioeconomic politics of regionalism—an additional layer not particularly relevant in other Caribbean territorial realities (excluding, perhaps, the southern equivalent, the Windward Islands).

An Imagined Regional Community

The Eastern Caribbean is an anomaly, with its colonial federalist roots and its socioeconomic and political pragmatism, that challenges normative perceptions of Caribbean nationhood, with its insistence that regionalism is contradictory to the insularity. Sir Shridath Ramphal describes this phenomenon as "different people of a different age renewing the effort to overcome the vicissitudes of smallness by building bridges across a dividing sea."[7] Antigua and Barbuda is a microcosm of this regional vision, a nation imagined as a regional community. This concept of community is based on the Western European philosophy that all humans are divided into groups called nations. Nationhood is therefore the ethical and philosophical doctrine that grounds and feeds nationalist ideologies, positing that members of a nation share commonalities in identity, origin, sense of history, ancestry, parentage, or descent.

In pondering on nationhood, however, several theorists maintain that nationhood is not that simple to define. Benedict Anderson contends that nations are "imagined communities ... an imagined political community—and imagined as both inherently limited and sovereign." Anderson argues that nations are imagined in the way unity is constructed and thereby expressed by its constituent believers. He states, "It is imagined because the members of even the smallest nation will never know most of their fellow-members, meet them, or even hear of them, yet in the minds of each lives the image of their communion." The nation is further imagined as limited, for it has "finite, if elastic, boundaries, beyond which lie other nations." Sovereignty is also an integral part of the imagination, for as Anderson asserts, "nations dream of being free, and, if under God, directly so. The gauge and emblem of this freedom is the sovereign state." Moreover, a nation is conjured up to be a community as, "regardless of the actual inequality and exploitation that may prevail in each, the nation is always conceived as a deep, horizontal comradeship."[8]

This imagination is based on the social, political, and cultural history of the group of people composing the nation. The stories that describe and define a nation may be the key reason for the composition of the particular nation by grounding the ideologies (i.e., nationalism) for the nation's existence. Quoting Gellner, Anderson made it quite clear that "nationalism is not the awakening of nations to self-consciousness: it *invents* nations where they do not exist." However, Anderson further suggests that all nations are not imagined in the same vein. He believes that each nation's imagination is unique and as such, "communities are to be distinguished, not by their falsity/genuineness, but by the style in which they are imagined."[9] And whether the imagination is deemed by the outsider wholesome, valid or not, Anderson contends that its adherent-citizens reckon it fixed.

Keeping Anderson's remarks in mind, what is clear is that Antiguans and Barbudans have conceptualized their nationalism in an open fashion, one that includes regionalist ideals and aspires to rise above the racial strictures imposed by the colonial experience. This nationalism differs from those varieties found in other Caribbean territories that were not so codependent on neighboring islands. The legacy of shared resources and institutions, which was central in colonial governance, is still present today within the lived experiences of the citizenry from this group of island nations, especially Antigua and Barbuda. Regionalism remains a prominent characteristic of the various territorial narratives of resistance, nationhood, and visions for their individual and collective futures. In exploring the ways in which independent states negotiated insular constructs of race, class, and nationalism through frameworks like cooperative regionalism, this chapter shows how these efforts have evolved, in the twenty-first century, into economic unions with intraregional supporting agencies, thereby creating possible alliances that the wider Caribbean community is yet to grasp. Island states like Antigua and Barbuda, as well as the other member states of the Organization of Eastern Caribbean States

(OECS), have unique perspectives on their colonial and postcolonial experiences that are reconfiguring their postindependent futures in ways that larger regional territories may never grasp.

A Regional Genesis

The Leeward Islands are central to understanding the history of the Caribbean. Whereas the Spanish attempted to occupy the larger islands in the Greater Antilles such as Cuba, Jamaica, Hispaniola, and Puerto Rico, the British and French pursued their colonial enterprises across the central and southern areas of the Caribbean. For the most part this gave rise to colonial experiences that were unique to individual territories. Yet regionalism too was a thread that weaved through the colonial politics of the British West Indies.

The idea for a regionalist approach to colonialism began with the settlement of Saint Kitts in 1624. For example, the commission to occupy the Leeward Islands granted by Charles I in 1625 was intended to ward off the Spanish in the Greater Antilles, as well as the French and the Indigenous Kalinagos locally. The commission gave Thomas Warner "the custodie of the aforesaid Islands, and of everie of them together with full power and authority for us."[10] Interestingly, the French Crown also granted their commission to Sieurs d'Esnambuc and du Rossey: a commission of the same nature, to claim, occupy, and Christianize the islands of Barbados and Saint Christopher and all other territories "situated at the entrance to Peru."[11]

There were also local pushes for regional solidarity. Settlers in Antigua were fearful of French incursion, which by 1662 had settled in Guadeloupe and Martinique. Lack of proximity to governance was also a concern. The settlers in the Leewards felt neglected by the Barbados-based governor, especially given French encroachment on Saint Kitts. In October 1667 a petition sent to the king requested "that Your Majesty will be graciously pleased to send over some person as Your Majesty's lieutenant for the islands of Nevis, St Christopher, Antigua and Montserrat and that they may be no longer under the government of Your Majesty's lieutenant of the Barbados." George Marsh, under whose hand the petition was raised, argued that this arrangement would be feasible since the four territories were in line of sight from each other, "whereas Barbados being a 100 leagues distant and many times five or six weeks before a ship can gain the Barbados from the Leeward Islands is rendered incapable giving any sudden relief." Distance was exacerbated by the belief that "Barbadians have wished these islands sunk declaring it would be better for them, for now there was so much sugar made [in Barbados], that it was a mere drugg."[12]

In 1668 Lord Willoughby visited the Leewards to show some interest in the subregion, but his failure to hasten the full return of British control in Saint Kitts did not comfort Leeward Islander colonialists. So in 1670 the Lords of Trade and Plantations instituted the Leeward Islands Colony as a separate entity. Charles II commissioned Sir Charles Wheler as governor-in-chief in January 1671 with charge over Saint Christopher, Nevis, Montserrat, Antigua, Barbuda, Anguilla, "and the other Leeward Islands, which His Majesty thought fit to separate from the Government of Barbados."[13] Interestingly, Wheler was directed to make Nevis the seat of his governance with his first order of business being to expel the French from neighboring Saint Kitts.

During this period Antigua grew in economic prominence. An increase in the importation of enslaved Africans commenced in the 1650s after the decimation and exodus of the Indigenous peoples. Sugar production on Antigua led to both growing interest and increasing wealth. By 1684 the governor, Sir Nathaniel Johnson, transferred the seat of the government from Nevis to Antigua, with Falmouth being the main town.[14] In addition to Johnson owning a large plantation on the island, Antigua was, by then, paying the largest amount of customs duty into the royal treasury. It had the largest population and strongest economy of all the territories in the Leeward Islands Colony. Additionally, Johnson considered this move a means of appeasing both the French in Saint Kitts and the new pro-Catholic monarch, King James II. In short, due to its location Antigua was well positioned to become a hub in the leadership, development, and defense of the Leeward Islands Colony. As I explain later, this regional experience would shape the island's perceptions of nationalism and the ways in which class and race were articulated within its borders and regional spaces.

Due to the plantation system, Caribbean societies are designed to be divided. Going as far as saying that "division is the heritage of the Caribbean," Sir Shridath Ramphal lists divisions of geography, colonialism and slavery, migration, and the insularity that frustrated movements toward a regionally encompassing independence. These divisions make it harder to form an extrastate national Caribbean identity: "The rivalries of Western Europe broke the region into segments; each tightly integrated into the trading system of the metropolitan power, sealed off in an almost watertight compartment and stocked with people brought together from Europe, a score of West African kingdoms and the central provinces of India. Nowhere else in the New World is there so sharp a juxtaposition of different races, languages, religions—different legal, educational and political systems."[15]

Geographic divides were exacerbated by inter-island prejudice intensified by colonial experience. Colonialism separated Caribbean societies from each other, while within each colonial society, class, race, and culture divided subjects. Andrés Serbin illustrates the partition colonialism instigated. "The colonial legacy of fragmentation hindered the construction of a wider identity than the insular ... by limiting and constricting efforts at nativisation or endogenisation [sic]. Parochial identities emerged, while the metropolitan *other* was mysticised and the geographical, cultural and ethnic differences of the neighbour disqualified. ... It was the differences and contrasts of the neighbour which were seen as a threat to identity because of linguistic, cultural, ethnic and colour differences."[16] The superciliousness that characterized inter-island relationships was also articulated in the relationships within the colony. Racism and structures based on class and color further divided Caribbean colonial societies. Although a dynamic system, the legacies of enslavement and colonialism created durable inequalities and entrenched hierarchies that in time came to hamper the pursuit of self-determination.[17] Induced social divisions, some of which I raised earlier, still weaken efforts to create collective identities. For example, Sam Selvon described the Trinidadian social relations as amicable yet tense. Still, "under the surface of affluence there is resentment, bitterness, tension and dissatisfaction between the Blacks and East Indians, and all the old handicaps standing in the way of a peaceful settlement."[18] This description could apply to many Caribbean societies.

Regionalism in Nationhood

As these brief preliminary remarks are intended to show, regional experiences shape the conceptions of collective identity in the Eastern Caribbean. Although federalism was a colonial imposition on the region, the movement toward self-government did nevertheless hinge on federalism. Shridath Ramphal notes that the 1705 law that imposed a "Federal Council that legislated on matters of common concern" was the first federal scheme in the British Empire, with a bicameral federal legislature with wide powers and a federal executive as the governor. This legislative relationship never lasted, however, and this body was last convened in 1798 to deliberate on the House of Commons' 1797 resolution on slavery. Other arrangements at federal governance were attempted in 1816 and 1833. These efforts were further consolidated in the 1869 appointment of Sir Benjamin Pine to lead the introduction of the Crown Colony system of colonial government with a federal mandate "to form these islands into one colony, with one Governor, one Superior Court and one Corps of Police."[19] This led to the 1871 Leeward Islands Act, which created six member presidencies: Barbuda, Saint Kitts, Nevis, Dominica, Montserrat, the Virgin Islands, and Antigua. The latter

> [retained] its premier position as the seat of the government. The island was also given more elected seats than the others in the General Legislative Council, [and] made liable for a larger share of the federal expenses. This Council, which had no independent source of revenue and could exercise no control over the fiscal affairs of the presidencies, assumed responsibility for matters such as education, policing, prisons, immigration, and the administration of justice (a supreme court being established, with three judges having jurisdiction in all the islands).... As the Governor resided in St. John's, and the General Council met there at least once a year, Antigua was more fortunate than the other five presidencies.[20]

This federal structure remained in place until 1957 when it was dissolved to make way for a large regional federation that was to be inaugurated in 1958.

With the demise of the West Indies Federation, in 1962 Antigua's then premier, Sir Vere Cornwall Bird, was one of the political leaders advocating for the continued pursuit of a federal nation, excluding Jamaica and Trinidad and Tobago, who sought independence. Deputy governor-general of the West Indies Sir John Mordecai, writing on his experiences negotiating for the West Indies Federation, quoted Premier Bird's commitment to the regional nation: "Shorn of all they were told, the people of the West Indies want Federation ... and are expecting their leaders to reach agreement."[21] Antigua's leadership and influence on regional matters, particularly among the Eastern Caribbean islands, would continue into postindependence. For example, Antigua articulates its independence and postindependence regional policies through an active role in the OECS, the legacy successor of the Leeward and Windward Islands Colonies.[22] Its participation in the 2010 Revised Treaty of Basseterre's Economic Union, which builds on its common currency and freedom of movement privileges for citizens of member states, further exemplifies this imbedded sense of regional nationalism.

The speeches of the political leadership throughout the 1970s, as an associated state and with independence in 1981, echoed what Gordon K. Lewis referred to as Antigua's "psychology of openness."[23] This openness is evident in several key pieces of state rhetoric. For example, on Antigua and Barbuda's independence on November 1, 1981, Prime Minister Bird's speech asserted that while Antiguans and Barbudans could claim other cultures and heritages, with the raising of the new national flag they are all now Antiguans and Barbudans. "My people, we are a multi-racial society. Our fore-fathers were Africans, English, Welsh, Scot, Portuguese and more recently Lebanese and Syrians.... We are all re-born Antiguans and Barbudans, each with a role to play, each with a contribution to make."[24]

This "psychology of openness" was to inform the future leadership policies on migration and citizenship issues. To wit, in a December 1995 national radio address, Bird maintained that migration was important to the development of the country. For those who choose to settle in Antigua, their commitment should be more than legal citizenship.

> There is no doubt in my mind that the majority of people who are born here, and those who have chosen to establish their citizenship here, do have a sense of commitment to this country. The fact that there is migration to other countries by Antiguans and Barbudans who are born here is not, in my view, an indication of a lack of commitment to the country. It is simply an expression of their desire to seek opportunities for self-satisfaction that cannot be fulfilled here. In the case of those who have chosen citizenship here, that act itself, in a general sense, is a demonstration of their wish for strong association with the country.

The prime minister argued that the attainment of legal citizenship and contribution to the economic life of the nation was not enough to be deemed good citizens. He suggested that full participation in the life and culture of the island was needed to be committed to the nation.[25]

However, some foreigners who have opted for Antiguan and Barbudan citizenship need to go beyond the mere acquisition of citizenship to display clearly that they are committed to the country. To do so, they need to show a readiness to integrate with the rest of the population, to participate in and support the activities that assert the culture of the country, and to be prepared to help promote our people and not berate them. "Bird was keen on the fact that the Antiguan society must embrace the immigrant settler for their commitment to the nation to grow and their contribution to be validated. He stops short, however, from encouraging the other to practice their own cultural heritages, seeking only that they embrace all the facets of Antiguan culture and that the local community encourage that process of cultural integration."[26]

Bird thereby called for an end to racism and the discrimination being voiced at the time toward immigrants and naturalized citizens. He posited that acceptance of the Other was as much a part of showing commitment to the nation as other expressions of Antiguan identity and patriotism: "I have noticed recently an attempt in some quarters of the local community to characterize differences of opinion in racial terms. I urge all Antiguans and Barbudans to spurn this development. Our people, regardless of what mix of blood runs through their veins, are all our people, and each person should be treated as equal, with the same rights, obligations, privileges and responsibilities as any other. We will not inculcate national commitment to our country without first accepting, without equivocation, the equality of all our people."[27]

Others in society were not as optimistic in their perspectives on the encouragement of the other settling in the society. The notable argument was, and still is, that while we encourage and support the "non-national" contribution to the development of the nation, their welcome should not be at the expense of opportunities for self-improvement and betterment of the "indigenous" population. Tim Hector listed the dangers the liberal immigration policy posed for the Antiguan populace, especially with regard of the widely discussed Caribbean Community (CARICOM) initiative, the Caribbean Single Market and Economy. In words laced with strong political furor, Hector argued that the nation needed to take stock of the implications of the policies. He asserted that while conditions were favorable for the skilled migrant, there were few opportunities for the local Antiguan to self-improve, thus forcing the national to emigrate.[28]

Hector suggested that a national skills training program is needed to offset the imbalance created by the emigration of Antiguan skilled laborers and the continued immigration of the skilled and unskilled Other.[29] Since then, several opportunities to develop the human resources in Antigua while still having favorable policies toward the other territories of the Eastern Caribbean have developed, such as varying hospitality training institutes and establishing the fifth campus of the University of the West Indies since 2019. Through these efforts Antigua has shown a commitment to addressing the fissures created by race, class, and nationalism through a Caribbean-oriented tertiary education.[30]

The policies of the political leadership and government, particularly from the 1950s onward, maintained, encouraged, and fostered regionalism among its populations in Antigua. The years leading up to full independence in 1981 saw the economic focus shift from the sugar industry to tourism and manufacturing sectors, which resulted in liberal "open-door" immigration policies and experimental economic decisions. Beginning with reference to the 1950s, Lewis posits that the Antiguan economic record was hopeful.[31]

This rapid development and the economic diversification attracted immigrants to the island's labor force. The *Antigua and Barbuda Bulletin* lists the Guyanese population as a well-established community in Antiguan society after a period of migration triggered by the economic policies of the time.

Mostly of African descent, the Guyanese date their history on the island to the 1940s and 1950s when migrants from that South American British colony arrived in Antigua to work in the rum industry as skilled operators. Following Guyana's attainment of independence in the 1960s, "many fled the political unrest and racial violence of the Forbes Burnham era, seeking refuge in Antigua."[32] Presently, the Guyanese are concentrated in the island's construction, private security, and tourism support services sectors as well as in the civil service. Like the other migrant groups, their culinary cultures have become a part of the local fare, thereby diversifying the cultural palate of the island.

Jessica Byron gives a brief synopsis of deliberate policies that encouraged the migration and settlement of the Other in Antiguan society. A regime encouraging new migrants sought to counterbalance the consistent outward migration of Antiguans and Barbudans to North America and Europe, while promoting an enabling environment for settlement and citizenship: "In the 1990s, between 70% and 75% of the GDP has been based on the output of the service sector. A high economic growth rate during the past two decades and relatively high rates of emigration of Antiguan nationals have led the country to rely to a greater extent on migrant labour, which currently accounts for over 20% of its overall workforce [in 1999]. The authorities have traditionally exercised a liberal policy on immigration and employment, recognizing the importance of such flexibility for the country's economy."[33]

These immigration policies are not restricted to labor and employment opportunities but arguably were favorable for the entire family unit. Regardless of the immigration status of the parent/guardian, admittance to school was easy, for example. This is not to deny that there are social conflicts. For example, one belief in the country is that these policies were pursued in order to shore up political support—the reasoning being that new immigrants are "badgered" into loyalty to the ruling party. One result of these allegations is that new immigrants can experience ostracization or taunting, which makes it harder for them to fully integrate into society. Thus, migration is impacting the contours of Antiguan nationalism.

Shared Services, Common Goals

Antiguan identity is distinguished by its ways of living and artistic expressions, like folklore, carnivals, festivals, music, and language, all of which are important means of maintaining national cohesion. Michael G. Smith argues that culture played a vital role in Caribbean independence movements, especially when claims of distinctiveness were graphed on the politics for autonomy.[34] Yet most of these movements invoked homogeneity for unity. Still, cultural critics have had hope the fragmented region could articulate a shared legacy, history, and future. This kind of Caribbean nationalism could rise above the circumstantial and inherited divisions, as Rex Nettleford argues: "Despite the diversity of Caribbean life and the surface fragmentation evident in multiple small sovereignties (all with standard bureaucratic rigidities), there are 'submarine' unities manifested in shared cultural identities and sense of community on which functional economic co-operation, if not immediate political integration, can be built."[35]

The colonial political arrangement had sociocultural consequences for Antigua, which continues to shape the postindependent nation. Antigua inevitably became the hub for the subjects of the Leeward Islands Colony. There was a constant movement in and out of Antigua, with islanders having a freedom of movement among the islands. It was commonplace for a Leeward Islander to hop on a schooner or fishing boat and sail to a neighboring presidency, leaving and returning at will. Bonham Richardson noted that inter-island movement was unrestricted, especially with reference to the seasonal migration to the Dominican Republic. "Travel back and forth from the Leewards to the Dominican Republic from 1900 into the 1930s was seasonal and by both steamship and sailing schooners. The voyages involved occasional stopovers at intervening islands both going and coming, and the individual departures and returns and numbers of people on board each vessel were therefore poorly recorded."[36] Carleen O'Loughlin further posits that inter-island movement was also reflected in family life and property ownership. "Many Leeward Island families have owned property in more than one island, and people of all origins have moved between the islands so that some of the most common names appear in all three."[37] This dynamic has certainly expanded and deepened, especially with modern modes of travel. Embedded in Antigua's nationalism are the deep family roots with many interregional connections, with histories and narratives dating back to the dynamics of colonial federalism.

Migration in and out of Antigua was a feature of the society, which also influenced the character of other local institutions. In addition to being home to a multiregional civil service, Antiguan schools, like the Antigua Girls High School and the Antigua Grammar School, were deemed the premier educational institutions for the subregion. Margaret Lockett, an English woman who spent her childhood in Antigua between 1920 and 1943, recalls in her memoir, *Antigua Then: Scenes from a West Indian Childhood*, that "like the

Grammar School, the High School applied no racial or colour bar to acceptance. The fees were low and affordable to many." She adds,

> The girls were drawn from all kinds of backgrounds. I suppose most were of essentially British origin, but there were a number of Portuguese and Arabs, for the most part the daughters of shopkeepers, Americans from the Virgin Islands of St. Thomas and St. Croix, a few East Indians whose fathers were employed by the Antigua Sugar Factory, and also the girls of Negro blood, ranging from very light to very dark. These might be the daughters of clergy, lawyers, government employees, all manner of occupations.... The school was sufficiently well regarded to draw boarders from St. Kitts and Nevis, Montserrat, Dominica, St. Croix and St. Thomas, Grenada [and] Anguilla.[38]

There were other institutions in Antigua that were regional in scope. The Holberton Hospital (now defunct) was considered the most advanced health care facility in the subregion and thus attracted medical migrants. Patients requiring special medical attention would journey from their various island homes to Antigua. This was also the case for private medical consultations and the mental asylum.

Education followed a similar pattern, particularly for secondary and tertiary learning. The first tertiary facility established and funded by the Mico Trust was regional in its remit. The Mico Charity Normal School was opened in St. John's in 1838 and trained ten to fifteen male teachers per annum from as far afield as British Guiana and around the Leeward Islands. The Moravians established a women's teacher training facility in the mid-nineteenth century that "became the highly respected Spring Garden Female Teachers' Training College, an institution which continued to produce teachers for all the Leeward Islands until its closure in 1958."[39] The Leeward Islands Teacher Training College was established in 1959 with facilities for migrant boarder students and pedagogical spaces on the same campus. This facility is the present-day site of the Antigua State College. Several other sectors that fostered this subregionalism within Antigua can be characterized as working within formal arrangements, based on the pillars of colonial governance: the church, the judiciary (including the police), and business enterprises.

Family and Social Ties

Other informal regional relationships established Antigua as the center for the Leeward Islands. From the small vendors who plied their trade selling fruits and vegetables in small boats, to inter-island cricket matches and interterritorial school debate tournaments, to other social and religious administrative relationships, Antiguans grew accustomed to persons from around the region landing on their shores, going about their business. Many of them settled and established families and enterprises. For that reason, many trace their family roots in migratory trajectories, as chronological routes, rather than in simple genealogical terms. Arvel Grant, a newspaper columnist, describes the impact migration has had on Antiguan society: "Here in Antigua and Barbuda, it is likely that a near majority of individuals living in these islands were not born in the country. More strikingly, it is likely that close to eighty per cent of all citizens are either children of immigrants, first generation immigrants, or grandparents of immigrants. To add to that, thousands of native Antiguans are either married to immigrants, cohabiting with immigrants, or otherwise intimately involved with immigrants."[40]

The roots of the society reside in journeys, arrivals, and departures. These routes are circumscribed by the experience of British colonialism and have impacted the daily lived experience in Antigua. Jacqui Quinn, a member of Parliament participating in a parliamentary debate on an immigration bill, stated that the villages and communities around the island are no longer monocultural Antiguan enclaves. Immigration and settlement have impacted every community on the island and in particular her suburban constituency. She described the cultural diversity that resulted from migration patterns there:

> We have in St. George our own little Roseau [i.e., the capital of the Commonwealth of Dominica], and on any given Sunday you may have cook-up rice, pellau, mettagie... coocoo, doucana... What we are seeing is that the composition and the whole cultural make-up of suburban communities like Potters, Herberts, Pigotts, Barnes Hill and some of the other areas in my colleagues' constituencies are rapidly changing. No longer will we find only native-born Antiguans in these communities [of political constituencies]. The suburban communities are comprised of small microcosms of multi-ethnic, multi-cultural pockets of Caribbean peoples and we, as a Government, feel that we are duty bound to facilitate these communities within communities.[41]

By being the federal center for the Leeward Islands, Antigua took this stance that favored immigrants coming to its shores to settle, as various groups of people did over the years, even with the colony's dissolution in 1957.

One prominent group with a long history of this migratory cultural relationship is the Montserratians. According to the *Antigua and Barbuda Bulletin*, Montserrat had always shared a close relationship with the twin-island state. In fact, in 1845 Montserrat's legislature proposed that their island be annexed to Antigua as an alternative to embracing the Crown Colony governance system.[42] From the colonial days Montserratians were part of the Leeward Islands Police Force stationed in Antigua, and according to the *Bulletin*, "Many came during the Second World War to work on the construction of American military bases. Montserrat also came to Antigua and Barbuda's aid during this period of food shortages and rationing, supplying much needed fruit and vegetables."[43] There is reportedly a strong Montserratian presence in the business sector of the Antiguan economy. As a result of these close geographic and sociohistorical connections, Antigua was the first port of refuge for the many evacuees during the volcanic eruptions of the mid-1990s.

The economic downturn in other CARICOM countries and the apparent stability and success of the Antiguan economy from the mid-1980s to the 1990s became another circumstance that attracted the Other to Antigua. Persons moved to the island to find work in the booming construction, tourism, and services industries. One notable example is the Jamaican community in Antigua. According to the *Bulletin*, the Jamaican population was approximately fifty persons in the mid-1980s. However, with the Jamaican economic slump in 1997–98, the number of Jamaican migrants increased. Today, in addition to serving as lawyers, "some Jamaican professionals are employed as teachers, nurses, and prison officers, while the majority of more recent unskilled arrivals are employed in construction, security or as domestics."[44] Prime Minister Gaston Brown notes that migrants have had a sociocultural significance on society: "Without our Caribbean brothers and sisters, the type of cultural diversity that we have in this country would not exist today."[45]

The present diversity in Antigua and Barbuda had its source in the circumstantial colonial formation of the Leeward Island Colony. This influence also shaped the wider regionalist and postindependent configuration of nationhood, which has imbedded a willingness toward inter-island cooperation and integration. Thus, the unique history of Antigua and Barbuda must be considered within the context of the other islands of the Eastern Caribbean, whose nationalistic visions are as regionally minded as that of Antigua and Barbuda.

Building on Legacies

While the Leeward Islands Colony is rarely mentioned in contemporary politics, the resultant countries did not jettison their federalist foundations when they gained their political independence. This colonial administrative infrastructure, though unjust given its historical origins and experiences, has shaped the present construction of regionalist sociopolitical, economic, and cultural outlook of the nation. Indeed, the economic, political, and social realities of the twenty-first century have validated the practicality of colonial-federalist ideals. Negotiations and representations on the global stage require this pooling of influence and resources. Moreover, this regionalism has reconfigured constructs of class and race in Antiguan society. Multinational/islander connections, heritages, and identities are key markers of citizenship, significance, and business prowess. In other words, race is no longer the social segregator as in colonial times. Instead, one's ability to, in subregional business, engender multinational identities via familial relationships and property ownership and promote favorable interregional community are hallmarks of social success.

The legacies of the Leeward Islands Colony are apparent in the sharing of technical resources and services in the Eastern Caribbean. From airspace to judiciary, the OECS has formed a tangible integration that differs in tone from the regionalism pontificated in the wider region. This regionalist relationship is cemented in the 1981 Treaty of Basseterre.[46] This treaty served as the basis for the increasing integration within the subregion, which initially included members of the former Leeward Islands Colony, namely, Antigua and Barbuda, Montserrat, Saint Kitts and Nevis, and former territories of the Windward Islands Colony: Dominica, Grenada, Saint Lucia, and Saint Vincent and the Grenadines. Earl Huntley states that this group of colonies sought to maintain the goal and vision of the defunct West Indies Federation (1958–62).[47] In so doing, these territories formed the West Indies Associated States Council of Ministers, which lasted for fourteen years and shaped the framework of the 1981 OECS, which, inter alia, sought "to promote unity and solidarity among the member states and to defend their sovereignty, integrity and independence." This group of island nations used the Treaty of Basseterre to create a common market while agreeing to "endeavour to coordinate, harmonize, and pursue joint policies ... in areas where functional cooperation was then existent—i.e. Civil Aviation, the Judiciary, Currency and Central Banking, Tertiary Education including the University, and those new areas where it hoped such cooperation would begin: audit, statistics; income tax administration, customs and excise administration; training in Public Administration and management; scientific technical and cultural cooperation, mutual defense and security."[48] The stability of the Eastern Caribbean dollar, freedom of movement within the community, and the establishment of the Eastern Caribbean Supreme Court, among other regional agencies and initiatives, have laid a solid foundation for greater and deeper relationships that would naturally evolve in the twenty-first century.

The revised 2010 Treaty of Basseterre builds on the vision for the OECS by setting out a framework for an economic union. The preamble illustrates the proposition of this chapter, that the present-day concept of class, race, and nationalism in the Eastern Caribbean is interwoven and shaped by regionalism. It states,

> RECALLING the links of their common history and the need to build on that history for the benefit of their peoples; RECOGNISING the progress that has been made towards their integration under the Treaty of Basseterre 1981 and the Agreement Establishing the East Caribbean Common Market; CONVINCED that at this time it is necessary to deepen the level of integration and the pursuit of a common economic purpose which has obtained under the Treaty of Basseterre 1981 and the Agreement Establishing the East Caribbean Common Market; MINDFUL of their obligations toward the wider grouping of the CARICOM Single Market and Economy; DETERMINED to enhance the level of regional co-operation between States that are parties to the Treaty of Basseterre 1981.[49]

In so doing, the OECS has crafted a "single financial and economic space where goods, people and capital move freely. [It] also allows the harmonisation of monetary and governmental policies relating to taxes and revenue. The countries of this economic union continue to adopt a common approach to trade, health, education and the environment, as well as the development of critical sectors such as agriculture, tourism and energy."[50] This group expanded to eleven members, with the associate membership of the British Virgin Islands, Anguilla, Martinique, and Guadeloupe, further diversifying its linguistic, cultural, and, more important, economic bases.

The 2010 treaty formalized centuries of colonial relationships and engendered new connections with the French Caribbean territories (Martinique and Guadeloupe) plus cemented an infrastructure for deeper interstate relationship. The OECS also has several organs to enable the vision of the treaty. There is the Authority, the supreme policymaking body of the organization composed of all heads of member governments, and a council of ministers (the second senior body) charged with reviewing policies and making recommendations to the Authority on legislation and policy. There is the OECS Assembly, which includes representatives of elected members from the various houses of Parliament and legislatures in the member states. The Economic Affairs Council focuses on the Economic Union Protocol of the Revised Treaty of Basseterre, with responsibility for the implementation of the Economic Union aspect of the organization. Finally, there is the OECS Commission, which coordinates the work of the various organs of the organization, headed by a director-general with ambassadorial commissioners from each member state represented.[51]

The OECS institutions, namely, the Eastern Caribbean Central Bank, Eastern Caribbean Supreme Court, Eastern Caribbean Civil Aviation Authority, and the Eastern Caribbean Telecommunication Authority, concurrently support and monitor the work of the OECS organs, under the leadership of the Authority. The Eastern Caribbean Central Bank (ECCB) was formed in 1983 as the Eastern Caribbean Currency Authority. Now a Central Bank, "the ECCB is the monetary authority for the seven OECS governments and the government of Anguilla (The British Virgin Islands uses the U.S. Dollar as their de facto currency). It issues the Eastern Caribbean Dollar and maintains its stability and oversees the banking system in the OECS states. The Bank is governed by a Monetary Council and a Board of Directors and is managed by a Governor" and is based in Saint Kitts.[52]

The Eastern Caribbean Supreme Court (ECSC) is a key feature of the autonomy of the subregional grouping of nations. The court succeeds the West Indies Associated States Supreme Court, which was established in 1967. It is a superior court of record for nine member states: six independent, namely, Antigua and Barbuda, Dominica, Grenada, Saint Kitts-Nevis, Saint Lucia, and Saint Vincent and the Grenadines; and three British Overseas Territories, namely, Anguilla, the British Virgin Islands, and Montserrat. The Eastern Caribbean Supreme Court has unlimited jurisdiction in the member states, in accordance with the respective national Supreme Court legislation. The court is a roving court, meeting in each territory accordingly, with the chief justice and two Supreme Court judges making the rules of court for the practices and procedures of the Court of Appeal and the High Court.

The Eastern Caribbean Civil Aviation Authority (ECCAA) is the oldest institution in the organization, having begun its role in 1957 as the Directorate of Civil Aviation. Its role is to "facilitate a collective and uniform approach to civil aviation matters of concern."[53] The ECCAA came into its current form in October 2004, when member states passed the Agreement Act. Thus, the ECCAA is now fully responsible for "regulating aviation safety and security within the OECS Member States in accordance with international standards."[54] This authority underpins all aviation movement and policy within the subregion, thus advancing and stabilizing the region's economy and livelihood.

The final entity with an Eastern Caribbean mandate was developed out of the need to diversity and revitalize the telecommunications sector in the Eastern Caribbean. The Eastern Caribbean Telecommunication Authority (ECTEL) was established in 2000 to provide legal and technical advice on telecommunications to all the member states. The ECTEL consists of a Council of Ministers, board of directors, and national telecommunications regulatory commissions in each member state.[55] With the proliferation of technology and communication methods and tools, the ECTEL "has been focusing within the recent past on educating consumers so that they become better informed and empowered to actively participate in their country's development through the electronic communications sector, in a meaningful way."[56] Thus, the subregion, through a unified approach, is enabling its citizens and economy for the emerging virtual age that is enveloping all sectors of life. Nevertheless, Antigua and Barbuda has been central to, and intimately involved in, regionalist thought and movements especially in the Eastern Caribbean. The work of these agencies is underpinned by the sociocultural and grassroots initiatives that drive the living experiences supported by these integration efforts.

Conclusion

The history of the colonial federation has certainly shaped a trajectory of mutual engagement and support that is still lacking in the wider Caribbean community. These organs exemplify the feasibility of economic unity in a region comprising postcolonial small island developing states. There has been some discussion about the possibility of a political union, for example, in 2008, a political union with Trinidad and Tobago, the southernmost island nation in the Caribbean archipelago.[57] The memory of the defunct West Indies Federation continues to haunt any effort toward that goal. A proponent of Caribbean regionalism, Sir Ronald Sanders posits that the OECS already has the basis and framework for the makings of a political union and would bolster the gains and infrastructure of the current economic union and hasten the possibility for a politically unified Caribbean community. He writes,

> If anything is to come of the OECS decision to form a political union with Trinidad, a series of steps suggest themselves. . . . The OECS should proceed to form a political union amongst themselves. This would be a natural progression since they already have a common currency, a common central bank, and a common judiciary. . . . It would be important for the union to be a federation and not a unitary state. . . . There should be free movement of goods, services, capital and people. . . . The door should be kept open for other CARICOM countries to join the political union if they wish to do so.[58]

Nonetheless, the island nations of the Eastern Caribbean have crafted a nationalistic ideal that is amenable to regional cooperation and union with other neighboring territories. This ideal continues the struggle to surmount the inequalities, legacies, and retentions colonialism imposed on constructs of class, race, and nationalism. These were further complicated by the pragmatism of subregional control and oversight. Yet the decolonization evolution taking shape in this subregion is using these hurdles as stepping stones to stronger socioeconomic and political futures for all member territories.

NOTES

1. There are not many works in this area. The following should be noted: Barry Gaspar's (1993) groundbreaking work examines master-enslaved relations from the 1730s. It details a society that was rigid in social and racial controls and hints at the root structures on which Antiguan society was built. Labor relations in Antigua have been a popular theme in Antiguan historical writing. Glen Richards, Susan Lowes, Keithlyn and Fernando Smith, and Natasha Lightfoot all provide insights into the various dynamics of labor relations and the development of unionism, especially after the 1930s. Paget Henry further chronicles the seeming underdevelopment of twentieth-century Antiguan society. Antigua's history focuses on group resistance and social reengineering by union leadership. The same could be said for historical literature for the other former territories of the Leeward Islands. This chapter is part of a larger work considering the cultural and historical constructs of the multiculturalism that is vibrant in Antigua and other parts of the Eastern Caribbean.

2. Stuart Hall, "Race—A Floating Signifier—Transcript," Media Education Foundation, 1997, audiovisual recording, http://www.slashdocs.com/nvkhs/stuart-hall-race-the-floating-signifier-transcript-407-1997.html, accessed August 18, 2013, 4.

3. See Frantz Fanon, "Black Skin, White Masks (Excerpts)," in *The Birth of Caribbean Civilisation: A Century about Culture and Identity, Nation and Society*, ed. O. Nigel Bolland (Kingston: Ian Randle, 2004), 228–35.

4. See Rex Nettleford, *Mirror, Mirror: Identity, Race and Protest in Jamaica* (Kingston: LMH, 1998).

5. See Howard Johnson and Karl Watson, *The White Minority in the Caribbean* (Kingston: IRP, 1998).

6. Hall, "Race—A Floating Signifier," 8.

7. Shridath Ramphal, "No Island Is an Island," in *No Island Is an Island: Selected Speeches of Sir Shridath Ramphal*, ed. David Dabydeen and John Gilmore (London: Macmillan Education, 2000), 17.

8. Benedict Anderson, *Imagined Communities* (London: Verso, 2006), 6, 7.

9. Anderson, 6.

10. Brian Dyde, *Out of the Crowded Vagueness: A History of the Islands of St Kitts, Nevis, and Anguilla* (London: Macmillan Education, 2005), 23–24. Granted, these commissions, Dyde suggests, do reflect a European total lack of appreciation of the geography, a misunderstanding that came to plague the Colonial Office in London.

11. Dyde, *Out of the Crowded Vagueness*, 25.

12. Dyde, 63, 64.

13. Brian Dyde, *A History of Antigua: The Unsuspecting Isle* (London: Macmillan Education, 2000), 26.

14. With the growth of the population and military defense on the island, Falmouth waned in its importance, and by the early 1700s a new main town was purposely de-

signed. St. John's was laid out in square grids in 1702, with a new market area and wharves constructed. Dyde posits that the inclusion of "a cage, pillory, stocks, whipping-post, and ducking-stool, put up at the public expense," which were common features in British towns, were evidence of the importance this town was designed to play in that colonial society. Dyde, *History of Antigua*, 43.

15. Ramphal, "No Island Is an Island," 15–16.

16. Andrés Serbin, *Sunset over the Islands: The Caribbean in an Age of Global and Regional Challenges* (London: Macmillan Education, 1998), 34.

17. Elsa Goveia, "Slave Society in the British Leeward Islands at the End of the Eighteenth Century (excerpts): The Ranks of Society," in Bolland, *Birth of Caribbean Civilisation*, 422–23.

18. As quoted in Stefano Harney, *Nationalism and Identity: Culture and the Imagination in a Caribbean Diaspora* (Kingston: UWI Press, 1996), 96.

19. Ramphal, "No Island Is an Island," 18.

20. Dyde, *History of Antigua*, 176.

21. John Mordecai, *The West Indies: The Federal Negotiations* (London: George Allen & Unwin, 1968), 358.

22. See "Our History: The Organization of Eastern Caribbean States," https://www.oecs.org/en/who-we-are/history, accessed January 15, 2020.

23. Gordon K. Lewis, *The Growth of the Modern West Indies* (Kingston: Ian Randle, 2004), 135.

24. Vere C. Bird Sr., "Masters of Our Own Destiny," speech at the Flag-Raising Ceremony, November 1, 1981 (St. John's: Government of Antigua and Barbuda, 1981), n.p.

25. Ronald Sanders, ed., *Antigua Vision, Caribbean Reality: Perspectives of Prime Minister Lester Bryant Bird* (London: Hansib, 2002), 237.

26. Sanders, 237.

27. Sanders, 237, 238.

28. Leonard Tim Hector, "This CARICOM Skilled Nationals Moving Here Now Is Fraught with Danger," *Fan the Flame*, January 31, 1997, www.candw.ag/~jardinea/ffhtm/ff970131.htm, accessed March 13, 2009 (no longer available).

29. Hector, "This CARICOM Skilled Nationals."

30. See "Five Islands Campus," University of the West Indies, Antigua and Barbuda, February 2021, https://fiveislands.uwi.edu/.

31. Lewis, *Growth*, 133.

32. *Antigua and Barbuda Bulletin*, 2008, 25.

33. Jessica Byron, "The Return of the Cocolos: Migration, Identity and Regionalism in the Leeward Islands," in *Beyond Walls*, ed. Simone Augier and Olivia Edgecombe-Howell (Saint Augustine: UWI School of Continuing Studies, 2002), 89.

34. Michael G. Smith, "West Indian Culture," in Bolland, *Birth of Caribbean Civilisation*, 364–65.

35. Rex Nettleford, *Inward Stretch, Outward Reach: A Voice from the Caribbean* (New York: Caribbean Diaspora, 1995), 10.

36. Bonham C. Richardson, *Caribbean Migrants: Environment and Human Survival on St Kitts and Nevis* (Knoxville: University of Tennessee Press, 1983), 124.

37. Carleen O'Loughlin, *Economic and Political Change in the Leeward and Windward Islands* (New Haven, Conn.: Yale University Press, 1968), 14.

38. Margaret G. Lockett, *Antigua Then: Scenes from a West Indian Childhood* (Washington: Antigua Press, 2003), 68, 74.

39. Dyde, *History of Antigua*, 152.

40. Arvel Grant, "Permanent Residents at Three Years—Voting Rights for Citizens," *Antigua Sun Online*, June 3, 2009.

41. Hon. Member for St. George, Dr. Jacqui Quinn-Leandro, Antigua and Barbuda, House of Representatives Hansard of Meeting, debate on the Millennium Naturalisation Bill, June 11, 2004, pp. 29, 30.

42. Douglas Hall, *Five of the Leewards: 1834–1870* (Bridgetown: Caribbean Universities Press, 1971), 164.

43. "Diverse Society Built from Many Cultures," *Antigua and Barbuda Bulletin*, July/August 2008, 25.

44. "Diverse Society," 25.

45. Hon. Member for St. John's City (West), Mr. Gaston Browne, Antigua and Barbuda, House of Representatives Hansard of Meeting, debate on the Millennium Naturalisation Bill, June 11, 2004, 20.

46. Earl Huntley, "The Treaty of Basseterre & OECS Economic Union," Paper no. OECS/AUT/03/38/17, 1, http://www.sice.oas.org/ctyindex/OECS/Treaty_e.pdf, accessed November 24, 2021.

47. For full discussion, see the memoir of former deputy governor-general of the West Indies, Sir John Mordecai's *West Indies*, 445–51.

48. Huntley, "Treaty of Basseterre," 1, 2.

49. Organisation of Eastern Caribbean States (OECS), Preamble to *Revised Treaty of Basseterre Establishing the Organisation of Eastern Caribbean States Economic Union*, June 2010, http://www.govt.lc/media.govt.lc/www/resources/legislation/revisedtreaty ofbasseterre.pdf, accessed November 30, 2021.

50. OECS, "About Us," https://oecs.org/en/who-we-are/about-us, accessed November 29, 2021.

51. For greater detail in the organs of the OECS, see "Our Structure and Organisation," https://oecs.org/en/who-we-are/our-structure, accessed November 28, 2021.

52. See "Our Institutions," https://oecs.org/en/who-we-are/institutions, accessed November 28, 2021.

53. See "Our Institutions."

54. Eastern Caribbean Civil Aviation Authority (ECCAA), "Our Origins," http://www.eccaa.aero/index.php?option=com_content&view=article&id=49&Itemid=56, accessed December 3, 2021.

55. See "Our Institutions."

56. ECTEL, "For Your Information," https://www.ectel.int/consumers/informational-guides/, accessed December 3, 2021.

57. The 2008 proposed political union was to take effect in 2013, which did not materialize. See discussion in "Moving Forward While Standing Still—Yet Another Attempt at Political Union," *Jamaica Gleaner*, August 29, 2008, http://old.jamaica-gleaner.com/gleaner/20080829/business/business7.html, accessed December 1, 2021.

58. Sir Ronald Sanders, "Political Union? The Devil Is in the Detail," September 12, 2008, http://www.sirronaldsanders.com/viewarticle.aspx?ID=49, accessed December 1, 2021.

PART TWO
HISTORY AND ACTIVISM

CHAPTER 4

Garifuna Deportees and Land Defense in the Bay of Trujillo

JUAN VICENTE IBORRA MALLENT
AND KIMBERLY PALMER

This chapter is the result of our encounters with young Garifuna men deported from the United States to Honduras.[1] Our combined research journeys entailed traversing ancestral pathways alongside these men who, after their forced return to their communities of origin, became involved in land struggles there. On two different but equally hot and torrid summer afternoons, we both arrived at the Wani Lee land recuperation (*wani lee* means "this is ours" in the Garifuna language), disembarking the refurbished yellow school bus that plies the route between Trujillo and Guadalupe in the Bay of Trujillo, Honduras. Wani Lee is on the outskirts of Santa Fe (Giriga) and across the road from a hotel and condominium complex called Banana Beach. The name Banana Beach alludes to the history of the banana enclave economy in Honduras, and the complex itself is constructed on lands seized by foreign investors from vulnerable Garifuna families with the complicity of the municipality. Despite the corruption and impunity involved in these sorts of land seizures, many young Garinagu are actively involved in recovering the lands of their ancestors. At Wani Lee and other recuperations in the Bay of Trujillo, we both met Garinagu who had been deported from the United States. The young men had all joined the land struggles in their home communities—forming land recuperation groups, claiming communal land tenure, occupying parcels of usurped land, and constructing abodes and cultivating food and medicine. Over the course of our time with them, they shared with us their experiences in Mexico and the United States. Migration and life abroad had allowed them to become familiar with other cultures and ways of life, which helped them demarcate new horizons after deportation.

The stories recounted to us were deeply moving and summoned our attention to the trajectories of resistance that young Garinagu manage to forge in the face of a life marked by expulsion. This chapter is an attempt to record these creative and courageous ways of imagining and enacting other worlds that we witnessed in Honduras. It forms part of a much larger collective and dialogic exercise in which we—as authors—play only a small role. We begin with a historical account of the complex regional processes that contextualize land seizures in Garifuna territory in Honduras today. As a result of historical cycles of dispossession, Honduran Garinagu increasingly migrated to the United States and formed transnational communities. Our research delves into the forced nature of Garifuna migration, identifying it as a result of forced displacement tied to extractivist economic activities such as tourism, drug trafficking, and the massive cultivation of African palm. In the 1990s the hardening of migration policies in North America heralded the intensification of deportation policies both in Mexico and the United States. This has held drastic consequences for young Garinagu, whose migration processes are increasingly interrupted by their forced removal from places where they have resided for most of their lives.

The experience of deportation or forced return is rife with encounters with the prison system, itself intimately linked to the immigration control system. Although some Garifuna deportees undertake new attempts to reach the North and seek opportunities denied to them in their communities of origin, other deportees reject the notion of the "American dream" and stay in Honduras, becoming involved in the recovery of ancestral lands seized by foreign investors. This has led to another type of return: to traditional cultivation and construction practices and a revaluation of ancestral knowledge. In Garifuna land recovery or recuperation processes in the Bay of Trujillo, a significant role has been played by the *Gari Rastas*, Garinagu who have incorporated Rastafarian imagery, beliefs, and worldviews into their organized resistance to land usurpation and concentration. In this chapter we center Gari Rasta experiences and reflect on the possibilities engendered by a return to the ancestors' way of life. A "return to the roots" signals a return to the community vis-à-vis land defense and becomes a method of revitalizing cultural practices that are being transformed and displaced by migratory processes. By participating in land recovery/recuperation processes, young Garifuna men overcome the stigma of deportation and lead lives that represent an alternative to seemingly inexorable and inevitable migratory processes.

Territorial Dispossession and the Garifuna Land Struggle

The Garinagu (plural of Garifuna) emerged as a distinct culture with African and Indigenous Kalinago roots on the island of Yurumein or Saint Vincent in the Eastern Caribbean. After successfully resisting the expansion of the plantation system into Saint Vincent, the Garinagu suffered a devastating loss to the British during the Second Carib War in 1795. In 1797 the British exiled the Garinagu to Roatán in the Bay Islands, from where they eventually established communities across the Caribbean littorals of Honduras, Guatemala, Belize, and Nicaragua. The oldest Garifuna communities in Central America are still to be found in Honduras. During the nineteenth century, Garinagu there developed key trade and smuggling routes between Trujillo, Balfate, Nueva Armenia, and La Ceiba, consistently forming community nuclei along the North Coast. These communities soon faced attempts by American fruit companies and groups of growers from other regions of the country (*poquiteros*) to appropriate land for banana cultivation.[2] Efforts to control the land were mirrored by similar efforts to control waterways, roads, forest resources, and commercial ports—all of the infrastructure necessary to export commodities to the world market.

Companies such as the Vaccaro brothers (Standard Fruit Company), the United Fruit Company (UFC), and the Cuyamel Fruit Company obtained vast concessions from Honduran governments such as that of Manuel Bonilla. By 1920 eighty-six kilometers of rail lines had been built in the North Coast department of Colón, from Puerto Castilla (Trujillo) to Bajo Aguán. That same year the banana companies controlled nearly 2,000 hectares in the region. By 1928 an additional 13,000 hectares were under pasture, demonstrating just how important this railway was to the transformation of the North Coast into an enclave economy. In total, the Truxillo Railroad Company—a subsidiary of the UFC—held dominion over 70,000 hectares in Colón.[3]

The first attempts to regulate land tenure in the Bay of Trujillo began in the late nineteenth century as a result of the expansion of cattle ranching into Garifuna communities. The Community of Morenos Naturales of Cristales and Río Negro (Trujillo) received titles that recognized full ownership of the community's lands, first from Luis Bográn (1886, 1889) and later from Manuel Bonilla (1901, 1904). In 1921 the Truxillo Railroad Company signed a lease agreement with the community for 239 hectares belonging to the 1901 La Puntilla title. After this contract expired on July 16, 1942, the community's lands continued to be coveted and usurped. The most egregious violation occurred in 1976 when Gen. Gustavo Adolfo Álvarez Martínez undertook a campaign of forced relocation of the Garifuna community of Puerto Castilla. Their displacement was deemed necessary for the installation and development of the National Port Company. Soon there would be repression of guerrilla and peasant movements within the country. In the 1980s, during the Roberto Suazo presidency, the Regional Military Training Center was created at the request of the U.S. government and within the framework of the National Security Doctrine. This military enclave, located in the vicinity of Trujillo, served the training and formation of Salvadoran troops and the Nicaraguan contras during the Central American civil war period. Events like these demonstrate the organic relationship between the agro-export economy and military interventionism.

Returning to the agro-economy, the 1954 strike aimed at improving worker rights and working conditions on the banana plantations resulted in the emergence of new forms of capital-labor cooperation embodied in the 1959 Labor Code. An increase in unionized workers followed, leading to higher wages and some benefits. However, introduction of machinery and techniques reduced labor needs. As there were few other employment opportunities, these layoffs prompted attempts to return to the land.[4] As a result, the demand for access to lots of land by peasant organizations intensified, and agrarian reforms were implemented during the 1960s and 1970s.

One of the key tenets of the reforms was that land now held a social function. This meant that there was differentiation between parcels of land that were being "effectively" used and those that were not. The National Agrarian Institute (INA) promoted the opening of new frontiers of agrarian colonization in the Garifuna communities of the North Coast, distributing lands deemed vacant or idle to landless ladino peasants from across the country. In cases where Garifuna inhabitants held titles that endorsed their historical and continuing possession of the community lands, authorities largely ignored their rights. Without sufficient legal checks, dispossession accelerated. Seizures of Garifuna lands intensified in community centers, while the massive appropriation of land for cattle ranching continued in rural zones. Starting in the 1980s and 1990s along the North Coast, the monoculture of African palm, the declaration of natural protected areas, and real estate development oriented to tourism further extended this trend. Notable examples include those of Vallecito in Limón, Punta Piedra, Nueva Armenia, the Bay of Trujillo, Triunfo de la Cruz, and surrounding communities in the Bay of Tela. In all of these places, Garinagu were confronted with the interests of African palm producers, drug traffickers, and cattle ranchers, as well as those of real estate speculators seeking land for the construction of luxury homes and tourism enclaves. Resisting these dynamics proved difficult: Garinagu did not always possess titles that guaranteed their ownership of land, and state authorities continued to refuse to enforce Garifuna rights in cases in which they did. As a result, migratory cycles progressively intensified.

Beginning in the late 1980s, so-called ethnic autochthonous policies were promoted in Honduras. These were in essence recognition policies that encompassed Indigenous and Black peoples, defining their differentiated condition in a complex and ambivalent way[5] and promoting a rhetoric sensitive to the cultural rights of minority groups convergent with hegemonic processes of regional and national development. Far from responding to the demands of Indigenous organizations regarding territorial rights and greater political autonomy, these policies set the stage for negotiation, becoming a way to legitimize projects of development that ensured the systematic violation of Black and Indigenous territorial rights. Dissatisfied, Black and Indigenous organizations continued to mount pressure against the state throughout the 1990s. Between 1992 and 1996 there was a groundswell of mobilization by Garifuna communities and organizations. A series of marches and petitions culminated in the October 1996 March for Justice and the Development of the Peoples (popularly known as the March of the Drums), convened by the National Coordinator of Black Organizations of Honduras. A series of agreements were eventually reached with the INA and the government, leading to a granting of collective property titles to Garifuna communities in the late 1990s and early 2000s.

The collective titles granted to the Honduran Garinagu excluded much of the land claimed by the communities as part of their ancestral geographies. Furthermore, the ancestral lands that were included have been fragmented in an unprecedented way: as we have both seen on the ground, there is near-constant curtailment and division of collectively titled Garifuna lands. Ethnic autochthonous recognition policies, by essentializing the cultural condition of the Garifuna and ignoring structural disparities, have become little more than a governmental device for the production of difference in complete alignment with the economic dynamics in the region. The formation of governmental organizations and institutions dedicated to ethnic autochthonous groups—such as the Directorate of Indigenous and Afro-Honduran Peoples (DINAFROH)—has been accompanied by the state's refusal to recognize organizations that actively defend the territorial rights of Black and Indigenous communities, such as the Black Honduran Fraternal Organization (OFRANEH) and the Lenca Council of Indigenous People of Honduras (COPINH). Recently these groups, as well as other legitimate community representatives, were excluded from the proposal for a Law of Free Prior and Informed Consultation (FPIC) pro-

FIGURE 4.1. Appropriated Garifuna ancestral territory "for sale" in the Bay of Trujillo

moted by the African palm businessman and deputy of the National Party of Honduras (PNH) Óscar Nájera.[6] This exclusion accompanied government attempts to promote so-called Special Development Economic Zones (ZEDE) in Garifuna territory. ZEDEs are zones oriented to tourism, extraction of natural resources, and the production of goods, ostensibly possessing administrative and economic independence and their own political and security systems. These controversial initiatives seek to increase foreign investment without attempting to control income, further damaging the territorial rights of populations such as the Garinagu who are considered little more than cheap labor.

Neoliberal geographies reproduce the enclave pattern in Honduras at the same time as they erode and displace Garifuna ancestral community, ritual, and economic geographies. This literal "emptying" of Garifuna territories makes visible the structural underpinnings of Garifuna migration and ongoing forced displacement. An active struggle for territory, political autonomy, and the recovery of ancestral geographies continues throughout the Garifuna communities of North Coast Honduras. OFRANEH is the Garifuna organization most involved in land defense, and land recuperations have emerged as a key strategy in their arsenal. The organization does not instigate these recuperations; rather, they support a network of grassroots land defense committees in the communities. Garifuna land recuperations entail processes of re-

FIGURE 4.2. Recuperated land being cleared for cultivation in the Bay of Trujillo

covering collectively titled lands that were illicitly acquired by *terceros* ("third persons" or community outsiders). In many cases these lands were "invaded," stolen, or illegally sold by corrupt leaders or community members with state complicity.

Recuperation groups are generally composed of young persons and at times entire families who identify and occupy parcels of collectively titled community land that have been acquired by outsiders. Recuperating land is frequently a difficult and dangerous process, and it is generally perceived as safer to recuperate appropriated land that has limited investment in terms of infrastructure and construction. Recuperation groups thus target land that is in the early stages of privatization—land that has barely been fenced off or is only signed as "for sale." Land recuperations are usually conducted in direct response to community needs for residential and farming lands in the context of growing land scarcity. However, there are community members in desperate need of housing and subsistence land who, fearing violence and other forms of retribution, decide not to participate in recuperation processes. Disinformation plays a fundamental role here, as land recuperation groups are sometimes accused of actually "invading" private property instead. This generates uncertainty around what constitutes legitimate processes of reappropriation of communal spaces. Recuperated lands belonging to Garinagu who live in the diaspora are frequently neglected, as these recuperation members are often unable to ensure the maintenance of their plots. There are also cases where recuperation members who reside in the community are unable, for various reasons, to cultivate their plot of land. Recuperation leaders can sanction people who are perceived to have "abandoned" their plots with a fine and revoke their membership in the recuperation. Mediation between community/recuperation members is thus essential to avoiding confrontations, and collective work a necessary means of maintaining recuperated land and avoiding abandonment. Recuperating a plot of land, working it collectively, and constructing a home demonstrates to the wider community that it is indeed possible to achieve "progress" without migration or assistance from governmental institutions or programs.

Migratory Logics, Incarceration, and Deportation

Garifuna migration from Honduras to the United States began with the establishment of agricultural companies in the region at the beginning of the twentieth century and continued after World War II. The strategic interests of the United States went hand in hand with transformations that were taking place in countries like Honduras in the 1960s and 1970s, affecting migratory dynamics and propelling another wave of Garifuna migration. Military interventionism and asymmetric trade agreements led to a deterioration in the standards of these economies, witnessed by rising inflation rates and a reduction of subsidies that increased the cost of basic goods and reduced purchasing power.[7] Simultaneously, the banana enclave declined and was replaced by colonial encroachment on Garifuna lands by ladinos and large landowners.

In the United States, industrial reconversion promoted the arrival of unskilled workers from economies historically linked to monoculture and sugar plantations. The dismantling of the manufacturing industry and industrial reconversion in cities such as Los Angeles or New York resulted in a mutation in labor markets and a transformation in the ethnic composition of the workforce, with new opportunities for unskilled migrant workers. The passage of the U.S. Immigration and Nationality Act of 1965 was crucial to this process: immigration restrictions were loosened, which led to a demand for labor from Caribbean countries such as Jamaica, Puerto Rico, the Dominican Republic, Cuba, and Haiti. During this time, Garifuna men enrolled in merchant companies and spent significant periods of time in cities in the United States. Belonging to the National Maritime Union guaranteed permanent residence status, a higher salary, and better benefits. This contributed to the formation of a pioneering Garifuna settlement in New York City, where the union's headquarters were located.[8] This migration of Garifuna men—which implied a continuity of certain dynamics of labor migration in search of salaried work—was soon augmented by the migration of Garifuna women, who found new employment opportunities.[9] This, in turn, led to the migration of different members of the same family with the goal of family reunification. In the early 1990s approximately 70 percent of Honduran migrants in New York were of Garifuna origin.[10]

Honduran migration captured the attention of the U.S. media and became a political vehicle for right-wing populists in the lead-up to the 2018 U.S. midterm elections. Honduras was not always associated with migration, however. Alongside Panama and Costa Rica, Honduras maintained some of the lowest migration levels in the region for years.[11] Internal and external migration increased after Hurricane Mitch in 1998. The United States granted some humanitarian visas, but the bulk of those affected by Mitch migrated irregularly, signaling a transformation of migratory patterns. Parallel to the post-Mitch outflux of irregular migrants from Honduras, there was a tightening of U.S. entry and reception criteria. The closure of the regular channels of migration led to not only a considerable increase in irregular migration but an increase in the number of deported persons as well.[12] From around 2000 onward, the Honduran migrant was socially coded as a criminal. The Garinagu were included in this criminalization as Black and undocumented, and forced return and state deportation became commonplace experiences.

Garifuna male deportees in the Bay of Trujillo recount that during the 1990s, they lived in depressed residential enclaves marked by territorial conflicts between the Crips and the Bloods. These gang rivalries infiltrated both the school and the neighborhood, making it near impossible to escape their influence. As a result, many young Garifuna men immersed themselves in what they refer to as a "black American life," losing sight of their roots. The *"guetto* street culture" exposed Garifuna migrants to criminalization, exploitation, marginalization, and the possibility of being deported to their communities of origin or spending periods of time in prison. Delcio, a Garifuna land defender active in several recuperations in the Bay of Trujillo, still remembers his life on the streets of Brownsville (Brooklyn). In his youth, he attended high school with members of the hip-hop group Mash Out Posse (M.O.P.) and experienced the confrontations between Jamaican groups and Black Americans in the streets of his neighborhood. He survived a shooting, and after being charged with a felony he was deported back to Santa Fe, his community of origin. There he became involved in land reclamation, being in desperate need

FIGURE 4.3. Delcio, at his home in Wani Lee, with his deportation documents

of land and housing. Sometime after, his wife and family in the United States convinced him to migrate again. Delcio was able to cross the U.S. border but was stopped at a highway checkpoint and deported a second time, spending a period in prison before returning to Honduras. That experience was a watershed moment in his life, after which he decided to embrace Christianity and heed the call of the ancestors to return permanently to his natal community.

In many ways, the prison industrial complex is the "logical extension" of both the plantation and urbicide.[13] While different, there are sufficient analytical similarities. Their being poor, Black men and irregular migrants places young Garifuna men in a sphere of vulnerability that can lead to their confinement, expulsion, or both, as related to the racialized dynamics of a prison-industrial complex that has a fundamental axis in deportation. The racial hierarchies of work, and the accompanying high levels of exploitation, means that "progressing" in Global Northern urban contexts often involves laboring in the construction or building maintenance industry. As a racialized, irregular migrant labor force, Garinagu are denied the job security, access to social services, or citizenship rights to which other groups are privy. This often leads young Garifuna men to seek other, faster ways to progress economically in the informal economy—a situation reflective of the structural conditions/institutional racism that shape the options available to them and place them at increasing risk for insertion into the prison spiral. The illegality of these subjects is legally constructed, placing the irregular worker in a space of vulnerability and leading to potential deportation.[14] Deportation regimes, in addition to preserving sovereign space along ethno-national and racial lines and excluding migrants from health care, access to education, or social protection, contribute to the disciplining of the workforce, promoting through exclusion or differentiated inclusion a greater extraction of capital gains.[15]

There are constant cases of deported Garifuna men who have been criminalized for being Black, wearing dreadlocks, and having tattoos. Facing prison sentences brings these men closer to the reality of the prison-industrial complex and mass incarceration, and many become keenly aware of the role these institutions play in both the economy and punishment of racialized populations. While serving prison sentences, being deported, or both, Garinagu like Julián also become increasingly conscious of the interconnectedness of the regimes of imprisonment and immigration/deportation. In his case, Julián was tricked into an illicit business and served a three-year prison sentence while living in the United States. After fighting his case, he finally accepted deportation in order to regain his freedom. On returning to his home community of Cristales and Río Negro/Trujillo, Julián decided against attempting to migrate anew to a country where Garinagu do not have the same access to social housing or government programs as other groups. As a Gari Rasta, Julián sees his permanent return to his community as an answer to "a call of the ancestors" demanding his participation in the struggle for Garifuna land and survival in Honduras.

It is best—in Julián's words—to avoid "confusion" and follow the path that the ancestors have dictated, staying in Honduras and defending Garifuna land rights. However, Garifuna deportees' awareness of the racialized dynamics of dispossession, forced migration, and the prison-industrial complex eventually converges with the difficult process of securing material survival in their communities of origin, as well as with desires to be reunited with family and community in the United States. Garifuna deportees in Honduras face the lived realities of racialized dispossession, high levels of unemployment, discrimination, and stigmatization as well as shame, isolation, and alienation because of their deportation experience.[16] Like Delcio, many deported Garifuna men thus seek to migrate again, leading to a cycle of migration, deportation, and migration.[17]

Repeated exposure to the informal economy of migration entails many risks. Although *coyotaje* (migrant smuggling) often solves the immediate needs of a migratory journey and might even involve members of the community, it nonetheless entails situations that compromise the safety of migrants—extortion and kidnapping by criminal groups or police entities during migratory transit are common occurrences, for example. The most vulnerable migrants are those who do not have the capacity to pay a *coyote*, nor the fines, *mordidas* (bribes), and transport costs entailed in independent migration. This typically means staying for extended periods of time in Mexico to save money and continue the journey northward. Typically these migrants work in construction, vulcanization, and other labor-intensive jobs where few questions are asked. In some cases they rely on charity (*charolear*). Take, for instance, the story of Rocky, another young Garifuna man deported to Santa Fe after living his youth in New York City. Once forcibly returned to Honduras, he tried to migrate again, suffering new episodes of imprisonment for his attempted reentry. After being deported again, he managed to build a home of his own at Wani Lee. However, in 2019 he was assassinated in the city of Veracruz while once more en route to the United States. This tragedy caused insurmountable damage to his relatives and fellow land recuperation members, who had to experience the pain of repatriating his body from a country he was transiting. Despite having been involved in territorial defense and building a life in the community, economic conditions forced Rocky to leave again, illustrating the difficulty of being able to return to the life of the ancestors from the fringes of the dynamics of the market and wage labor.

Honduran Garifuna migration patterns continue to demonstrate a trend of "emptying," with recent figures indicating that more than half of the inhabitants reside outside the community. Educational and employment alternatives are scarce in the Bay of Trujillo and explain, beyond the perceptions of young people, how structural conditions drive the new generations' decisions to seek opportunities outside of their home communities. Thus, while several deportees become resigned to staying in Honduras, other community members continue to irregularly migrate, usually with the objective of saving enough money to construct a house. Many of these young persons are perceived by deportees as having lost sight of the "community horizon" and the cultural significance/importance of the land. For these younger Honduran Garinagu, farming and fishing are largely seen as "backward" and shameful undertakings. It is this perspective—as well as the dynamics entailed—that Garifuna deportees involved in community land defense ultimately aspire to transform. Involvement in the land struggle thus allows Garifuna deportees not just to have a piece of land and a home but to rejoin local processes and shed the stigma of deportation by assuming a leadership role in community problems as "warriors."

Edward Kamau Brathwaite offers a set of distinctions that help us better understand deportee aspirations to transform the racialized dynamics of dispossession, forced displacement, migration, and return. Brathwaite proposes there is both an "inner" and "outer" plantation.[18] Viewed through this lens, two prominent dynamics installed in Garifuna society come into focus. There is a long-term trajectory defined by dependency, underdevelopment, the impact of foreign investment, accumulation cycles based on territorial dispossession, and the appropriation of natural resources—symptoms of the subordination of the national economy to foreign capital and the implementation of hegemonic development models that involve the exclusion and displacement of the inhabitants. In the Bay of Trujillo, this "outer plantation" is exemplified by North American real estate speculators who appropriate Garifuna lands for the construction of residential enclaves, Banana Beach being but one example. Across the Honduran North Coast, the export-oriented monoculture of African palm also reinscribes the legacy of the outer plantation. This outer plantation is accompanied by an "inner plantation," akin to a form of mental colonialism that is evident in the loss of a territorial and community roots and the internalization, and even legitimation, of the unjust, racialized dynamics that territorial dispossession encompasses. It is this inner plantation that is most difficult to transform, since it requires a transformation of values and a return to the way of doing things before. Gari Rasta philosophy and practice rejects and disassembles the inner plantation. As Julián states: "The white man, the man on earth wants to wash our minds so that we can live as they want. I became a Rasta because I abandoned the life that white people want to give me, I don't accept their mentality. We become stronger when we live what our mind tells us."[19]

Garifuna Resistance and Post-plantation Geographies

To further delineate the trajectories of resistance forged by Garifuna deportees in Honduras, we focus on the political, pedagogical, and community work carried out by the Gari Rastas. The Gari Rastas are a particular group of Garifuna land recuperation leaders in the Bay of Trujillo—Julián being a founder of the group—who comingle Garifuna and Rastafarian cultural forms and practices. Rastafarianism is rooted in Blackness, and the incorporation of Rasta becomes a way to challenge Eurocentric modernity and all that it entails. Rastafarianism here is not just an aesthetic by any means, as it presupposes practices deeply rooted in the experience of slavery and the plantation. Approached from this angle, the land recuperation movement in the Bay of Trujillo appears to encompass a set of decolonial practices that span both Rastafarianism and Garifuna ancestral worldviews. Recuperations such as Wani Lee might thus be understood as Black place-making projects holding radical potential, with antecedents in what Sylvia Wynter named "the plot."[20] Plots were parcels of land that were given to enslaved persons in the plantation complex to cultivate their own food and reduce costs/maximize profits for the planters/enslavers. Food was cultivated in the plot, with the plot becoming at once "the root of culture." The plot was also where the enslaved literally *plotted* against the system: Brathwaite reminds us in that "sacred plot of land where slaves wd plot," they found "groundation."[21] Roots of many kinds are thus sown in the plot: yams (and cassava in the case of the Garifuna) engender a connection to both the land and ancestral pasts, signaling a process of making ground or space from which to exist and imagine/create decolonial futures.

There are debates, contradictions, and divergences between Rastafarian and Garifuna practices in the context of the land defense movement in the Bay of Trujillo. The Gari Rastas do not wholesale adopt and reproduce a "Jamaican" way of life. For example, for Julián it is a mistake to promote "false idols" like Emperor Haile Selassie. There are also convergences between other spiritual forms/religious practices and Garifuna spirituality and Rastafarianism. Some young people from Roatán are part of groups such as *Nation of Judah*, promoting gospel readings that dovetail with Rastafarianism and dialogue with the evangelical interpretations of Garifuna that are part of different denominations such as Baptist or Mennonite. Although the Garifuna community is predominantly Catholic, hybridizing Catholicism with traditional ritual forms in its practices, there has been a recent and growing tendency to adhere to evangelism. In cases such as that of Delcio, evangelical conversion has become a way of leaving behind his "bad" life lived in the Brownsville (Brooklyn) *guetto*. As we detailed earlier, in Brownsville Delcio experienced the confrontation between gangs, insurance scams, drug sales, and a traumatic deportation that eventually took him away from his children and family. Entering the church is the start of a new path, along which emerge new ways of living that involve a return to the way of life of the ancestors, traditional cultivation practices, and living in a more harmonious way with nature. Although it is common for evangelical pastors to maintain more conservative views in relation to opposition to government institutions or even land recuperation, this is not always the case. For example, Pastor Melesio and his wife Magdalena have constructed the Ministerio Trabajadores de Dios (Ministry of God's Workers) at the land recuperation Laru Beya in Cristales and Rio Negro/Trujillo. From there, they promote a moral and spiritual reform that allows the community members "to leave the mental colonization that puts them on their knees in the face of injustice, and leads them to reproduce the messages of the same executioner who has them prostrate."[22] In this sense, there is an amalgam of religious interpretations that find their commonality in being deeply rooted in the recovery of land.

Leonard B., who has family members in Miami and New York, affirms: "I am not interested in migrating because my ancestors were free human beings. I believe in spiritual, mental and physical freedom. United States is the land of slavery."[23] "Slavery" is here conveyed as a component of the erosion of community practices, and a result of migration to the United States. However—and as we have demonstrated in this chapter—the assimilation of experiences garnered in the United States and its influence on the ways of life and imaginations of Garifuna deportees has not necessarily led to a destruction of traditional ways of life.[24] In fact, the incorporation of certain religious and cultural forms such as Rastafarianism signal the ways in which diverse belief systems are incorporated in dialogical, relational, and heterogeneous ways by social movements in the Caribbean. These cosmopolitical vernacular imaginative reinventions have strong roots among those people determined to return to the ways of life of the ancestors that suppose a respect for nature and forms of community work.[25] This explains how the Gari Rasta movement both emerges from land recuperation processes and ideologically nurtures the struggle. As García points out, individualized perceptions of the territory have permeated Garifuna families, both local and migrant, and caused land to be viewed as a commodity.[26] But these perceptions coexist with ways of life that suggest a continuity, rescue, and revitalization of ancestral life forms. This signals a constant dialogue between traditional ways of life, practices that emerge from contact with other Afro-diasporic Caribbean cultures, ways of understanding the reality that emerges from the diffusion of Afro-American culture and the migratory experience and certain visions of progress that are more modern and individualistic. These frameworks, far from being fixed, pose a multiplicity of ways of living that, although they may differ and present contradictions to each other, have territorial and community roots, which explains why in one way or another they are experienced and acted out on the boundaries of the ancestral communal territory.

Returning to the Roots

In the Bay of Trujillo, returning to the way of life of the ancestors sets the guidelines for a dissolution of the dynamics of the internal plantation. At the same time, this "return to the roots" offers alternatives to the inexorable destinies marked by dependency and imperialism—the outer plantation. Mobilized into the land defense movement, Garifuna deportee men "stay on the land" and reclaim it for community housing and sustenance needs. At land recuperations, traditional food crops such as cassava, squash, banana, and coconut are cultivated. While cultivation becomes a very real means of material survival—providing food for those at the recuperation and beyond in a context of deteriorating food security—it also becomes a way for returnees to connect to the land and their ancestors/ancestral practices. As well, it becomes a way to "use" land in line with dominant, Eurocentric spatial imaginaries in Honduras and prevent further invasions.[27] But cultivation becomes a way to resist these same logics, as land recuperations become, in effect, place-making projects that construct a "history in place" by demonstrating the necessity of the land for cultural survival vis-à-vis traditional subsistence agriculture. Diasporic Garifuna involved in the land struggle in the Bay of Trujillo suggest that reclaiming and working the land could even lead to an eventual coastal network/Garifuna economy that challenges Eurocentric notions of "development." For these men, recuperations have the potential to turn into Garifuna development zones in line with Garifuna world views, promoting community businesses creating employment opportunities for Garinagu at home and abroad, furthering Garifuna cultural and material survival in a transnational context.[28]

Besides traditional cultivation practices, recuperations often feature houses constructed with indigenous materials such as adobe and timber (mahogany or bamboo). The revival of indigenous technologies—such as ancestral Garifuna building techniques involving *abüdürühani* ("cover with mud")—allow for economically viable ways of building houses that are in line with maintenance of traditional ecological knowledge. The ready availability of these materials means that recuperation members can avoid postponing construction until enough money is saved to get the cement or *lamina* (galvanized sheeting). This in turn leads to the valuation of traditional construction techniques. However, a significant number of Garinagu prefer "a modern home" and admit that they do not work in the fields—perhaps explaining a tendency to devalue these jobs and knowledges and consider migration an option. In addition, the lack of technological means for the processing and cultivation of the land constitutes a crossroads by preventing greater productivity as well as the commercialization of crops.

In the context of the COVID-19 pandemic, there was an attempt to return to the traditional medicinal practices practiced by the ancestors. A lady from Giriga (Santa Fe) returned infected from New York and was a victim of stigmatization, later announcing that she and her family had recovered from

COVID-19 through remedies they had learned from their ancestor, an important *buyei* (spiritual priest and healer) from Trujillo. This led many community members to seek medicinal herbs such as grass, avocado leaf, lemon leaf, holy cane, chamomile, calaica, lizard's hand leaf, man's stick, cuculmeca, nutmeg, cinnamon, clove, panela, eucalyptus, moringa, ginger, and cotton. Faced with the incapacity of the government to face the situation, community self-organization occurred. In the absence of respirators, medicines, or even face masks, the residents turned to natural remedies, which demonstrated the value of traditional ecological knowledge in a context where sanitary protection is not guaranteed. Collection centers were set up, both for food and for teas and antibacterial soap made by hand, supported by OFRANEH and also by community members living in New York. At the same time, community members continued to plant cassava and other traditional food crops in the land recuperations, since agricultural production could not be limited by confinement and mobility restriction measures, and even less in a context of scarcity and shortage.

Given the generalized economic and health crisis that is ongoing, the path of the ancestors became an effective possibility of life for many, considering the existing restrictions on mobility that prevented many young people from migrating or significantly delayed the arrival of relatives visiting from abroad. Remittances play a fundamental role in the local economy, as does the local spending of family members when they return to visit the community. The lockdown transformed the ways of life of many and reduced the influx of money into the Garifuna communities in Honduras. However, for the Gari Rastas, daily life took its cyclical course, punctuated with the harvesting and planting of cassava. The virtual way of life imposed on much of the world, too, was already a forced condition for the deportees. For them, video calls had long been one of the only ways to keep in touch with their families and loved ones after they were forced to leave the United States. Beyond the dynamics of enclosure and expulsion, practicing territorial resistance through cultivation and the construction of houses for future generations, the Gari Rastas lead lives that represent an alternative to forced migration. In fact, the Canadians and other North Americans who reside in protected luxury homes left the Bay on a repatriation flight, reflecting how finally, despite the incessant process of land and resource grabbing, the Garinagu continue and will continue to live in their ancestral territory.

Conclusion

In assessing the forced displacement of Garifuna communities, an intersection is observed between unequal development, imperialism, demand for labor, and forced migration. The attempts to impose an enclave model such as the Special Development Economic Zones show the close relationship between migration and territorial dispossession. The recent announcement of the incorporation of Roatán and Puerto Satuyé (La Ceiba) to the Prospera ZEDE project is one more example of the intention to promote foreign investment without attempting to control the income that said tourist activities might generate.

Migration, violence, and displacement have characterized the experiences of Garifuna communities in Honduras. These experiences are not incidental. Rather, they are a direct consequence of the implementation of mechanisms created structurally and maintained through imperial subjugation: the criminalization of migration, the racial hierarchy of citizenship, and the state promotion of labor exploitation.[29] Deportation mechanisms become supplementary mechanisms oriented to the organization of living labor, becoming instrumental for the disciplining of both the labor force and the reserve army of labor. Surplus plays a fundamental role in the reproduction of labor power, with necessary labor power always available and capable of being mobilized according to productive needs. Border control, containment, and organization of the labor force perpetuate dynamics of racial division of labor that have their origin in the slave trade and the plantation economy. In addition, certain policies of innocence and "respectability" play a priority role in discerning between those subjects who can be deported and those who are deserving of refugee status through avenues such as political asylum.[30]

These policies of protection and containment perpetuate an organic link between expulsion processes functional to the labor markets, processes of territorial dispossession, and the production of geographies of confinement of the prison-industrial complex, revealing how the control and exploitation regimes are articulated in a joint way. At the same time, they exacerbate the racial lines along which the division of labor, extractivist regimes on a global scale, and citizenship are sustained. Therefore, the intimate connection between settler colonialism and the plantation model that had its genesis during the slave mode of production has maintained its continuity through new forms of exclusion and appropriation. Even so, just as the plantation was subverted through flight and the constitution of Maroon geographies, the current conditions of dispossession, expulsion, and racialized exploitation make possible the formation of abolitionist geographies through new forms of interdependence and encounter with the territories inhabited,[31] facing seemingly inevitable processes of annihilation, subjugation, and erasure of Black geographies in America. So even though the slave plantation functioned according to logics of nonplace of descendants of Africans in America, as well as their illegitimacy to claim their right to inhabit the territories in which they lived, the multiplication of forms of appropriation, reproduction of the means necessary to live, and relationships with the multispecies tissues that make up the territory reveal the institution of alternative imaginaries beyond the plantation and those imposed by the gaze and the colonial archive. These fugitive geographies reveal modes of postplantation resistance that, in addition to honoring and recovering the ancestors' ways of life, reflect ways of living after deportation. From these interactions and encounters with the ancestors emerge more livable worlds, drawing Black geographies beyond settler colonialism and the political economy of racialized migration.

NOTES

1. We dedicate this chapter to Delcio Odil Roches (Gombiri), a Garifuna land defender and recuperation leader in the Bay of Trujillo, and a friend of both authors.

2. Antonio Canelas Díaz, *El estrangulamiento económico de La Ceiba 1903–1965* (La Ceiba: ProCultura, 2001), 22–24.

3. John Soluri, *Banana Cultures: Agriculture, Consumption, and Environmental Change in Honduras and the United States* (Austin: University of Texas Press, 2005), 50–51.

4. Darío A. Euraque, *Reinterpreting the Banana Republic: Region and State in Honduras, 1870–1972* (Chapel Hill: University of North Carolina Press, 1996), 95–105.

5. Mark Anderson, *Black and Indigenous: Garifuna Activism and Consumer Culture in Honduras* (Minneapolis: University of Minnesota Press, 2009), 104–71.

6. Juan Vicente Iborra, "Los límites a las políticas del reconocimiento y el derecho a la consulta previa en Honduras: El caso garífuna," *Estudios de Historia Moderna y Contemporánea de México* 60 (2020): 51–77, https://doi.org/10.22201/iih.24485004e.2020.60.71405.

7. For an analysis that links geopolitics with regional migration, see Sherri Grasmuck and Ramón Grosfoguel, "Geopolitics, Economic Niches, and Gendered Social Capital among Recent Caribbean Immigrants in New York City," *Sociological Perspectives* 40, no. 3 (September 1997): 339–63, https://doi.org/10.2307/1389447. For the garifuna case, see Sarah England, *Afro Central Americans in New York City: Garifuna Tales of Transnational Movements in Racialized Space* (Gainesville: University Press of Florida, 2006), 55.

8. England, *Afro Central Americans*, 44.

9. Nancie L. Gonzalez, "Garifuna Settlement in New York: A New Frontier," *Interna-

tional Migration Review 13, no. 2 (June 1979): 255–63, https://doi.org/10.1177/019791837901300205.

10. England, *Afro Central Americans*, 55.

11. Ricardo Puerta, "Entendiendo y explicando la migración hondureña a Estados Unidos," *Población y Desarrollo: Argonautas y caminantes* 2 (2004): 65–84, https://doi.org/10.5377/pdac.v2i0.829.

12. Puerta, "Entendiendo," 75.

13. Katherine McKittrick, "On Plantations, Prisons, and a Black Sense of Place," *Social and Cultural Geography* 12, no. 8 (October 2011): 955, https://doi.org/10.1080/14649365.2011.624280.

14. Nicholas P. De Genova, "Migrant 'Illegality' and Deportability in Everyday Life," *Annual Review of Anthropology* 31, no. 1 (October 2002): 419–47, https://doi.org/10.1146/annurev.anthro.31.040402.085432.

15. Juan Vicente Iborra, "Migración garífuna, deportaciones y asilo político en un contexto de desplazamiento forzado," *Andamios, Revista de Investigación Social* 18, no. 45 (January–April 2021): 47–76, http://dx.doi.org/10.29092/uacm.v18i45.810.

16. See Shahram Khosravi, *After Deportation: Ethnographic Perspectives* (New York: Springer, 2017); Tanya Golash-Boza, "Forced Transnationalism: Transnational Coping Strategies and Gendered Stigma among Jamaican Deportees," *Global Networks* 14, no. 1 (January 2014): 63–79, https://doi.org/10.1111/glob.12013.

17. Victoria Rietig and Rodrigo Dominguez-Villegas, "Stopping the Revolving Door: Reception and Reintegration Services for Central American Deportees," Migration Policy Institute, December 2015, https://www.migrationpolicy.org/research/stopping-revolving-door-reception-and-reintegration-services-central-american-deportees.

18. E. Kamau Brathwaite, *Caribbean Man in Space and Time: A Bibliographical and Conceptual Approach* (Mona: Savacou, 1974).

19. Interview conducted in Trujillo on June 18, 2018.

20. Sylvia Wynter, "Novel and History, Plot and Plantation," *Savacou* 5 (June 1971): 95–102.

21. Elizabeth DeLoughrey, "Yam, Roots, and Rot: Allegories of the Provision Grounds," *Small Axe: A Caribbean Journal of Criticism* 15, no. 1 (March 2011): 63, https://doi.org/10.1215/07990537-1189530.

22. Interview conducted in Trujillo on August 7, 2019.

23. Interview conducted in Trujillo on January 20, 2020.

24. Anderson, *Black and Indigenous*; Paul Christopher Johnson, *Diaspora Conversions: Black Carib Religion and the Recovery of Africa* (Berkeley: University of California Press, 2007).

25. Shelene Gomes and Scott Timcke, "Observations on Rastafari Cosmopolitics from the Caribbean," *Anthropology News*, April 8, 2019, https://www.anthropology-news.org/articles/observations-on-rastafari-cosmopolitics-from-the-caribbean/.

26. Doris García, "Place, Race, and the Politics of Identity in the Geography of Garinagu Baündada" (PhD diss., Louisiana State University, 2014), 9.

27. Sharlene Mollett, "A Modern Paradise: Garifuna Land, Labor, and Displacement-in-Place," *Latin American Perspectives* 41, no. 6 (February 2014): 27–45, https://doi.org/10.1177/0094582X13518756.

28. Interviews conducted by Skype on January 10, February 17, and April 11, 2018.

29. Harsha Walia, *Border and Rule: Global Migration, Capitalism, and the Rise of Racist Nationalism* (Chicago: Haymarket, 2021).

30. Iborra, "Migración garífuna," 63–70.

31. Ruth Gilmore, "Abolition Geography and the Problem of Innocence," in *Futures of Black Radicalism*, ed. G. T. Johnson and A. Lubin (New York: Verso, 2017), 226–40.

CHAPTER 5

Labors of Love

Returnee Women's Care-Motivated Migration

SHELENE GOMES, ANTONIA MUNGAL,
AND MARIA THÉRÈSE GOMES

It's a balancing act. A real balancing act. —Lisa

Basically, I will do anything for my mom. —Janet

This is a labor of love. —Janet

In *Ageing the Caribbean* Joan Rawlins and Nicole Alea note "the current and projected rapid growth in the number of older adults in our region."[1] They connect this "regional ageing phenomenon" with the common "migration of family members." The result is that "it leaves some older persons without relatives to provide the necessary oversight."[2] Against the backdrop of the formation of the Caribbean political economy, we examine in this chapter the convergence of two primary aspects of care work and the gendered division of labor: caregiving for older adults or aging populations in Trinidad with the voluntary return of their adult children to provide proximate care.[3] We center the ongoing lived experiences of women return migrants to Trinidad from locations abroad in this microlevel, empirical study. Guided by social reproduction theory, we too recognize that women's work is typically undervalued and rendered invisible. These are central issues within the politics of Caribbean feminisms.[4]

While the persistent undervaluing of women's labor is a cross-cultural pattern associated with capitalism and remains a significant concern for women globally, we examine how it plays out in the experiences of return migrant women (or returnees) within the cultural milieu of Trinidad and twenty-first-century neoliberal capitalism.[5] We propose that this undervaluing emerges when the cultural logics of kinship are co-opted by the capitalist logics of work when women provide proximate care or the "hands-on or physical (feeding, bathing), practical (advice, assistance), emotional, financial and material (remittances or goods) and accommodation (providing shelter)."[6] Typically the cultural logics of kinship provide cover for the capitalist logics of work. For example, the tolls of this unwaged work were largely left out of women's descriptions of their caregiving. Intervieewes rarely spoke of their difficulties in caregiving. When they did speak of the everyday bodily, financial, and emotional tolls, it was in terms of obligation and duty, rather than "work," signaling the persistent "valorization of housework."[7]

Historical factors matter in contextualizing women's return to provide proximate care for aging parents and relatives. The moral and cultural expectations of reciprocal care between children and parents at the beginning and end stages of the life course were conditioned within the plantation society historically in the Caribbean, on which we will expand in a later section, to situate cultural patterns and social expectations that have shaped gendered citizenship into the "postcolonial" present. As such, we concur with feminists who argue that the treatment of social reproductive activities reveals the persistent undervaluing of women's labor and its invisibility. Therefore, the invisibility of "women's work" remains a major concern for women globally, even while various liberal gains have had some positive changes in dulling the gendered division of labor.[8]

To develop this argument, we first provide an overview of our participants. Then we discuss health care in Trinidad and Tobago as well as the formation of Caribbean family structure within plantation society with its pertinent migration trends. We analyze participants' experiences in providing proximate care with the conflicting emotions and family interactions around their everyday care work for relatives, paid professional work, and personal goals and ambitions.

Five Trinidadian Women

Today this care work in Trinidad takes place against the backdrop of a local economic recession managed by a neoliberal state that is drastically cutting back social security and welfare services such as health care. We focus on the unpaid caregivers or care workers—those viewed as "children" and therefore subject to parental authority, as one of our authors described, as well as normative expectations. We are also attentive to the financial concerns of these two groups of older adults—older retired parents and their employed mature children—the care receivers and caregivers. Our study explores the reconfiguring of duties, burdens, and responsibilities in Trinidad and Tobago. We offer a perspective on social reproduction from the Global South and the family relations in which they are entangled.[9]

Participants in this study lived in Jamaica, the United States, and the United Kingdom, of which the latter two are typical migration destinations for persons from the English-speaking Caribbean. From semistructured interviews with five women returnees we highlight their motivation for return migration to do this sort of caregiving. We are also attentive to the reconfiguration of these women's duties, as the opening epigraphs from two participants, Lisa and Janet, indicate. How does a woman's educated status affect her ability to care for parents? How do women's financial positions enable choices between public and private medical facilities? In examining the gendered and intergenerational power dynamics within the "private" sphere of the home and its implications for the public domain, the reproduction of systemic inequalities and affective effects can be seen in the participants' testimonies.

Below we provide more details about the participants, but they had several common characteristics. They had all completed tertiary-level education and worked in "professional" sectors. In short, they can be categorized as "highly skilled" return migrants. Aged in their twenties as well as early fifties to midsixties, they returned with the economic, social, and cultural capital to navigate the household, everyday, and institutional challenges they confront. The family members for whom they cared were all aged in their seventies to early nineties. All participants, who self-identify as Trinidadian, returned within the past ten to fifteen years; one interviewee, Janet, resides seasonally in Trinidad and the United States.

In focusing on this specific group, we present the challenges, negotiations, and responses to cultural expectations, highlighting that if this class of women are unable to meet these expectations, then those with significantly less privilege or advantage are even less likely to do so. We are not suggesting that care work of this sort is easy, but that these women's position and capabilities differed from the norm in Trinidadian society even while "skilled" and "highly skilled" groups of women confront these prevailing cultural expectations for caregiving. This raises questions about how the women framed and/or accepted their caregiving as an obligation, continuing the invisibility of their work as well as the possible diminishing quality of geriatric care in Trinidad and Tobago and the wider Caribbean.

By examining returnees, we intentionally selected those who can successfully navigate regimes of mobility to provide proximate care for aging parents and relatives. Cognizant that these regimes of mobility and immobility have unequal impacts and effects on peoples' ability to physically move across territories, our focus is on these highly skilled women and the varied privileges they have to return to countries of origin, find comparatively well-paid jobs with flexible hours or live largely on retirement funds, and secure safe, comfortable housing in order to fulfill their aims of providing care.

As our participant group was a small one, we introduce our interlocutors before delving into the background and literature for this chapter. We conducted these interviews before the COVID-19 pandemic. Sadly, but not unexpectedly, some elderly relatives have died. At the time of writing, some professional work has shifted to remote forms, but this reveals layers of inequalities as "essential workers" have not been able to socially isolate, and women typically have had to do the additional work of routine care like daily cleaning.[10] Periods of self-isolation, especially when a household member was exposed to the coronavirus, have added stress to returnees.

In terms of our participants, as previously mentioned, they were all educated at the tertiary level and held postsecondary qualifications. From the most recent 2011 Trinidad and Tobago census, 6.2 percent of Trinidad and Tobago's population had acquired "tertiary non-university level education and 8.4 [percent] tertiary university-level education," emphasizing their relative educational privilege.[11] Severine, Lisa, and Janet live in the largely residential suburb of Diego Martin, north of Port of Spain. Ashley resides in the suburb of Bel Air in San Fernando and Flora in the northeastern neighborhood of Valsayn, which is in proximity to Saint Augustine and the regional university campus. These are all middle- to high-income locations.

Ashley is a medical intern in her twenties who lives with her natal family. Fulfilling the role of the dutiful (grand)daughter, she felt obligated to return to Trinidad from Europe to help take the pressure off her older parents, who are caring for her grandparents in declining health. Ashley moved into her parents' home in San Fernando. Ashley refers to herself as ethnically Indian and "Hindu on paper," often using her prayers learned in Catholic school for spiritual support. She contributes modestly to her family's household expenses.

Like some of the other returnee-participants, Severine is in her fifties. Although she has lived in the United Kingdom for more than thirty years, when her retired parents decided to return to Trinidad from England, she accompanied them. Severine lives in the family home with a separate entrance to her self-contained living space. Before Severine "fell out," as she explained, with her sister, the family would gather at her parents' family home for "Sunday lunch." Her accent is distinctly English and distinguishes her from the average Trinidadian. Severine calls herself Black, and in the context of Trinidad she is considered "light" or "fair" skinned, a status that brings positive and negative popular reactions within a social privileging of "lightness." Most of her time is dedicated to doing care work for her parents. This entails attending to daily needs, such as helping her mother cook, cleaning, attending to her father's basic needs, arranging and accompanying them to doctor visits, buying medication, and spending leisure time with them (usually indoors) chatting and sharing meals.

Unlike our other participants, Janet, now in her late fifties, lives seasonally in Trinidad and the United States, spending half the year in each country. This practice began when her father died and her mother remained alone in the family house. As Janet explains, "It was decided among the [three] brothers and I . . . I'd be the one to make the sacrifice" to return home as the only daughter. Having lived in London from her teenage years, after attending university and working, Janet immigrated to the United States. She did administrative work in both countries and now works in event planning and interior design in Trinidad. Her work in Trinidad allows flexible hours where she can prioritize care work for her mother. Despite her brother's recent return to live in Trinidad and his financial support of their mother, Janet does most of the care work. Janet identifies as Christian. She spoke about how churchgoing presented opportunities to socialize and find emotional and religious support from other congregation members.

Flora is in her early sixties and returned from the United States (Florida and Georgia) to Trinidad. Like the other participants, she lives in the family home but in urban northeastern Trinidad. Flora is trained in senior care and developmental care and worked in insurance in the United States. Her pension sustains her financially in Trinidad, allowing her to spend a great deal of time with her mother.

Lisa, in her late fifties, returned to Trinidad from Jamaica with her immediate family, which included her husband and two children. She is now divorced, her children themselves adults (in their twenties) with children of their own. They live in separate households. Lisa lives in her parents' family home with her sister and aging parents. Lisa's father died shortly before the pandemic was declared, but her mother is mostly mobile. After working in management in a public organization, she now works in insurance, which also gives Lisa some flexibility to care for her mother and, more important, to spend leisure time with her. Lisa is Catholic and has an active role in the nearby church.

These profiles set the stage for a more detailed discussion of these "highly skilled" participants' experiences in providing care for relatives. Amid the COVID-19-associated conditions and circumstances, there are continuities in these women's socially reproductive labors.

Methodology

Our objective was to elicit participants' detailed experiences of the everyday, emotional, and institutional labors they undertook in caregiving. In early 2019 we advertised and held a public roundtable discussion at a university in Trinidad on this topic. Five return migrants (four women and one man) joined the discussion with three of the women volunteering to participate further. We used purposeful snowball sampling to recruit other interviewees. We interviewed four additional persons, two of whom we have included in this chapter. At this stage of our project, our interview data came from five female participants. Envisioned as a phenomenological study broadly speaking, we conducted in-person interviews that incorporated semistructured and conversational techniques. Many of the participants were familiar with one of our authors, whose own experiences are incorporated into this chapter. Building a good rapport with participants in a study such as this one, which delves into intimate spheres of life, is essential. Therefore, we view our author's familiarity with the first three women as a strength that allowed us to affectively connect with participants, rather than a limitation. The author's inclusion as participant and as researcher out of necessity included a degree of reflexivity. Validity of the interview data arises out of the analysis and the instruments for data collection, such as the interview questions as well as the talking points for our roundtable discussion, rather than the numbers of participants.

We agree with Andrew Beatty's argument that first-person accounts can counteract the abstract typifying that comes from certain ways of practicing cultural analysis. But whereas he argues that these accounts are "unreliable" and that "shared experience turns out to be an illusion," we suggest that this critique underemphasizes how narrative analysis of these accounts can show the ways in which people reconcile roles and navigate identities.[12] A more suitable description of our approach is what Andrew Sparks and Brett Smith describe as "embodied engagement with the lives of others."[13] In this spirit, we sought to understand the social production of symbolic interactions vis-à-vis the difficult demands of elderly and end-of-life care for close family members. We attempt to elucidate the contextual expectations that frame our participants' conduct and conflictions. We looked at how these ideals were manifested in attitudes, values, beliefs, and behaviors as well as self-perceptions.

Our interview guide provided interviewees with the opportunity to situate their responses and narrate events as they felt necessary. Consent forms were provided during these face-to-face interviews. Follow-up conversations were held remotely by telephone and WhatsApp. Direct quotes from interviewees are indicated using quotation marks in the text. Some of the codes we identified from the interview data were responsibility, family, love, dependency, independence, self-care, and support, on which we expand in the following sections.

In terms of our own positionalities, in this multidisciplinary research team we are trained in anthropology, social work, and human communications. To a degree, these disciplines share a "family resemblance," but there is enough distance to provide differences in assumptions and attention. These diverse perspectives improve our analysis. Age and life stage also shape our positions, as we are in our early twenties, late thirties, and early sixties. Two of us identify as ethnically "mixed" and one of us as ethnically "Indian." We all confront the same Caribbean cultural expectations and scripts around respectability, which impacted our empathy as well as how we conducted the interviews. All three of us are Caribbean women, with insights and cultural conditioning that have accrued from growing up, living, and working in the region. We share the class background of many of our participants. Two of us have experience with emigrating from the Caribbean for work and study.

While one of our authors was working in the United States she had a critical role in her natal family for "looking after" her elderly mother, who required regular medical attention. This care entailed frequent telephone conversations with her mother as well as siblings in Trinidad and Canada, constituting a translocal network of caregivers. Our coauthor also visited Trinidad each year, with a focus on caring for her mother's health. Our coauthor and her family exchanged news and information on medical visits, changes to medication and her mother's diet, and the aches and pains that accompanied diminishing physical mobility. The changing facilities in the home to accommodate these differing needs such as a mobility aid or walker and an exercise bicycle fitted for seniors were expensive, but collectively she, her siblings, and mother were able to buy all the items.

Our coauthor decided to "return home" to Trinidad, as she says, to provide in-person care for her mother. Resigning from her academic position at an American university without employment in Trinidad, she moved into the family home and eventually secured a job at a local university. With her own physical health challenges that accompany aging but overall in good health, our coauthor acted as a "good daughter." She simultaneously functioned as mother and then grandmother, as her four children in Trinidad, Canada, and the United States were having children of their own. She continued these transnational patterns of care toward her children from Trinidad. Overall, these experiences allowed us as researchers, adults, children, and Caribbean women to engage in self-reflexivity throughout the research process.

Family Structure in the Caribbean

Following the systematic extermination of Indigenous groups with the European conquest of the Caribbean, African enslaved and Indian indentured labor, among others imported, sustained plantation production well into the twentieth century. Histories of migration matter. Colonial labor immigration and enslavement of Africans and Asians in the sixteenth to nineteenth centuries in particular, as well as postcolonial emigration from the Caribbean predominantly to the Global North in the search for individual and family betterment, has had lingering effects on social reproduction. Within the multicultural plantation society that developed over these centuries, race was entrenched within this stratified social ordering, and ethnically specific as well as common family and kinship patterns developed, as we briefly review.

"Slave proto peasantry" of plantation society (as termed by Sidney Mintz) set the stage for African-Caribbean household production. In the postemancipation Caribbean economy, household production became a means of safeguarding against turbulence in the labor market and starvation more generally, while also supplementing the minuscule incomes that came from plantation labor. Mintz characterized household production as a "mode of response" as well as a "mode of resistance."[14] This household production typically incorporated waged labor, subsistence farming, and small animal rearing with surpluses sold in markets.

In the postemancipation/indentureship era in the British West Indies following emancipation in 1834, male wage outmigration became part of Caribbean social life. West Indian men's work on the American-owned fruit plantations in Central America, in building the Panama Canal, and in the twentieth century in the oil sector of Trinidad provided higher income for families and households as compared to wage work on local plantations.[15] Men were encouraged to undertake foreign wage labor to remit funds to families, households, and children's mothers.

Regarding the family, men's wage migration financed the construction of homes, while women managed the households. Mother-centered or matrifocal families within these patriarchal societies also characterized African-Caribbean families and households, in the presence or absence of a father.[16] Women themselves also migrated with mothers leaving older female relatives to care for children in what are now well-established patterns of child shifting.[17] This is a translocal pattern that continues with the commodification of care, which often sees Black and Brown women from the Global South in care work (for children and the elderly) and domestic work as integral to the functioning of economies.[18]

Children also became important for labor.[19] They contributed to domestic work and subsistence farming, which provided necessary supplemental food and income in a wider context of underpaid plantation wage labor. Daughters in particular were valued because they produced laborers and were a dependable source of assistance in households with fewer men in the context of male outmigration. In short, the reproduction of the family was a strategy to secure livelihoods in an unequal and unfair market society.

Immigrant Indian women's labor under the indentureship program following emancipation was also necessary for plantation production. "The bulk of the population in the Caribbean was brought here from Africa and India to provide labour," Merle Hodge explains, inclusive of women.[20] However, the devaluing of women's labor encased in the high cultural value of women's roles as mothers and wives left the latter as the ideal. Indian women in a dominant Hindu religious system were encouraged to prioritize these roles, subordinate to both the colonial European and the Indian patriarchy. While there are historical examples of women's resistance and autonomy, domestic organization and family structure facilitated this social organization.[21] Occupation, income, and residence were all factors that determined domestic organization.

Indian and subsequently Indo-Caribbean households were male-headed and multigenerational, similar in the latter respect to African-Caribbean households but different in the gender composition given patrilocal residence patterns, with wives residing in the family homes of their husbands. Indo-Caribbean and specifically Indo-Trinidadian nuclear households came later with male emigration, Western education, urbanization, and increased wealth and buying power as well as labor and feminist movements.

Linda Peake and Alissa Trotz also discuss multiethnic Caribbean women's historical relationship to labor. During slavery "women worked alongside men in the fields for equally long hours and were equally subjected to the routine physical torture that accompanied resistance."[22] They trace the beginnings of the division of labor to plantations whereby men were exclusively occupied in the most prestigious skilled trades, preventing women from accessing equal sources of income. At that time women were engaged in domestically oriented work. Their work is helpful in thinking through the historical connections between women's identity and labor, and how labor continues to underscore contemporary constructions of women's identity, in this case enmeshed in an ethic of care for elderly relatives. The self-identified African, Black, Indian, and mixed women participants in our study share these obligations.

In the lines under which society had been stratified, factors such as race, gender, class, and capital ought to be considered. Although these are all interrelated, any one relation may take precedence over another depending on the context. For this study, while the norms governing behaviors of the sort we describe have weakened in the twenty-first century, our participants are of an age where these norms were still influential—in families and society—and very much still shaped their life chances. So notwithstanding changes in the labor market that allow women to work, daughters continue to be valuable for their assistance in the care of elderly parents, even if the daughters themselves have migrated.

Caribbean men and women continue to emigrate, some to undertake undervalued wage labor and others in high-earning sectors. Like countries such as India and China, the Caribbean is characterized by "bi-modal emigration—highly paid professionals and low-wage workers."[23] Thus, migration remains an important route to improvement for persons and families. But with daughters abroad, it does raise an issue of caring for aging parents. "Concerns about shared values ... networks for mutual support, and who does what, when and where, continue to be as relevant today as in the 1950s and 1960s [in the Caribbean]."[24]

Aging in Neoliberal Times

Aging populations are a feature in many middle-income developing countries.[25] Around the world, older populations are growing. The global population of older persons is expected to rise from 901 million in 2015 or 12 percent of the global population, to 1.4 billion by 2030 and 2.1 billion by 2050, when "for the first time there will be more older persons in the world than children under the age of 15." Additionally, the number of older persons is projected to grow fastest in Latin America and the Caribbean with an expected 71 percent increase in the population aged 65 years and over.[26] In 2000, persons 60 years and over accounted for approximately 9 percent of Trinidad and Tobago's population. By 2020, it was projected that the number of persons aged 60 years and over would be about 230,000 or 15 percent of the total population. While Trinidad and Tobago is classified as a high-income developing country, the patterns of emigration mean there are even fewer people able to support older adults and undertake caregiving.

The issue of caring for aging relatives more generally becomes important not only in how families function but also how the state allocates resources for this population. With dwindling state-provided social security, for example, the public health care sector is strained and of poor quality, while private health care is excessively costly with only marginally better health outcomes. On small islands like Trinidad and Tobago, the ability to pay for medical treatments and preventive health care determines life and death chances. There are inequalities of all kinds that compound one another.[27]

Ongoing debates about increasing taxes in Trinidad and Tobago to cover the state's pension fund for an aging population and private-sector encouragement for working people to "save more" rather than "burdening" the state demonstrate how neoliberal values are entrenched.[28] Economic advantages can (and do) buffer diminishing social services as our study illustrates, but if privileged persons are strained, vulnerable groups are even more exposed given their multiple inequalities. The reproduction of unwaged and undervalued labor ensures a continued "reserve army of labor" as well as the mystification of these processes by classifying domestic and care work, historically done by women, as obligation or duty rather than "work."

All participants recounted their harrowing experiences with their parents' treatments in public health care facilities as compared to private hospitals, both of which employ the same doctors in Trinidad. The long wait times for basic tests or procedures such as X-rays, or to see a doctor or receive results of urine or blood tests, were commonplace in public hospitals, in contrast to the efficiency of the private facilities. Lisa and Janet, two of our participants, commented on the lack of diligence of public institutions' nursing and technical staff, who in turn are significantly underpaid in contrast to physicians and surgeons.

In one memorable example, Lisa relates going into the emergency room at a public hospital in Port of Spain with her father and confronting a nurse who explained the long wait time: "we came at a bad time because there were few doctors on duty." These are the realities for the average aging person in Trinidad. Our participants, however, were either able to combine public and private medical care or predominantly pay the high costs of private care. Flora, Severine, and Janet were selective in which type of institution they patronized, depending on the circumstance. For instance, Lisa's family has a general practitioner who makes the occasional house call. This practice helped Lisa access medical care for her father when he was confined to bed. Lisa and her sister also paid a physiotherapist to do house calls for their father to minimize muscular atrophy during this time. These examples show the various facilities and strategies on which this group of returnee women draws to fulfill duties of care.

Migration has been a notable feature of Trinidad and Tobago's society. For example, the relative wealth of the oil industry brought intra-Caribbean migrants in the twentieth century. Patterns of emigration have also developed. Following formal decolonization from the British Empire in the 1960s, a multiethnic middle class formed. Political power generated new upward socioeconomic mobility for this class as well as a set of associated ambitions. This new class and ambition had to reconcile aspirational entrenched neoliberal values of individualism with consumerism and accumulation impulses in a context of unemployment and underemployment. As such, emigration continued. Given this experience of migration, the family remains a constant key locus of support and identity. For example, scholars have found that duty to one's elders and relatives is a recognizable core value, which we relate to our empirical data in the following section.[29]

Compared to return migrants, "skilled" Caribbean migrants in the Global North, often underpaid women in the service, domestic, and care industries whose labor is integral to the functioning of global capitalism, remain in the destination countries instead of returning before retirement age. Unable to draw a livable wage in Trinidad and Tobago, their remitted monies and goods demonstrate care rather than their full-time presence.

The Cultural Logics of Kinship

Following emigration from the Caribbean, there has also been return or circular migration. Studies have noted the return of Caribbeans as older adults and retirees as well as second- and third-generation Caribbeans in the Global North "returning" to their parents' and grandparents' country of origin.[30] If labor migration is a collective strategy toward social and self-improvement, care-motivated return migration of the sort we examine is also organized collectively among kin, but to ensure the comfort and safety of the aging relative, often at the end-of-life stage.

In the Caribbean, migration to economically wealthier countries whether in the Global North or within the Caribbean is usually a "family strategy."[31] The goal of such migration is usually bettering or improving the material condition of a family or household rather than solely one person—the migrant. Consequently, migration involves "dual obligations" to the immediate family unit and extended family members in multiple locations.[32] These translocal dynamics of duty and responsibility are evident in participants' decision-making as well as daily activities and emotional responses in Trinidad. Janet, Lisa, Severine, Flora, and our coauthor all chose jobs with flexible working times, with Lisa even changing careers from management to insurance, in order to maximize their availability to do care work. These changes come with resentments, as we will discuss.

The financial implications of these decisions are shown in Severine's case. Because her primary reason for moving to Trinidad was to care for her ailing parents following their return after five decades in the United Kingdom, Severine works part-time only or takes short-term administrative work to meet her recurring expenses. Most of her time is dedicated to her parents—attending to their daily hygiene, meal, and exercise needs, buying and sourcing medication, going to doctors, visiting regularly during periods of hospitalization, and spending leisure time with them. Their pensions as well as financial contributions from her siblings cover their care-related costs. However, since her father's passing in 2019, Severine has begun working full-time as her mother requires less attention. She also has more time at present to attend to her own health care. Earning money through her short-term administrative jobs was meant to ensure that Severine could contribute her time, attention, and love to her parents as she herself had minimal expenses while living in their family home.

It is women who continue to prioritize family well-being, specifically that of parents and grandparents in this study, over careers and individual well-being. One example is Janet, who agreed with her brothers that she would "make the sacrifice" to care for their mother, as quoted previously. As Tracey Reynolds notes based on her study of Caribbean migrants in the United Kingdom, "Migration also has negative consequences for the migrants' experience. People who migrated from Jamaica to the UK during the 1990s highlighted the burden of care and expectation that migrants feel in providing for family 'back home.' This burden of care creates stress for migrants particularly those on limited earnings who are struggling to make ends meet in their new country. Some migrants who are unwilling or unable to meet demands of family members left behind decide to cut or weaken their contact with them."[33]

Flora also cares for an uncle, her mother's brother, since his children reside abroad and, like those whom Reynolds interviewed, they were unable to physically return. Other migrants, such as our participants, were financially able to return and fulfill the "demands" of care for relatives in Trinidad.

Regarding family relationships that cross borders, as Reynolds notes, such relationships come with conflict as well as support. The frequent contact that Lisa, Severine, Ashley, Flora, Janet, and our coauthor kept remotely and in person with relatives in Trinidad fostered their reintegration into Trinidadian society and relative ease with daily tasks. Our interlocutors' active participation in religious organizations as well as the knowledge, ideas, and habits they brought with them also fostered their reintegration and the social as well as emotional support that helped in undertaking this sort of caregiving. Even if returnees did not arrive with substantial savings or then acquired assets in Trinidad, their local networks facilitated their reentry into Trinidadian society and into specific communities.

In Flora's case she lives in the family home with her mother. She is satisfied that she is without major expenses like a mortgage, although her modest income limits what she can do in terms of consumptive power and group leisure activities. But she maintains contact with relatives and friends from church as well as neighbors, who are Flora's primary social group for support, leisure, and time away from care work.

As one of the quotations from participants highlights, care work can be viewed as a "labor of love," a phrase that both Lisa and Flora used verbatim. Indeed, Janet's comment "I will do anything for my mom" reflects the stance of all the participants when issues about the reciprocity of care emerged during interviews. Their parents cared for and raised them in childhood. Now as parents and relatives were less able to take care of themselves "independently," as one participant remarked, so it was incumbent on the adult children to take on the role of caregiver. A gradual decline in parents' health or a specific event such as an illness or fall precipitated these women's move back to Trinidad. Lisa, Flora, and Janet gave examples of an incident that resulted in a parent's hospitalization and advanced participants' decisions to return. While Lisa was living in Jamaica, her father collapsed in the bathroom, and family members were unaware he had fainted for some time. Participants all spoke of feeling as though their parent or parents "needed them." When it became more difficult to provide long-distance care, the women felt that their physical presence was the best solution to this "need" for care from them.

The language about labor prompts us to think about the additional costs of these decisions. Such daily "labors of love" exact physical and emotional tolls on familial care workers. Ashley, who is the youngest participant in this study, thinks of caring for her grandparents as a "privilege." They are ambulatory but with chronic heart conditions. This situation makes her training in medical care valuable as she is the only member of the family with this kind of knowledge. While Ashley does not live with her grandparents, she resides with aging parents who are largely self-sufficient but require care on occasion. But Ashley explains that she feels "constantly tired." Her daily routine involves working long shifts in the hospital, "checking in" on her grandparents in the morning or evening (depending on her schedule), and going home to sleep. Ashley's leisure time is severely curtailed. As she explained, she feels obligated to fulfill these responsibilities. If at this age Ashley is already chronically tired, what will the next thirty years of care work for her parents and her own prospects for career advancement, reproductive labor, and general well-being hold? How will she balance these obligations with longer life expectancy?

Ashley's experience is not unique. Janet echoes this feeling of fatigue. "I know I don't get enough sleep," she admits, always staying alert during the night, listening if her mother calls for assistance to use the washroom or worse, listening for an emergency. She struggles to sleep soundly because the prospect of an emergency is very real. Flora and Dawn shared these experiences regarding lack of nightly rest. Flora was adamant that sleeping at most for ninety minutes each night is enough for her. In addition to the damaging psychological effects of such hypervigilance and lack of sleep, such circumstances have further potentially harmful consequences. In one instance our coauthor recalls "nodding off" while in traffic on her way to work in the morning, resulting in a minor vehicular accident.

Another result of lack of sleep that Lisa, Severine, Janet, and Flora pointed to was lack of patience. Our coauthor concurred with this "short fuse" that she sometimes had with her eighty-plus-year-old mother. The women spoke about being more attentive to "self-care" in addition to an ethic of sacrifice in caring for their aging parents. Caribbean societies and cultures, arguably influenced by the hyperindividualism of contemporary neoliberal capitalism, demonstrate a degree of modern capitalist individualism as well as collectivism and communalism.[34] Asserting that self-care is not only important for her mother, our coauthor added she pursues pleasurable leisure activities such as yoga and swimming as well as "limin" or socializing with friends and going to an art class with her adult daughter, who resides separately. In the latter example, not only is this activity an enjoyable one but also part of her role as a mother to care for a daughter by "bonding," as our collaborator explained.

The "balancing act" to which Lisa refers involves managing the care of parents, her waged work as an insurance agent, domestic duties, and family responsibilities with her children, themselves adults. To manage these responsibilities and practice self-care more effectively—or at least to incorporate time for regular exercise—Lisa had employed a care worker during the day for her parents, prior to her father's death. Cognizant of her own hypertension, Lisa would like to exercise more but is usually unable to with all her duties, though she does especially point out that during the annual Carnival festivities in

Trinidad she sets aside leisure time. Ashley also noted that in being more attentive to her own well-being, spending time alone is an important aspect of self-care. As we previously noted, in the Caribbean "lineage and kinship are foregrounded as structuring practices, through and in which the individual and his/her sense of self is inextricably bound."[35] In this study the participants' references to self-care, then, are seen as indicative of the valuing of the self to better perform care work for aging relatives.

No one directly expressed regret at the decision to re-migrate. This was quite surprising given our empathetic standpoint. We suggest that such a silence demonstrates the adherence to one component of a Caribbean value system that valorizes children's reciprocity to parents. Ashley explains, "When it came to the point in time whether to take a job away or to come back home, my grandpa fell ill so it kind of made its decision for itself." After studying for many years in preparation for a career in Europe, Ashley felt resentful at the work opportunities that she missed abroad by returning to Trinidad. However, she went on, "now I'm happy I made that decision."

Rather than thinking of "giving up" prospective opportunities abroad, Ashley looks toward the prospects for new professional opportunities in Trinidad. Flora, likewise, is happy to see her grandchildren grow and to care in person for her mother, although at times she misses her independence abroad. For instance, Flora had planned to drive in Trinidad to facilitate moving around but found that she is uncomfortable driving and has lost the freedom of movement that driving in the United States provided. She uses public transportation, especially the bus, and arranges transport with friends and relatives when necessary. The compromises and negotiations that these returnees make are evident in terms of affective and everyday concerns.

Caregiving also brings physical challenges. Lisa details her shoulder pain from lifting her parent to sit up in bed or moving from the bed to the wheelchair. Flora's chronic back pain now limits her ability to sit with her mother and provide company. This is emotionally painful for all involved as Flora's mother initially interpreted this behavior as a rejection of sorts. What we find in these experiences is, for lack of a better term, precarious social reproduction. Within the historical conditions of Caribbean values and a modern gendered division of labor, the conditions and expectations of social life are also shaped by the present-day hierarchies of public versus private medical care within reduced state-provided social security.

Ashley, Janet, Severine, and Lisa undertake multiple jobs and duties, which when accumulated limit their ability to even care for themselves. It is worthwhile for us to ask about the cumulative costs—social, physical, emotional, friendship, general opportunities—that stem from the cultural norms surrounding these "labors of love" for relatives. When we preface the "labor" bit with "love," this allows us to elide the emotional, financial, and social costs of this type of work.

Conclusion

Our discussion has highlighted the cross-sectional structural vulnerabilities and everyday experiences of these return migrants in how they perform intimate labors of care within specific cultural contexts. The women's silence regarding the emotional and physical costs of providing this proximate care for aging relatives signaled ideology at work—the capitalist and cultural logics of work and care. The eliding of socially reproductive labor remains as important for populations and societies today as well as for the social sciences, even within the egocentrism that characterizes much scholarship at present. To link back to the capitalist logic of work, these physical and emotional tolls can be interpreted as expressions of alienation thereby highlighting the contradictions between values and value as relationships are configured around labor, its extraction, and valorization of housework.

NOTES

This project is funded by the University of the West Indies Campus Research and Publication Fund. We are grateful to Scott Timcke for his sustained editorial work.

1. Joan Rawlins and Nicole Alea, eds., *Ageing in the Caribbean* (Greenacres, Fla.: Lifegate, 2014), 11. The names in the epigraph are pseudonyms, as are those of all interviewees in this chapter.

2. Rawlins and Alea, *Ageing in the Caribbean*, 11, 20.

3. Following the United Nations definition, we categorize elderly persons as sixty years of age and over, as cited in Denise Eldemire-Shearer, "Caribbean Ageing—the Jamaican Situation," in Rawlins and Alea, *Ageing in the Caribbean*, 49–76. We use "care work" and "caregiving" interchangeably throughout this chapter.

4. Also see Silvia Federici, *Revolution at Point Zero: Housework, Reproduction, and Feminist Struggle* (Oakland, Calif.: PM Press, 2012); Tithi Bhattacharya, ed., *Social Reproduction Theory: Remapping Class, Recentering Oppression* (London: Pluto Press, 2017).

5. Maria Mies and Veronika Bennholdt-Thomsen, *The Subsistence Perspective* (London: Zed Books, 1999); Federici, *Revolution at Point Zero*; Friedrich Engels, *The Origin of the Family, Private Property, and the State* (London: Penguin, 2010 [1884]); Maria Mies, *The Lace Makers of Narsapur* (London: Zed Books, 1982).

6. Laura Merla, Majella Kilkey, and Loretta Baldassar, "Examining Transnational Care

Circulation Trajectories within Immobilizing Regimes of Migration: Implications for Proximate Care," *Journal of Family Research* 32, no. 3 (2020): 514–36.

7. Federici, *Revolution at Point Zero*, 1.

8. As one tweet during the COVID-19 pandemic read: "The economy isn't closed, people. The economic activities we're doing—childcare, cooking, cleaning etc—just aren't considered valuable by most economists #feminist #economics #Covid_19." @DrJenCohen, Twitter, April 7, 2020.

9. By "Global South" we mean former European colonies, now independent states across Africa, Asia, the Pacific, Latin America, and the Caribbean. While this term elides economic, political, and cultural diversities among this grouping, the historical conditions of plantation monocrop production from diverse forced labor point to certain persistent legacies.

10. Scott Timcke and Shelene Gomes, "Essentially Disposable," *Exertions*, November 2, 2020, https://doi.org/10.21428/1d6be30e.f3d5cda3.

11. Government of the Republic of Trinidad and Tobago, Ministry of Planning and Sustainable Development Central Statistical Office, "Trinidad and Tobago 2011 Population and Housing Census Demographic Report," 2012, https://cso.gov.tt/wp-content/uploads/2020/01/2011-Demographic-Report.pdf.

12. Andrew Beatty, "How Did It Feel for You? Emotion, Narrative, and the Limits of Ethnography," *American Anthropologist* 112, no. 3 (2010): 430–43.

13. Andrew Sparks and Brett Smith, "Narrative Analysis as Embodied Engagement with the Lives of Others," in *Varieties of Narrative Analysis*, ed. James Holstein and Jaber F. Gubrium (London: SAGE, 2012), 53.

14. Sidney Mintz, "Reflections on Caribbean Peasantries," *New West Indian Guide/Nieuwe West-Indische Gids* 57, nos. 1–2 (1983): 8.

15. See Bridget Brereton, "Society and Culture in the Caribbean," in *The Modern Caribbean*, ed. Franklin W. Knight and Colin A. Palmer (Chapel Hill: University of North Carolina Press, 1989), 85–119.

16. M. G. Smith, "Kinship and Household in Carriacou," *Social and Economic Studies* 10, no. 1 (1961): 455–77.

17. Elizabeth Thomas-Hope, *Freedom and Constraint in Caribbean Migration and Diaspora* (Kingston, Jamaica: Ian Randle, 2009); Irma Watkins, "Early-Twentieth-Century Caribbean Women: Migration and Social Networks in New York City," in *Islands in the City: West Indian Migration to New York*, ed. Nancy Foner (Berkeley: University of California Press, 2001), 25–51; Elsa Chaney and Constance Sutton, *Caribbean Life in New York City: Sociocultural Dimensions* (New York: Center for Migration Studies, 1987); Lara Putnam, *The Company They Kept: Migrants and the Politics of Gender in the Caribbean* (Chapel Hill: University of North Carolina Press, 2002).

18. See Rhacel Parreñas, "Long Distance Intimacy: Class, Gender and Intergenerational Relations between Mothers and Children in Filipino Transnational Families," *Global Networks* 5, no. 4 (2005): 317–36; Bridget Anderson, *Doing the Dirty Work? The Global Politics of Domestic Labour* (London: Zed Books, 2000); Helma Lutz, *The New Maids: Transnational Women and the Care Economy* (London: Zed Books, 2011); Pier-

rette Hondagneu-Sotelo, *Doméstica: Immigrant Workers Cleaning and Caring in the Shadows of Affluence* (Berkeley: University of California Press, 2001).

19. See Smith, "Kinship and Household in Carriacou."

20. Merle Hodge, "We Kind of Family," in *Gendered Realities: Essays in Caribbean Feminist Thought*, ed. Patricia Mohammed (Mona, Jamaica: Centre for Gender and Development Studies, 2002), 474–85.

21. Patricia Mohammed, *Gender Negotiations among Indians in Trinidad, 1917–1947* (London: Palgrave Macmillan, 2002).

22. Linda Peake and Alissa Trotz, *Gender, Ethnicity and Place: Women and Identity in Guyana* (London: Routledge, 1999).

23. Saskia Sassen, "A Savage Sorting of Winners and Losers: Contemporary Versions of Primitive Accumulation," *Globalizations* 7, nos. 1–2 (2010): 23–50.

24. Harry Goulbourne, *Caribbean Transnational Experience* (London: Pluto Press, 2002).

25. United Nations Department of Economic and Social Affairs, Population Division, *World Population Ageing Report*, 2017, https://www.un.org/development/desa/pd/sites/www.un.org.development.desa.pd/files/files/documents/2020/May/un_2017_worldpopulationageing_report.pdf; World Bank, *Approach Paper: World Bank Support to Aging Countries*, May 28, 2019, https://documents1.worldbank.org/curated/pt/870611561130594816/text/World-Bank-Support-to-Aging-Countries-Approach-Paper.txt.

26. United Nations Department of Economic and Social Affairs, *World Population Ageing Highlights*, 2015, https://www.un.org/en/development/desa/population/publications/pdf/ageing/WPA2015_Highlights.pdf.

27. See Sassen, "Savage Sorting."

28. Yvonne Baboolal, "Trinidad and Tobago's Aging Population," *Daily Express*, January 23, 2020, https://trinidadexpress.com/newsextra/t-t-s-aging-population/article_56c147fe-3ddc-11ea-bbaf-6724991400c6.html.

29. Harry Goulbourne, ed., *Families, Social Capital and Ethnic Identities of Caribbeans, South Asians, and South Europeans* (London: South Bank University, 2006); Wilma Fletcher-Anthony, Kerri-Ann Smith, and Mala Jokhan, "Transnational West Indian Mothers: Narratives of Parent-Child Separation and Subsequent Reunification Abroad," *The Global South* 12, no. 1 (2018): 14–32; Christine Barrow, *Family in the Caribbean: Themes and Perspectives* (Kingston, Jamaica: Ian Randle and James Currey, 1996); Christine Ho, "The Internationalization of Kinship and the Feminization of Caribbean Migration: The Case of Afro-Trinidadian Immigrants in Los Angeles," *Human Organization* 52, no. 1 (1993): 32–40; Mary Chamberlain, "Family and Identity: Barbadian Migrants to Britain," in *Caribbean Migration: Globalised Identities*, ed. Mary Chamberlain (London: Routledge, 1998), 148–61.

30. Dwaine Plaza and Frances Henry, eds., *Returning to the Source: The Final Stage of the Caribbean Migration Circuit* (Mona, Jamaica: University of the West Indies Press, 2006); Polly Patullo, *Home Again: Stories of Migration and Return* (London: Papillote, 2009); Margaret Byron, "Return Migration to the Eastern Caribbean: Comparative Experiences and Policy Implications," *Social and Economic Studies* 49, no. 4 (2000): 155–88; George Gmelch, "Work, Innovation, and Investment: The Impact of Return Migrants in Barbados," *Human Organization* 46, no. 2 (1987): 131–40; George W. Roberts and

Donald O. Mills, "Study of External Migration Affecting Jamaica, 1953–55," *Social and Economic Studies* 7, no. 2 (1958): 1–126; Tracey Reynolds, "Families, Social Capital and Ethnic Identities of Caribbeans, South Asians, and South Europeans: Report on the Caribbean," in Goulbourne, *Families, Social Capital and Ethnic Identities*, 6–17; Plaza and Henry, *Returning to the Source*; Goulbourne, *Caribbean Transnational Experience* and *Families, Social Capital and Ethnic Identities*; Dennis Conway and Robert B. Potter, eds., *Return Migration of the Next Generations: 21st Century Transnational Mobility* (London: Routledge, 2016).

31. Mary Chamberlain, *Family Love in the Diaspora: Migration and the Anglo-Caribbean Experience* (Piscataway, N.J.: Transaction, 2006).

32. Karen Fog Olwig, "Narratives of Home: Visions of 'Betterment' and Belonging in a Dispersed Caribbean Family," in *Caribbean Narratives of Belonging: Fields of Relations, Sites of Identity*, ed. Jean Besson and Karen Fog Olwig (London: Macmillan Education, 2005), 189–205.

33. Reynolds, "Families, Social Capital and Ethnic Identities," 11.

34. Sidney Mintz, "Enduring Substances, Trying Theories: The Caribbean Region as Oikoumene," *Journal of the Royal Anthropological Institute* 2, no. 1 (1996): 289–311.

35. Chamberlain, *Family Love in the Diaspora*, 6.

CHAPTER 6

The Politics of Civic Ascription and Self-Fashioning in Contemporary Cuba

JULIO CÉSAR GUANCHE AND MAIKEL PONS-GIRALT

The social protests that erupted in July 2021 in Cuba were the largest of their kind since 1959. Spatially, they covered about sixty locations in six provinces, with thousands of people demonstrating in the streets. While the actions of the U.S. government and the responses of the Cuban government contributed to the protests, undeniably racial issues were a central factor too. This is evident in the social composition of the protestors and the slogans used.[1] Videos and photographs of the protests show a very large number of Black and mestizo people, among both the protesters and the Cuban police.[2] The only death officially recognized as a direct result of the protests was that of Diubis Laurencio Tejeda, an Afro-Cuban.[3] The soundtrack of much of the demonstrations was the song "Patria y Vida," a "rapper anthem" performed by six Black musicians, released with a video clip that highlights the racial conflict in Cuba.[4]

Analyzing the role of race in the protests is complicated. This is because the U.S. government has funded "regime change" programs to spread critical discourses against the Cuban government, making use of anti-racist contested subjects like Cuban rap groups.[5] Similarly, in the face of the protests, the official discourse used terms such as "vandals" and "criminals" to describe the protesters, while official and para-official operators deployed racist speeches against those who defended the right to peaceful protest, highlighting strategies that revisit and renew old narratives about the "debt" owed by Afro-Cubans to the revolution.[6]

While Cuba is firmly located in a Caribbean sociocultural area, we look to

Latin American literature to inform the Cuban treatment of race. Cuba has not been the exception in Latin American history on the issue of race. The emerging field of Afro–Latin American studies seeks to show how "during most of the twentieth century was installed the idea that race was not an essential dimension in Latin American societies."[7] In that context, the national ideology of "racial harmony" contributed to appeasing subordinates on racial grounds, and racial discourse communicated "that there was really no power relationship with respect to race."[8] However, in Cuba, as in Latin America, race increasingly occupies a central place in studies about its national society.

In this chapter we approach race not as a "convenient" factor to analyze but as central to shaping ideas about society. To achieve this task, we focus on a few key issues that can help explain how race mattered in the July 2021 protests: (1) the long-standing debate on race and color more generally, (2) the revolutionary experience on the racial issue after 1959, (3) the problems of the debate on racism in Cuba, (4) the political background of the discussion about "Blacks vs Afro-Cubans," and (5) the tensions about the idea of "racial harmony" as a national ideology. To that end, we identify a political map of Cuban anti-racism and the current needs of activism in this field.

Ethnicity, Race, Color, and Anti-racism

Cuba is a multiethnic nation that currently perpetuates a single racialized national ethnos.[9] The predominant theoretical line in academia, government reports, and Cuban education is that different ethnic components that make up the nation—ingredients melted in an "Ortizian ajiaco" ready to taste after the "national cooking." From this perspective, any insistence on a racial identity prior to Cuban ethnicity, like self-identifying as Afro-Cuban or Black, is sidelined as rhetorical nonsense. For their part, the Cuban revolutionaries of the independence era offered key articulations of Cuba as a racially integrated nation.[10] The idea is assumed as the core of Fernando Ortiz's interpretation of the national conformation while moving away from it in an antidialectical way. For Ortiz, "Cubanness is not only in the result but also in the very complex process of its formation, disintegrative and integrative, in the substantial elements entered into its action, in the environment in which it operates and in the vicissitudes of its course. The characteristic thing about Cuba is that, being 'ajiaco' [a typical Cuban dish that represents a diverse mix of ingredients], its people are not a stew made, but a constant cooking."[11] In the Ortizian logic of diasporic and cross-cultural counterpointing, Cubanness is not *stew premade*.

Current genetic research demonstrates the miscegenation of Cuban nationalism. The Cuban National Center for Medical Genetics, after measuring melanin indices present in the epidermis, concluded that Cubans "in a range of one to one hundred—that is, from the whitest to the blackest—are distributed between twenty-three and eighty-five, on average." For Beatriz Marcheco, director of that center, this type of research shows that "this miscegenation is going to increase more and more, and that the mixture of our population is going to be more and more intense."[12] According to Fernando Martínez Heredia, the war of 1895–98 was a turning point. "For nonwhites, this was an especially positive event, because it gave them an identity they shared with all other Cubans.... The Blacks of Cuba became the Black Cubans with the Revolution of '95, and the order of identity was that, from then until today," he writes.[13]

However, anti-Black racism is a central component of Cuban national formation. About a million Africans arrived in Cuba in the nineteenth century. During enslavement, the island became the world's leading producer of sugar and, after Brazil, the country with the second largest population of enslaved people in Latin America. After 1860 slave smuggling introduced a further 350,000 enslaved people into Cuba.[14] Each people/ethnicity involved in the slave process was fixed in certain social places, a fact that marked the mono-ethnic nation that emerged from such foundations but structurally influenced by a racialized social formation. To this day, the word "Black" has specificities and consequences different from those of "white" in Cuban society. The language of official documents, such as the census, uses the word "color." The color of the skin is "the first of the elements with which Cubans form the images of the Other."[15] The amount of melanin is one way people are marked and positioned.[16]

Currently, new anti-racist discourses give a critical account of this fact. Roberto Álvarez, Afro-Cuban rapper and stylist, produced a song marked by racial consciousness whose refrain repeats:

> I am Black.
> Blessed is melanin.
> I am Black!
> How rich it is to be Black, "asere."[17]

It is an approach that produces a conceptual shift on "race," in favor of skin color, although the notion of race is still used within Cuban artistic expressions to formulate anti-racist discourses, ironically, with no less powerful meanings.[18]

The Cuban folk language has elaborated a vast set of representations about the color of the skin. To refer to Blacks there are expressions such as "black-blue," "black phone color," "black coconut timba," "black tiptoe head," or "black." For whites there is "white," "blond," "white orillero," or "milky white." Just as with Blacks and whites, for other groups such as mulattoes, Cuban popular language has also developed a variety of expressions such as "mulato claro" (lighter skinned), "mulato blanconazo" (big white mulatto), and "mulato oscuro" (darker skinned). All these terms shift "according to the context, an affective or derogatory connotation," but color matters for social differentiation.[19] It is another way of saying that races do not exist, but racism exists.

While expressed as a catalog of prejudices, racism is primarily a pattern of power that accumulates differences to organize, distribute, and justify advantages and disadvantages in a systematic way. It unfolds in individual and institutional actions and defines the order of opportunities by being part of the social structure. In history founded on slavery, race behaved as "a category of difference, as an engine of stratification and inequality and as a key variable in the processes of national formation."[20] The Cuban Revolution of 1959 impacted the structure and culture of racism; at the same time, the revolutionary process has a problematic history in recognizing this problem.

Race in the Revolutionary Experience after 1959

With the Cuban revolutionary triumph of 1959, the principle of equality, recognized in the letter of the 1940 Constitution—put into effect by the Basic Law of 1959—began to materialize in all spheres of the country's life. From the governmental discourse and political practice, the challenge of the "battle against racial discrimination" was assumed. The fact implied subverting the racialized social order imposed by more than three centuries of colonialism and neocolonialism, and marked by the coloniality of the capitalist power existing on the island until that date.

In January 1959 the newspaper *Revolution* published the text "Blacks no ... citizens!" in which several Black people explained the meaning of what they considered their new life under the nascent revolution. An analysis of Fidel Castro's interventions between 1959 and 1960 yields no less than seven direct allusions to the racial problem within the country, which imply a severe social condemnation of racism. Two of those speeches from March 1959 ended the existing segregation against Blacks in being allowed to access public places such as beaches. Such political legitimacy facilitated that in 1959 itself "about forty works related to the racial issues [were published] by Cuban academics and intellectuals." In the long run, such production would make up about 85 percent of what was produced in Cuba on the race issue until 2005.[21]

After 1959, photography, cinema, theater, historical research, painting, publications, institutional work, sociocultural research, music, and literature show a repertoire of great quality and wide circulation that re-elaborated in Cuba the image of the Black as part of an effort to dignify historically marginalized subjects. Examples of the avant-garde include "Suite yoruba" (1964), by Ramiro Guerra; "Palenque y mambisa" (1976), by the Conjunto Folklórico Nacional; and "La última cena" (1977), by Tomás Gutiérrez Alea (with the collaboration of Manuel Moreno Fraginals and Rogelio Martínez Furé). Within this logic of cultural decolonization, the National Theater of Cuba, of the Department of Folklore, and the Institute of Ethnology and Folklore were created. These two institutions were concerned with recognizing and preserving artistic and religious practices of African origin.[22] A landmark example of this cultural history is the play *María Antonia*, which premiered in 1967, written and directed by Eugenio Hernández Espinosa. The work marked a decolonizing milestone in the scenic projection, subjectivities, and artistic-teaching-methodological conception of Cuban theater. Hernández Espinosa's intention was to provide "to our people an exact vision of themselves, in which they can recognize themselves. Because there was still the deformed image through clichés: the Galician, the negrito, the mulatto ... And you still longed for that." The work generated contradictions, along with ovations from the audience, and was attacked with violence even though "the setting ... is not artistically questioned, but the different vision of the Black and the theater that was being written."[23]

In *María Antonia*, as documented by historian Lilian Guerra, Hernández Espinosa chose to treat the characters as "complex people who grew up in a culture of violence that exemplified the legendary Havana life of Black slums." The work thus had a radical aspect: "Its insistence on a culture derived from Africa as the definitive source of freedom and a brake on all forms of oppression—a position that broke completely with the great narrative and the official position of the Communist Party at that time expressed by itself as 'criticism within the Revolution,' although it received challenges to the contrary from official instances."[24]

The great initial measures of the revolution—land reform, rent cuts, scholarship schemes, and job creation—benefited Blacks and whites alike. The Black intellectual Serafín "Tato" Quiñones would recognize that he did not feel affected or benefited when he learned of the revolutionary triumph on the morning of January 1, 1959. Quiñones affirmed that his adhesion to the process occurred "when Fidel Castro first referred ... to the problem of racial discrimination and racism.... There it did seem to me that what was happening had to do with me."[25] The testimony of Quiñones, also an Abakuá religious, makes it possible to assess the magnitude of the challenge assumed by the Cuban Revolution with respect to the issue of race and racism.

Problems of the Debate on Racism in Cuba:
The "Vestige" and the "Mulatto Culture"

In February 1962 Fidel Castro declared that Cuba was "the Latin American country that has ... abolished discrimination on the basis of race or sex."[26] According to the intellectual and anti-racist activist Gisela Arandia, with the announcement that "racial discrimination had been eradicated, perhaps unintentionally, the revolutionary project was canceling the opportunities to find solutions to a historical and strategic issue of the Cuban nation: racism and racial discrimination."[27] These beliefs are some of the central problems in the debate on race as they seem to suggest that there is no need for debate in the first place.

The belief about the elimination of racism in Cuba was present not only in political discourse but also in anti-racist leaders. Nicolás Guillén argued, "As the class division of society disappeared, racism lost its most efficient breeding ground." Guillén goes on to add that the absence of "the line of color ... is indispensable for the strengthening of national unity."[28] The revolutionary nationalist project required "national unity" and therefore used a well-earned social legitimacy so that the racial debate was subsumed in the class and anti-imperialist struggle in search of equality, before which racism received connotations of backwardness or taboo.

In the early 1970s another problem was added to the racial debate: the "cutting of the revolution," of its programs and scope, which marched in parallel with the new Cuban insertion in the world socialist field marked by selfish individualism, the formation of privileged groups, and notable setbacks in revolutionary ideology.[29] The racial issue would be included in the process called "rectification of errors" in the second half of the 1980s, with the first revolutionary outlines of developing policies of "affirmative action," which in the long run were insufficient or unfulfilled.

All of these factors contribute to the silencing of the racial issue, but this silencing has generated harmful and lasting effects on the possibility of public debate on race, to which are added those that we consider political-conceptual errors in contemporary debates: presenting racism as a "vestige" and promoting an uncritical vision of miscegenation and "mulatto culture."[30]

The presentation of racism as a vestige affirms that the present contributes to eradicating it, not reproducing it. That idea understands racism as a cultural issue, an aggregate of ideas and prejudices. Racism has both a cultural and structural nature.[31] To claim that racism exists but is only "cultural"—with no structural component—reveals a poor theoretical understanding, anchored in a politically self-interested use that ignores the mechanisms of reproduction of racism. This approach denies the existence of a structural, social, and cultural heritage that at the same time is "reconstructed in moments of crisis, in which competitive spaces appear."[32]

Various investigations developed since the late 1990s found that the Black and mestizo population had the worst houses, received fewer remittances from abroad, depended more on their personal effort and scarce resources to earn complementary income, and had less access to emerging sectors; in tourism this population was mostly hired for "indoor" jobs, not directly linked to the client. These investigations agreed that, taking into account the proportion of Blacks and mestizos in the total population, such groups were also underrepresented in the private agricultural sector (2 percent) and the cooperative sector (5 percent).[33]

A decade later, other research yields similar findings. Currently, groups of Blacks and mestizos (who have specifically experienced inequality in income in convertible currency) have fewer accounts and amounts of savings in banks, travel less, have less access to the Internet, and receive fewer remittances from abroad than Cubans who identify as white.[34] Other research shows how the structural dimension coexists with discrimination of cultural attributes, like stereotypes about Blacks and mestizos, with negative consequences for their labor, economic, and educational attainment.[35] In this, they observe that Black and mestizo women are the majority in areas of informal employment like street vending, elderly care, bathroom care, housecleaning, and nonformal businesses.[36] There is no information on the profile of the Cuban prison population, but it seems to be the majority Black and mestizo, and there is evidence of police undertaking racial profiling of possible violators of the law.[37]

In this regard, the Committee on the Elimination of Racial Discrimination (CERD) highlighted in 2016 and 2018 reports "the State party's interpretations as regards the non-existence of institutional and structural discrimination in the State party." However, the document considers "that, as a result of the historical legacy of slavery, people of African descent in the State party continue to be the victims of racism and structural discrimination, as evidenced by the inequality gap in the exercise of their economic, social, and cultural rights by comparison with the rest of the population." Therefore, the observations recommend that the Cuban government "intensify its efforts to adopt and implement the special measures required to put an end to the structural discrimination that affects the population of African descent."[38] Despite this evidence, the standard way of presenting racism as a "vestige" reinforces the tendency to relativize, at the social and official level, the structural dimension of racism in Cuba, the inequality it generates, and the systematicity of its pattern of unfair distribution of opportunities and resources.[39]

Miscegenation, on the other hand, is seen in the Cuban debate on racism as denying inequalities that originate with race. The idea of Cuban culture as "mulatto culture," a concept that names and synthesizes Cuban miscegenation, is a strong core of Cuban racial ideology.[40] One of its main creators, the poet Nicolás Guillén, proposed it as the "dream of a Cuban color." Fernando Ortiz is another of the central authors of the mulatto culture thesis. But does this conceptualization stand up to scrutiny? The last population census conducted in Cuba (2012) includes indicators that show different distribution between Blacks and whites: in some the former have advantages, others have similar proportions, and still others have differences in favor of whites, but in a good number of cases they are discrete. The official study of the census by skin color concludes—based on its indicators, which leave out, for example, the comparison with income in convertible currency—that the existing differentials between whites, Blacks, and mulattoes cannot "concretely ratify that this problem [racism and racial discrimination] is indeed quantitatively present in a critical way in Cuban society today."[41] That is, the census recognizes differences in several fields but considers that they are not critical.

At other levels, one fact reinforces this criterion: education, health, and social protection systems have remained universal for more than six decades. The 2013 Labour Code expressly prohibited discrimination based on skin color. The 2019 Constitution also prohibits it, and a National Program against Racial Discrimination has been approved. However, while the notion of mulatto culture celebrates a nation without racial differences, the 2012 census, ironically, throws up majority disadvantages precisely for mestizos (mulattoes). On the other hand, the idea of the mulatto "as a representative of cultural synthesis and national unity" brings with it other problems. Cuba is "a version—although socialist—of the Latin American model of race relations, whose essence is ethnic mixing and an unjustified paternalistic integrationism, which only leads to reinforcing the invisibility of the negro."[42]

The Political Background of the Discussion about "Cubans vs. Afro-Cubans"

Paradoxically, the Cuban government's discourse asserts that the term "Afro-descendant" is "not suitable for the Cuban social context."[43] It is an affirmation that contains several conflicts regarding the uncritical celebration of miscegenation, identity politics, and citizen participation based on self-identification. However, there is a "high intensity" discussion that presents the terms "cubano" and "afrocubano" as dichotomous. In this debate, those who defend the "incorrectness" of the term "Afro-Cuban" are usually authors committed to the racial policies of the Cuban state. For example, to say "Afro-Cuban" in Cuba is, in the words of Martínez Heredia, "a serious mistake if one is going to refer precisely to the most general, to the very existence of people. There is no such thing, there are Cubans; but it was because of this, the origin is revolutionary and nobody donated them to them, they earned it, they conquered it."[44]

However, drawing a line of political distinction of the type "for or against" the "Cuban Revolution"—which is often presented as synonymous with its constituted state, from the use of the expression "Cuban" versus "Afro-Cuban"—is misleading. Also, a subset of those "committed to the racial policies of the Cuban State" represent critical anti-racist discourses in the national context, as was the case of Martínez Heredia himself.

In the Cuban debate, several authors assume these terms ("Afro-Cuban," "Afro-descendant," "black subject") are "perfectly interchangeable," while others make an exclusive, and conscious, use of each of these terms, either "Black" or "Afro-Cuban."[45] Odette Casamayor uses the term "negros," within a perspective that in turn criticizes the racial policies existing in Cuba. In her opinion, "The Blacks of Cuba, in one way or another, all come from a resounding violence.... Neither of the fugitive Lucumí of whom stories were told in my family, nor of any of our African ancestors, do we retain an exact memory. We do, however, have memories of the flesh; and from there out to the world, in our gaze."[46]

Colectivo Cuba Liberación Negra does something similar, when it presents itself as "We are Black people *cuir* Cubans." That space has denounced "the invisibility of the realities of Cuban Black people, especially in the context of the economic crisis that is being experienced in Cuba."[47]

Other researchers prefer the term "Afro-Cuban." A paradigmatic example is the book *Afrocubanas: historia, pensamiento y prácticas culturales*, which emerged from a blog of the same title, edited by the Black intellectual Inés María Martiatu. "The impact of both projects," she writes, "generated a group of Afro-descendant women to fight against sexism and racial discrimination."[48] Through the concept of "Afro-Cubans," Martiatu and her colleagues examine their experiences "using an approach that analyzes race, gender, class, sexual orientation, ability, religion, and geographic location" all as part of an interrelated set.[49] Specifically, Yesenia Selier, one of the authors in *Afrocubanas*, claims, against the theses of Fernando Ortiz, that "the reviled Afro-Cuban identity bloodily chastened in the Massacre of the Twelve, the Massacre of the Ladder, and the Conspiracy of Aponte," while qualifying the Afro-Cuban miscegenation of Ortiz as an "escape valve to digest the noisy and fearsome omnipresence of the drum and the key in the Cuban."[50]

The preference for "Afro-Cuban" is not confined to scholarly debate. Musicians like Roberto Fonseca, Cimafunk, Brenda Navarrete, and DJ Jigüe explicitly claim identity as the distinctive concept of their cultural expression. A recent event sets off alarm bells regarding this debate, when the Afro-Cuban poet Georgina Herrera received a tribute from the Nelson Mandela Chair of Afro-descendants, belonging to the Center for Psychological and Sociological Research in Havana. The state-owned newspaper *Tribuna* covered the event with the title "Afro-Cuban poetesses receive the honorary distinction of Mandela Chair," and the comments on the newspaper's Facebook post about the article show that the use of the term "Afro-Cuban" generated disgust and surprise.[51] Later the title of the article was censored to appear without the term "Afro-Cuban," which provoked various reactions.[52]

This exchange illustrates the political issues that underlie the debate of "Cubans vs. Afro-Cubans." According to official logic, the concept of "Afro-Cuban" undermines the concept of "Cubanness" in its Ortizian conception and supposes a discursive strategy that copies demands of the African American movement in the United States. The U.S. government is taken over by movements of intellectual and artistic activism opposed to the Cuban government, all with the purpose of dividing whites and Blacks, or more generally, the "Cuban nation." The official Cuban criteria ignore the political implications of this debate by imposing the label of "incorrect" on the concept of "Afro-Cuban." According to Alberto Abreu, the rejection of the term "transcends the mere terminological question and presupposes a debate not only political but also epistemological about the way in which the colonial heritage and its ways of thinking to the Other of raciality continue to be reproduced in the discursive paradigms of our social and humanistic sciences."[53] When reproduced by official bodies, the discourse that denies any possibility of the "Afro-Cuban" implies restrictions on the expression of identity and imposes a single possible format on possible political participation based on it.

Cuban Racial Ideology and Harmony

"Racial harmony" is the Cuban national ideology around race. Historian Danielle Pilar Clealand has shown the existing incentives for its continuity as an ideology: "Talking about racist actions or beliefs can be considered unpatriotic and contrary to the national image of equality.... Both whites and non-whites have reasons to advocate racial democracy both inside and outside Cuba and their support is crucial for the maintenance and survival of the ideology."[54] However, the idea of "racial harmony" presents more complexity than that of being a mere resource to appease and hide racial differences. One way to identify this conflict is to distinguish between "racial harmony" as a language of harmony versus its uses as a language of contention.

In the first sense, fraternal discourse presupposes the absence of racial problems in Cuba. This old idea came to life after the founding of the Cuban Republic in 1902, since the new political context legally prohibited "privileges and privileges," including racial ones. Manuel Sanguily, a prominent fighter for independence and later also an important republican politician, shared the anti-racist ideal of independence, but he considered the Black problem already solved after the conquest of independence. Historian Raquel Mendieta analyzed the "pejorative charge" of Sanguily's critique of the Black poet Plácido as an illustration "of the variety of nuances with which within the pro-independence sectors themselves—and even anti-imperialist—the sociopresidential problems of Cuba were analyzed."[55] Sanguily's proposal was that of racial fraternity as "harmony," as a silencing of the intersections between power and race in the nascent republican scenario.

The idea that Black Cubans have a "historical" debt to the nation—whether it is specified as "debt to the Republic" after 1902, or as "debt to the Revolution" after 1959—has been a persistent theme in the country's political discourse. It is a very conflicting thesis regarding the idea of fraternity as "harmony," since it implies dependent, and paternalistic, integration within that fraternity. In a 1910 text the Independent Party of Color (PIC)—a movement that suffered in 1912 the largest massacre in Cuban republican history—already questioned the existence of such a "debt." In that context, the idea referred to the liberation of the slaves—thus denying Black agency in their own liberation, whose emancipation was identified as the conquest of the white Cuban patriciate. The idea was formulated in this way: "We should not request anything as Blacks, but demand everything as Cubans." However, *Previsión*, the newspaper of the PIC, said that phrases like that "will have to confess their guilt before the altar of their conscience for the immense damage they have produced. Phrases like those have killed the just and legitimate aspirations of the Black element to the point of having cowed it in such a way that it feels incapable of claiming what in fact and right corresponds to it."[56]

The idea of "debt" has had successive transmutations in Cuba. Among the most recent, it is stated that "the revolution made Black people." Yotuel Romero, another of the authors of the song "Patria y Vida," received racist comments such as "if it were not for the revolution, you would be shining shoes," while social media profiles associated with the Cuban government reminded him that because of his skin color he should be grateful for revolutionary racial policies. The jazz singer Daymé Arocena, who released a song in defense of the protestors of July 11, experienced similar reactions. The racist attacks against Arocena were interpreted as part of the "repertoire of mantras according to which, Cuban Afro-descendants must place ourselves as individuals, in the XXI century, in the same genuinely and slavishly grateful position that the Creole slavers expected and claimed from our ancestors."[57]

According to Black collectives, phrases such as "the revolution made Black people" "reinforce the myth that the revolutionary process ended racial inequality and discrimination and aim to place Black people in a place of subordination and helplessness and eternal and uncritical gratitude. In addition, it ignores the achievements and struggles of the Black populations in Cuba prior to 1959 and dehumanizes them, [because before] 1959 they were already people."[58]

In Cuban history, another meaning of racial fraternity has disputed that language of harmony and debt. It is a conception of fraternity understood as a language of contention. *Previsión* put it this way: "We come from slavery, of course the principles of democracy are our principles. But not a Greece-like democracy... but a democracy that does not see colors, that does not distinguish races, but that looks at men... that does not quarrel with the notion of Law proclaimed in our giant twentieth century."[59]

Something similar was done, together with the revolutionary and reformist Black sectors, by the most heterodox and sophisticated Cuban Marxism of the time. When in 1925 a group of whites shot Blacks in a park in the province of Villa Clara, communist leader Julio Antonio Mella said: "We want and love fraternity among all races and among all peoples, but on an equal footing. A fraternity between tyrants and slaves is an abjection, like the camaraderie between exploiters and prostitutes. Justice is conquered, or slavery is deserved."[60]

Now, when the term "racial harmony" is mentioned as a national ideology in Cuba, its most common reference is that of the language of harmony, not that of strife. This fact has historical explanations. Zuleica Romay asserts, "The radicalism of the new revolutionary order [after 1959] canceled minority and opprobrious privileges and redeemed non-whites, seven decades after their formal liberation." The daily reality was seen "full of examples of social equity and racial fellowship," which "rearticulated the myth of racial equality [that] ceased to be manipulative historical construction to become a partial reproduction of reality and a moral incentive for its definitive transformation."[61] At the same time, this majority use of fraternity as "harmony" explains how "after forty years of Revolution, Cubans still widely believe that there are no racial hierarchies in Cuba."[62]

The renewed notions of fraternity as a *language of strife* that can be seen in today's Cuba continue to be belligerent against harmony, which makes differences invisible, and against the "debt," which subjects the national membership of the Afro-Cuban to dependence and gratitude. The new ideas remain within the framework of "fraternity," because they do not claim a "nation within the nation" for Cuban Blacks, nor separate or hierarchical identities between Blacks and Cubans, but they do intervene on the specific profile of the Afro-Cuban within the national community against the invisibilizations of their historical legacies and the inequality they suffer in the present.

The concept of "cultural maroonage" is one of the instruments of belligerence that turns racial fraternity into a language of contention. Cuban Black feminism has questioned the origin of national feminism in the first decades of the twentieth century—then with liberal and socialist versions—to place it in the palenques of former enslaved people who "fled to the mountains" in search of freedom, and there, also with the presence of women, maintained life practices as liberated beings to themselves.[63]

The work of contemporary Black creators, such as the essayists and poets Nancy Morejón, Excilia Saldaña, and Georgina Herrera, has been read as "intellectual maroonage," while their texts subvert the double subordination of race and gender and confront the Manichaean discourses of the patriarchal paradigm. From their identity as Afro-Cuban women, these works re-create the link with Africa as a matrix and the rescue of women in the national identity project. From a decolonizing discourse, they project the image of women within a framework of resistance that deconstructs and transcends "the avant-garde parameters of the misogynistic negrism of the first half of the twentieth century."[64]

Although the figure of the *cimarrón* has had great weight in revolutionary Cuban culture since 1959—as a counterpoint to what was the main image of dignification of the Cuban Black in the republican context, that of the "veteran" of the war of independence—there seems to be a resurgence of uses of *cimarrón* in our day. Cuban music is a fruitful example of this: "Cimarrón" is the title of songs by the troubadour William Vivanco and the pianista Harold López-Nussa. The theme "Raza," by Alexander Abreu, begins this way: "Let go of the dog, mayorá, cuidao con el cimarrón." A song by Leonardo Diago, with his group La Nueva Era de Cuba, which has a concert broadcast via streaming by the Ministry of Culture of Cuba, mentions "there is no one to stop this Black; when he seeks his destiny the Black no longer respects the majority."[65]

Before the July 11 protests in Cuba, Maykel Osorbo, one of the rappers participating in the song "Patria y Vida," starred in a typically Maroon image: when escaping the police persecution that sought to stop him, a photograph captured him waving one of his arms with semi-open handcuffs, from which he had freed himself. The also rapper Tito Pakín released after July 11 a song whose title is also "Cimarrón." Its lyrics are evocative:

> the barracks is full of slaves who live
> singing to the master they hate
> who traded with their master

Here "master" refers to the current Cuban authorities. In this vein, the Cuban-American plastic artist Lilí Bernard has reformulated the classic painting *Liberty Leading the People*, by Eugène Delacroix. If in the French original appears the image that became a universal allegory of the Marianne, in Bernard's work appears a Black Marianne: a real Cuban Black woman, named Carlota, leader of a slave uprising held in the Ingenio Triunvirato (Matanzas) in 1843.

The tensions that exist regarding "Cuban Black vs. Afro-Cuban" are also experienced with the definition of maroonage. With this concept, Ana Cairo Ballester exalted "the emancipatory options, with which the ability to rebel or resist is defended. And the cult of freedom is legitimized, endearingly fused with justice and solidarity." From that understanding, Cairo can place José Martí as "the most remarkable of our Maroon intellectuals."[66] On the other hand, another type of approach "blackens" the Maroon tradition. The researcher Irina Pacheco considers that in "the construction of the story and experiences of the Cuban nation, the places of maroon not only have their particularities, but change over time," and she associates maroonage with the concept of "national formations of otherness," in the way that has been outlined by the Argentine anthropologists Claudia Briones and Rita Laura Segato. With this, Pacheco recalls the differences in power within the Cuban racialized social formation and identifies the "diversity of others within the nation" as well as the "inequalities constituted in the name of hierarchical cultural differences."[67]

The elaboration of cultural maroonage, which we propose here as a current of "fraternity as a language of strife," is also familiar conceptualizations, applied to Cuba, of "internal colonialism" and "epistemic racism." With the first concept, the essayist Roberto Zurbano aims to "de-idealize the hegemonic practices of socialism as a political system and introduce the possibility that, from within and despite its emancipatory efforts, socialism also generates its own internal colonialism, promotes a colonial space within its structures, from which it is oppressed or excluded (consciously or not)" with respect to specific groups, in particular Cuban Blacks.[68] Regarding "epistemic racism," the essayist Alberto Abreu also points out: "From the genesis of the nation and our literate city, the idea was established about the inability of Afro-Cubans for the grammatological and symbolic order. It reaches our days as a stereotype that conceives of Blacks as good athletes, musicians, dancers but never as great thinkers," an issue that, Abreu believes, has not been overcome in the present.[69]

Cuban Anti-racism and the Needs of Citizen Activism

Finally, another dimension of ethnic-racial relations was provided by the Cuba-U.S. conflict after the revolutionary triumph of 1959. According to Devyn Spence Benson, any Afro-Cubans who may have "disagreed with the new government [were] less likely to immigrate to the United States, a country known for its own racial tensions." Soon thereafter emerged "revolutionary discourses claiming ownership over plans to end racial discrimination along with language depicting opposition groups as racist." The event was accompanied by a "strong silence regarding racial equality within a large portion of the U.S. exile community."[70] From this horizon, Eliseo Altunaga argues: "The racist Cuban nation is formed, consumed, and created when only whites go to Miami," where the "idyllic idea that there could be a Cuba without Blacks was conceived."[71] Some of these issues, reinforced by policies of social equalization and the increase in U.S. hostility toward the island, led to the identification of racism as an "enemy ideology" of the revolution. Racism became an expression of anti-communism and was treated as a dangerous sign of ideological backwardness. However, "if openly racist acts were judged as counterrevolutionary, any attempt to debate in public the limitations of Cuban integration was regarded as the work of the enemy."[72] This is still a core problem in contemporary Cuba: the denial that one's race shapes one's treatment.

Since the early 1990s various initiatives began to expand on what Alejandro de la Fuente and Bárbara Oliveira called an Afro-Cuban movement: the gestation in 1995 of the community project Concha Mocoyú in the neighborhood of La California, directed by the Black leader Bárbara Oliva Micado; between 1997 and 1999, the cycle of exhibitions called *Keloids: Race and Racism in Contemporary Cuban Art*, organized by the plastic artist Alexis Esquivel; in 1998 the anti-racist civic-citizen project known as the Brotherhood of Negritud, directed by Norberto Mesa; during 2001 the Cuban Color Project, led by researcher and university professor Gisela Arandia; and as a means of disseminating the various activities, the *La Ceiba Bulletin* stands out, promoted and directed by Tato Quiñones.

In 2012 a concert was held at the Acapulco cinema in Havana, according to the official CubaSí website, with "the most heretical representatives of Cuban hip-hop, Raudel from Escuadrón Patriota, Al2, Soandry Hermanos de Causa, Silvito el Libre, Maykel Xtremo, Barbarito el Urbano Vargas, and Carlitos Mucha Rima." The concert took place within the framework of the XI Havana Biennial, as part of a performance by the plastic artist Michel Mirabal. The rappers covered the song "Créeme" by Vicente Feliú, an icon of the revolutionary protest song. Feliú then said about that concert: "And this critical, uncomfortable, bold, and public concert, supported by the institutions of the State, was the least they wanted—those who are always eager to find a crack in the walls of Cuban culture, among whose defenders, a word raised high as a shining sword, are the hip-hop boys who led this concert, next to the flags of the Homeland of Michel [Mirabal]."[73] That is, according to Feliú, the way not to allow spurious instrumentalizations to participate in the critical cultural expression that was Cuban hip-hop was to give them public space.

At the current juncture, Cuban anti-racism presents a well-diversified panorama. There is (1) an anti-racist activism that, facing resistance, managed to place the issue on the national agenda in the 1990s, with critical positions toward the Cuban government, while recognizing it as an interlocutor and demanding channels of dialogue; (2) an anti-racism, assumed by the government, whose spokesmen appear on national television and in the press, and integrate most of the anti-racist spaces recognized by the State; (3) an anti-governmental anti-racism, typical of the "traditional" dissidence from the 1980s, created by Afro-Cubans; (4) movements such as San Isidro, openly placed against the Cuban government, among whose speeches appear calls for military intervention in Cuba, with criticisms that are part of the "anti-communist" cultural universe, at the same time that they have built neighborhood and intellectual networks that do not exist in the other anti-racist dissident movements; (5) an anti-racist activism that is not always defined politically but rather as an expression of civil society movements, crossed in some cases by interconnected demands of race and gender, among them the Network of Afro-Cuban Women, the Neighborhood Network of Afro-descendants, the Afro-descendant Network, and political-cultural projects such as *Afro-Cuban* magazine and the Cimarronas collective.

As a Cuban saying goes, "Nothing is just what it seems." A demonstration held in Trillo Park in November 2020, which had official support but was organized by left-wing youth groups, officially launched, in a novel way, anti-racist demands along with others related to gender and sexual diversity. The event was attended by President Díaz Canel, and his gesture contains novelties: this type of activist discourse breaks, in a certain way, with the plot of the debt of the "Cuban Blacks with the Revolution" by explicitly claiming the anti-racist struggle as a lack and a revolutionary necessity.[74] In the field of Cuban citizen activism there are serious problems. Actors linked to demands for race, gender, and animal protection and other subjects such as young people, academics, the artistic and intellectual sector, journalists, athletes, and the religious field were identified in the report to the most recent Congress of the Communist Party of Cuba—the only party, which governs over the Cuban state and society—as the target of the "subversive component of U.S. policy toward Cuba." Then, with respect to the July 11 demonstrations, a good part of those who demonstrated were described in the same way, thus limiting more democratic political ways of metabolizing the conflict. This fact adds to a trajectory: CERD has pointed out shortcomings with respect to the investigation of complaints about racial discrimination, as well as cases of police mistreatment of Black and mestizo people and anti-racist activists.

Regarding the events of July 2021, the anti-racist intellectual Zuleica Romay states that she is uncomfortable with the dissonance between "the images of the protests that took over the public space in several Cuban cities on July 11 and 12, 2021, and the speeches about them . . . because one of the dominant elements in the audiovisual scene—the majority presence of Black and mestizo people—was persistently ignored, instrumented or criminalized by interpretations whose arguments or silences, omissions or exaggerations, half-truths or total lies, respond to the struggle between emitters of an increasingly diverse, intertwined, and complex ideological spectrum."[75] Consistent with these concerns, an editorial of the Cuban blog *La Tizza* points out the erratic nature of ignoring the complexity of the events that occurred, giving priority to the narrative that those who demonstrated are "criminals" or "marginals," because "if we resist understanding the processes of marginalization and if we do not recognize the debts with the most humble toward the inside of our society, we will never understand what happened that Sunday."[76] Undoubtedly, the racialization of the protests corresponds to a notable increase in inequality gaps in

Cuba that "settle on racialized women and men, from peripheral neighborhoods, with health and universal education . . . that even its realization with quality also goes through unequal mediations. The apparent tranquility and security in coexistence, where racial inequalities lay beneath, were abruptly interrupted by the events of July 11th, 2021."[77]

The situation poses a dilemma: it establishes a line of continuity between citizen action, and at least a part of politics from below, with the interventionist management of U.S. politics. The latter is real and proven to act, but it is not all-encompassing, nor does it subordinate the entire existing fabric of national civil society, which has in its anti-racist demands a long and legitimate path to travel in pursuit of rights of social, cultural, and material inclusion. As we have shown so far, the available evidence on inequality and skin color shows modes of reproduction of anti-Black racism today in Cuba. In that context, limiting oneself to the idea of equal opportunities is problematic. It is more reasonable to defend equality of outcome. This is not a question of equalizing downward but of closing inequality gaps and overcoming discriminatory ideas and practices that reproduce injustices. It is also problematic to persevere in uncritical notions of "mulatto culture" and of racial fraternity as a *language of harmony*. In this, anti-racist activism is crucial to give its own shape to the necessary solutions to these problems.

NOTES

1. El proyecto Inventario, with data from the period (https://proyectoinventario.org/), created a map of the protests, available here: https://www.google.com/maps/d/u/o/viewer?mid=1AQAArlWutvq3eqA2nK_WObSujttknlxZ&ll=21.66153107712415%2C-80.20082207193147&z=6, accessed August 28, 2021.

2. In this text, we use the terms "Blacks" and "Afro-Cubans" interchangeably.

3. José Raúl Gallego Ramos, "Videos muestran momentos finales de la vida de manifestante ultimado en las protestas del 11J," last updated August 19, 2021, https://proyectoinventario.org/videos-muestran-momentos-finales-vida-diubis-laurencio-tejeda-protestas-11j/, accessed August 28, 2021.

4. Yotuel Romero (composer), "Patria y Vida," performed by Descemer Bueno, Gente de Zona, Maykel Osorbo, and El Funky, YouTube, https://www.youtube.com/watch?v=pP9Bto5lOEQ&ab_channel=Yotuel, accessed August 27, 2021.

5. Santiago Pérez and José de Córdoba, "'Patria y Vida': The Dissident Rappers Helping Drive Cuba's Protests," *Wall Street Journal*, July 13, 2021, https://www.wsj.com/articles/cuba-protests-dissidents-san-isidro-patria-y-vida-11626198332, accessed October 6, 2021.

6. Rosa Marquetti, "Neo-racismo en Cuba: Crónicas del desparpajo," *La Joven Cuba*, August 5, 2021, https://jovencuba.com/neo-racismo-cuba-desparpajo/, accessed October 5, 2021.

7. Alejandro de la Fuente and George Reid Andrews, *Afro-Latin American Studies: An Introduction* (Cambridge: Cambridge University Press, 2018).

8. Danielle Pilar Clealand, *The Power of Race in Cuba: Racial Ideology and Black Consciousness during the Revolution* (Oxford: Oxford University Press, 2017).

9. Jesús Guanche Pérez, "Etnicidad y racialidad en la Cuba actual," *Raza y racismo en Cuba*, ed. Marianela González (Havana: Ediciones Temas, 2015), 53–74.

10. Alejandro de la Fuente, *A Nation for All: Race, Inequality, and Politics in Twentieth-Century Cuba* (Chapel Hill: University of North Carolina Press, 2001); Rebecca Scott, *Slave Emancipation in Cuba: The Transition to Free Labor, 1860–1899* (Princeton, N.J.: Princeton University Press, 2000); Ada Ferrer, *Insurgent Cuba: Race, Nation, and Revolution, 1868–1898* (Chapel Hill: University of North Carolina Press, 1999); Aline Helg, *Our Rightful Share: The Afro-Cuban Struggle for Equality, 1886–1912* (Chapel Hill: University of North Carolina Press, 1995).

11. Fernando Ortiz, "Los factores humanos de la cubanidad," in *Fernando Ortiz y la cubanidad*, ed. Norma Suárez (Havana: Ediciones Unión, 1996), 16. Translations are by the authors unless otherwise noted.

12. Nancy Morejón, Miguel Barnet, Fernando Martínez Heredia, María del Carmen Barcia, Beatriz Marcheco, and Denia García Ronda, "Qué pretendemos," in *Presencia negra en la cultura cubana*, ed. Denia García Ronda (Havana: Ediciones Sensemayá, 2015), 17–18.

13. Fernando Martínez Heredia, "De los negros de Cuba a los cubanos negros," in García Ronda, *Presencia negra*, 210–11.

14. Manuel Moreno Fraginals, *El Ingenio: Complejo Económico Social Cubano del azúcar* (Madrid: Editorial Crítica, 2001), 158.

15. Mayra Espina, "Desigualdades en la Cuba actual: Causas y remedios," in García Ronda, *Presencia negra*, 480.

16. Guanche Pérez, "Etnicidad y racialidad."

17. Roberto Álvarez, "Negro," YouTube, https://www.youtube.com/watch?v=CDOg7B-8NBsc&ab_channel=Roberto%C3%81lvarezRobeLNinho, accessed June 10, 2021. "Asere" is a Cuban term "loosely translatable in usage as 'brother,' meaning good or trusted friend." According to Pedro Pérez Sarduy, for the Abakuá culture of Cuba, as in the ancient Carabalí religion, it is a form of greeting. For Sergio Valdés Bernal, its use is part of the sub-Saharan linguistic legacy in Cuban Spanish, "another identity nuance of our variant of the Spanish language." See Pedro Pérez Sarduy and Jean Stubbs, eds., *Afrocuba: An Anthology of Cuban Writing on Race, Politics, and Culture* (Melbourne: Ocean Press / New York: Center for Cuban Studies, 1993), 157; Sergio Valdés Bernal, "¡Ay, qué felicidad!: ¡Cómo me gusta hablar español!," *Catauro* 4, no. 6 (2002): 95.

18. Alexander Abreu y Habana de Primera ft. Osain del Monte, "Raza," YouTube, https://www.youtube.com/watch?v=j9vtPX3Nd4s&ab_channel=SINPoseNiEtiquetaMusic%2FYuniorAlvarado, accessed March 10, 2021.

19. Guanche Pérez, "Etnicidad y racialidad," 67–69.

20. Fuente and Andrews, *Afro-Latin American Studies*, 11.

21. Clarisbel Gómez, "Las ciencias sociales cubanas en el torbellino revolucionario: Relaciones interraciales y discurso científico-social," *Revista Universidad de la Habana* 273 (2012): 137.

22. Lázara Menéndez, "Las religiones de origen africano en la Revolución," in García Ronda, *Presencia negra*, 395–96.

23. Alberto Curbelo, *La pupila negra* (Havana: Editorial Letras Cubanas, 2019), 114–15.

24. Lilian Guerra, "Raza, negrismo, y prostitutas rehabilitadas: Revolucionarios inconformes y disidencia involuntaria en la Revolución," *América sin nombre* 19 (2014): 127–28.

25. Dimitri Prieto, "Tato, Cuba y la libertad," *La Tizza*, July 21, 2020, https://medium.com/la-tizza/tato-cuba-y-la-libertad-87386e141ea6, accessed August 25, 2021.

26. Fidel Castro, "Discurso en la Segunda Asamblea Nacional del pueblo de Cuba," February 4, 1962, http://www.cuba.cu/gobierno/discursos/1962/esp/f040262e.html.

27. Gisela Arandia, "Estudio teórico crítico del racismo: Un modelo de análisis epistemológico y político para el contexto cubano" (PhD thesis, Universidad de La Habana, 2017), 91–92, http://eduniv.mes.edu.cu, accessed July 30, 2021.

28. Nicolás Guillén, *¡Aquí estamos! El negro en la obra guilleneana* (Havana: Ediciones Sensemayá, 2017), 274.

29. Martínez Heredia, "De los negros de Cuba," 16–17.

30. Maikel Pons Giralt and A. Laó-Montes, "Raza y Revolución cubana en los años sesenta: Notas de discusión sobre lo (in)visible," *MERIDIONAL: Revista Chilena de Estudios Latinoamericanos* 15 (2020): 15–36.

31. According to Silvio Almeida, "structural racism" refers to social, political, historical, ideological, economic, legal, symbolic, space/territory, discursive, educational, ethical, and aesthetic structures that condition and determine the manifestations of racism, its consequences, tensions, latencies, and/or emergencies in a given context. It does not try to reduce the individual responsibility of the subjects, let alone the institutional responsibility and public policies against racism. However, it seeks to understand comprehensively that racism as a historical and political process creates conditions for society to become a reproducer of prejudices and racist attitudes through structural channels. Silvio Almeida, *O que é racismo estrutural? Belo Horizonte* (MG: Letramento, 2018).

32. Pablo Rodríguez Ruiz, Lázara Carrazana Fuentes, and Ana J. García Dally, *Las relaciones raciales en Cuba: Estudios contemporáneos* (Havana: Fundación Fernando Ortiz, 2011), 48.

33. Rodríguez Ruiz et al., *Las relaciones raciales en Cuba*, 48; Esteban Morales, *La problemática racial en Cuba: Algunos de sus desafíos* (La Habana: Editorial José Martí, 2010), 129.

34. Some of specific data: 11.5 percent of Black people said they have a bank account, 70 percent do not connect to the Internet, 96.7 percent do not travel abroad, and 71.5 percent do not access remittance. Katrin Hansing and Bert Hoffmann, "Cuba's New Social Structure: Assessing the Re-stratification of Cuban Society 60 Years after Revolution," GIGA Research Programme: Accountability and Participation, Working Paper no. 315, February 2019, https://pure.giga-hamburg.de/ws/files/21197393/wp315_hansing_hoffmann.pdf, accessed March 10, 2021.

35. Sandra Abd'Allah-Álvarez Ramírez, "¿Racismo 'estructural' en Cuba? Notas para el debate," *Negra cubana tenía que ser* (blog), August 28, 2018, https://negracubanateniaqueser.com/2018/08/28/racismo-estructural-en-cuba-notas-para-el-debate/; María Magdalena Pérez Álvarez, "Los prejuicios raciales: Sus mecanismos de reproducción," *Temas* 7 (July–September 1996): 44–50; Daybel Pañellas Álvarez, Cabrera Ruiz, and

Isaac Irán, eds., *Dinámicas subjetivas en la Cuba de hoy* (Mexico City: ALFEPSI Editorial, 2020); Maikel Pons Giralt, "Cubanas/os negras/os en su laberinto educativo: Un análisis pedagógico-crítico de ausencias/emergencias" (PhD thesis, Universidad Federal de Minas Gerais, 2021), http://hdl.handle.net/1843/37148.

36. Alina Herrera Fuentes, "Desigualdades de las mujeres negras y mestizas en Cuba: Desafíos ante la covid-19," El Toque, 2020, https://eltoque.com/desigualdades-de-mujeres-racializadas-cuba-desafios-covid-19, accessed February 10, 2021.

37. Sandra Abd'Allah-Álvarez Ramírez, "Denuncia: La policía, el 'asedio al turismo' y el neorracismo cubano," *Negra cubana tenía que ser* (blog), 2017, https://negracubanateniaqueser.com/2017/02/06/denuncia-la-policia-el-asedio-al-turismo-y-el-neorracismo-cubano/, accessed September 28, 2021.

38. Committee on the Elimination of Racial Discrimination, "Consideration of reports submitted by States parties under article 9 of the Convention, Nineteenth to twenty-first periodic reports of Cuba," July 28, 2016, https://tbinternet.ohchr.org/_layouts/15/treatybodyexternal/TBSearch.aspx?Lang=en&TreatyID=6&CountryID=44&DocTypeID=29; Committee on the Elimination of Racial Discrimination, "Concluding observations on the combined nineteenth to twenty-first periodic reports of Cuba," 2018, https://tbinternet.ohchr.org/_layouts/15/treatybodyexternal/TBSearch.aspx?Lang=es&TreatyID=6&CountryID=44&DocTypeID=5.

39. An example of the discourse's insistence on the "cultural" character of racism can be found in the program *With Wire*, conceived as an effort to dismantle "negative opinion matrices" about Cuba. The program is broadcast three times a week on Cubavision, Cuba's main state-owned television channel. Available at YouTube: https://www.youtube.com/watch?v=UmeemsutDCQ&ab_channel=ConFilo.

40. Fernando Ortiz, *Epifanía de la mulatez: Historia y poesía*, ed. José A. Matos Arévalos (Havana: Fundación Fernando Ortiz, 2015).

41. ONEI, *The Color of the Skin according to the Population and Housing Census 2012 in Cuba* (Havana: Center for Population and Development Studies, 2016).

42. Aymée Rivera Pérez, "El imaginario femenino negro en Cuba," in *Afrocubanas: Historia, pensamiento y prácticas culturales*, ed. Daisy Rubiera Castillo and Inés María Martiatu (Havana: Editorial de Ciencias Sociales, 2011), 227.

43. CEPAL, "Cuba: Informe a la Tercera Reunión de la Conferencia Regional sobre Población y Desarrollo de América Latina y el Caribe," 2018, p. 50, https://crpd.cepal.org/3/es/documentos/informe-nacional-cuba.

44. Martínez Heredia, "De los negros de Cuba," 210–21.

45. Alberto Abreu Arcia, *Por una Cuba negra: Literatura, raza y modernidad en el siglo XIX* (Miami, Fla.: Hypermedia Ediciones, 2017), 23; Devyn Spence Benson, *Antiracism in Cuba: The Unfinished Revolution* (Chapel Hill: University of North Carolina Press, 2016); Alejandro Leonardo Fernández Calderón, "¿Cubanos o afrocubanos? En la encrucijada del sujeto negro," Cuba Posible, 2016, https://cubaposible.com/cubanos-afrocubanos-encrucijada-sujeto-negro-cuba/, accessed September 9, 2021.

46. Odette Casamayor Cisneros, "Gazes of the Black Woman," *On Cuba News*, June-July 2019, https://ufdcimages.uflib.ufl.edu/AA/00/06/92/09/00009/06-2019.pdf.

47. Colectivo Cuba Liberación Negra, "Declaración del Colectivo Cuba Liberación Negra," July 31, 2021, Medium, https://medium.com/@cuba.liberacion.negra/declaración-del-colectivo-cuba-liberación-negra-d33a545375a7.

48. Martiatu and Rubiera Castillo, *Afrocubanas*; Sandra Abd'Allah-Álvarez Ramírez, *Negra Cubana tenía que ser* (Barcelona: Ediciones Wanáfrica S.L., 2021), 61.

49. Devyn Spence Benson, "Afrocubanas," *On Cuba News*, July 24, 2020, https://oncubanews.com/cultura/afrocubanas/, accessed October 10, 2010.

50. Yesenia Selier Crespo, "La habitación propia de la negra cubana," in Martiatu and Rubiera Castillo, *Afrocubanas*.

51. Raquel Sierra Liriano, "Recibe poetisa cubana distinción honorífica Cátedra Mandela," *Tribuna de La Habana*, August 7, 2021, http://tribuna.cu/cultura/2021-08-07/recibe-poetisa-afrocubana-distincion-honorifica-catedra-mandela?platform=hootsuite, accessed September 29, 2021; Tribuna de La Habana, Facebook, August 7, 2021, https://m.facebook.com/story.php?story_fbid=3138625989705727&id=1600236706878004, accessed September 9, 2021.

52. Maikel Pons Giralt, "Ser afrocubano: ¿(anti)tesis de un debate sobre prefijos o sobre origen?," *On Cuba News*, September 6, 2021, https://oncubanews.com/cuba/ser-afrocubano-antitesis-de-un-debate-cubano-sobre-prefijos-o-sobre-origen/, accessed September 21, 2021.

53. Abreu Arcia, *Por una Cuba negra*, 23; Benson, *Antiracism in Cuba*, 23.

54. Clealand, *Power of Race in Cuba*, 22, 1, 11.

55. Raquel Mendieta Costa, *Cultura, lucha de clases y conflicto racial, 1878–1895* (Havana: Pueblo y Educación, 1989), 61.

56. "Nuestra campaña en Oriente," *Previsión*, April 1901.

57. Marquetti, "Neo-racismo en Cuba."

58. Colectivo Cuba Liberación Negra, "Declaración del Colectivo Cuba Liberación Negra."

59. "Ellos y nosotros," *Previsión*, September 30, 1908.

60. Julio Antonio Mella, "Los cazadores de negros resucitan en Santa Clara," in *Mella: Textos Escogidos*, ed. Julio César Guanche, vol. 2 (La Habana: Ediciones La Memoria, Centro Cultural Pablo de la Torriente Brau, 2017), 87.

61. Zuleica Romay, *Elogio de la altea o las paradojas de la racialidad* (Havana: Fondo Editorial Casa de las Américas, 2014), 78–79.

62. Mark Q. Sawyer, *Racial Politics in Post-Revolutionary Cuba* (Cambridge: Cambridge University Press, 2016).

63. Martiatu and Rubiera Castillo, *Afrocubanas*.

64. Lissette Corsa, "Palabra inédita género, raza, e identidad: Estrategias de la memoria cultural en la poesía de Georgina Herrera, Nancy Morejón, y Excilia Saldaña" (MA thesis, University of South Florida, 2007), v–vii.

65. Leonardo Diago y la Nueva Era de Cuba, "Reflexiones de un Negro," 2021, https://youtu.be/OcawfUXJfkY?si=keGegyYD3Sx-yRZh.

66. Ana Cairo Ballester, *Bembé para cimarrones*, ed. José A. Baujin (Havana: Editorial UH, 2019), 16.

67. Irina Pacheco Valera, "El imaginario del cimarronaje en el itinerario de la historiográfica cubana," *Temas* 93–94 (January–June 2018): 126.

68. Roberto Zurbano Torres, "Racismo vs. socialismo en Cuba: Un conflicto fuera de lugar (apuntes sobre/contra el colonialismo interno)," *MERIDIONAL: Revista Chilena de Estudios Latinoamericanos* 4 (April 2015): 17–20.

69. Alberto Abreu Arcia, "El racismo en Cuba no es solo estructural, también es

epistémico," *Hypermedia*, December 9, 2019, https://www.hypermediamagazine.com/dosieres-hm/contra-el-racismo/racismo-en-cuba/, accessed August 20, 2021.

70. Devyn Spence Benson, "Owning the Revolution: Race, Revolution, and Politics from Havana to Miami, 1959–1963," 15, https://escholarship.org/content/qt5sb9d392/qt5sb9d392_noSplash_a6f55d3b2a90d720bc16faeb0e88eab5.pdf?t=mfsppa); Devyn Spence Benson, "Not Blacks, but Citizens! Racial Politics in Revolutionary Cuba, 1959–1961" (PhD diss., University of North Carolina, 2009), 76.

71. Eliseo Altunaga, "Diálogo con Eliseo Altunaga," in *¿Racismo en Cuba?*, ed. Heriberto Feraudy Espino (Havana: Editorial de Ciencias Sociales, 2015), 79–80.

72. Alejandro De la Fuente, *Una nación para todos: Raza, desigualdad y política en Cuba, 1900–2000* (Havana: Ediciones Imagen Contemporánea, 2014), 355–57.

73. "CRÉEME en la XI Bienal de La Habana," CubaSí, 2012, https://cubasi.cu/es/cubasi-noticias-cuba-mundo-ultima-hora/item/6962-creeme-en-la-xi-bienal-de-la-habana, accessed September 15, 2021.

74. Roberto Zurbano Torres, "Contra la rabia política: Una vacuna y una propuesta," *Sin Permiso*, April 25, 2021, https://www.sinpermiso.info/textos/contra-la-rabia-politica-una-vacuna-y-una-propuesta, accessed August 9, 2021.

75. Zuleica Romay Guerra, "Cuba: Sincronizando narrativas sobre el 11-J," *Sin Permiso*, May 9, 2021, https://www.sinpermiso.info/textos/cuba-sincronizando-narrativas-sobre-el-11-j, accessed September 21, 2021.

76. "Tendremos que volver al futuro," *La Tizza*, July 15, 2021, https://medium.com/la-tizza/tendremos-que-volver-al-futuro-21721dc2ffaa, accessed September 21, 2021.

77. Alina Herrera Fuentes and Milay Burgos Matamoros, "Cuba y las protestas sociales del 11J," *La Tizza*, July 30, 2021, https://medium.com/la-tizza/cuba-y-las-protestas-sociales-del-11j-95bc930f6f6c, accessed September 21, 2021.

CHAPTER 7

Masculinism and Gendered Power Relations in the Caribbean Left

AMÍLCAR PETER SANATAN

In 2018 the Sir Arthur Lewis Institute for Social and Economic Studies hosted the symposium "Whither the Left in the Caribbean?" With hindsight, the primary purpose of the symposium was quite explicit in assessing the legacies of canonical leaders in the independence movement such as Forbes Burnham, Maurice Bishop, Fidel Castro, Hugo Chavez, Cheddi Jagan, and Michael Manley. These male icons were centered and given pride of place. While they were all renowned, these figures were complex persons and personalities, with mixed policy records due to living in, and wrestling with, politics at a time of imperial aggression and limited resources for postcolonial development. But it is also true that all of these names have become iconographic signifiers standing in for a definitive leftist male occupant of state power in the Caribbean and the Americas. Effectively, the symposium provided a misleading representation of the Caribbean Left, one that solely relied on male icons. Still, it is worth pausing here to pointedly ask how our understanding of the Caribbean Left might shift when we refocus the frame to include people like Janet Jagan, Viola Burnham, Celia Sanchez, Beverley Manley, and Jacqueline Creft. Might a different analysis of the historical legacies of the Caribbean Left emerge? And if so, what are the advantages of this historiography? What intellectual space and programmatic agenda might such a historiography provide?

The masculine frame of understanding the Caribbean Left contains three primary errors.[1] First, it is partial and unduly selective because it does not reasonably interpret the concrete actions on the ground in many Caribbean liberation movements, movements in which the participation of women was crucial. Next, it gives little attention to the diversity of leftist politics, branches that included socialist feminisms, which critiqued revolutionary projects for sidelining gender dynamics. Finally, it promotes an intellectual heritage in which at least half of the population of the Caribbean do not see themselves.

The chapter illustrates the masculinist character of leftist political organizations in the Caribbean. Masculinism can be defined as an "ideology that justifies male domination."[2] In political practice it is also understood to be "constituents of antifeminism, including religious, conservative, nationalist, and other currents."[3] The concept typically refers to the ideological domination of men in institutions, especially in the public sphere. In the case of social movements and revolutionary projects, masculinism not only excludes women for real or perceived threats to their patriarchal power but also constructs masculine identities and mobilizes and recruits men to this form of gender politics.

Intellectual projects that reproduce androcentric narratives of the Caribbean revolutionary projects, even if done by error and without malicious intent, underscore how the figureheads of revolutionary movements during the 1970s and 1980s with their masculine character of politics have become so naturalized. The ease with which this frame has power and influence is a kind of domination itself. In my view, contemporary leftist historiography should certainly recover women from historical obscurity but also has a duty to elucidate the internal structures and reactions of power within the movement to bring to light male paradigms and institutions of power. There is another charge: by being statist, the analyses of the Caribbean Left magnify the masculine persona of its leadership, giving a social license to patriarchal relations in venues where the highest political stakes are decided.

The chapter explores why the Caribbean Left failed to adequately address gender inequalities in their revolutionary agenda. I highlight a pervasive sexism in scholarship that involves nonengagement with feminist theorizing and gender issues in the analysis of revolutions and Caribbean studies. The central reference point in this chapter is the Grenada Revolution. Calling back to the earlier question, this chapter sets out to work through the trifecta of assumptions about class, gender, and the state and show how they continue to shape scholarship produced in the twenty-first century.

In terms of organization, I first discuss the significance of feminist historiography to contemporary analyses of the Caribbean Left. Next, I provide a background to the political developments of the Grenada Revolution. Examining the feminist literature on the revolution, I illustrate the masculinist structure of the state and party during the revolution. Then I discuss the ongoing gender omissions from contemporary scholarship that fail to embrace critical insights about gendered power relations and masculinity in the Caribbean Left in the twenty-first century.

Feminist Historiography as a Method for Understanding Masculinism

The study of Caribbean history pre-1960s did not reflect a careful awareness of gendered analysis.[4] Therefore, the feminist movement sought to "recover" and "retrieve" information about women in past societies in history. Women's increased participation in higher education in the postindependent Caribbean and expansion of feminist activism that transformed the academy brought about historiographies that examined new evidence, new questions to old archives, and new voices of historical subjects. Thus, feminist historiography is as much a methodological approach of women scholars to engender historical analysis as an assertion of their social group within the political order. This led to the development of the "women's history approach" that concentrated on women's special historical experiences. However, contemporary studies employ a "gender history approach" that highlights the gender roles and ideologies that constituted and transformed the historical experiences of women and men over time. Feminist scholarship began to resist the isolation of women's experience and elected to explore the social relations of gender that are constituted in the society. The latter tendency fits in the broader scholarship on social and cultural history in the Caribbean.[5] Brian Meeks notes that Caribbean feminist theory in the last quarter of the twentieth century has led the academic trends in reconceptualizing Caribbean social and political thought.[6] Gender history in the Anglophone Caribbean does not always apply "new" methodologies and draw from unknown historical sources. Instead, scholars apply different questions to traditional sources and dominant historiographies and thereby bring to the fore accounts of the past that were previously excluded, marginalized, or silenced. Male scholars and the male agents of the past about whom they write ultimately leave little room for women in the production of mainstream scholarship on the Caribbean. The outcome of this tradition is that it reifies male domination in knowledge production about the Left and Caribbean history.

In the specific case of the Grenada Revolution, the universalizing of Marxist and socialist ideas without adequate interrogation and application to Third World countries generally reproduced Eurocentric notions about development without taking into consideration the "messy historical realities of colonialism, dependency and continuously reproduced heterogeneity or hybridity."[7] The

People's Revolutionary Government's promotion of Marxism-Leninism, the centralized state, and the principality of the party put them in conflict with the mass of Caribbean people and their understandings of political institutions and cultures. For Eudine Barriteau, gender is not a subsystem of a broader political and economic system; rather, it is "the core of all subsystems" and "social relations between women and men are socially constituted to perpetuate male dominance."[8] Accordingly, she rejects the notion that socialist feminism can adequately explain the complex experiences of women's lives. There is some value in the first part of Barriteau's observations, but also inaccuracies that perpetuate the errors she wishes to avoid; her critique flattens all socialist feminism and Marxist theorizing by not paying due attention to the diversity of socialist feminist voices. By contrast, Zillah Eisenstein maintains that Marxist methodological approaches continue to offer pertinent frameworks for understanding unequal social relations. For Einstein, a Marxist analysis offers "tools to understand any expression of particular expression of power" and requires rigor in its application to interpreting social relations.[9] Effectively, Barriteau makes an essentialist argument, not a conditional one.

Historiographies of women Caribbean revolutionaries and women in Caribbean revolution have opened further possibilities to understand socialist feminisms and the Caribbean Left in practice. Reddock's work on Elma Francois or Carole Boyce Davies's pioneering text on Claudia Jones challenged the androcentric analyses of revolutionary figures and movements.[10] Nicole Phillip has established herself as a leading contemporary scholar on women and the Grenada Revolution.[11] Although it can take time for work to disseminate—especially in the intensely politicized neoliberal environments of the academy—this scholarship demonstrates that there are ample *existing* resources for studies of the Caribbean Left, Marxism, and revolutionary theory to draw on to address gender relations and otherwise complete the analysis of the totality of social life. A feminist historiography is crucial to understanding the ways male dominance is perpetuated in the past and present, a core task for any radical theorizing that can generate an emancipatory political project.

The Movement for Social and Economic Transformation from an Ex-Colony

To appreciate the Grenada Revolution in 1979, it is important to consider the context of colonial and postcolonial Grenada. Eric Gairy emerged on the political scene in 1950 as a populist anticolonial leader. In 1950 he founded the Grenada Manual and Mental Workers Union. One year later, he established the

Grenada United Labour Party (GULP), a party that had a dedicated women's group, the Grenada Women's League. Together these organizations were part of the wider movement that helped lead the country to independence from the British. With universal suffrage granted in 1951, Gairy's tools to challenge the governor-general, the local ruling class, and the colonial order resided in his ability to mobilize union power for political ends, primarily advocating for the interests of the Black urban poor and peasant groups. The capacity to mobilize takes extraordinary, sustained effort, and so it is unsurprising that women were actively involved in organizing for Eric Gairy. Although their level of involvement in leadership ranks was insufficient by the standards of our time, women were incorporated into the political fold: Gairy appointed the first female governor of Grenada, Dame Hilda Bynoe; appointed two female ambassadors; and included women in the cabinet and Parliament.[12]

In Grenada, GULP was able to redistribute social benefits to the poor and invest in the small local Black petit bourgeois class. Despite challenges Gairy and the party mounted to the Grenadian colonial political order and plantocracy of Grenada, the postcolonial social order and dependent economy remained intact with little moves for redress. Relying on a cult of personality, erratic decision-making, and entrenching clientelist relations in Grenadian politics, "a new authoritarian state emerged."[13] Opposition to Gairy's government came primarily from the Grenada National Party and the New Jewel Movement (NJM). The NJM was able to politically organize with a coalition of workers' unions, the local business class, and civil society groups against Gairy's repression. The socialist-oriented NJM drew support from returning nationals from abroad and the discontented youth from urban poor sections. Merle Collins is one of the few observers to identify the role of student activism in the lead-up to the Grenada Revolution.[14] When key figures in the NJM leadership were beaten, arrested, and charged with the possession of arms, secondary school students mobilized alongside civil society to oppose political victimization. As the social legitimacy of the group grew, so the NJM movement gained the confidence to stage a coup d'état in March 1979 when they were threatened by escalating state violence. The NJM announced itself as a socialist government and declared it the People's Revolutionary Government (PRG).

The Grenada Revolution cannot be understood as an isolated political development in the Caribbean region. The events in Grenada are tied to a wider geopolitical context in which the Iranian and Nicaraguan Revolutions of 1979 effectively challenged the projection of U.S. imperial power in the Third World.[15] The proximity of Nicaragua and Grenada to the United States of America in addition to the socialist rhetoric of the revolutionary political leadership firmly placed these geographically small nations on the U.S. political radar, fearing further political successes of liberation movements in the Third World that sought alternatives to neocolonial and capitalist development. Thus, the Grenada Revolution is by no means insignificant to global history due to the geographic size nor the short time span of the revolutionary process. The revolution is related to a major geopolitical shift in the twentieth century.

The Grenada Revolution, in a short space of time, was able to make significant achievements to the benefit of ordinary Grenadians. With multilateral aid and technical cooperation from the Soviet bloc and countries in the Non-Aligned Movement, the PRG was able to expand access to education at all levels, address illiteracy, and enhance the capacity of the teaching force. The most outstanding example of this effort was the development of the Centre for Popular Education, which was instrumental in developing curricula for place-based learning and pedagogy. In addition, the formation of mass-based organizations such as the National Women's Organisation (NWO) and National Youth Organisation (NYO) were indicative of the efforts of the PRG to use volunteerism to drive policy change in areas like health care, public transportation, and housing, areas that were crucial to building legitimacy in the NJM and PRG.

The NWO in Grenada did not identify itself as a feminist organization, sticking to an orthodox Marxist-Leninist line. The stance was, "The NWO is not a feminist organization. We have taken the egalitarian approach. Women make up at least 50 percent of our people; they therefore make up half of Grenada's potential for development."[16] It was thought that the NWO would function as a mass-based organization to educate women about programs and projects of the PRG and solicit views from grassroots women on their lived conditions and experiences. It was not uncommon for women then, as it is now, to hold misconceptions about feminism. Interestingly, the NWO's emphasis on women's leadership, partially autonomous organizational structure and women-targeted projects and programs, represents a form of rights-based and gender-conscious activism and organization in the revolution. One of the NWO's most difficult tasks that persisted was to "break through the patriarchal and macho attitude embedded in the fabric of Grenadian society."[17] The NWO was instrumental in building the case for a Women's Desk in the Ministry of Education, Youth and Social Affairs that birthed an autonomous Ministry of Women's Affairs in 1983. Finally, the NJM as led by Maurice Bishop championed women's rights in government more vigorously than his predecessor.[18]

By 1980 the global economic recession limited the scope of economic transformation for the PRG and their allies to support the developing nation with multilateral aid. The popularity of the NJM and PRG waned, and intrafactional contests erupted. In 1983 the two factions, one in support of Bernard Coard and the other Maurice Bishop, drew fault lines. In a dramatic turn of events, the dispute culminated in the assassination of Maurice Bishop and core members of the NJM leadership such as Minister of Health Norris Bain, Minister of Education Jacqueline Creft, and Minister of Foreign Affairs Unison Whiteman. This created a pretext for U.S. invasion on the island with the support of Caribbean governments such as Barbados, Dominica, and Jamaica. The revolution fell, never to return, and only lessons can be drawn from the experience today.

Entrenched Male Power in the Leadership of the Caribbean Left

Several women's organizations have been documented in the nineteenth- and early twentieth-century Caribbean. Most were linked with religious orders. These groups were significant because they were the "main mechanism for transferring and inculcating Western European values of women's place in society, for determining the post-emancipation sexual division of labour."[19] To skip forward a few decades, after 1970 activists and organizers in "second wave" feminism in the Caribbean were typically associated with leftist organizations like the Committee of Women for Progress in Jamaica, the Committee for the Development of Women in Saint Vincent and the Grenadines, the Democratic Women's Association in Trinidad and Tobago, and the Red Thread in Guyana. But this ideological affiliation was not without difficulties as male-dominated political organizations permitted views in which concerns about gender were deemed "bourgeois," "foreign," or "irrelevant."[20]

The result was that opportunities for women's leadership in leftist political parties were narrow.[21] At times there were strongly worded condemnations of this phenomenon. In Guyana, Forbes Burnham acknowledged the prevalence of the political discrimination against women and promised to eradicate these barriers in the People's National Congress. But little political action was forthcoming.[22] For the People's Revolutionary Government in Grenada, between 1979 and 1982, there existed one female minister (Jacqueline Creft) and two female deputy ministers (Phyllis Coard and Claudette Pitt). In spite of public expressions supporting women's equal participation across all tiers of the government, follow-through was lacking. Additionally, women were relegated to ministries involved in community development and social welfare, spheres traditionally associated with women's roles as caregivers. So while Dessima

Williams was the ambassador to the Organization of American States, this appointment to a prominent diplomatic position can be regarded as atypical. What remained was that men were given high-status ministries such as economic planning, national security, and foreign affairs. Thus it is argued that "states have historically institutionalized male interests" and left little room for women to strategically address women's issues in public life.[23]

As stated earlier, women's roles, their relationship to the economy, and the myth of women's inferiority were challenged on the grounds that women were equal citizens in a revolutionary process and/or state. However, these ideological lines were contained within an often socially conservative framework that had not transformed the unequal gendered structures of the state and political parties for women involved in decision-making. Commenting on the Grenada Revolution, Merle Hodge said, "Men had one thousand meetings, sitting around conference tables all the time and they had women cooking the food and washing their clothes. We need to look at revolutions and all the issues of gender as it relates to changing the division of labour."[24]

As the new revolutionary situation developed, women sometimes felt burdened with their double duties of being committed to maintaining the care work of the household and participating in party meetings, consultations, and initiatives of revolutionary groups. Yet by 1981 members of the Women's Committee of the Party found the divide unacceptable and formally complained about "overwork" and its impact on the well-being of women members. A leader of the NJM and PRG, and one of the main characters in the Grenada Revolution's undoing, Bernard Coard observed: "In late 1981, NJM Women's Committee members, led by Phyllis Coard, sought to persuade the Party leadership that there were unique difficulties women faced. These complaints were treated no differently than the complaints of overwork by members of the Youth and Workers' Committees of the Party and indeed many other members engaged in many areas of Party work simultaneously. The Party women's line of reasoning was not accepted."[25] Interestingly, Bernard Coard's account offers a glimpse of the critical self-reflection that might have been possible if leading figures of the revolution were alive today.

Phyllis Coard was the only female member of the Central Committee. She listed issues of exhaustion; growing illness among women members, especially those in leadership positions; and the men's lack of contributions to household care and the nurturing of children. Later, Bernard Coard reflected: "My reaction to Phyl's and the Women's Committee members' complaints, criticisms and proposals was the same as the rest of the [male] leadership. Our first response was denial: we did not acknowledge the gravity of the crisis facing women Party members. The women were exaggerating, we felt; it really was not as bad as they were making it out to be. Everyone, we said, was overworked; there was nothing exceptional about the women's situation."[26]

In April 1982 the Women's Committee submitted a memorandum highlighting their grievances in the party. These concerns included work hours, the challenge of mothers delivering party work and childcare, men's lack of responsibility in household work, and the nonrecognition of the Maternity Leave Law for women party members and leadership.[27] Indeed, the unequal gendered division of labor was not unique to the Grenada Revolution. Andaiye points out how in the Working People's Alliance when Yvonne Benn objected to the overwhelming responsibility of women in care work, the complaint was dismissed by party leaders, including Walter Rodney.[28]

What Hodge, Phyllis Coard, and Benn allude to in their respective ways are how discourses of revolutionary women were framed by their roles as mothers and wives; they had to meet the demands of national liberation in public while simultaneously adopting conservative gender roles in private. Fundamentally, there was no complete revolution of women's social roles. Men tended to downplay the charge of sexism; the masculinist structure of their groups anchored them to gendered exclusions. Despite the significant level of women's participation in leftist movements and organization—indeed, many women were committed to the eradication of economic, racial, and sexist inequalities—they nevertheless were subjected to the masculinist culture that confined their political power and expression.

The cases of masculinism in the Caribbean Left provide historical evidence of the problematic nature of the rhetoric of women's liberation and empowerment in political institutions, movements, and the state in postcolonial societies. The emphasis on fostering improved conditions for women, and the promotion of women's leadership without a wider transformation of the masculine norms and institutional practices limited the political possibilities of revolutionary politics. Furthermore, in the case of the Grenada Revolution, the centrally organized, top-down, state-led approach to the enshrinement of women's rights may have first appeared to be indicative of progressive political leadership but ultimately privileged a new but narrow political class of men and some women. Autonomous, democratic, and politically independent political action needed to be more seriously encouraged by the Caribbean Left in order to redress cultural biases, exclusion in political leadership, and social and economic inequalities that oppress women. The true potential of a revolutionary process also involves the transfer of power from privileged men to women.

(Mis)Reading of the Grenada Revolution: The Limits of Androcentric Scholarship

One would hope that nearly four decades after the Grenada Revolution, the inclusion of women's experiences and gendered analyses of the events would be commonplace. Unfortunately, this is not so. What stands are discrete readings of the Grenada Revolution where women scholars have advanced analysis attentive to gender and male scholars who, for the most part, gesture toward the issue or otherwise ignore it completely. Given the extent of feminist scholarship and the sheer labor undertaken to provide evidence for feminist revisionism, these omissions illuminate narrow frameworks of scholars that reproduce gaps in Caribbean studies. Arguably, they stem from wider gender exclusionary approaches and positions in Caribbean academic culture.

In a similar fashion to androcentric readings of the Grenada Revolution, Tennyson Joseph charges a critique of the party and state organization of the NJM in Grenada through the Marxist political thought of C. L. R. James. His analysis exposes the epistemic flaws of the intellectual leadership of the NJM in their propensity to centralize the state based on the Russian socialist model and their failure to meaningfully embrace Caribbean-based Marxist thought, which is considered to promote deepened democratic practices and political participation. Yet the discussion Joseph leads is fundamentally androcentric with references to the working class, state bourgeoisie, and division of labor. These are all fine in and of themselves, but they are partial when one considers how there is no attention to unequal gendered power relations. Therefore, it is unsurprising that he concludes that the main contributing factor and issue of internal conflict arose from the differences among populist politics and institutionalizing Marxism-Leninism in the party and party discipline, a conclusion that remains wanting at this time.[29]

Campbell differs in his approach from Joseph on his analysis of the Grenada Revolution. Whereas Joseph mediated political thought connecting C. L. R. James's Marxist analysis and the pronouncement of the revolutionaries in Grenada, Campbell examined contemporary developments in leftist movements in the Caribbean and Latin America region to foreground the role of Indigenous peoples and the effective challenge to European hegemony in the form of development models as fundamental forces for revolutionary activity. Herein popular movements like the Zapatistas, landless workers' movements, and women's movements proffer political possibilities for revolutionary change in the Caribbean. Campbell does acknowledge the need to construct societies "freed from the complexes of racial, gendered and sexual hierarchies," but this seems like an easy slogan because he does little to expand on his ideas of gendered and sexual freedom. He scantily references "another aspect of the narrative of the Cuban Revolution" to refer to the conditions of women revolutionaries "grappling with the heritages of patriarchy and misogyny" in Cuba and the significance of contemporary women's rights activism in the Global South.[30] These critiques of patriarchy and machismo are rendered as particular to the culture and impediments to democracy. Much like Joseph, Campbell ignores the mechanics of patriarchal power and masculinity in revolutionary organizing itself that serve to expose some of the contradictions within movement building.

As an alternative to the perspectives offered by Joseph and Campbell, Laurie Lambert's *Comrade Sister*, published in 2020, is perhaps the most comprehensive account of gender and sexuality, particularly women's experiences and voices, in the Grenada Revolution. Through an examination of the revolutionary process that attends as much to women's experiences, Lambert focuses on aspects that illustrate the gendered dimensions of power in the revolution but might also be synecdoche for a "class postcolonial condition" in which women are simultaneously included in political movements and structures yet excluded from high-stakes decision-making.

One of Lambert's creative contributions is her analysis of the rise of the "new" Black revolutionary masculinity of the NJM leadership. "A different kind of masculine authority, one informed by the Black Power movement, arose in the late 1960s and 1970s," she writes. "It was not Victorian. It was a more macho form of masculinity, one tied to black consciousness, and it marked a generational difference between Bishop and writers such as Lamming and Walcott. Bishop and his party comrades in the New Jewel Movement (NJM) represented a younger generation that did not care to prove that they were English as the English. They wanted to express pride in their Caribbean identities."[31]

It is common enough that observers point out the middle-class and "top-down" nature of the Grenada Revolution; however, there has been little discussion on the discourses, body politics, and Black revolutionary masculinity in the Caribbean Left. Lambert adds that these revolutionaries "were rebellious": "They wore shirt jackets and military fatigues instead of suits. People found Bishop magnetic, even sexy. These young radicals prided themselves on both being cosmopolitan and connected to the [grass roots]. They were educated abroad but spoke plainly in the kind of 'nation language,' to borrow a term from Brathwaite, with which the general public could identify."[32]

The point is not to single out Joseph and Campbell and chide them. Nor even to praise Lambert. The point is that questions like "How does male power reproduce undemocratic institutions?" or "What specific challenges are required to address the entrenchment of male power in a revolutionary situation?" remain unanswered in overtly masculine studies of the Grenada Revolution. One of the difficulties about writing about the revolution, and perhaps why some analysis tends toward individualistic heroic tropes, is because so much of the archives were destroyed during the U.S. invasion in 1983, or were taken abroad, only to be returned later. Other sections of the archive reside in the Global North. It is for this reason that Lambert employs techniques from literary analysis. "So many more Caribbean women achieved voice and context in the creative literature produced about this revolution than is discernible in the archives," she writes.[33] Literature allows Lambert to add to as well as counter the partiality of what documents remain and instead build historical narratives with literary imaginaries.

The Grenada Revolution sought to redefine social and economic relations of development as much as it did to redefine manhood from a new group that posed a challenge to an older generation of masculine authority. Maurice Bishop was from the capital of Grenada and attended law school in the United Kingdom. Unison Whiteman studied economics at Howard University in the United States. Leaders such as Bishop and Whiteman were a new cohort of educated and middle-class leaders who challenged the hegemony of the earlier independence leaders. These insights are part of an understudied but hopefully growing field of masculinities in liberation movements.

These arguments about historiography are not "academic." They concern the very vitality of contemporary political life. Let me explain by recounting one of my experiences as a socialist student organizer at the University of the West Indies (UWI). Between 2016 and 2021 the UWI Socialist Student Conference in partnership with the Grenada Students' Association of Trinidad and Tobago organized an annual Maurice Bishop Lecture. The purpose of the lecture was to reflect on the Grenada Revolution and raise current questions about youth, organizing strategy, gender, sexuality, and democratic freedom for the speakers to learn from and exchange with each other. Ultimately, the goal was movement building. At one event an elderly activist man who actively supported the solidarity events in Trinidad and Tobago for the Grenada Revolution urged us, "Remember this is about Marxism and the universal principles of Marxism. Feminism and all the other issues are okay but Marxism is about the history of humans and the total revolution of all." Statements like these suggest that Marxist revolution can in and of itself repair all social divisions while also rendering gender relations as peripheral to the conversation about liberation. While I too will be an old activist sooner than I would like, if Caribbean leftist scholarship fails to adapt and make good on its aspiration to undertake an analysis of the totality of social life, inclusive of issues around gender, then it may well be me or someone of my ilk that perpetuates the idea that Marxism and feminism are essentially incompatible frameworks of analysis.

Conclusion

The leadership of the Grenada Revolution and, more widely, the Caribbean Left relied on an anticolonial and class-based politics embedded in—and supportive of—a drive for male leadership and masculinist political structures. This occurred even as women exercised leadership and were a critical force in the political, economic, and social spheres of revolutionary planning and activity. The Left failed to radically transform an inherited ideology of power between women and men during a revolutionary process. At the same time, this is not to say that women's organizing did not grapple with issues of difference and inclusion in their movement.[34]

What provides men, more specifically masculine ideology, with its social power is its legitimacy in the environments where men dominate, secure power, and exercise social power over women, reproducing social inequalities.[35] Contemporary leftist movements are challenged to reexamine the role men play in transforming unequal gender relations, which requires a transformation of masculinist politics and institutions. For the most part, if women and men occupy differentiated and unequal positionalities in a revolutionary process, they may have different feelings, memories, hopes, and concerns about revolution itself. Today, with the establishment of feminist organizations and institutions and a wave of new women's voices in social organizing, women's issues and women cannot and should not be represented by an exclusive and masculinist order of men—whether as a political party or a movement. Decolonial and liberation movements without depatriarchal thought and action reduce and confine the political possibilities for change.

Organizations such as the National Women's Organisation in Grenada and similar revolutionary women's organizations in the Caribbean Left require further study. The growth of these organizations was based on revolutionary women's desire to create a political vehicle to empower women. However, the extent to which these organizations sought structural change and challenged power relations between women and men varies across contexts. This chapter's intervention emphasizes the need to understand patriarchal power, male privilege, and masculinity in political institutions and scholarship, yet it is equally important to understand women's organizing, subversion of patriarchal power, and complicity, which illustrate the complexity of gendered power relations during revolutionary periods and political processes. Such studies enhance our understanding of "state-society relations."[36]

The issues that women faced within the Caribbean Left show that machismo and patriarchal manhood shaped the culture of many of our radical political organizations. Male solidarity for women was confined to limited legislative reforms and a handful of select women for executive leadership. There is yet to be seen a political movement in the Caribbean Left that promotes male solidarity in the form of men taking on more responsibility in the home and a recognition of womanhood outside of conservative gender ideals. That said, many of these men received loyal support from women and were also encouraged by some women to sustain conservative relations of gender. In the end, men did little to transform the culture of masculinism within their organizations. Scholarship needs to catch up to this reality, to sustain the recovery of women from historical obscurity while taking steps to take on the inner logics and exclusions of male dominance, advantage, and power. The goal, however, is not to construct "accuracy" and more just representations in scholarship. The goal is still to transform material inequalities and advance a concrete political project of emancipation attentive to racial, class, and gender inequalities. Halfway revolutions lead to halfway results. Feminist historiography is one of the tools available to a new generation of scholars and activists invested in greater social, economic, and political change.

NOTES

A version of this chapter was delivered at the SALISES symposium "Whither the Left in the Caribbean? Assessing the Legacies of Forbes Burnham, Maurice Bishop, Fidel Castro, Hugo Chavez, Cheddi Jagan and Michael Manley" at the University of the West Indies, St. Augustine Campus, Trinidad and Tobago, March 12, 2018.

1. For this discussion, the Caribbean Left broadly refers to social movements, organizations, and political parties in the Caribbean that struggle for alternatives to the dominant postcolonial racialized, classed, gendered, social, and political order through a range of political actions. The Caribbean Left, as did many of its revolutionary counterparts throughout the Third World, sought to eradicate class exploitation and racial oppression.

2. Satoshi Ikeda, "Masculinity and Masculinism under Globalization: Reflections on the Canadian Case," in *Remapping Gender in the New Global Order*, ed. Marjorie Griffin Cohen and Janine Brodie (London: Routledge, 2007), 112.

3. Melissa Blais and Francis Dupuis-Déri, "Masculinism and the Antifeminist Coun-

termovement," *Social Movement Studies: Journal of Social, Cultural and Political Protest* 11, no. 1 (2012): 23.

4. Verene Shepherd, *Engendering Caribbean History: Cross-Cultural Perspectives* (Kingston: Ian Randle, 2011).

5. Bridget Brereton, "Women and Gender in Caribbean (English-speaking) Historiography: Sources and Methods," *Caribbean Review of Gender Studies* 7 (2013): 2.

6. Brian Meeks, *Envisioning Caribbean Futures: Jamaican Perspectives* (Kingston: UWI Press, 2007).

7. Cecilia Green, "Caribbean Dependency Theory of the 1970s: A Historical-Materialist-Feminist Revision," in *New Caribbean Thought: A Reader*, ed. Brian Meeks and Folke Lindahl (Kingston: UWI Press, 2001), 41.

8. Eudine Barriteau, "The Construct of a Postmodernist Feminist Theory for Caribbean Social Science Research," *Social and Economic Studies* 41, no. 2 (1992): 15.

9. Zillah Eisenstein, "Some Notes on the Relations of Capitalist Patriarchy," in *Capitalist Patriarchy and the Case for Socialist Feminism*, ed. Zillah Eisenstein (New York: Monthly Review, 1979), 42.

10. Rhoda Reddock, *Elma Francois: The NWSCA and the Workers' Struggle for Change* (London: New Beacon, 1988); Carole Boyce Davies, *Left of Karl Marx: The Political Life of Black Communist Claudia Jones* (Durham, N.C.: Duke University Press, 2008).

11. Nicole Phillip, *Women in Grenadian History, 1783–1983* (Kingston: UWI Press, 2010).

12. Nicole Phillip-Dowe, "Women in the Grenada Revolution, 1979–1983," *Social and Economic Studies* 62, nos. 3–4 (2013): 45.

13. Wendy Grenade, "Party Politics and Governance in Grenada: An Analysis of the New National Party (1984–2012)," in *Grenada: Revolution and Invasion*, ed. Patsy Lewis, Gary Williams, and Peter Clegg (Kingston: UWI Press, 2015), 229.

14. Merle Collins, "What Happened? Grenada: A Retrospective Journey," in Lewis et al., *Grenada*.

15. Patsy Lewis, Gary Williams, and Peter Clegg, "Introduction: Grenada Revolution and Invasion in Perspective," in Lewis et al., *Grenada*, 2.

16. Rita Joseph quoted in Phillip-Dowe, "Women in the Grenada Revolution," 45.

17. Phillip-Dowe, 54.

18. Laurie Lambert, *Comrade Sister: Caribbean Feminist Revisions of the Grenada Revolution* (Charlottesville: University of Virginia Press, 2020), 28.

19. Rhoda Reddock, "Women's Organizations and Movements in the Commonwealth Caribbean: The Response to the Global Economic Crisis in the 1980s," *Feminist Review* 59 (1998): 57.

20. Rhoda Reddock, "Diversity, Difference and Caribbean Feminism: The Challenge of Anti-Racism," *Caribbean Review of Gender Studies* 1 (2007): 24, 13.

21. Barriers to women's executive leadership were not uncommon on the Left and in revolutionary struggles during the post–World War II era. In El Salvador the FMLN's inclusion of women in the armed militia did not transform the machismo cultures and masculinist structure of the party. Further afield, Salamishah Tillet's study of the Black Panther Party in the United States identified several "founding gender contradictions,"

such as the fact that "as women increasingly reached all levels of the organizations, male leaders had mixed responses to their push for equality." Salamishah Tillet, "The Panthers' Revolutionary Feminism," *New York Times*, October 2, 2015, https://www.nytimes/com/2015/10/04/mobies/the-panthers-revolutionary-feminism.html, accessed March 11, 2018.

22. Cecilia McAlmont, "The Participation of Guyanese Women in Politics and Parliament during the Administration of the People's National Congress," *History in Action* 2, no. 1 (2011): 5.

23. Jane Parpart, Shirin M. Rai, and Kathleen Staudt, "Rethinking Em(power)ment, Gender and Development: An Introduction," in *Rethinking Empowerment: Gender and Development in a Global/Local World*, ed. Jane L. Parpart, Shirin M. Rai, and Kathleen Staudt (London: Routledge, 2003), 14.

24. Merle Hodge, lecture delivered at the Second Annual Maurice Bishop Reasonings: Decolonising Education, hosted by the UWI Socialist Student Conference, the University of the West Indies, St. Augustine Campus, March 12, 2017.

25. Bernard Coard, *The Grenada Revolution: What Really Happened?* (Kingston: McDermott, 2017), 76.

26. Coard, 77.

27. Coard, 79–80.

28. David Scott, "Counting Women's Caring Work: An Interview with Andaiye," *Small Axe* 15 (2004): 123–217.

29. Tennyson Joseph, "C. L. R. James' Theoretical Concerns and the Grenada Revolution: Lessons for the Future," *Journal of Eastern Caribbean Studies* 35, nos. 3–4 (2010): 4–31, quotation on 20.

30. Horace Campbell, "The Grenadian Revolution and the Challenges for Revolutionary Change in the Caribbean," *Journal of Eastern Caribbean Studies* 35, nos. 3–4 (2010): 32–74, quotations on 43, 52, 68.

31. Lambert, *Comrade Sister*, 6.

32. Lambert, 6.

33. Lambert, 7.

34. Andaiye, "The Angle You Look at Determines What You See: Toward a Critique of Feminist Politics in the Caribbean," lecture delivered at the Lucille Mathurin-Mair Lecture, the University of the West Indies, Mona Campus, March 8, 2002.

35. Linden Lewis, "Masculinity, the Political Economy of the Body, and Patriarchal Power in the Caribbean," in *Gender in the 21st Century: Caribbean Perspectives, Visions, and Possibilities*, ed. Barbara Bailey and Elsa Leo-Rhynie (Kingston: Ian Randle, 2004), 236.

36. Marella Bodur and Susan Franceschet, "Movements, States and Empowerment: Women's Mobilization in Chile and Turkey," in Parpart et al., *Rethinking Empowerment*, 113.

PART THREE

DOMINATION AND EXPRESSION

CHAPTER 8

Perceptions of Ethnicity and Language Use in Suriname

GERALD STELL

Ethnicities and Their Linguistic Indexing

Ethnicity, defined as the "shared belief in common descent and culture," has increasingly been regarded as a largely relational construct, partly inherited, partly negotiable.[1] Ethnicity finds expression through "diacritic features," which can be phenotypical or rooted in a variety of behaviors, including linguistic ones. Depending on situations, variable combinations of these diacritic features may be made salient to draw a symbolic "boundary," which—in Fredrik Barth's view—signals ethnic distinction.[2] Sociolinguistics has long assumed that language reflects ethnic distinctions, or in other words, that it carries ethnic "indexicalities."[3] "Hard" ethnic boundaries, typically found in socioeconomic hierarchies defined by rigid phenotypical and/or religious classifications, may translate into categorical linguistic distinctions. Sociolinguistic manifestations of hard ethnic boundaries include the maintenance of heritage languages or the preservation (or even creation) of distinctive linguistic features endowed with ethnic indexicality. Conversely, "soft" ethnic boundaries are found where assimilation into a dominant group, or integration (which implies the combination of distinct ethnic identities for individual identity construction purposes), is a plausible option.[4] Soft ethnic boundaries are conducive to fluid multilingual practices that may be hard to characterize in terms of established language labels.[5] Whether ethnic boundaries are hard or soft depends on traditional patterns of economic and political intergroup competition, possibly combined with salient religious and phenotypical differences. Sociolinguistic studies suggest that linguistic interactions between ethnolinguistic groups are likely to occur via the language of the dominant ethnolinguistic group, if that group is inclined to assimilate others. This is a scenario typical of immigration contexts where traditional ethnicities are encouraged to dissolve. By contrast, lingua francas form a defining linguistic attribute of multiethnic states, especially postcolonial states where incipient nation building is not yet able to offer viable alternatives to ethnicity for identity construction purposes.

Postcolonial nation building often involves promoting an ethnically neutral nationhood whose reason for being is to minimize risks of ethnic conflict. Retaining the former colonizer's language as an official language has been deemed compatible with ideals of ethnically neutral nationhood as the expatriate elites that spoke that language natively often lost their social preponderance in the wake of national independences. Where they exist, indigenous lingua francas have also often been promoted as low-function official languages, as, for example, Swahili has been in East African countries. In the postcolonial world, high-function and low-function lingua francas generally coexist with heritage languages within multilingual repertoires to degrees that vary with social class. Whether social class supersedes ethnicity in postcolonial identity construction has visibly been debated in urban studies—such as Bekker and Leildé—premised on Glazer's distinction between "dual" cities (where social stratification is primarily class-based) and "divided" cities (where social stratification is based on ethnicity).[6] Where ethnic boundaries are superseded by class boundaries, one may expect lingua francas to develop an association with ethnically diverse middle classes, among which these lingua francas may eventually become nativized. If, on the other hand, ethnicity remains a prominent factor of distinction, one may expect heritage languages to remain part of linguistic repertoires and leave their imprint on lingua francas via substratal transfers and emblematic lexical or phonetic features, which carry ethnic indexicalities.[7] European-dominated immigrant societies, where traditional ethnicities are dissolved into "melting pots," exemplify the former scenario. The latter is typical of former multiethnic exploitation colonies, where the former colonizer's language tends to develop distinctive ethnic varieties, as studies of "New Englishes" have abundantly shown.[8]

Communication accommodation theory (CAT) offers one theoretical perspective on how ethnicity and language interact. CAT predicts language shift among minority groups and language choice in interactions between members of different ethnolinguistic groups. Its predictions are based on "ethnolinguistic vitality." Inferred from intergroup differentials in demographics, socioeconomic status, and institutional support, it copredicts how soft or hard ethnic boundaries are, and, by extension, to what extent they are linguistically indexed.[9] A different theoretical perspective on how language and ethnicity interact comes with Myers-Scotton's markedness model (MM).[10] The MM generally posits that conversational alternation between high- and low-status languages occurs to situationally index distance and solidarity, respectively. In the African contexts described by Myers-Scotton, ethnically neutral languages are endowed with high status and "ethnic" languages with low status. In contrast to CAT and the MM, ethnographic approaches do not seek to link linguistic behaviors to macrosocial indicators. Instead, fluid multilingual practices, which involve the situational—and largely unpredictable— combining of various linguistic resources, are regarded as a linguistic hallmark of many ethnolinguistically diverse settings.[11] A theoretical assumption of this chapter is that ethnic boundaries are indexed by linguistic features and that unsystematic linguistic distinctions between traditionally defined ethnic groups suggest that ethnic boundaries are becoming increasingly negotiable. This chapter proposes to test this assumption against perceptions of ethnicity and language use in Suriname, a postcolonial society still marked by a segregationist heritage.

Ethnicity and Language in Suriname: General Background

In 2012 the population of Suriname, a South American country of little more than half a million inhabitants, consisted of mostly Hindustani (27.4 percent), followed by Maroons (21.7 percent), Creoles (15.7 percent), Javanese (13.7 percent), and individuals declaring a "mixed" ancestry (13.4 percent). The other categories (that is, mostly Europeans, Chinese, Amerindians, and Brazilians) accounted for 8.2 percent.[12] Descending from slave populations imported during the British and Dutch colonial periods (1630–67 and 1667–1975, respectively), the Creoles and Maroons form a demographic majority in the northeastern extremity of the country; in Paramaribo, the capital city; and in the interior. By contrast, Hindustani and Javanese form the dominant ethnic groups along the coastline stretching from Paramaribo up to the western border. Half of Suriname's population is currently concentrated in Paramaribo, and two-thirds in greater Paramaribo.[13] Originally a European and Creole city, Paramaribo began to acquire substantial Hindustani and Javanese populations from the first half of the twentieth century, through either immigration or the absorption into the agglomeration of Hindustani and Javanese settlements. In 2012 the largest ethnic group in Paramaribo was the Creoles (25.5 percent), followed by the Hindustanis (22.9 percent), the Maroons (15.9 percent), and the Javanese (9.8 percent). A large portion of the population (18.3 percent) claimed a "mixed" ancestry. It is noteworthy that the Maroon component had grown significantly.[14] The main religions in Suriname are Christianity (with which 48.4 percent of Suriname's population identify), Hinduism (22.3 percent), and Islam (13.9 percent). The geographic diffusion of religions suggests a strong association between Hindustani and Hinduism, between Javanese and Islam, and between Afro-Surinamese and Christianity.[15]

Surinamese society in late colonial times was characterized by an ethnically stratified socioeconomic hierarchy, described in detail by Kruijer.[16] Europeans stood at the top of the socioeconomic ladder, followed by the Chinese, Creoles, Hindustani, Javanese, Maroons, and Amerindians.[17] Since World War II this hierarchical order has been considerably disrupted by several factors. One was the "Surinamization" policies implemented in the public sector, which saw the Europeans gradually lose their visibility in favor of the Creoles.[18] Meanwhile, accelerating urbanization and increased exposure to education have led to a reduction in socioeconomic gaps between ethnic groups. Schalkwijk and de Bruijne's Paramaribo survey showed that the Hindustani, and to a lesser extent the Javanese, have caught up with the Creoles in terms of levels of educational attainment, while high-ranking professions are now distributed evenly among ethnic groups. Additionally, Paramaribo's emergent multiethnic middle class shows signs of residential concentration. However, there remain suggestions of strong ethnic polarization. The historical racialized socioeconomic hierarchy seems to still be manifested in the fact that Europeans remain socioeconomically preponderant while the Maroons and Amerindians are marginalized. Additionally, ethnic endogamy is strong among Asians and Maroons.[19] The persisting salience of ethnicity is reflected at a political level, with ethnic clientelism a pervasive practice.[20] Altogether, the indicators discussed above suggest that ethnic boundaries in Suriname remain hard and spatially salient at a national level, although they seem to be softening at a socioeconomic level, as well as at a residential level in the specific case of Paramaribo.[21]

The historical patterns of social stratification in Surinamese society, and, more specifically, its internal ethnic divides, partly account for its linguistic complexity. Despite Dutch being the only official language, each population group has to various degrees preserved its heritage language: Sarnami (a local form of Bhojpuri), Sranan, Javanese, Chinese dialects, Maroon, and Amerindian languages.[22] Historically rooted in the Creole population, Sranan is described as a society-wide medium of interethnic solidarity.[23] The most comprehensive accounts of Surinamese language practices are the surveys conducted among Surinamese school pupils by Léglise and Migge as well as Kroon and Yagmur.[24] Unlike these surveys, in which geographic location and type of school were treated as the main independent variables, other sociolinguistic surveys systematically included social and situational variables in their design. Westmaas inferred from his urban data that ethnicity, age, gender, social class, and communication settings copredict language behaviors.[25] Apart from Léglise and Migge, none of the surveys named above attempted to describe the patterns of code-switching widely reported in Suriname, which often make use of established language labels irrelevant to describing local sociolinguistic reality.[26] The only attempt to situate patterns of language use within the perspective of interethnic boundaries was made by Menzo, who focused on interactions between Hindustani and Creoles. This chapter proposes to follow Menzo's lead while taking account of more ethnic groups. The data it uses are formed by sociolinguistic perceptions elicited from an ethnolinguistically representative young sample recruited in Paramaribo, where the country's main ethnic groups are all represented.

Methodology and Sample

This study examines perceptual data that were collected via semidirected interviews conducted between 2015 and 2017 with a sample of fifty-seven Paramaribo residents, aged between seventeen and twenty-three, recruited from Anton de Kom University's campus in Paramaribo using the "friend of a friend approach."[27] The sample included slightly more women than men, and comprised the following self-declared ethnicities: Creole, Maroon, Hindustani, Javanese, Euro-Surinamese, and Chinese. It also included individuals declaring a "mixed" ethnic background. Table 1 shows the proportions of ethnic backgrounds and genders in the sample. The Maroon informants all specified their ethnic background as Aucan, except for one who declared a Kwinti background. Some individuals declared an ethnically mixed background while still self-identifying with a specific ethnic group. In such cases those individuals were treated as members of the ethnic group with which they self-identified. Most informants were born and had uninterruptedly been living within Greater Paramaribo. Two informants had spent most of their lives in Nieuw Nickerie, and three in Saramacca. These informants had moved to Paramaribo for their tertiary education.

TABLE 8.1. Informants by Ethnicity and Gender

	Creole (CR)	Maroon (MA)	Hindustani (HI)	Javanese (JA)	Euro-Surinamese (EU)	Chinese (CH)	Mixed (MI)
Male	7	5	5	5	-	-	4
Female	6	7	6	6	1	1	4

The interview questions were designed to prompt discussions of ethnicity and language in the context of Paramaribo and Suriname in general. The informants were led to discuss their views on social distinctions in Surinamese society, whether ethnic, linguistic, or other. The questions on ethnicity asked during the interview broadly fall into the following themes:

- The informants' ethnic background
- The informants' history of exposure to other ethnic groups
- The ethnic profile of the informants' close social network
- Perceptions and experiences of intergroup discrimination
- Perceptions and experiences of ethnic distinctions in Surinamese society

The informants were regularly prompted to identify nonethnic social distinctions that they perceive as salient, such as between wealthy and poor, urban and rural, and different religious groups. Questions designed to elicit such perceptions are, for example, "In what ways do you feel that people from rural areas behave differently from people in urban areas?," "Who and where are the wealthy in town and how do they typically behave?," "How do you as a Christian Javanese relate to a Muslim Javanese?," and so on.

The linguistic questions asked during the interview were phrased to elicit the following information:

- The informants' linguistic biographies
- The informants' macrosociolinguistic perceptions with an emphasis on the perceived linguistic attributes of Surinamese ethnic groups
- The informants' linguistic behaviors—expressed in terms of patterns of language choice—across intra- and interethnic contexts, as well as across a range of interactional contexts identified as linguistically relevant in the sociolinguistic literature on Suriname (that is, formal/informal, intra-/intergenerational, intra-/intergender)[28]
- The informants' linguistic behaviors, described in terms of intraconversational code-switching practices. Efforts were made to focus the informants' responses on characterizing the totality of linguistic resources that they draw on

across interactional contexts and on the pragmatic functions that they assign to these resources.

The analysis first discusses how the informants perceive their own ethnicities and those of others while relating these perceptions to other social categories that the informants describe as salient. It then focuses on the perceived macrosociolinguistic attributes of ethnicities, and of other salient social categories, expressed mostly in terms of language knowledge, language maintenance, and language shift to Dutch and/or Sranan. The analysis then goes on to describe the perceived interplay between social categories, interactional contexts, and patterns of language use. Finally, it describes the perceived interplay between salient social categories, interactional contexts, and "codes"—by which I refer to the varieties of languages or multilingual styles identified by the informants. The discussion section draws tentative conclusions on ethnolinguistic dynamics in Suriname. The informants are referred to via the capitalized abbreviations introduced in table 8.1 (e.g., "CR"), prefixed with "M-/F-" to indicate their gender, and suffixed with a number (e.g., "M-CR-2").

Perceptions of Ethnicity and Other Social Categories

The informants perceive ethnic boundaries at both macro- and microsocial levels. Some professions remain stereotypically associated with specific ethnic groups, as previously reported by de Bruijne and Schalkwijk.[29] Most informants associate Hindustani with agriculture, retail trade, and catering; Creoles with the public sector; and Maroons and Javanese with agriculture and the construction sector. There is also a perception that schools are ethnically segregated, especially primary schools, where Hindustani majorities are likely to be found if they are Hindu or Muslim schools. Some areas of Paramaribo are characterized as ethnic enclaves: Hindustani are associated with Kwatta Road, Javanese with Leonsberg and Blauwgrond, and Maroons with Latour and Pont Buiten. The informants agree that the Hindustani form the ethnic group most inclined to social self-insulation. Indeed, seven out of the eleven Hindustani informants describe their circles of friends as mostly Hindustani. Additionally, ten describe feeling pressure from their families not to marry those of a non-Hindustani background, especially Creoles and Maroons. The Javanese, Euro-Surinamese, and Chinese informants report similar pressure from their families to maintain social distance vis-à-vis Creoles and Maroons. The Maroon informants agree that the Creoles maintain a degree of social distance toward Maroons: they perceive Creoles as being condescending toward them, mostly due to their historically more urban character. That is the reason, in F-CR-1's opinion, why "a Creole would take offence if you called him a Maroon." Experiences of ethnic discrimination come to the fore in two main forms: discriminatory comments on social media (reported by fifteen informants), and patterns of group formation on campus, whereby Hindustani student groups are repeatedly described as maintaining their distance from other ethnic groups (reported by thirty-nine informants).

Despite perceived patterns of separation, the informants see some scope for mobility across ethnic boundaries. Most perceive the historical association of Creoles with employment in the public sector as eroding ("These days you find more and more Hindustani in the public services," M-HI-2). There is also little perception of rigid ethnic segregation at the educational level beyond primary school, or at the residential level in Paramaribo, as most informants describe their streets as ethnically mixed. Except for the Hindustani, most informants describe their social networks as ethnically mixed. There also seems to be scope for situational ethnic repositioning or "crossing,"[30] subject to the presence or absence of certain phenotypical features, in particular skin color, hair texture, and eye shape. F-MA-1 remarks that urban Maroons "sometimes pretend they are Town Creoles," a strategy of blurring ethnic boundaries that is facilitated by the African phenotypical features Maroons share with Creoles. Generally, it seems that full self-categorization as Creole can be justified simply by at least partial Creole parentage and the presence of African phenotypical features. For example, M-CR-1 and M-CR-2 do not include in their self-categorization their partial Javanese backgrounds due to what they say are their dominant African features. A clear-cut boundary is also lacking between light-skinned Creoles and Euro-Surinamese to the extent that the two categories are sometimes even treated as synonymous. A case in point is provided by F-EU, who in her self-categorization as "white" distances herself from her mother's Javanese ethnicity due to what she claims are its "negative connotations."

Ethnic disidentification can translate into the situational adoption of another ethnicity, but it can also translate into the situational rejection of established ethnicities in favor of "Surinameseness," which, for M-MI-1, provides an escape route from what he calls "the pressure to join one specific group." There are indirect indications, however, that "Creoleness" forms a defining dimension of Surinameseness due to the intrinsically inclusive values it conveys. This perception is perhaps best epitomized in F-MI-1's observation that "we Douglas are rejected by the Hindustani but accepted by the Creoles." Openness to other ethnicities on the part of the Creole population, according to F-CR-3, has to do with a strategy of "whitening," as "the Creoles are maybe not happy with their skin color, so they want to have Bonkoro and Dougla children."[31] By indexing hybridity, Creoleness can be appropriated into an oppositional identity set against ethnic traditionalism. Although she self-categorizes as Hindustani, F-HI-4 prefers associating with Creoles rather than with Hindustani, whose ethnocentric behaviors she finds oppressive. Additionally, projecting Creoleness more than other ethnic identities offers an avenue for social self-promotion. This is evident in the case of the Maroon informants, who tend to apply to themselves the Dutch label *Creool* rather than the officially used labels *Boslandscreool* (i.e., "Bushland Creole") or *Marron*. Calling oneself *Creool*, in F-MA-3's opinion, neutralizes the rural stigma historically attached to Maroons. Similarly, M-MI-1—who is of mixed Creole-Javanese parentage—feels strongly inclined toward "the Creole side" of his identity, as in his opinion "you get nowhere in life if you act like a traditional Javanese."

Parallel phenotypical hierarchies seem to be found among Creoles and Hindustani. The Creole informants describe a Creole phenotypical continuum ranging from *blaka* ("black") to *redi* ("red," meaning "fair"), with *bonkoro* forming a transitional category between the two. Hindustani may—according to the Hindustani informants—be categorized as either *kariya* (the Sarnami term for "black") or *safa* ("white," "fair"). In both cases, being "fair" suggests that one belongs to the higher social classes. Religious affiliations also seem, at first sight, to cut across ethnic boundaries: Islam is shared by sections of the Hindustani and Javanese populations, and Christianity by sections of the Javanese population and most Afro-descendants.[32] Additionally, the informants named Winti (or Winta in Aucan) as a set of religious beliefs and practices shared by Afro-descendant groups. However, the informants perceive religious practices as strongly ethnicized. The Javanese informants stress the "Javanist" component of Javanese Islam and emphasize that Christian Javanese typically identify with a Protestant denomination that specifically accommodates the Javanese. The Creole and Maroon informants agree that Winti/Winta rituals strongly differ across their respective communities. Finally, a social distinction regularly named while qualifying ethnicity is the urban-rural divide, especially when describing the Hindustani, Javanese, and Maroon populations, whose rural components pursue a more "traditional" lifestyle. However, certain ethnicities remain perceptually polarized across the urban-rural divide. The non-Maroon informants associate Maroons with rural areas, and Maroons regard Creoles as essentially urban. I examine in the next sections how the social distinctions reported by the informants play out at a linguistic level.

Perceived Ethnic Factors in Patterns of Language Knowledge and Dominance

There is an obvious connection between ethnicity and patterns of self-reported language knowledge in the sample in that the active knowledge of specific languages—namely, Sarnami, Javanese, Chinese dialects, and Maroon languages—is ethnically bounded. The informants also stress a symbolic connection between these languages and senses of ethnic belonging. For example, it is inconceivable in the view of all informants to be Creole and not speak Sranan: "The Creoles own Sranan," according to f-cr-5. Also, for a Hindustani to not at least understand Sarnami is likely to raise questions as to their membership in the Hindustani community, as explained by m-hi-3 and m-hi-4, who describe their competence in Sarnami as low or nonexistent. Self-reported modes of acquiring heritage languages vary considerably across ethnic groups. The Aucan informants and the seven Hindustani informants with active knowledge of Sarnami claim to have acquired their respective heritage languages from their parents. By contrast, two out of the three Javanese informants with active knowledge of Javanese acquired their language skills from their grandparents. Finally, the Creole informants all claimed to have picked up Sranan mostly outside of their homes, more specifically in the neighborhood or at school. These patterns of language transmission reflect perceived society-wide dynamics of language maintenance and shifts. The Javanese informants describe what they see as a near-complete shift from Javanese into Sranan and Dutch among younger Javanese generations. The Creole informants describe Sranan as largely absent in intergenerational communication in Creole households. The heritage languages perceived as best maintained in the home sphere are Maroon languages and Sarnami, although cases of urban Hindustani and Maroon children not understanding their heritage languages are reported.

When a given heritage language is not dominant in the home sphere, Dutch is. Most informants (as well as most informants from each ethnic group) reported that Dutch is their dominant home language, the exceptions being four of the eleven Hindustani informants, five of the twelve Maroon informants, and one of the eleven Javanese informants. Even when not described as dominant in the home sphere, Dutch is described as present, except by two Maroon informants. Overall, having Dutch as a home language seems to be an attribute of Creole and Euro-Surinamese identity. However, the suggestions by the informants that Dutch nowadays also functions as an identity marker among other ethnic groups and among "mixed" individuals (especially in urban areas

Ethnicity and Language Use in Suriname   171

and among the middle classes) seems to give it the trappings of an ethnically neutral language. The informants ascribe the dominance of Dutch in their home spheres to a strategy consciously pursued by their parents to enhance their children's performance at school, where Dutch is always the dominant medium of instruction. The informants also perceive a correlation between speaking mostly another language than Dutch at home and underperforming at school (e.g., "You can tell school kids who only speak Javanese at home because they struggle with Dutch," F-JA-4). Except for two of the eleven Hindustani and two of the twelve Maroon informants, the informants intend to make Dutch dominant in their future households. The main reason named by the Maroon informants for the limited presence of Dutch in their homes is that their parents grew up in remote rural areas and thus did not have access to Dutch-medium education.

Aside from Dutch, Sranan is the other language that—at first sight—seems to be known across ethnicities: all informants claimed to have at least partial knowledge of it. There is a wide consensus that Sranan is the most widespread language in Suriname (e.g., "It is everyone's language," M-HI-2). By contrast, knowledge of the other heritage languages seems confined to the ethnic in-groups, although mention is made of Hindustani and Javanese individuals fluent in one another's heritage languages, often as a result of being part of a mixed union. Also, all Creole informants claim a passive knowledge of Aucan (attributed to the fact that it closely resembles Sranan), which—according to the Maroon informants—is also widely known among the non-Aucan Maroons.[33] Not speaking Sranan is linked to an attitude rather than to an ethnicity ("There are some that just don't like to speak it," M-MI-4). Sranan is in all cases acquired in the early years and, as already mentioned above, mostly outside the home sphere, especially on the street. Only three (Creole) informants stated that they had acquired Sranan partly from their parents, and even then, only indirectly. Three of the eleven Hindustani informants stated that they began to learn it on joining secondary school. Most Creole informants reported that they began to use Sranan at home with their parents once they were halfway through school, as "it becomes acceptable as one gets older" (M-CR-1). Overall, there is a perception that speaking Sranan is less stigmatized past primary school, where acquiring Dutch is essential. Still, only one informant (F-CR-3) is of the view that Sranan should be made an official language, which shows that Dutch holds more overt prestige.

Ethnicity may not necessarily predict whether someone knows Dutch or Sranan. Yet ethnicity is seen as having an impact on degrees of competence in these languages. The informants mostly named the Creoles as most likely, and the Maroons and Hindustani as least likely, to speak "good" Dutch, while "good" Sranan was associated with Creoles and to a lesser extent Maroons. Other factors the informants mentioned as impacting levels of competence in Dutch are the urban-rural divide, social class, and age: competence in Dutch is perceived as highest in urban areas, among middle and upper classes, and among younger generations, and as lowest in rural areas, among lower classes, and among elderly individuals. Competence in Sranan is perceived as highest in rural areas, among lower classes, and among men, and as lowest among middle and upper classes, and among women. Eight informants indicated having only limited competence in Sranan (e.g., "When I try Sranan it just doesn't sound right," F-JA-5). Out of these informants, seven are female, four are Hindustani, two are Javanese, one self-identifies as being of "mixed" ethnicity, and one is Creole. Three of the eleven Hindustani informants ascribe their limited competence in Sranan to their parents' bias against the language (e.g., "My father doesn't want me to speak it as he thinks it sounds too rough," F-HI-5) and to having attended Hindu primary schools where Sarnami and Dutch were the mediums of socialization. The other informants cite social pressure to project an educated image as a factor limiting their scope for improving their Sranan. F-JA-6 claims that her competence in Sranan remains limited because "if you are of a certain standing, you have to keep it Dutch." Generally, F-MI-1 links low competence in Sranan to high academic attainment ("The more people have studied, the less they can speak Sranan").

Perceived Ethnic Factors in Language Choice

The informants were generally able to link the use of specific languages, especially Sarnami, Javanese, and Maroon languages, with specific social contexts where projecting ethnicity is expected. One is the home sphere, especially in the case of mono-ethnic households. As it often displays an ethnic character, religious worship forms another context where the use of especially Sarnami and Javanese is reported. Finally, intra-ethnic socialization with age peers outside of the family unit is recurrently mentioned as a context where Sarnami, Javanese, and Maroon languages are typically used. To some extent, the use of Dutch correlates with Creole ethnicity in that all Creole informants describe it as their dominant linguistic choice at home. Ethnic factors at work in language behaviors are also revealed in comments that the informants make on ethnic groups other than their own. Sixteen informants explicitly relate the frequent use of Sranan to being Creole. Some informants also identify interethnic contexts in which heritage languages other than Sranan are used for various purposes that involve projecting one's ethnicity. One of these purposes is the situational exclusion of ethnic others. For example, F-MA-5 observes that "it is a typical Hindustani thing to speak Sarnami when they don't want others to join their groups." Another purpose is identifying the background of unknown interlocutors via what Myers-Scotton calls exploratory code-switching.[34] This strategy is mostly deployed by the Aucan informants when interacting with dark-skinned interlocutors, who may turn out to be Creoles ("The dark ones [Creoles] may as well be Maroons, so you can try Aucan first," M-MA-2).

Certain patterns of situational language choice are seen as ensuring ethnic neutrality. According to F-CR-1, if only Creoles are taking part in a conversation, then Sranan is the norm, whereas "if the group is mixed, then it is mostly Dutch." This suggests that choosing Dutch as a medium of interaction helps shape ethnically neutral communication settings. One alternative to Dutch or Sranan as lingua francas involves both interacting parties maintaining their respective heritage language during the exchange. The Maroon informants report using this strategy in their interactions with Maroons of different linguistic backgrounds and with Creoles. Four of the twelve Maroon informants reported regularly using Aucan with Creoles. Their motivations for doing so are the close resemblance between Aucan and Sranan ("Aucan is Sranan with an accent," M-MA-5) and a belief that Creoles are more fluent in Sranan than others. However, the maintenance of Aucan in interethnic communication does not seem to meet with universal acceptance: F-MA-1 remarks that "Creoles sometimes get annoyed when you start talking to them in Aucan." The Maroon informants have mixed perceptions of linguistic norms of interaction between Maroons of distinct linguistic backgrounds. Four of the ten Maroon informants believe that Aucans and Saramaccans generally maintain their respective heritage languages when mutually interacting, yet only when the Aucan speaker is familiar with Saramaccan. By contrast, the other eight Maroon informants believe that Sranan remains the ethnically neutral medium between the various Maroon subgroups, as regular exposure to other Maroon languages is not widespread outside of specific settlements.

The patterns of language choices reported by the informants sometimes aim to invoke ethnic solidarity or to mark ethnic boundaries. They also occasionally derive from cognitive considerations: in which language is the interlocutor most proficient? They also derive from linguistic conventions of deference. These factors become apparent when an intergenerational perspective is taken on language choices within the home sphere. Even though Sranan is known across generations, its use is described as mostly restricted to intragenerational interactions, as it is ascribed connotations of "roughness." All thirty-two informants who declare that they ever use Sranan in their home spheres specify it as a medium for interacting with their siblings. Dutch seems to be the dominant choice for intergenerational interactions in the home spheres, unless the addressee's competence in Dutch is low. In that case, two options present themselves. One is to use the heritage language, as in the case of F-HI-3, who speaks Dutch with her father, but Sarnami with her mother, "because her Sarnami is better." Using mostly heritage languages with parents is the norm for seventeen of the informants (nine Maroons, six Hindustani, and two Javanese), while using Dutch is the norm for the rest. Using Sranan for intergenerational communication is also motivated by competence. Four informants (two Javanese and two Hindustani) use it with their grandparents, whose knowledge of Dutch is limited, and with whom Sarnami and Javanese cannot be used as mediums of interaction by the informants as their own competence in these languages is low. Exploratory code-switching outside the family provides another illustration of linguistic conventions of deference. For most informants, except the Maroons, addressing (older) strangers in their presumed heritage language or in Sranan might convey an assumption that the interlocutor is uneducated.

In summary, language choices in the Surinamese context experienced by the informants do not only index ethnicity. They also index specific attitudes or assumptions. The informants clearly associate Dutch with deference, an attitude they feel cannot be conveyed through heritage languages. For example, all Javanese informants with competence in Javanese admitted to not mastering the "polite" register of Javanese, otherwise called "High Javanese." In the words of M-HI-4, Sarnami is no more than a "hotchpotch," a "coarse language" that is not as refined as Hindi, itself a "pure" language, in which only two informants claim to have competence. In opposition to Dutch, Sranan—a "street language" (M-CR-2)—is assigned a [-deferential] and [-distant] value. Outside of the home, Sranan is—irrespective of ethnicity—the language used with age peers, or the language you speak with your friends (M-CR-3). These contrasting indexicalities are reflected in linguistic norms of deference in intergender interactions. Most informants agree that it is more appropriate to address women in Dutch. It is, in the words of M-MA-1, "an indication that things are neat and tidy," while speaking Sranan to a woman would send potentially unwelcome "macho" signals. The "manliness" attached to Sranan explains why Dutch is regarded as more apt to index femininity, and why women correspondingly tend to speak more Dutch than men in the view of the informants, especially when they are "not emancipated" (M-JA-1), and Hindustani, as Hindustani women are noted for being "ashamed to speak Sranan" (F-HI-1). The link between Dutch and deference, distance, and femininity seems to be less strong among Maroons, as they see Maroon languages as not inappropriate in intergender interactions.

Perceived Ethnic Factors in the Use of Linguistic Varieties and "Mixed" Codes

While ethnicity cannot straightforwardly predict who can and cannot speak Dutch and Sranan, it can to a higher degree predict how one's Dutch or Sranan is likely to sound. According to the informants, each ethnic group speaks Dutch with an "accent," especially when they speak their heritage languages fluently and their competence in Dutch is correspondingly low. The Hindustani are stereotypically perceived as speaking Dutch with a "singing tone": "It is like they add a question mark to the end of every sentence" (M-HI-4). A widely held view of the Javanese accent in Dutch is that it is overaccented ("They draw it out a lot," M-MI-2). Similarly, there is a perception of a "Maroon accent," characterized, among other things, by the confusion between the phonemes [g] and [k] (M-HI-2 gives the example of the word *gat* ["hole"] that Maroons would pronounce as *kat* ["cat"]). Varying degrees of competence in Dutch are usually measured by the ability to distinguish between the definite articles *de* (the "common" gender article) and *het* (the "neutral" gender article). Hindustani stand out as often using the Dutch definite articles incorrectly. "They make crazy mistakes," according to F-JA-4, also in terms of confusing present and past tenses.

Apart from ethnicity, the rural-urban divide, social class, and age are named as salient social factors that have an impact on the ways of speaking Dutch: second language learner errors are more likely to be encountered among individuals with a rural background and lower levels of education and older individuals. Contact with the Netherlands is also named as a factor: there is a widespread negative stereotype of Surinamese returning from the Netherlands with a contrived Netherlandish accent. "Overdoing" the European Dutch accent may have ethnic overtones: it tends, according to M-HI-2, to be more frequent among Hindustani and Javanese, whereas Creoles "only just learn new words" but "don't catch the accent."

Ethnicity is less salient as a predictor of variation in Sranan. Primary impressions are that Sranan sounds the same across all ethnic groups ("There is only one Sranan," F-CR-2). However, ethnicity (alongside education levels, social class, and gender) does manifest itself indirectly as a prominent factor in variation through levels of competence. Most informants agreed that there is a contrast between the "native-like" Sranan spoken by Creoles and the Sranan spoken by others, especially Hindustani (whose competence in it is deemed lower).

An important aspect by which the informants measure variation in Sranan is knowledge of "deep words" and expressions, such as *odos* (proverbial statements), which in the view of the informants tend to be hallmarks of the Sranan spoken by Creoles. Although some think that Maroon ways of speaking Sranan are lexically marked by Maroon languages ("The Saramaccans sometimes use Saramaccan words in their Sranan," F-MA-2), the dominant opinion among the informants is that the Maroons speak a conventional form of Sranan. Still, it could be that an urban Maroon variety of Sranan might be emerging in an Aucan guise, in the sense that urban Aucan varieties might be merging with Sranan. That possibility is most clearly indicated by the observation made by F-MA-2 that "many [urban Aucan speakers] think they speak Aucan while it is actually Sranan that they speak." In turn, the large presence of Aucan speakers in urban areas could be leaving a lexical imprint on urban Sranan, as the Creole informants were aware that they use Aucan borrowings in their Sranan.

All informants describe intraconversational code-switching as widespread. Its patterns vary across ethnolinguistic groups but tend to uniformly display a combination of Sranan and Dutch. Code-switching involving Sranan and Dutch alone is more likely to be found among Creoles, while other ethnic groups' code-switching patterns are likely to also involve their respective heritage languages. Whether these heritage languages are present in code-switching patterns largely depends on whether the exchange takes place in intra- or interethnic settings. Still, there are indications that Sarnami, Javanese, and Maroon languages occasionally feature in code-switching patterns deployed in interethnic settings. Some Hindustani, Javanese, and Maroon informants describe how they occasionally insert emblematic words from their heritage languages into Dutch and/or Sranan while interacting with members of other ethnic groups, such as F-HI-5, who claims to "sometimes" use Sarnami words in her Dutch as "an ice-breaker" while interacting with Creoles. Such self-reported behaviors indicate ethnicity projection strategies. Patterns of Dutch-Sranan code-switching are more likely to covary with location, age, and social class than with ethnicity. The informants agree that code-switching practices include more Sranan and less Dutch in rural areas, as well as among lower classes and older individuals. Irrespective of the urban-rural divide, age, and social class, some informants feel that there is a limit to how much Dutch can be combined with Sranan (e.g., "Too much Dutch in Sranan is confusing: one should stick to one or the other," F-MI-3).

Topic and conversational frame are perceived as impacting code-switching patterns. The only language perceived as usable across topics is Dutch. Except for Aucan, the informants consider their respective heritage languages to be of more limited conversational use. Sarnami and Javanese can never be used for discussing school-related topics, for which Dutch is in all cases seen as the more appropriate language choice. Among those who provide more detail on their use of Sarnami, F-H-2 claims to use it in connection with community-related topics. Sranan is felt as more appropriate for "macho-themed" conversations, which is the reason that F-HI-2 says she uses it "to discuss football" with her brother. Sranan is also described as appropriate for indexing specific conversational frames (F-JA-5: "If you want to tell a story, then you do it in Sranan, because it is more fun"). Additionally, it is used for "cracking jokes" or "hurling insults" (F-CR-1). Perhaps due to their low levels of competence in it, the Javanese informants seem to use Javanese more for emblematic purposes within otherwise Dutch or Sranan exchanges with ethnic peers. For example, F-JA-4 says she mostly uses Javanese for questions such as "How are you?" or "Have you finished eating?" While the examples of code-switching discussed so far seem to involve stylistically salient transitions between languages, there is also a widespread opinion that code-switching "happens automatically" (F-MI-3) and is "unconscious" (M-CR-2). This type of code-switching, referred to as "language-mixing," is likely to occur between typologically close languages.[35] This explains the perception that Aucan and Sranan could be merging in urban areas.

Discussion and Conclusion

The data reveal that ethnic boundaries are salient in Suriname. These ethnic boundaries could be discerned in perceptions of segregation in Surinamese society, ethnic stereotyping, and socialization patterns. There is a perception that the Hindustani, Euro-Surinamese, and Chinese maintain hard ethnic boundaries. There is also a perception that Surinameseness carries connotations of Creoleness, or in other words, that the Creoles form Suriname's socially dominant ethnic group. The hypothesis that ethnic boundaries are linguistically manifested holds true to some extent. Ethnicities are associated with specific heritage languages, which are used especially in the home sphere. There could also be some ethnic indexicality to the Dutch language as it is perceived as the only home language of the Creoles and Euro-Surinamese. Ethnic boundaries are also reflected in group-specific levels of competence in Dutch and Sranan, with the lowest levels of competence attributed to the Hindustani and the highest to the Creoles. Finally, code-switching practices can also index ethnicity, as some informants report combining their heritage languages with Dutch and Sranan as a strategy of ethnic identity projection.

Despite the above observations, there are suggestions that ethnic boundaries might be eroding, as Menzo proposed, albeit perhaps more between specific ethnic groups. For example, urban Maroons tend to identify with Creoles, as the two groups share similar phenotypical features. One can infer potential for ethnically neutral Surinamese identities to develop from biographies of exposure to other ethnic groups, the propensity to maintain ethnically mixed social networks, and, more generally, widespread identification with Surinameseness. At a linguistic level, eroding ethnic boundaries are suggested by the fact that Surinamese linguistic practices are linked to not only ethnicity but also other factors. In particular, the process of language shift to Dutch partly explains patterns of language choice more than do strategies of ethnic identity negotiation: low competence in Dutch among older generations is why heritage languages are maintained in intergenerational interactions.[36] Additionally, the scope for speaking Sranan seems constrained by linguistic conventions of deference. Finally, code-switching outside intra-ethnic settings involves only Dutch and Sranan by default and is mostly described as a topic and frame management strategy, or as unconscious language mixing.

Based on perceptions, the findings suggest that Surinamese ethnic boundaries are enduring, with signs of erosion in urban areas. Erosion is visible at a linguistic level with a general shift in urban areas toward Dutch and Sranan. Erosion could be proceeding fastest among those ethnic groups most inclined to identify with Surinameseness (and its Creole component), most notably the Maroons, and slower among the others, most prominently the Hindustani. As a salient social category in Surinamese society, ethnicity still seems reflected in ways of speaking Dutch and Sranan, determined by ethnically variable levels of linguistic competence. Whether these differential levels of competence are producing fossilizing features that over time could acquire an emblematic value remains to be established based on directly observed linguistic usage.

NOTES

1. Andreas Wimmer, "The Making and Unmaking of Ethnic Boundaries: A Multi-Level Process Theory," *American Journal of Sociology* 113 (2008): 970–1022; Michael Banton, *What We Know Now about Race and Ethnicity* (New York: Berghahn, 2015); Richard Jenkins, *Rethinking Ethnicity: Arguments and Exploration* (London: Sage, 1997).

2. Fredrik Barth, "Introduction," in *Ethnic Groups and Boundaries: The Social Organization of Cultural Difference*, ed. Fredrik Barth (Oslo: Universitetsforlaget, 1969).

3. Carmen Fought, *Language and Ethnicity* (Cambridge: Cambridge University Press, 2006); Michael Silverstein, "Indexical Order and the Dialectics of Sociolinguistic Life," *Language and Communication* 23 (2003): 193–229.

4. Howard Giles, Richard Y. Bourhis, and Donald M. Taylor, "Towards a Theory of Language in Ethnic Group Relations," in *Ethnicity and Intergroup Relations*, ed. Howard Giles (London: Academic Press, 1977); Howard Giles, "Ethnicity Markers in Speech," in *Social Markers in Speech*, ed. Klaus R. Scherer and Howard Giles (Cambridge: Cambridge University Press, 1979); John Berry, "Immigration, Acculturation and Adaptation," *Applied Psychology* 46, no. 1 (1997): 5–34.

5. Jan Blommaert, *The Sociolinguistics of Globalization* (Cambridge: Cambridge University Press, 2010); Ben Rampton, "Contemporary Urban Vernaculars," in *Language, Youth, and Identity in the 21st Century*, ed. Jacomine Nortier and Bente A. Svendsen (Cambridge: Cambridge University Press, 2017).

6. Simon Bekker and Anne Leildé, *Reflections on Identity in Four African Cities* (Oxford: African Minds, 2006); Nathan Glazer, "Divided Cities, Dual Cities: The Case of New York," in *Managing Divided Cities*, ed. Seamus Dunn (Newcastle-under-Lyme: Keele University Press, 1994).

7. Michael Clyne, *Dynamics of Language Contact: English and Immigrant Languages* (Cambridge: Cambridge University Press, 2003); William Labov, *Principles of Language Change: Social Factors* (London: Wiley, 2001).

8. Edgar W. Schneider, *Postcolonial English, Varieties around the World* (Cambridge: Cambridge University Press, 2007).

9. See Martin Ehala, "Ethnolinguistic Vitality and Intergroup Processes," *Multilingua* 29 (2010): 203–21; Cindy Gallois, Tania Ogay, and Howard Giles, "Communication Accommodation Theory: A Look Back and a Look Ahead," in *Theorizing about Intercultural Communication*, ed. William B. Gudykunst (Thousand Oaks, Calif.: Sage, 2005); Giles, "Ethnicity Markers in Speech."

10. Carol Myers-Scotton, *Social Motivations for Codeswitching: Evidence from Africa* (Oxford: Clarendon, 1993).

11. Blommaert, *Sociolinguistics of Globalization*.

12. Algemeen Bureau voor de Statistiek, *Censusstatistieken 2012*, vol. 1: *Presentatie definitieve resultaten census 8* (Paramaribo: ABS, 2012).

13. Algemeen Bureau voor de Statistiek, *Suriname Census 2004*, vol. 1: *Sociale en demografische karakteristieken* (Paramaribo: ABS, 2005).

14. Algemeen Bureau voor de Statistiek, *Censusstatistieken 2012*; Ad de Bruijne and Aart Schalkwijk, "The Position and Residential Patterns of Ethnic Groups in Paramaribo's Development in the Twentieth Century," *New West Indian Guide* 79 (2005): 239–71; Aart Schalkwijk and Ad de Bruijne, *Van Mon Plaisir tot Ephraïmszegen: Welstand, etniciteit en woonpatronen in Paramaribo* (Paramaribo: Leo Victor, 1999).

15. Algemeen Bureau voor de Statistiek, *Censusstatistieken 2012*.

16. G. J. Kruijer, *Suriname: Neokolonie in rijksverband* (Meppel: Boom, 1973).

17. Also see Rudolf Asveer Jacob van Lier, *Samenleving in een grensgebied: Een sociaal-historische studie van de maatschappij in Suriname* (The Hague: Martinus Nijhoff, 1949); Rudolf Asveer Jacob van Lier, *Frontier Society: A Social Analysis of the History of Surinam* (The Hague: Martinus Nijhoff, 1971).

18. Rosemarijn Hoefte, *Suriname in the Long Twentieth Century: Domination, Contestation, Globalization* (New York: Palgrave Macmillan, 2014).

19. Schalkwijk and de Bruijne, *Van Mon Plaisir tot Ephraïmszegen.*

20. Rivke Jaffe, "Hegemonic Dissolution in Suriname? Recent Challenges to Pluralist Politics," in *M. G. Smith: Social Theory and Anthropology in the Caribbean and Beyond*, ed. Brian Meeks (Kingston: Ian Randle, 2011); Hans Ramsoedh, "Playing Politics: Ethnicity, Clientelism and the Struggle for Power," in *20th Century Suriname: Continuities and Discontinuities in a New World Society*, ed. Rosemarijn Hoefte and Peter Meel (Leiden: KITLV Press, 2001).

21. See Monique Menzo, "Ethnic Group Boundaries in Multicultural Suriname" (MA thesis, Tilburg University, 2012).

22. Eithne B. Carlin, "Of Riches and Rhetoric: Language in Suriname," in Hoefte and Meel, *20th Century Suriname.*

23. Jacques Arends, "The History of the Surinamese Creole: A Socio-Historical Overview," in *Atlas of the Languages of Suriname*, ed. Eithne B. Carlin and Jacques Arends (Leiden: KITLV Press, 2002).

24. Isabelle Léglise and Bettina Migge, "Language Practices and Language Ideologies in Suriname: Results from a School Survey," in *In and Out of Suriname: Language, Mobility and Identity*, ed. Eithne B. Carlin, Isabelle Léglise, Bettina Migge, and Paul B. Tjon Sie Fat (Leiden: Brill, 2015); Sjaak Kroon and Kutlay Yagmur, "Meertaligheid in het onderwijs in Suriname," 2012, https://taalunie.org/publicaties/67/meertaligheid-in-het-onderwijs-in-suriname.

25. A. Y. Westmaas, "De Taalkeuze als Meter van Intimiteitsrelatie Tussen Veeltaligen," in *De Talen van Suriname*, ed. Eddy Charry, Geert Koefoed, and Pieter Muysken (Muiderberg: Coutinho, 1983).

26. Although the term "translanguaging" has to a large extent eclipsed the term "codeswitching" in the current sociolinguistic literature, I am still using the latter as I consider it more compatible with my aims of identifying grammatical types of Surinamese language practices.

27. Lesley Milroy, *Observing Natural Language* (Oxford: Oxford University Press, 1987).

28. See Westmaas, "De Taalkeuze als Meter."

29. See de Bruijne and Schalkwijk, "Position and Residential Patterns."

30. The term comes from Ben Rampton, "Contemporary Urban Vernaculars," in Nortier and Svendsen, *Language, Youth and Identity.*

31. *Bonkoro* is a Sranan term meaning "light brown." *Dougla* is a Bhojpuri term referring to individuals of mixed African and East Indian ancestry.

32. Algemeen Bureau voor de Statistiek, *Censusstatistieken 2012.*

33. Four of the twelve Maroon informants did, however, claim knowledge of Saramaccan, in one case due to the mother being Saramaccan.

34. Myers-Scotton, *Social Motivations for Codeswitching.*

35. Peter Auer, "From Codeswitching via Language Mixing to Fused Lects: Toward a Dynamic Typology of Bilingual Speech," *International Journal of Bilingualism* 3 (1999): 309–32.

36. As observed by Léglise and Migge, "Language Practices and Language Ideologies."

CHAPTER 9

Thinking beyond the Coloniality of Power with Patrick Chamoiseau

SAVRINA CHINIEN

> The power of a man or of a nation can be measured only in its capacity to be in interaction with the Places of the world, to harness from them the resources and the diversities in order to constitute the best of exchanges. Power lies in the radiance of correlation, in what binds, rallies, connects, relays these potentialities, individuals, and worlds.
> —Patrick Chamoiseau

Martinique and the Coloniality of Power

Martinique is in an ambivalent situation.[1] Sociopolitically and legally, it forms part of France, but through a shared history of enslavement and colonialism, culturally it is closer to other Caribbean islands. Patrick Chamoiseau (1953–) is a Martinican novelist, essayist, theorist, playwright, and scriptwriter who has spent the bulk of his professional career conceptualizing this ambivalence.[2] As a leading figure of the Créolité literary movement, he has become an engaged political activist who does not hesitate to make his voice heard within Martinique and France and on world affairs.

Much like Césaire was the embodiment of a mid-twentieth-century anticolonial reasoning, so too is Chamoiseau the same for the early twenty-first century. This is where we start to see differences between Césaire and Chamoiseau, and between the Négritude and Créolité movements.[3] For example, Chamoiseau has deplored the aftereffects of the 1946 law of departmentalization and the continuing economic and political dependence of Martinique on France. To this end, in *Écrire en pays dominé*, he criticizes the "incoherence" between Césaire the politician and Césaire the anticolonial poet: "Out of the hope of his work *Cahier*, Césaire has chosen departmentalization." Chamoiseau continues, "While the poet was invoking freedom, his political moves provided only certain material comforts instead of a new national identity."[4]

As part of seeking to move beyond the limitations of Négritude, the central claim of this chapter is that Chamoiseau has redefined the identity of the Martinican Black man. In doing so, he reconstructs narratives and discourses that not only put forth but question a sense of "nationness," to use Homi Bhabha's term.[5] The driving forces behind Chamoiseau's call for a "dialogic" approach around coloniality are also examined.

For Chamoiseau, it is evident that Martinique still suffers from the "coloniality of power" from France as well as from "global coloniality."[6] According to Ramón Grosfoguel, "coloniality of power" refers to a crucial structuring process in the modern/colonial world-system that articulates peripheral locations in the international division of labor with the global racial/ethnic hierarchy and Third World migrants' inscription in the racial/ethnic hierarchy of metropolitan global cities. Peripheral nation-states and non-European people are currently living under the regime of global coloniality imposed by the United States through the International Monetary Fund (IMF), the World Bank (WB), the Pentagon, and NATO.[7] Given their pervasiveness, these colonialities shape politics, race, class, and nationalism in Martinique. It is of interest how Chamoiseau's contemporary works discuss how the reality of these colonialities shapes his political position/vision.

In this chapter I examine the historical background of Martinique to explain why Chamoiseau still perceives his native island as being dominated by France, despite its status as an overseas department (DOM or *département d'outre-mer*) putting an ocean between the two. The second part deals with how Martinicans, Chamoiseau included, believe that their voice is silenced. I then discuss the impact of the 2009 strikes in Martinique and Guadeloupe, which brought to light the socioeconomic divide with metropolitan France. In the third part, through Chamoiseau's concept of the "warrior of the imaginary," I will delve into the interplay of race and class within the Martinican context. I continue these themes when analyzing the notions of "territory," borders, nation, and "nationness" in the fourth part. Finally, I investigate how Chamoiseau thinks beyond the "coloniality of power." Through his guidance, perhaps we might be able to do the same.

Chamoiseau's poetics is important to politics as it represents the politically voiceless. Poetics does possess a greater fineness of perception than politics, whence arises its capacity to represent the politically excluded (and included). Chamoiseau's works eschew the mostly binary vision of politics (left- and right-wing parties), seeking instead to portray human reality in all its complexity. In so doing, the author is able to enrich and illuminate political issues, highlighting the ambiguities and nuances that politics may overlook or is ignorant of. For Chamoiseau, the "Taubira law" whereby slavery was declared a crime against humanity (May 10, 2001) is representative of the fact that intellectuals can make an impact on the political arena.[8]

Martinique: The Making of a "Nation"

One stable element in the various political narratives and cultural traditions that form part of diverse European historiographies is the self-perception of superiority over all other colonized civilizations, especially those in the Global South. Marc Ferro, in *L'Histoire sous surveillance*, pointed out that the inventory of values supposedly defining civilization provided a sort of code to enter in history.[9] History and occidental law had codified what civilization was to the exclusion of many other civilizations.[10] There has been a Western will to establish an ontological and epistemological distinction with the aim to dominate, restructure, and acquire more power. As Chinua Achebe explains in *Hope and Impediments*, the primary pedagogical aim of all his works is to put forth a "revised" and "corrected" historical memory: "I would be quite satisfied if my novels (especially the ones I set in the past) did no more than teach my readers that their past—with all its imperfections—was not one long night of savagery from which the first Europeans acting on God's behalf delivered them."[11] For civilizations that, for a long time, have been oppressed and dispossessed of their own history, their foremost task would be to examine the concordances and discordances with the dominant European ideology or "the symbolical capital, to discover the latent collective memory behind the apparent 'institutional' memory, the non-visible through the visible and to undertake the historical work of dehistoricization."[12]

Through the critique of Eurocentrism in the early twentieth century, the model of civilization was no longer considered as singular and solely appertaining to European empires but as plural and encompassing other cultures with their diversities. In the Martinican context, Aimé Césaire challenged the European discourse on colonized countries through focusing on the representative colonized, subjugated man in the figure of Caliban, claiming recognition and acceptance for his newly self-forged identity.[13] Although he was the mayor of Fort-de-France and deputy to the French National Assembly (where he was instrumental in paving the way for Martinique to become a DOM in 1946), Césaire frequently voiced concern about the imperial and cultural domination of France, which can bring out "a special aura of legitimacy to any idea emanating from the Center."[14] Césaire and other Martinican intellectuals like Frantz Fanon, Édouard Glissant, Raphaël Confiant, and Patrick Chamoiseau have deplored the political, economic, and cultural dependence of Martinique on France. As Martinique relies heavily on France for economic assistance and aid, this perpetuates the imperialist dynamics of the capitalist world-system. Though Martinicans became French citizens in 1946, they only obtained the same social welfare rights as the rest of the French population in France much later. Césaire, as an engaged artist and politician, always tried to "deconstruct" the dominant Eurocentric discourse about the Martinicans while simultaneously "reconstructing" their history and forging a more informed political consciousness, as attested by some of his "political" works.[15]

The works and political position of Césaire had a profound influence on Édouard Glissant and Creolists like Patrick Chamoiseau. In Martinique, Césaire's Négritude movement began in the 1930s, followed by Glissant's Antillanité movement in the 1960s. Glissant reiterates that Martinicans do not have access to their own specific history but rather that of France and points out in *Le Discours antillais* that Martinique has known only a "history without accumulation ... a history plunged in the history of the Other (France). There is thus no historical memory enabling us to achieve a collective memory."[16] The contribution of Glissant to the conceptualization of Antillean identity is significant. To the notion of "root identity" put forth by Césaire, Glissant draws on Gilles Deleuze and Felix Guattari's ideas of a rhizome based on polysemy and polymorphy.[17] He criticizes former empires with their "universal" ideology or uniformity based on a monolingual territory that is fixed and authoritative and proposes a "diversal" "poetics of Relation" that is "multilingual and baroque, churned by the chaotic and disorderly mixing of cultures, ignoring the intolerance of the territory, animated by the thought of mobility."[18] In doing so, Glissant redefined the whole concept of a nationalist identity founded on Martinique's own specific history and cultural specificities.

The Créolité movement in the late 1980s produced *Éloge de la Créolité*, a major literary manifesto that presents a theoretical/political framework co-written by Jean Bernabé, Raphaël Confiant, and Patrick Chamoiseau. The Creolists acknowledge the influence of Glissant and Césaire; they even describe themselves as being "forever Césaire's sons." They clearly praise the Négritude movement for paving the way for their own engaged political writings: "To a totally racist world, self-mutilated by its own colonial surgeries, Aimé Césaire restored mother Africa, matrix Africa, the Black civilization. He denounced all sorts of dominations in the country, and his writing, which is committed and derives its energy from the modes of war, gave severe blows to postslavery sluggishness. Césaire's Négritude gave Creole society its African dimension, and put an end to the amputation that generated some of the superficiality of the so-called doudouist writing." The Creolists perceive the Négritude movement as a "necessary dialectical moment, an indispensable development," and they likewise reject the (neo)colonialism and the cultural, intellectual, racial, and moral hegemony of France.[19] However, for Chamoiseau the identity construct of the Martinican Black man is more complex than merely acknowledging the African and French influence. He therefore proceeds to explore questions of voice/silence through asking whether the formerly marginalized are presently being silenced.

The Politics of Voice

In a lecture provocatively titled "Create Dangerously," Albert Camus pointed out that to "create today is to create dangerously. Any publication is an act." He adds, "Today everything is changed and even silence has dangerous implications."[20] This sentiment applies to Chamoiseau when he denounced the "coloniality of power" that France exerted and still exerts over Martinique, pointing out that "France has to get rid of its colonial mindset."[21] Chamoiseau conceptualizes three types of political dominations: "the Brutal," "the Silent," and "the Furtive." The brutal domination is the "One and Universal Truth that [empires] imposed on us through genocides, violence, and auto-sanctifications to exploit the world."[22] This more visible form of colonialism was replaced by the "silent" form of domination.

Chamoiseau points out that in Martinique, like in many formerly colonized countries, the great achievements of "Progress" were instrumental in advancing colonial exploitation, particularly through the churches, schools, and hospitals of the former empires.[23] This silent domination is established on a symbolic principle that is known and acknowledged by the dominant as well as the dominated people, as Pierre Bourdieu explains in *La Domination masculine*.[24] Likewise, Chamoiseau agrees that this silent, surreptitious domination becomes possible as the colonizer "disposed of the arms of his victory: a Nation-Territory, a language, a skin color, an identity, a flag, a dominating expansion."[25] All these elements contribute to a myth of historical genesis that can lead to silent domination.

The most surreptitious form of domination is the "furtive" one, which is "invisible"—the colonial power matrix has morphed into "global coloniality." Grosfoguel points out that the "mythology of the 'decolonization of the world' obscures the continuities between colonial past and current global colonial/racial hierarchies and contributes to the invisibility of 'coloniality' today."[26] This "coloniality" is an aggression without violence; it is the "invisible" imperialist army and the impact of neoliberal capitalism, which is much more difficult to resist on the socioeconomic level. Chamoiseau is concerned that not addressing the issue of finding alternatives to capitalism and means of economic development will lead to a totalitarian system that will deny humane values.[27] In *Frères Migrants* Chamoiseau denounces the capitalist system, the "paradigm of maximum profit" whereby "profit at all costs becomes immanent" to the exclusion of anything else.[28]

Though Martinique is a department of France, Chamoiseau has deplored that the socioeconomic and political rapport between both countries is a sort of "sterile monologue" where all major political decisions are taken in France.[29] Chamoiseau's political views are often expressed in his novels, plays, and literary and political manifestos, and so his ideas about the sterile monologue make an appearance. In the novel *Biblique des derniers gestes*, the protagonist Balthazar Bodule-Jules, the old "revolutionist," is concerned about the status of Martinique: "[The country] had become a department of the faraway metropolis. It has been submerged by allowances, subsidies, and financial assistance, generosity and alms. The price of living has exponentially gone up like that of a castle in a fairy tale. Schools have been implanted a bit everywhere so as to better learn to become an 'overseas person.'"[30] In the Martinican context based on economic dependence, Chamoiseau highlights that culture and politics are intricately linked, and one serves as the instrument of the other. Grosfoguel elaborates on this complex link: "Post-colonial studies conceptualise the capitalist world-system as being constituted primarily by culture, while political-economy places the primary determination on economic relations. In the 'coloniality of power' approach, what comes first, 'culture or the economy,' is a false dilemma, a chicken-egg dilemma that obscures the complexity of the capitalist world-system."[31] Economic dependence, a major component of this complex capitalist world-system, is one of the factors that led to the 2009 French Caribbean general strikes in Guadeloupe and Martinique.

The general strikes can partly be explained by the fact that Martinique and Guadeloupe had one of the highest unemployment rates in the European Union in the preceding years.[32] According to Insee statistics, 34 percent of Guadeloupeans were living below the poverty line in 2017.[33] Income inequality is significantly compounded by wealth inequality, inherited from the slavery era. In Martinique, the cost of living is 17 percent higher than in France because of import laws,[34] which explains the high cost of staple goods. Imports constitute three times more of the trade economy than exports because the industrialization process has been incomplete, with sugar refinement being the most developed industry, followed by the tourism industry. Hence, the economy remains unbalanced and is heavily dependent on France.

The high price of living, prices of basic commodities, and monthly salaries of low-income earners are all factors that contributed to the growing feeling that there was a divide between how French citizens in France and those of the DOM were considered from a socioeconomic point of view. Following the 2009 strikes, together with seven other engaged writers, Glissant and Chamoiseau wrote a short political manifesto, *Manifeste pour les "produits" de haute nécessité*, whereby the authors denounce capitalism as a "blurred, globalized system" that victimizes most people.[35] They also criticize France for not considering the socioeconomic and cultural reality/specificity of Martinique.[36]

The 2009 social unrest and pressure from Martinican political parties, like the Movement Indépendantiste Martiniquais seeking independence or others seeking more political autonomy from France, resulted in a promise for constitutional reform. As Johan Galtung points out, imperialism "is a sophisticated type of dominance relation which cuts across nations, basing itself on a bridgehead which the center in the Center nation establishes in the center of the Periphery nation, for the joint benefit of both." This can cause a "disharmony of interest" as is attested by the rapport between France and Martinique.[37] In a bid to create more of a "harmony of interest," a bill was passed in early 2016 granting Martinique the additional status of a *collectivité territoriale*, which facilitates policymaking at the local level. This policymaking is divided into two sections, the first comprising the social, economic, and environmental aspects and the second the cultural and communication aspects. Martinique is represented by four deputies to the French National Assembly and two senators to the French Senate.

Considering this relatively recent bill that enables Martinican politicians to decide about local policies, where does Martinique really stand? What kind of voice does it have? If it does not form part of the CARICOM or Françafrique, even though it has a shared collective history with these Caribbean and African countries, it is part of the Outermost Regions (OMR) of the European Union and by extension can be represented by NATO, of which France is a member state.

The Warrior of the Imaginary

As a Martinican author, Chamoiseau does consider himself as subaltern. In *Eloge de la Créolité* he demonstrates the determination to be decolonized intellectually within the literary space and hence accede to an autonomous, "local" literature that would be more authentic without the gaze of the Other and also without the "domination of another place."[38] Thus Chamoiseau symbolically inverts the debate between Centre and Margin (the formerly colonized countries of the Centre), between France and Martinique. In *Écrire en pays dominé* this discussion is renewed and the intellectual resistance toward the Centre is enhanced. Moreover, in his works Chamoiseau often opposes the symbols of the South (Martinique and other Caribbean countries) to those of the North. The systemic ideologies of the North concerning the southern countries are challenged and presented with a new ethos from the South. This process allows for the creation and control of an Antillean Centre, of which the author ensures the exegesis. Indeed, the Creole storyteller, who according to Chamoiseau has played a fundamental role of "resistance" during the slavery era, is considered a hero as his words are a source of inspiration. Furthermore, the notion of orality (which forms part of the culture of many African nations) defines the Caribbean societies better, as the authors of *Éloge de la Créolité* point out that "orality is our intelligence; it is our reading of this world, the experimentation, still blind, of our complexity. Creole orality, even repressed in its aesthetic expression, contains a whole system of countervalues, a counterculture; it witnesses ordinary genius applied to resistance, devoted to survival."[39]

In a culture where the transmission from the storyteller to the writer, from the unique oral, spoken words to the written words assumed by a writer, has not yet taken place, the discourse can only be fragmented, stretched between the spoken and the written words. Chamoiseau describes his works as being closer to the verve of the storyteller as he would like his writing to be free from the "constraints" of Western writing, which, according to him, is marked by the seal of universality.

Grosfoguel points to the "ego-politics of knowledge" of Western philosophy, which has always privileged the myth of a nonsituated "Ego" to produce a Truthful universal knowledge. Hence all non-Western knowledge is dismissed as being particularistic and subsequently unable to achieve universality. For Grosfoguel, this forms part of global designs articulated to the simultaneous production and reproduction of an international division of labor of core/periphery that overlaps with the global racial/ethnic hierarchy of Europeans/non-Europeans.[40] Like Glissant before him, Chamoiseau has questioned that notion of "universal knowledge" and the epistemic hierarchy of Western knowledge and cosmology and has endorsed instead the notion of "Diversality," which would be inclusive of the particularities of different cultures. The epistemic hierarchy of knowledge is intricately linked to a linguistic hierarchy, and Chamoiseau has pointed out the divide that this creates.[41]

The schism, the "break ... gap ... deep ravine between a written expression pretending to be universal-modern and traditional Creole orality enclosing a great part of our being," is one of the issues that Chamoiseau tries to resolve in his literary works. He explains that "this non integration of oral tradition was one of the forms and one of the dimensions of our alienation." Chamoiseau describes himself as a "marker of speech" rather than an author.[42] His primary source of inspiration is the traditional Caribbean storyteller (inspired by the African *griot*). In his writing he often adopts the role of the narrator/narratee, the "marker of speech" who "collects," takes notes, reports, and brings forth ancestral or popular sayings. In *Biblique des derniers gestes* the narrator is retelling the life of the protagonist, Balthazar Bodule-Jules, but his challenge is to face his own uncertainties: "subjugated to the maelstrom of notes I had brought back, I was forced to write in a polycentric, disseminated, dispersed instability, plunged in a confusion of multiple evocations."[43] The act of narrating is problematized and becomes transparent, evident, and curiously uncertain. The narrator often doubts his own memory and his notes, and he reveals his angst during his writing process as he feels torn about not being able to transcribe faithfully what he has witnessed.

In both Chamoiseau's fictional and quasi-autobiographical writings, the storyteller will change into the "marker of speech" and subsequently into the "warrior of the imaginary," a character who is also recurrent in his literary and political manifestos. As an empirical author giving interviews, lectures, and keynote speeches at conferences, Chamoiseau also assumes the role of the "warrior of the imaginary."[44] As Aníbal Quijano points out, the coloniality of power, expressed through political and economic spheres, is strongly associated with a coloniality of knowledge that has been deeply imbricated in the structures of European colonial domination.[45] María Lugones expounds on Quijano's concept of "coloniality of power" by arguing that not only did colonization invent the colonized but it also disrupted the social patterns, gender relations, and cosmological understandings of the communities and societies it invaded.[46] The role of the "warrior of the imaginary" that Chamoiseau assumes both in his works and in real life is to deconstruct the coloniality of knowledge by identifying and acknowledging the Francophone sources of knowledge while affirming modes of knowledge that have been denied as the key role and influence of the storyteller.

Walter Mignolo points out that a decolonial epistemic shift should enable the histories and thought of other places to be understood as prior to European incursions and to be used as the basis of developing connected histories of encounters through these incursions.[47] This "decolonial epistemic shift" ties in with Chamoiseau's intentions as he questions narratives reinforcing the conceptualizations of epistemic power and proposes instead other (counter)narratives, based on the memories and experiences of the Martinican people who have suffered from slavery, colonialism, and ongoing socioeconomic inequalities. Chamoiseau also describes himself as a "cartographer of the wounds" of his country and as such tries to delve into the "authentic" Martinican identity both for him as an author and for the people of the lower social strata.

The enactment of the colonial matrix of power is clearly shown in Chamoiseau's trilogy on his childhood[48] as "le petit négrillon" (the little negro boy) becomes more and more aware as he grows up of the painful divide between the logic of coloniality (poverty, misery, inequality) and the rhetoric of modernity that France represents (progress, development, growth).[49] France and its culture is exalted in the colonial school system, and as such the French language is given preeminence over the Creole language. This is a cause of trauma for the children as well as "le petit négrillon" as their teacher would chastise them for speaking Creole and for their poor pronunciation of French.[50] Many of the children would start feeling alienated and drop out of the school system. Anyone, usually the descendants of the former slaves, unable to speak French (the language of the Creole white class and wealthy mulattos) with a decent accent was discriminated against. To date, this "subtle" discrimination still pervades the Martinican society.

In *Eloge de la Créolité* the authors point out the cultural alienation arising from the imposed use of the French language during colonization: "Creole, our first language ... is the initial means of communication of our deep self, or our collective unconscious, of our common genius, and it remains the river of our alluvial Creoleness. We dream in it. In it we resist and accept ourselves. It is our cries, our screams, our excitements. It irrigates each one of our gestures.... The absence of interest in Creole language was not a mere mouth silence but a cultural amputation."[51] In *The Location of Culture*, Homi Bhabha reiterates the dominant power of language, particularly concerning theoretical discourse: "Is the language of theory another power ploy of the culturally privileged western elite to produce a discourse of the Other that reinforces its own power-knowledge equation?"[52] Does the Western world then exploit what Bourdieu defines as its "symbolical capital"? According to Bourdieu, all art represents a "conflict of class struggle,"[53] and if a text is canonized and studied, the dominant group can proscribe its perspective of the world to all societies. Bourdieu explains that there is a symbolical violence at the basis of all valorization. Does the process of political and economic colonization morph into an intellectual colonization through the dominant language? Is there, as Grosfoguel points out, a pedagogical hierarchy where the Cartesian Western forms of pedagogy are considered superior to non-Western concepts and practices of pedagogy?[54] Finally, in this hybridity and diversity of cultures and languages, how can an authentic discourse or writing be forged?

In *La Langue créole force jugulée*, Dany Bebel-Ghisler examines this problematic and states that the French language disposes of the arsenal of ideological weapons imbricated in French imperialism; this contributes to the reinforcement of France's political and economic domination, and this acknowledged legitimacy has as correlation the suppression of the Creole language.[55] Even as an author, Chamoiseau admits he has struggled with what language to use in his works, French or Creole.[56] The narrator in *Écrire en pays dominé* expresses his angst at his dual heritage.[57] Chamoiseau integrates the defense of Creole language as a vector of authenticity in the confrontation of languages as according to him, the idolized dominant language ignores the personality of the colonized speaker, falsifies his history, and denies his freedom.[58]

This choice of Chamoiseau implies an appropriation of the dominant language of the Centre and its adaptation in a discourse that is entirely his. He has transcended the debate by finding his own voice and forging a unique "chamoisified" language whereby he seamlessly uses the French language while incorporating Creole expressions, onomatopoeia, and words. This idea is also expressed in *Eloge de la Créolité*: "Creoleness left its indelible mark on the French language, as did other cultural entities elsewhere. We made the French language ours. We extended the meaning of some of its words, deviated others. And changed many. We enriched the French language, its vocabulary as well as its syntax. We preserved many of its words which were no longer used. In short, *we inhabited it*."[59] Hence, dominant structures of Western knowledge and language are questioned and symbolically "appropriated" by Chamoiseau. For instance, his novel *L'Empreinte à Crusoé* is a critical rewriting of the vicissitudes of Daniel Defoe's Robinson Crusoe as well as Michel Tournier's Crusoe (in *Vendredi ou Les Limbes du Pacifique*, 1972) to prise out a counternarrative. Through the silenced castaway of history, Chamoiseau delves into the inner depths of the very notion of humanity and explores the dissolution of nation and culture through the protagonist. He weaves several layers of ideological subtexts in his novel, one of which is the subversion of the colonizer's perspective (as he also does in *L'Esclave vieil homme et le Molosse*). This novel illustrates how Chamoiseau strives for a "decolonial epistemic shift" (to quote both Mignolo and Grosfoguel). If Chamoiseau as the "warrior of the imaginary" tries to deconstruct dominant structures of knowledge, he is also concerned about how to map out a "new" Caribscape in a globalized world.[60]

Mapping Out the Caribscape

Paul Jay argues that globalization is a historical process beginning "at least in the sixteenth century and covering a life span that includes the long histories of imperialism, colonization, decolonization and postcolonialism." Globalization has spurred on an inevitable and ongoing phenomenon as "every culture is always shaped by other cultures and agency has more to do with the intelligent and imaginative negotiation of cross-cultural contact than in avoiding such contact."[61] The dynamics between a global homogenizing culture and an endogenous heterogenizing one is rife with multiple (re)definitions of the cultural complexities of the self as globalization requires "us to define who we are, or strive to be, within an ever-broadening spectrum of contexts [by] stepping out of the narrow, self-incarcerating traditions of 'belonging.'"[62]

In the Martinican society where there has been the imbrication of cultural and linguistic micro- and macro-climates, Chamoiseau points to the significance of conceiving all cultures as exerting simultaneously a unified and diversified "action" without a dilution or loss of the diverse populations in contact. For this to be achieved, Glissant and Chamoiseau suggest that a "poetics of Relation" becomes necessary to "conceive the elusive globalized chaos-world."[63]

The notion of rhizome as expounded on by Félix Guattari and Gilles Deleuze provides the analogy for both Glissant and Chamoiseau to develop the concept of the "poetics of Relation"—the rhizome, being a root that has multiple horizontal sprouts without any one of them being vertical and "totalitarian." The rhizome thus privileges a "mise-en-relations" (putting-in-relation) whereas the unique, single root privileges a "mise-sous-relations" (putting-under-relation), thus tying in with the notions of Diversality versus Universality. According to Chamoiseau, the rhizome-identity would enable individuals to be in total fluidity as the old systems of belonging, of identity markers, of relating to oneself or to others would be completely modified.

Hence, a neutral space of interaction whereby reigns tolerance but also the dialectic between confrontation/harmony, conciliation/opposition, rupture/coalescence among different cultures is essential for a constructive exchange/dialogue among different societies. Identity is no longer confined to one geographical location but rather to an individual experience that increasingly involves several spaces in a mobile, interconnected, recomposed world, and the cultural referents also have to be reconfigured accordingly to what Glissant terms the "Tout-Monde."

Subsequently Chamoiseau states that there is no territory in Creole land and that there are fundamental differences between the notion of "territory" and "place"/space: "the implacable Territory holds on a unique root. A place/space represents Diversity; the Territory arms itself of Unicity.... The Territory imposes Universality. The Place/space is only perceived through a thousand imbricated stories; the Territory comforts itself in one History."[64] These notions of "poetics of Relation," "territory," and "place" may seem controversial and utopian, considering the sociopolitical and economic construct of the Western world. Karl Marx did denounce this kind of "imaginary absence of class relations."[65]

In the political manifesto/pamphlet *Quand les murs tombent* (2007), Chamoiseau and Glissant condemn the silence of Europe for walling itself within its borders and hence being against crowds of migrants in exodus, fleeing war, misery, and oppression, arising from socioeconomic and political exploitation. *Frères Migrants* (2017) was compellingly composed, following the testimonies of Parisian friends expressing their deep concern about how migrants were being treated and the lack of compassion from public authorities. Grosfoguel rightly explains that the idea of race or arranging the world's population into a hierarchical order of superior and inferior people becomes an organizing principle of the international division of labor and the global patriarchal system and that contrary to the Eurocentric perspective, race, gender, sexuality, spirituality, and epistemology are not additive elements to the economic and political structures of the capitalist world-system but an integral, entangled, and constitutive part of the broader "package" called the European modern/colonial capitalist/patriarchal world-system.[66]

Thus race and racism are not superstructural or instrumental to an overarching logic of capitalist accumulation; they are constitutive of capitalist accumulation on a world scale.[67] Likewise, Chamoiseau condemns neoliberalism and capitalism as being an integral part of the worldwide issue of immigration and the base immigration policies of most Western countries in *Frères Migrants*. The book, through its poetic dimension, is political in its discourse and a plea for humanity to be respected in a dignified manner. Chamoiseau clearly positions himself in solidarity with migrants, as for him the French Republican values of "liberté, égalité et fraternité" are essential for the progress of any society: "Liberty, equality, brotherhood, sharing, equity, human dignity are forces that are constructed against barbarities." He denounces the neoliberal system, resulting in "exclusion, rejection, violence, nonsense, hate, and indecency that ferment everywhere."[68] For Chamoiseau, the violence suffered by migrants affects a falsely sealed "us" (that of Europeans or the Western world).

If both Glissant and Chamoiseau project a world, a "Tout-Monde" whereby the "walls will fall" and human beings have total freedom of movement, implying that no border can be materialized (other than by representation on a map), what kind of "Caribscape" (the suffix *-scape* referring to the deeply perspectival constructs pointing to the fluid, irregular shapes of landscapes) are they then mapping out?[69] Homi Bhabha has proposed the idea of nationalism as boundaries not as simply the space between one nation and another, oneself and another, but as a way of seeing the boundaries also as always facing inward, as a kind of internal liminal space; this space would then enable people to rewrite their own "nationness."[70]

However, this new globalized cultural landscape must be perceived as a complex, overlapping, disjunctive order (what Glissant terms as "chaos") that cannot any longer be understood in terms of existing center/periphery models such as postcolonialism, which provides a narrower perspective "focused strictly on re-imagining the nation."[71] Does the Caribscape for Chamoiseau, then, imply a nonphysical space, "a kind of internal liminal space," as Bhabha has suggested?

Thinking beyond the Coloniality of Power

After centuries of domination and exploitation of non-European labor from the South, wealth has been accumulated and remains concentrated in the North. Chamoiseau has pointed out that the most active motor of globalization up to now has been the capitalist system, which creates a very particular kind of globalization based on poverty, suffering, and rupture, as well as standardization and uniformity through consumerism.[72] Globalization has superseded economic imperialism and goes even further by peeling this facade to reveal its intrinsic nature: fascism as multinational corporations exercise more control and power than governments.[73]

Neoliberal policies represent a continuation of the "accumulation by dispossession."[74] Alain Badiou makes the overall point eloquently as follows:

> The fall of the Berlin wall was supposed to signal the advent of the single world of freedom and democracy. Twenty years later, it is clear that the world's wall has simply shifted: instead of separating East and West it now divides the rich capitalist North from the poor and devastated South. New walls are be-

ing constructed all over the world: between Palestinians and Israelis, between Mexico and the United States, between Africa and the Spanish enclaves, between the pleasures of wealth and the desires of the poor, whether they be peasants in villages or urban dwellers in favelas, banlieues, estates, hostels, squats and shantytowns. The price of the supposedly unified world of capital is the brutal division of human existence into regions separated by police dogs, bureaucratic controls, naval patrols, barbed wire and expulsions.[75]

How viable is, then, the concept of "Tout-Monde" proposed by Glissant and endorsed by Chamoiseau, which indicates a dissolution of the "walls" of territories?

The 2009 strikes serve as a reminder that there is an economic divide/"wall" between metropolitan France and its overseas departments. If Chamoiseau asserts the need for a metaphorical dissolution of those walls, the limits of his conceptualizations are that he does not propose a concrete political/economic vision as to how this can be achieved except through what can be perceived as "abstract" notions of "diversality" and borders (or rather nonborders) being a place of exchange and enrichment where pluralist identities can flourish and human dignity is respected. However, he does point to the urgency of the rethinking of the notion of borders as wars, poverty, and systematic violations of human rights are pushing millions of people to seek asylum.

Dora Kostakopoulou has proposed a more concrete, viable solution: that of "civic registration." Under this model, the only condition for residence would be demonstrated by willingness to live according to democratic rule plus some set requirements for residency and the absence of a serious criminal record. Such a citizenship model requires a reconceptualization of territorial space as a "dwelling space" for residents and thus a move away from the nationalist narratives that cultivate the belief that territory is a form of property to be owned by a particular national group, either because the latter has established a "first occupancy" claim or because it regards this territory as a formative part of its identity.[76]

However, Jonathan Seglow proposes another solution instead of open borders: that of global redistributive justice, as he believes it is better to shift resources to people rather than permitting people to shift themselves toward resources.[77] This ties in with Quijano's proposal of "the socialization of power," which implies the formation of global institutions beyond national or state boundaries to guarantee social equality and justice in production, reproduction, and distribution of world resources.[78] While this socioeconomic/sociopolitical solution is viable, stimulating and sustaining economic development in situ, the struggle cannot be just anticapitalist but also an antisystemic decolonial liberation, requiring "a broader transformation on different other levels as well (racial, epistemic, political, linguistic, pedagogical and aesthetic amongst others)." How can this social antisystemic change involving so many diverse aspects of power hierarchies be achieved in a nonreductionist way? This could be achieved by decolonizing "Marxist/Socialist perspectives from [their] Eurocentric limits" and by adopting "Diversality as a universal project."[79] What I mean is a universal that is pluriversal, which would include all epistemic particularities within a "transmodern socialization of power."[80]

How, then, does Chamoiseau think beyond the "coloniality of power"? I suggest that he does so by questioning and examining all the ramifications of the "colonial power matrix" within Martinique but by also analyzing the power hierarchies within the whole world-system. It is for this reason that Chamoiseau's ideas are more relevant than ever in both Martinique and France. He has proposed for a sustainable, organic agriculture to be developed in Martinique so that it starts to achieve more economic independence from France, which is currently being considered and put in practice by the local authorities. He pinpoints all the areas that need to be addressed and has conceptualized possible solutions: "diversality," "Tout-Monde," "the warrior of the imaginary," among others. For him, the notion of identity construct transcends space and should not be limited to any particular territory: identity can no longer be rooted but is rhizomatic and mosaic.

Though some of Chamoiseau's conceptualizations do have limitations in that they remain abstract notions in current societies, they do represent the stepping stones to thinking what Chamoiseau terms as "l'impensable" ("the unthinkable"). Today, in a world where there is little normalcy, where social structures need to be reframed and redefined, "thinking the unthinkable" and "thinking about the unthinkable" are no longer abstract notions but reality.

NOTES

1. The epigraph is from Patrick Chamoiseau, *L'intraitable beauté du monde* (Paris: Galaade, 2009), 54. All translations in the chapter are the author's, unless otherwise stated.

2. Chamoiseau is a versatile artist. He has also written comic books for children and lyrics for songs. He is a social worker by profession and is the town planner for the towns of Saint Pierre, Trois Ilets, and the capital Fort-de-France in Martinique.

3. Though Césaire had a considerable influence on Pan-Africanists like Nkrumah, Chamoiseau criticizes him for his "relationship with the French language" as well as for his political stance.

4. Patrick Chamoiseau, *Écrire en pays dominé* (Paris: Gallimard, 1997), 200.

5. For Bhabha, "nationness" is constitutive of narrative constructions that arise from the "hybrid" interaction of contending national and cultural constituencies. See Homi Bhabha, *The Location of Culture* (New York: Routledge, 1994), 2.

6. Aníbal Quijano differentiates between colonization and coloniality. For him, "coloniality" refers to "colonial situations" in the present period in which colonial administrations have been almost eradicated from the capitalist world-system. Aníbal Quijano, "Coloniality and Modernity/Rationality," *Cultural Studies* 21, no. 2 (2007): 173.

7. Ramón Grosfoguel, "The Epistemic Decolonial Turn," *Cultural Studies* 21, nos. 2–3 (2007): 14.

8. Literature can have an impact on politics: Joseph Conrad's *Heart of Darkness* generated momentum for the campaign against King Leopold's regime in the Congo; *Oliver Twist* by Charles Dickens, in its depiction of the impoverished Victorian underclass, outraged the British public and prompted social changes. Likewise, *Uncle Tom's Cabin* became instrumental in energizing the abolitionist cause in the United States.

9. Marc Ferro, *L'Histoire sous surveillance, science et conscience de l'histoire* (Paris: Calmann-Lévy, 1985), 41.

10. Some of the writings of the Enlightenment philosophers such as Montesquieu and Voltaire, while advocating for freedom for slaves and respect for other civilizations, were also controversial. Henri Moniot, "L'histoire des peuples sans histoire," in *Faire de l'histoire, I—Nouveaux problèmes*, ed. Jacques Le Goff and Pierre Nora (Paris: Gallimard, 1974), 106.

11. Chinua Achebe, *Hope and Impediments* (London: Heinemann, 1988), 30.

12. Pierre Bourdieu, *La Domination masculine* (Paris: Seuil, 1998), 114, 132.

13. Savrina Chinien, "Memory of Trauma and Trauma of Memory" in *Caribbeing: Comparing Caribbean Literatures and Cultures*, ed. Kristian Van Haesendock and Theo D'haen Theo (Amsterdam: Rodopi, 2014), 98.

14. Johan Galtung, "A Structural Theory of Imperialism," *Journal of Peace Research* 8, no. 2 (1971): 91.

15. *Cahier d'un retour au pays natal* (Paris: Présence Africaine, 1948); *Discours sur le colonialisme* (Paris: Présence Africaine, 1955); and his triptych of political plays: *La tragédie du Roi Christophe* (Paris: Présence Africaine, 1963), *Une Saison au Congo* (Paris: Présence Africaine, 1966), and *Une Tempête* (Paris: Présence Africaine, 1969), among other works.

16. Édouard Glissant, *Le Discours antillais* (Paris: Gallimard, 1981), 293.

17. Gilles Deleuze and Felix Guattari, *Mille Plateaux* (Paris: Les Editions de Minuit, 1980).

18. Glissant, *Le Discours antillais*, 773.

19. Jean Bernabé, Raphaél Confiant, and Patrick Chamoiseau, *Eloge de la Créolité* (Paris: Gallimard, 1993), 79, 80, 82. "French ways forced us to denigrate ourselves: the common condition of colonized people" (86). The Creolists still consider Martinique as being neocolonized. Note: all translations from this book are by M. B. Taleb-Khyar.

20. Albert Camus, "Create Dangerously," lecture, University of Uppsala, Sweden, December 14, 1957, https://www.brendanhart.com/content/files/2022/06/Create-Dangerously-2.pdf.

21. "Guadeloupe: le LKP reprend les négociations mais se méfie," *L'Express*, February 20, 2009.
22. Chamoiseau, *Écrire en pays dominé*, 23, 29.
23. Chamoiseau, *Écrire en pays dominé*, 49, 34.
24. Bourdieu, *La Domination masculine*, 58. Bourdieu expounds that dominated people contribute, often unknowingly, sometimes against their will, by tacitly accepting this relationship.
25. Chamoiseau, *Écrire en pays dominé*, 62.
26. Grosfoguel, "Epistemic Decolonial Turn," 14.
27. Patrick Chamoiseau, "L'individu placé dans les grands vents de la Relation," in *La Caraïbe, chaudron des Amériques*, ed. Jean-Michel Devésa and Savrina Chinien (Limoges: Presses Universitaires de Limoges, 2017), 229.
28. Patrick Chamoiseau, *Frères Migrants* (Paris: Gallimard, 2017), 33.
29. "Martinique: The Question of Autonomy," interview in *AlterPresse*, July 2, 2002.
30. Patrick Chamoiseau, *Biblique des derniers gestes* (Paris: Gallimard, 2002), 698.
31. Ramón Grosfoguel, "Colonial Difference, Geopolitics of Knowledge and Global Coloniality in the Modern/Colonial Capitalist World-System," *Review* 25, no. 3 (2002): 203–4.
32. BBC News, February 16, 2009, "French Isles Top EU Jobless Table," http://news.bbc.co.uk/2/hi/europe/7892773.stm.
33. L. Demougeot, N. Kempf, and B. Raimbaud, "Niveaux de vie en Guadeloupe en 2017: La pauvreté touche un tiers de la population guadeloupéenne," Insee, July 1, 2020, https://www.insee.fr/fr/statistiques/4623253.
34. The importation rates are high and trade is encouraged within France.
35. Patrick Chamoiseau et al., *Manifeste pour les "produits" de haute nécessité* (Paris: Editions Galaade), 7.
36. Chamoiseau, *L'intraitable beauté du monde*, 5.
37. Galtung, "Structural Theory of Imperialism," 81.
38. Bernabé et al., *Éloge de la Créolité*, 14.
39. Bernabé et al., *Éloge de la Créolité*, 95.
40. Ramón Grosfoguel, "Decolonizing Post-Colonial Studies and Paradigms of Political-Economy: Transmodernity, Decolonial Thinking, and Global Coloniality," *Transmodernity: Journal of Peripheral Cultural Production of the Luso-Hispanic World* 1, no. 1 (2011): 4, 6.
41. Walter Mignolo, *Local Histories/Global Designs: Essays on the Coloniality of Power, Subaltern Knowledges and Border Thinking* (Princeton: Princeton University Press, 2000), 94.
42. Bernabé et al., *Éloge de la Créolité*, 96.
43. Chamoiseau, *Biblique des derniers gestes*, 396.
44. Chamoiseau, *Écrire en pays dominé*, 303.
45. Quijano, "Coloniality and Modernity/Rationality," 168.
46. María Lugones, "Toward a Decolonial Feminism," *Hypatia* 25, no. 4 (2011): 742.
47. Mignolo, *Local Histories/Global Designs*, 469.
48. Chamoiseau, Antan d'enfance (Paris: Gallimard, 1990); Chemin d'école (Paris: Gallimard, 1994); A bout d'enfance (Paris: Gallimard, 2005).

49. I am here referring to Mignolo's article and his argument that the colonial power matrix is the inextricable combination of the rhetoric of modernity and the logic of coloniality.

50. Chamoiseau, *Antan d'enfance*, 92. The small negro boy reveals that it was more natural for him and other children of his socioeconomic background to speak Creole as it was their "natural" language.

51. Bernabé et al., *Éloge de la Créolité*, 104.

52. Bhabha, *Location of Culture*, 20–21.

53. Pierre Bourdieu, *La Distinction, Critique sociale du jugement* (Paris: Éditions de Minuit, 1979), 50.

54. Grosfoguel, "Decolonizing Post-Colonial Studies," 9.

55. Dany Bebel-Ghisler, *La Langue créole force jugulée* (Paris: L'harmattan, 1981), 157, 161.

56. Chamoiseau, *Écrire en pays dominé*, 66–67.

57. "My primary suffering was in the tragedy of languages: between Creole language and French language. The old challenge of authenticity. In which one write correctly and how?" Chamoiseau, *Écrire en pays dominé*, 274.

58. Bernabé et al., *Éloge de la Créolité*, 47.

59. Bernabé et al., 107.

60. Béatrice Boufoy-Bastick and Savrina Chinien, *Caribbean Dynamics: Reconfiguring Caribbean Culture* (Kingston: Ian Randle, 2015), xii.

61. Paul Jay, *Global Matters: The Transnational Turn in Literary Studies* (Ithaca, N.Y.: Cornell University Press, 2010), 3.

62. Berthold Schoene, *The Cosmopolitan Novel* (Edinburgh: Edinburgh University Press, 2009), 21.

63. Édouard Glissant, "Le cri du monde," *Le Monde*, November 5, 1993. The term "chaos" is used in the sense that the "creolisation" of cultures has brought about unpredictable results.

64. Chamoiseau, *Écrire en pays dominé*, 227.

65. Karl Marx, *Class Struggles in France, 1848–1850* (New York: International, 1984), 91.

66. Grosfoguel, "Colonial Difference," 11.

67. Grosfoguel, "Colonial Difference," 11.

68. Chamoiseau, *Frères Migrants*, 35, 20.

69. Arjun Appadurai, *Modernity at Large: Cultural Dimensions of Globalization* (Minneapolis: University of Minnesota Press, 1996).

70. Gary Olson and Lynn Worsham, eds., *Race, Rhetoric, and the Postcolonial* (Albany: State University of New York Press, 1999), 28.

71. Schoene, *Cosmopolitan Novel*, 130.

72. Maeve McCuster, "On Slavery, Césaire, and Relating to the World: An Interview with Patrick Chamoiseau," May 10, 2008, https://warwick.ac.uk/fac/arts/english/currentstudents/postgraduate/masters/modules/resourcefictions/oil09/13.3.mccusker.pdf.

73. This has been made more explicit with the COVID-19 pandemic with multinational corporations exercising more control and power and dictating to governments what to

do through the use of nonpolitically elected bodies (funded by the said multinational companies who also lobby elected government officials). These companies also make large financial contributions to both right- and left-wing parties.

74. David Harvey, *The New Imperialism* (Oxford: Oxford University Press, 2003).

75. Alain Badiou, "The Communist Hypothesis," *New Left Review* 49 (January-February 2008): 38.

76. Dora Kostakopoulou, "Thick, Thin and Thinner Patriotisms: Is This All There Is?," *Oxford Journal of Legal Studies* 26 (2006): 73.

77. Jonathan Seglow, "The Ethics of Immigration," *Political Studies Review* 3 (2005): 229.

78. Quijano, "Coloniality of Power."

79. Grosfoguel, "Colonial Difference," 12, 29; Mignolo, "Local Histories/Global Designs."

80. Quijano, "Coloniality of Power."

CHAPTER 10

Cultivating Black Authenticity in Jamaican Popular Music

NADIA WHITEMAN-CHARLES

Caribbean music has been likened to a semantic battle between the colonizer and the enslaved.[1] For example, Keith Nurse views Caribbean popular music as a site of resistance where the subjugated can contest their control.[2] Similarly, Paul Gilroy argues that during colonialism music was important because other modes of literacy were denied to the enslaved. Without schooling, their "bad English" became the primary means for ordering their world, thoughts, and feelings. Thus, Creole language is a motif in the production of Black music.[3] Supriya Nair stipulates that in the Caribbean, folk orality creates a unique idiom that can be found in sounds like reggae, dancehall, and dub poetry.[4]

A key motif in Jamaican reggae and dancehall is *nation music*, which is centrally linked to Black nationalism to accentuate the rhetoric of Jamaican national identity. By nation music I mean the process of syncretism local music undergoes to be treated as "authentically Jamaican."[5] Whereas reggae and dancehall were once deemed undesirable musical forms by the Jamaican bourgeoisie, as these sounds became profitable they gained wider acceptance. By contrast, alternative musical forms practiced in Jamaica, like rock music, are construed as antithetical to the nation.

Keeping these topics and themes in mind, this chapter describes how value is assigned to Jamaican musical forms. I suggest local rock music is situated between two communities: the mainstream music industry and the alternative music scene, with each mapping onto Victor Turner's concept of structure and antistructure.[6] I describe the mainstream as principally housing the production and consumption of reggae and dancehall, while the alternative label signifies music and other cultural products that are not construed as emblematic of the nation. While I add nuance and qualifiers to this argument, my primary evidence comes from two years of ethnographic fieldwork I conducted in Jamaica.

My ethnographic inquiry into the Jamaican alternative scene, specifically its rock music scene, was conducted between August 2013 and October 2015. The members of the rock scene typically lived in Kingston, were between the ages nineteen and fifty-one, and descended from various socioeconomic brackets. Using a critical lens, I analyzed data collected via participant observation and interviews. I focused on narratives of taste in "local" and "foreign" music and used discourse analysis to evaluate issues related to race, nationalism, and the politics of difference.

A Brief Overview of the Rock Scene Culture

Music scenes define a group of people who enact their musical tastes in various ways such as in their fashion, dancing, and listening and/or playing music in various spaces (club, bar, school, or sidewalk).[7] Most important, scenes are a part of the social network and so impact the social system in which they belong. They should never be discounted as truly separate from dominant culture/s or class structures.[8] Will Straw defines music scenes as "actualizing a particular state of relations between various populations and social groups, as these coalesce around specific coalitions of music style." Straw further argues that scenes "may be both local and trans-local phenomena, a cultural space which may orientate as much around stylistic and/or musicalized association."[9] Some criticize the use of terms like "subculture" and "scenes" as they privilege pop music as "obviously connected" to the youth experience and undermine the "true" representation of the impact of music on groups. Hesmondhalgh acknowledges the importance of music in sustaining terms associated with youth such as "scene," "subculture," and "tribe" but argues that they "overestimate the coherence and fixity of youth groups."[10] Consequently, Jenks explains that subcultural research embodies a capricious landscape: "the idea of subculture becomes no more than opinion—everyone has one and, as the cliché runs, they are entitled to it!"[11]

Jamaican music scenes are defined in this chapter as finite groups of individuals who express their tastes in local and foreign music through their discourses, the production and consumption of sounds, and their musicianship.

I chose "scene" to describe the groups of this research because of the term's strong connection to scholarship on popular culture and music. Additionally, when my participants talked about their own groups and activities, they often used the term "scene." Members of both the rock and alternative music scenes generally described their activities as "a bunch of friends who want to play music. People like Tony with his bar and Dominique Brown and Joan with Nanook are people who have the resources to create infrastructure. And then there is us, the performers, we are just the people who stumbled across music and fell in love. Stumbled across each other along the way and just fed off of each other's energy. The scene is like an intangible thing. The energy that holds us together, that's really what the scene is to me."[12]

There have been many cultural intersections with global and Jamaican scenes. In the late 1960s and 1970s British mod and skinhead subcultures incorporated elements from Jamaican rude boy culture for its fashion and music consumption. Jamaican immigrants in the 1950s and 1960s and record companies like Island Records and Trojan brought an interest in Jamaican music to the British public. In fact, it was Island Records artist Desmond Dekker's ska song "The Israelites" that got ska into heavy rotation on British radio in 1969. Don Letts's written account of the culture clash between Jamaican dread and British punk cultures in the 1970s describes the fluid identities that Letts himself negotiated within these two scenes. The rude boy and dread cultures of Jamaica synthesized with the European punk scenes and birthed various expressions like ska punk.[13]

Ska punk was a very popular style in the 1970s with British bands such as the Specials and the Clash. Arguably, later practitioners of ska punk are 1990s U.S. bands like No Doubt, Rancid, and Blink-182. Additionally, classic rock bands like Led Zeppelin and the Police were influenced by ska and reggae. Many bands saw Jamaica as a creative source. The quintessential example is how in 1973 the Rolling Stones recorded tracks for their *Goats Head Soup* album at Dynamic Sounds Studio in Kingston, where they utilized local conga and timbales players.[14]

Concurrently, Jamaican acts borrowed in kind from their rock brethren. Jamaican record producer Chris Blackwell is viewed as one of the visionaries who married rock and reggae in the twentieth century. His label Island Records signed acts like U2, the Cranberries, and Melissa Etheridge. He is seen to have had a hand in making punk and new wave music popular. The music from the Jamaican acts on his label, such as Bob Marley, Peter Tosh, Jimmy Cliff, and Third World, were influenced by classic rock and pop rock sounds.[15]

Bob Marley was one of the major reggae artists to utilize rock in his musical compositions. His lead guitarist, Albert Anderson, is said to have been purposely recruited for his rock skills. Along with Blackwell, Marley was inducted into the Rock and Roll Hall of Fame, though in 1976 he was reluctant to class his craft as rock: "Me have to laugh sometimes when dem scribes seh me like Mick Jagger or some superstar thing like that.... Dem have to listen close to the music, 'cause the message not the same. *Nooo*, mon, the reggae not the twist, mon!" For Rolling Stones reporter Robert Palmer, Bob Marley's life story of struggle and redemption and his musical legacy represent rock and roll philosophies and make him a perfect candidate for the Rock and Roll Hall of Fame. Additionally, the Rock and Roll Hall of Fame has officially stated that more than Marley's stylistic influences drew from the rock genre, as reggae "is legitimately part of the larger culture of rock and roll.... In Marley's own words, 'Reggae music, soul music, rock music—every song is a sign.'"[16] Presently, the popular pop rock and reggae mixes of Justin Bieber, Chris Brown, Nicki Minaj, and Rihanna synthesize these sounds to earn international success. However, Chang and Chen see that these success stories do not deter Jamaican audiences who feel that their best artists should concentrate on Jamaican music and not succumb to foreign influences, which dilute the authenticity of Jamaican music.[17]

Rock music in its many forms has infiltrated Caribbean popular culture for decades. The terms reggae fusion and reggae/rock or rock/reggae describe the synthesis between reggae and pop, rock, hip-hop, and other foreign musical influences. They have been applied to many musical acts since the 1970s. Jamaican singer Tessanne Chin is widely known to infuse rock, reggae, and dancehall in her local musical style. As the season 5 winner of the American music show *The Voice*, Tessanne's rock abilities have been promoted globally. She is one of the products of the Jamaican rock music scene.

The rock music scene in Jamaica is situated between the nation's mainstream music industry and the alternative music scene. The latter was made up of music styles like local rock, rap/hip-hop, and jazz, which were not popular in Jamaica. Popular tastes were aligned with reggae and dancehall. There was heavy criticism for tastes in rock music regardless of its fusion with reggae. Some of these criticisms stemmed from stereotypical assumptions of the genre's connection to occult practices, which conflicted with the widely held Christian morals of the society. In an online post, the fusion between dancehall and Goth was identified in the music of Jamaican dancehall artist Tommy Lee. The disapproving writer even went so far as to say that Mr. Lee was dancehall's Marilyn Manson, a "demon praising rapper" who used "dark elements to boost his career."[18]

Despite being in the shadow of reggae and dancehall, rock music is present in the tastes of some Jamaicans in the twenty-first century. Rock was heard sparingly on radio stations in the late 1980s and 1990s. The children and teens of this era, particularly in upper-middle- and upper-class homes, also had access to foreign music through cable television and the Internet. More than this, live performances at Jamaican hotels included a repertoire of rock and pop music to appease the tastes of expats and tourists. These enclaves provided avenues for locals to nurture their interests in different styles of rock and resulted in youth formulating the rock scene in 1995.

The fusion between rock styles and Caribbean music is evident not just in Jamaica but also on other islands. Trinidadian soca and chutney soca acts like Kes the Band and Karma have included rock music in their musical repertoires, and soca artists such as Faye-Ann Lyons, Patrice Roberts, and Destra Garcia have also incorporated the movement's fashion into their acts. Rock music has long been present within the popular culture of the Caribbean. During the mid-twentieth century, Best explains, music from Barbados was influenced by technological and creative developments in international music: "[The] Farfisa [accordion's] portable and relatively compact organs became very popular among rock and roll bands and other combos during the early 1960s.... Barbadian musicians therefore aspired to own and play the instrument." This interest was also sustained in the 1980s and 1990s, as soca artists, in an attempt to make themselves viable for the international market, explored and exploited the fusion between local and foreign sounds.[19]

Trinidad has the largest rock music following in the Caribbean. There are three radio stations (HOTT 93 FM, 95.1 FM the Ultimate One, and STAR 94.7 FM) that play various rock styles, and since the late 1990s there have been music festivals devoted to rock fans during July and August, such as the SKYY Rock Festival. There are also venues that exclusively cater to rock tastes such as the bar Rock of Ages, now called Phoenix Park, in Chaguanas. Many bands populate the rock music scene in Trinidad, such as the heavy metal group Orange Sky, death metal band LYNCHPiN, and alternative rock group Brain Coral. Alternative rock music has infiltrated the playlist of many mainstream radio stations in not just Trinidad but also Jamaica, Barbados, and Saint Lucia.[20]

One of the earliest works on rock in the Anglophone Caribbean is Robin Balliger's 1999 study of popular music consumption in Trinidad in the 1990s. Here, the rock music scene was described as the fans of rock, metal, and alternative music. Balliger described the group's tastes as tied to class and race distinctions as both typifications were used to allocate divisions in public spaces. She stated that popular music was used as a divisive force as nightclubs were a source of overt racist and class-conscious policing. Youth of different races were given specific nights to attend, and the high price of entry restricted the lower classes. Balliger positioned the rock scene as populated by "mainly white and mixed, middle class and above, from the North and West [of Trinidad]; the other is largely working-class Indians, many from Central and South."[21]

The older generation's disapproval of rock music is motivated by a fear of being imperialized by Western states. The Caribbean youth's interest in rock music is therefore believed to be in opposition to local traditions. As a result of the social pressure to conform to local tastes, few fans in the Caribbean maintain their allegiance to rock in their adult years.

Not many works have explored the intersection of Caribbean music with styles of rock or tried to complicate the production of local music with its global counterpart. Barbadian scholar Curwen Best's comparison of the directorial and technological similarities between American alternative rock music videos and dancehall music videos is among the few.[22] In light of the deficit in knowledge conducted on rock music in the Caribbean, my research brings awareness to a hidden social performance. The realities of Jamaicans with a taste for rock give a fair representation of the glocal reality we must contend.

Despite a history of hybridization in foreign and local music, rock music was seen by mainstream Jamaica as a symbol of white colonialism, while the reggae and dancehall sounds were artefacts of resistance and Black excellence. For many of the older generation, the interest of millennials and Gen Z in rock music was an example of Western imperialism. Michael "Ibo" Cooper, past member of the reggae band Third World and president of the Jamaica Reggae Industry Association at the time of this study, affirmed this perspective: "Uptown kids live in a virtual lifestyle. They were never a part of Jamaican society.... In many ways, their class does not relate to our culture easy. Then came the expansion of media and communications and everybody started to get cable and Internet. In the digital communication age, the United States has an amazing jack of cultural imperialism."[23]

There is a superficial acknowledgment of rock music's contribution to reggae. Many scholars have stressed the importance of hybridity in Caribbean music.[24] Still, many have highlighted how local sounds—built on foreign styles—are not an easy sell to Caribbean audiences.[25] On the ground, rock music lingers as an uneasy symbol of Western oppression.

Mainstream versus Alternative

Jamaican tastes in music are decidedly allocated to two realms: the mainstream (audiences and music industry professionals of the popular domain) and the alternative (audiences and music professionals outside the popular). All artistic expressions and experiences that differed from dancehall and reggae were deemed "foreign," "different," "inauthentic," and "alternative music." These ascribed values signified the boundaries between national and foreign tastes and lifestyles. Additionally, mainstream audiences' dispositions were not limited to music but also sentiments surrounding politics and religion. Consequently, dancehall and reggae represented these individuals' choice of music as well as their acceptance of the genre's authenticity.

Bourdieu described social capital as assigned to individuals who belong to specific social groups in society. A group's social distinction hinges on the network of individuals and their institutional roles. Capital is accrued when, in the words of Bourdieu, "exchange transforms the things exchanged into signs of recognition and, through the mutual recognition and the recognition of group membership which it implies, reproduces the group. By the same token, it reaffirms the limits of the group, i.e., the limits beyond which the constitutive exchange—trade, commensality, or marriage—cannot take place."[26]

Consumptive choices for Bourdieu convey the act of selection of cultural products that communicate the individual's relative position in struggles for distinction. For Bourdieu, tastes and lifestyles (social dispositions) are strategies and constraints within the economic class struggle.[27] Consequently, Jamaican consumer practices were oriented and stylized into lived choices. Alternative and mainstream music represented the tastes and lifestyles of two opposing groups who conflicted with each other. The struggle between mainstream and alternative music tastes highlighted the logic of sociocultural distinctions between "local" and "foreign" identities.

These kinds of distinction making can be seen in how the members of the Jamaica Reggae Industry Association (JaRIA) conducted their business. For example, they primarily focused their lobbying on issues such as the Noise Abatement Act, the termination of payola, and the application of the Entertainment Encouragement Act. However, JaRIA's major activity was the planning and organizing of the nation's Reggae Month, which featured mainly dancehall and reggae acts and history.

To fully understand the distinction in terms like "alternative scene" and "rock music scene," it may be best to describe how my participants consciously and unconsciously threw the tag around. It was quite implicit that "alternative music," "alternative musician," and "alternative audience" were terms used to describe entities outside the reggae and dancehall circle and were contingent on the context of an event or practice. For example, dub poetry was aligned with the alternative scene, not because dub poetry was seen as a "foreign" music style but because of its lack of popularity in the public domain. Dub poetry is a Jamaican artform, but its creative practice is regarded as an alternative to reggae and dancehall.

The Cosmic Rotation event on October 26, 2013, showcased both rock music acts Kat C.H.R. (lovers rock) and the band Skygrass (pop, reggae rock) along with reggae singers Bryan Art and Timeka Marshall. However, promoters did not describe this event as connected to the rock or alternative scene. It was principally cast as music from new and upcoming artists in Jamaica. Thus the allocation of the label "rock" or "alternative" was not an exact science. Why certain persons, music, or events were depicted by Jamaicans as such was highly contextual, but more times than most the "imagined" alternative was aligned with U.S. music.

Unpopular local sounds were pigeonholed as "Other" music that was not considered native to the country. Though rap is said to have been influenced by Jamaican dancehall, it is nevertheless treated as an external, and hence threatening, cultural product.[28] The consumers and producers of the Jamaican rap or hip-hop music scene bonded their interests and pooled resources to produce the Pay Attention event, which was featured at the South Beach Café two to three times a year. This event along with infrequent house parties were where the rap community congregated between 2013 and 2015. The rock and rap music scenes were both part of the alternative music community—the alternative to reggae and dancehall.

THE ROCK COMMUNITY

Kingston was home to the rock community. Participants spoke of learning about rock (and other "foreign") music through cable television and the Internet. Some pursued this interest by attending live performances at hotels, which included a repertoire of rock and pop music meant to cater to the tastes of expats and tourists.[29] Still, the scene sought out venues for local Jamaican rock music. I spent a considerable amount of time in two establishments, these being Tony's Bar and Nanook. At a conceptual level, scenes impact the social system in which they belong and so should never be treated as truly separate from dominant culture(s) or class structures. Jamaican music scenes are defined in this work as finite groups of individuals who express their tastes in local and foreign music through their discourses, the production and consumption of sounds, and their musicianship.

Rock music events were rooted in Kingston's buzzing nightlife and considered an "uptown" experience. It earned this label because the events within the scene took place at uptown venues in Kingston. Uptown-downtown is a spatial division that reflects class boundaries connoting rich and poor neighborhoods. For instance, Burlington Avenue was regarded as a street that offered premier musical performances in the uptown scene. Many mainstream and emergent music events were held at this location. The rock community utilized the venue Nanook on this street for many of its shows when Tony's Bar closed in 2014. Though traditionally dancehall shows are depicted as restricted to downtown areas, a few uptown areas hosted these events. For instance, the Stone Love Movement, a popular dancehall sound system, held Weddy Weddy (a dancehall party) a short distance away from Nanook on Burlington Avenue.

The uptown label was also attached to the scene because its members, musicians and nonmusicians alike, were perceived as rich expatriates, tourists, or Jamaicans belonging to the upper-middle and upper classes. I was told by one of my participants that the scene held "more white and Brown bodies" than other local music zones. Brown and white skin colors signified upper-class positions in the society according to Jamaica's postcolonial prescriptions.[30] Furthermore, the fact that the music played at the scene differed from reggae and dancehall, which had been the traditional vehicles used to tell the stories of the lower classes, created a distance between popular local music and alternative music: "Reggae is of the Black poor masses and the alternative scene is smaller and usually has lighter-skin people."[31]

CLASS, COLOR, TASTES, AND TRADITION

Many members of the rock scene were seen by the mainstream to belong to families who owned businesses or were themselves employed at jobs considered an enclave for the upper classes, such as law or interior design. Additionally, their familial homes were in uptown rather than downtown areas, making them more likely to be members of the Jamaican ruling class. The class struggle in capitalist societies can be understood as the antagonism between the capitalists and workers. These dominant groups, like the government or capitalists, wield social, economic, political, and moral power by owning the means of production and enlisting the use of dominant ideologies to conventionalize their social control. The working class is exploited to further the interests of the ruling classes.

As a brief aside, the class system in Creole societies is racialized. Those who do not hold economic power are perceived as Black, descendants of the enslaved, while white and Brown groups occupy the upper echelons in society.[32] In Jamaica I found that my participants viewed white and Brown groups as symbols of the plantocracy. Consequently, the upper- and middle-class groups' cultural tastes have been stereotyped as foreign and juxtaposed with the urban sounds of the Black lower classes like dancehall and reggae. The Jamaican distinctions in sociocultural capital applied oppressive ideas of color and class to people. The Jamaican social sphere has been plagued with race/class/color conflict. A history of colonialism, slavery, and creolization certified that individuals were assigned their social positions based on their skin's hue.[33] It is not surprising that the production and consumption of rock music would also bear this logic.

Ibo Cooper's many accolades include being a senior lecturer at the Edna Manley College of Visual and Performing Arts (EMC). Beyond his professional credits, Cooper is respected in Jamaica's music community and addressed as an elder by his younger compatriots. Cooper insists there is alienation between the rock musician and the realities of the Jamaican political economy because of U.S. media imperialism. Reggae producer Paul Love, with over thirty years in the business, also expressed his opinion of the hopelessness of the art form surviving outside of traditional Jamaican tastes:

> **NWC:** So what do you think about rock music in Jamaica?
> **Paul:** Personally, I hear some people doing rock. But I don't think we should be doing rock.
> **NWC:** How come?
> **Paul:** Because we have our own music. Not saying you couldn't play something or do one track on an album. But doing a whole rock album, I don't see it happening.
> **NWC:** Why?
> **Paul:** Because we barely have the market for reggae. Reggae is there but reggae does have a big, massive market like the R & B and the soul. And reggae is big. Cuz when you even think about calypso and soca, they really behind reggae . . . so we don't have the market for rock. Rock isn't our thing.
> **NWC:** Why do you think Jamaican youth are into that whole rock scene?
> **Paul:** They just wanna do something, they just thinking that will make them big. The rock people have their own market. . . . If a youth in Jamaica wants to make it, he has to go the traditional route. You pass ska, you pass rock steady. We are in reggae, we are in dancehall. This is what you have to do. You can't do anything else. You don't have the market for it. You

have nothing you can sell the rock songs to. You have a rock reggae band, you not in the rock company. You have the rock market? You have the country market? You have a limited reggae market.[34]

Members of the public agree with Cooper's and Love's sentiments. Nineteen-year-old Crystal remarked that the young uptown community fixated on a Western lifestyle while the downtown crowd "did not focus on American things as much."[35] Many individuals within the mainstream and rock audience explained that specific color distinctions like Brown, Black, and white were used to categorize the difference between the dancehall and rock music events. Rock music was viewed by the average Jamaican as an uptown scene, where individuals bear a lighter skin tone and are from a higher economic rung. Dancehall on the other hand was stereotyped as a downtown product; its singers, musicians, and audience had dark skin tone.

Alternative music also symbolized to the public a moving away from local traditions, as Ibo Cooper implied. From my observations, Jamaican rock music was "indigenized" with reggae and dancehall to create a unique product that also reflected Jamaican social life despite being labeled as alternative music. When it came to his own music, Ibo Cooper explains, "The difference with Third World is though we were influenced by rock and jazz we kept reggae on the brain, we kept Jamaican consciousness. And we produced original music. We were the first reggae group to use a cello . . . but we didn't take the cello and just play traditional cello music. They took out the cello and played dancehall. At that time it was a serious piece of innovation." Yet he was not willing to entertain the idea that younger musicians' innovation was consistent with their own comprehension of "Jamaican consciousness": "So it has to do with the culture of imperialism. You must still produce from your own creativity. Many of the guys they copy and alienate themselves from their culture. . . . Youth is sliding back into colonialism without realizing it. Utilizing rock will be us willing giving ourselves back to slavery."[36]

Persons were also assigned the alternative label if they were viewed by rock scene members as not fitting squarely into the flux of activities that were specifically deemed rock, hip-hop, R & B, dub poetry, or jazz. For instance, Joan Webley, the owner of the social enterprise Nanook, hosted rock, reggae, and rap events. Her establishment was continuously referred to as a site for the alternative scene but never the "rock" or "hip-hop" scene. Conversely, Tony's Bar, which was also a site for rock, rap, and reggae events, was given the seal of approval as a rock site. Tony, the owner of the bar, had a personal relationship with rock scene members as well as a longer history of hosting rock events.

The "alternative" label distanced Joan from the rock community. This gave her stronger footing within the business of the mainstream. Being assigned the "rock" tag could have undermined her prestige, as rock events did not earn as much income as mainstream events and the musical efforts of rockers were not taken seriously by businessmen in the reggae and dancehall industries.

The various styles of rock were blurred in the local landscape and simply represented by the label "rock music." Emo kids, metalheads, EDM lovers, punks, and goths all gathered and shared the rock space. The complex matrix of musical tastes and fashions inside the rock scene was ignored by the public. The group accepted its generic categorization by the mainstream as it allowed solitary figures to connect with people who had other tastes. This built a communitas based on a general interest and perceived tolerance. More important, rock members accepted their alternative status, as it was explicitly understood by the group that their activities were aligned with other subgroups that were not accepted by the mainstream. Pierre Bourdieu explains that social contradictions are not in opposition to the established order but reflect the homologous principles of the habitus. The permanence of class structures is ensured by the symbolic reconversion of ideological markers into products, dispositions, and identities.[37] The ideological markers of difference (local vs. foreign) in Jamaica maintained the historical poles for identifying "Black music" and "white music."

Steven Grosby defines nationalism as "the belief that the nation is the only goal worthy of pursuit—an assertion that often leads to the belief that the nation demands unquestioned and uncompromising loyalty."[38] When these sentiments are widely held, nationalism limits individual liberties and may incite hatred of all things foreign given nationalists' propensity to promote divisiveness in service of their political goals.[39] The divide enacted in the production and consumption of music within a Black nation is theorized by Neil Lazarus as firmly embedded within debates about authenticity. Authenticity in predominantly Black nations betrays a preoccupation with popularity, degrees of Blackness, and local traditions.[40]

A Fear of Imperialism

My interviews with stakeholders within the reggae industry uncovered proud sentiments about "authentic" sounds originating from the Black experience. Ibo Cooper and other over-thirty-year veterans of the music industry such as Charles Campbell and Paul Love vehemently sought to maintain the tradition of creativity and ingenuity inherited from the local reggae industry. The critical discourses of traditionalists in JaRIA policed the social arena and muffled conversations on Other musical styles. Furthermore, Cooper was adamant that Jamaicans had the capacity to develop their own music and should reject foreign offerings.

Any reference to the fact that dancehall and reggae inherited their form from European sounds was dismissed in my interviews with traditionalists. Quips like "It's ours now" echoed debates about the indigenization of goods.[41] However, the fact that rap and hip-hop began through the contributions of Jamaican migrants reinterpreting the dancehall form in the 1980s was acknowledged by traditionalists like Paul Love, Ibo Cooper, and Charles Campbell and then quickly dismissed as a "weak" argument that only substantiated U.S. imperialism. These sentiments were also applied to descriptions of American Black culture being the impetus for rock and roll.

Individuals like Ibo Cooper and Paul Love represented Bourdieu's logic of opposing groups and how their symbolic and material distinctions encouraged producers to become absorbed in class struggles by forwarding opposing creative strategies. The tension between artists and their critics becomes the material and symbolic capital of taste.[42] Traditional producers of reggae maintained an opposition to "foreign" sounds. Reggae music producer Paul Love and Yacob, an emerging reggae music producer, felt quite strongly that the use of American accents and narratives rather than Jamaican Creole and Black Caribbean motifs in Jamaican rap and rock music explained the genre's unpopularity.[43]

Consequently, from the perspective of traditionalists, differences in tastes in music articulated one's value to the nation. The rightness or wrongness of taste was measured in one's adherence to local authenticity. The genealogy of Black nationalism in the production and consumption of Jamaican music was the foundation of authentic local music. The narrative of oppressive forces against Black agency is symbolically produced in local music.[44] But the nation's strict preoccupation with authenticity delimited the creative imagination, for when "in the exercise of his [Caribbean person] creative imagination, [he] shuts out his own indigenous experience," Nettleford writes, "what he produces is not likely to earn him the status of prophet or visionary, guide or 'artist.'"[45]

U.S. imperialism was a constant fear within the music industry. Expressions of this fear echoed trauma from a contentious past. The plantation economy as well as Jamaica's interaction in the global cultural economy has yielded many hardships that are still yet to be overcome. Though American popular music styles like rap, pop, and R & B were consumed nationally, the society still held on to past resentments. The ability to consume American pop and rap yet criticize the producers of Jamaican rock and rap is quite the contradiction. Nevertheless, my mainstream participants in no way saw the irony. They held on to resentments that drew on a history of political and economic domination by the United States in the 1970s and 1980s. The communal memory also held on to past injustices carried out by foreign music executives on local talents. Vigilance through hypernationalism was used as a cultural antibody against U.S. imperialism. Discrediting Other styles of music as un-Jamaican and oppressive was a discursive technique employed to maintain the nation's borders. Whereas nationalists perceived a negative influence of U.S. culture on Jamaican youth, musical exchanges with Cuba, Haiti, and Nigeria were looked on as creative and powerful alliances that enhanced Jamaican musical culture.

Calhoun stipulates that tangible cultural heritage is authenticated between the performances of ethnic and civic nationalism.[46] Though Ibo Cooper insisted that one cannot predict the next popular sound in Jamaica, he saw that local rock music could never be a contender for popularity. The "imagined" Black nation articulated through dancehall and reggae was threatened by "real" global processes (rock music). These "real" effects signified a return to slavery and the debilitating economic crisis of the 1980s. Local rock music, then, as a projection of popular music from the United States and United Kingdom, was an artefact of modern-day imperialism.

Criticism toward the consumption of rock music was used to censure occult beliefs and homosexuality:

> **Wayne:** Seriously tho. For the first time in a long time I am feeling a bit happier about the future of Jamaican Rock
> **Brian:** Zeen . . . rock naah dead . . . nuh worry yuseself bro
> **Jodi:** Yeah I really hope it goes far. And really reach ppl, especially the ones who choose not to expose themselves to it out here. Til they can't ignore it anymore
> **Brian:** Zeen
> **Wayne:** Jones can tell u. we been dealing with closed minded fucks since the 90s
> **Brian:** Fi real breda . . . real ting . . . suh hear wah . . . Anytime wi have a show all wi have to do is continue kickin out den troat . . . and wi good to go
> **Jodi:** Even before I started music on a level like this I've seen it. So I know.
> **Wayne:** Back in the day. The cry was "gweh wid di batty boy music." And mi did get a bokkle or 2 sometime. Now here it is. Yaaaay.
> **Brian:** Satan music me use to get

Wayne: Yeah. Mi get dat too
Jodi: Lol I heard demon music. Yeah
Brian: Now dem mi a satan himself... lol... rassclaat
Jodi: And white people music later down
Wayne: Being called a devil worshipping faggot ain't cool
Brian: Lololol. Daaaaaaaaamn[47]

The positioning of rock music as "Satan music" illustrates that the predominant Christian and Rastafarian beliefs of the nation sidelined rock music much in the same way dancehall music was dispelled in its early history for its slack lyrics. The stereotype that rock is an artefact of occult practices was derived from American media and used to justify the genre's incongruity to Jamaica's moral sphere. This is further depicted when Wayne remarks, "Being called a devil worshipping faggot ain't cool." Rock music was further stereotyped as engaged by homosexuals because a key condition of nation music is its mythologized Black heteronormativity. Consequently, producing alternative content suggests to the public a moving away from heterosexual scripts.[48]

This is not to say that every Jamaican adored reggae and dancehall, but both forms of production and consumption were intrinsically tied to Jamaican nationalism. Members of the local Christian factions described dancehall as endorsing "slackness" and "lewdness." Nineteen-year-old Allain explained that from his religious standpoint (Apostolic), music styles like dancehall and reggae were conduits to improper sexual feelings, which a young man and woman should only experience in marriage. This was why he did not attend bars and clubs and only listened to music with "positive" lyrics. These attitudes showed that reggae and dancehall within the public domain were not effortlessly accepted by citizens. However, Allain in no way felt that the music did not reflect the Jamaican identity. He strongly agreed that despite the religious faux pas, the genres were intrinsically "Jamaican" music while sounds like rock and rap were not.[49] Crystal agreed, explaining, "Reggae is Jamaican, is the music from Jamaica, so we must hear it."[50]

The Thursday Night Jam

The alternative music groups are treated as abject to the mainstream in Jamaica. But the factions within it, rock, rap, and dub poetry, fluidly articulated mainstream and alternative ideas. Moving from a lower to a higher status, from opposition to structure, is the life cycle of social transitions. To experience freedoms, humans create a liminal space where they can play and create without fear of structural recriminations. I assessed the rock and rap scenes as liminal groups that may eventually transition into the postliminal (structure) or become a site of opposition. My analysis highlights the rock scene's liminal status as a negotiation of both the structure (mainstream) and antistructure (alternative). Consequently, though the rock scene's performances were viewed by the mainstream audience (Allain, Crystal, Ibo Cooper) as outside the national construct because it resided within the alternative music scene, the ideologies and music produced and consumed by the rock group also adhered to mainstream values.

The in-between status of the rock scene was further evidenced in the Thursday Night Jam. The Jam reflected a constant flux between structural and antistructural opinions on the authenticity of musical expressions. The Jam allowed mainstream and alternative musicians and audiences to interact in one space through the improvisation of local and foreign music styles. These were time-honored rituals of the event, inherited from the earlier period of "bottle parties" in the rock music scene in the late 1990s and early 2000s.

Jazz, hip-hop, R & B, dub poetry, various types of rock music like heavy metal, grind core, punk rock, screamo, pop rock, and world music were all staged at the Jam either through live music or deejayed sounds. As Other styles of music were not popular with the mainstream audience, various alternative musics in the Jamaican landscape collaborated to produce Thursday Night Jam. The Jam was very clearly controlled and regulated by adherents from the rock scene. The venue, rental of equipment, and marketing of the event were done by members of this group. Most of the musicians and stable audiences were from this scene. However, the growth in interest in rap, hip-hop, R & B, jazz, pop, and funk allowed for a multiplicity of musical contributions to the Jam's stage outside of rock music. This meant that the Thursday event mirrored the Jamaican "one pot."

AUDIENCE AND PERFORMERS

The Thursday Night Jam's transition from Tony's Bar to Nanook instituted changes to the composition of performances and the audience. I have defined the Jam's audience as Schechner's touring and stable audiences.[51] Touring audiences were described as those persons who take in various theater performances but were not constant visitors to the event. The touring audience within the Jam was made up of various foreign nationals, tourists vacationing in Jamaica, expats who worked locally, researchers, and individuals in the music management and production business looking for interesting acts they could collaborate with. Local personnel from music management and production groups were also a part of this clique as well as the few curious locals who were interested in the goings-on of the rock scene. Additionally, up-and-coming reggae artists trying to break into the industry used the rehearsal format of the night's performances to showcase their work. These individuals were not consistent attendees.

The stable audience members were musicians from the rock community, elders or regulars who helped maintain the event like Omar, Dominique, Jeremy, Spyda, Tony, Vernon, Petros, and Brian. These individuals had been present at various installations of the Jam. The touring and stable audiences dressed in any fashion that suited their tastes. Tattooed arms mixed with jewelry shaped as ankhs; black jeans, black T-shirts, and black Converse shoes mixed with bohemian chic accessories and flowing brown cotton. Navel breakers, halter backs, and miniskirts were aligned with shirts, metal chains, and sandals. Stable audiences were the elders and regulars of the Jam. These elders instilled the ritualized structure that upheld traditions. They had been a part of the rock scene from its earliest period and now regulated the Jam's alternative structure. They perpetuated the importance of improvisation, the spontaneous flow of mostly foreign music sounds and tempo by musicians.

The ritualized performances on the stage were structured like a rehearsal. This meant that most of the activities, interactions, and relationships were contingent on live music, informality, and improvisation. The live music structure at the Jam incorporated skilled DJs at times. But though the Jam was envisioned as a space of creative equality, just as in any rehearsal, the musicians were the major driving force of most interactions, musical and social.

Cookie merged the lyrical flow of hip-hop with jazz and alternative rock sounds. At twenty-one years old he was working to become a successful artist. Cookie became friends with Vernon and Omar, who introduced him to the Jam session. By attending the Jam, Cookie became less shy as he was encouraged to perform onstage and share his art. He said he felt comfortable on his first try and spontaneously improvised a rap verse with the musicians on stage. Though the rock and hip-hop scene had its own intimate groups, the Jam to many like Cookie represented the essence of the alternative music community. This mix of sounds highlighted to him that music was not pure, and the incorporation of difference suggested that "all are welcome," although it never drew a big crowd.

The separation between the musician and performer and nonmusician was brokered by the DJ in the rock scene. Though the musician was held in high regard, there was a feeling of fandom assigned to all who attended rock events. This resulted in the rock musician and his/her audience describing themselves as rock fans. In the rock scene, the roles of the musician and the nonmusicians were quite distinct and implied an economy of social labor. Musicians and singers possessed a skill to entertain the crowd. The audience listened and rewarded creativity and skill with applause and loud words of encouragement. The DJ with his unique mixing skills contributed foreign rock styles to the mix. However, at the Jam the boundaries between these roles were blurred. The musician played music and/or sang, and the nonmusicians listened and/or sang and played an "unchallenging" instrument like a drum or tambourine. All were creators and fans of the music produced in the Jam.

GOOD VIBES

The Jam was a project in creativity and acceptance of different musical styles. The business place, the social site, and the performance stage were all hitched to the caravan of memories that had authenticated a spirit of democracy. The traditional program of the Thursday night event insisted on eclecticism in the music played (rap, hip-hop, heavy metal, pop rock, and very little dancehall and reggae) and the importance of improvising to create the right "vibe" at the event. It also scripted the statuses of various attendees: who was given the seat of honor, a nod of respect, a free drink, the ability to play more than one set—and who was not. Advice was sought from elders like Petros, Omar, and Wayne McGregor, and they were allowed to play a bit longer on stage than other musicians and performers.

At Tony's Bar the Jam's typical program began at 10 p.m., with a soundboard playing rock music. Musicians and audience slowly arrived between 10 and 11 p.m., during which time the musicians would set up while audiences drank, conversed, and/or smoked marijuana. When ready, the musicians played well-known rock, jazz, reggae, and hip-hop-infused music at their leisure throughout the night. Most of the audience arrived after midnight. As sets progressed, the bands improvised or spontaneously created new lyrics to a conventional melody. As the Jam was a space of eclectic tastes, reggae was welcomed. In keeping with the spirit of improvisation, audience members could sing on stage, although the order (and permission) was decided by elders within the rock scene, usually Dominique or Omar. By 3 a.m. the Jam began to end.

At Nanook the Jam was different. First, it was a more structured program of reggae performers, which reduced the number of alternative songs played, improvisation, or synthetic blending of styles. Furthermore, the reggae singer became the focal point on the stage, accompanied by a "backing band" of alternative musicians who played mostly reggae. This climate was specific to the

Nanook space. At Nanook the reggae singer controlled the musical climate, while in the improvised setting of Tony's Bar the musician was king:

> **Cookie:** If you come to the Jam the only thing that will make you unwelcomed is if you disrespect the Jam.
>
> **NWC:** How can you disrespect the Jam?
>
> **Cookie:** I have my personal pet peeves. I mean, the Jam is supposed to be, at least in my mind and experience, a stream of energy that just flows. And who decides to come on stage should just commit themselves to keep that energy flowing. But sometimes, somebody might feel like coming on the stage and the musicians might be doing something amazing... I mean it's like... when you think about it all of human history has to happen for you and I to be having this conversation. It's the same with the Jam. It might start off awkwardly and then it gets to a point where all the musicians are perfectly in sync and playing something that is so amazing and so colorful, you can't place it in a genre. And the thing is the whole Jam had to happen just for them to get to that moment. And then somebody would come on and say "Yo, stop playing that and play this thing." I feel like that disrespects the Jam.[52]

The elders and regulars at the Jam did not support its placement at Nanook. Many said that it "did not feel like the right fit" and "was the wrong vibe." Spyda explained how he saw the differences in the Jam between the two spaces: "Tony's is a gathering of weirdos, here [Nanook] is more like live karaoke."[53] Dominique explains: "You know when you entered Tony's you just listened to music and Tony don't care. If Omar came to Tony's and played jazz [the] whole night, Tony's would be in heaven, heaven! You can come there and play the most random shit and Tony don't care. You see if you put on dancehall Tony would be like 'mmmm' and then he goes to Omar and say 'Okay, we've had enough of this.' Because he plays dancehall on a Wednesday, he plays dancehall on a Tuesday and for him Thursday is not the average."[54] She concluded that the scene did not have "enough open and free venues" like Tony's Bar. The Jam was abandoned at Nanook by its stable audience while Tony's Bar held a firm grip on the loyalties of the group. As a result of the abandoning of the scene's rituals, its elders and traditional organizers took a less active role in putting on the show. Some left because, again, they felt that "Nanook was not a good fit," others because they had poor working relationships with the management of the bar. Still, the playing of reggae at the beginning of the Jams signaled the direction of the night's music toward the mainstream and the loss of "good vibes." It symbolized mainstream tastes and creative re-

FIGURE 10.1. The band plays with French reggae artist at Nanook's Thursday Night Jam. Photograph by author, February 2014

strictions. Mostly, the Jam ended at Nanook because of the management's concern about the meagre revenue.

"Good vibes" were consistently undermined at Nanook. Stable members remarked that they were bored by the night's regimented reggae program, which left the alternative musicians as a backing band. The dominance of reggae inhibited the sense of freedom in the choice of music but also ruptured the creative flow of the musicians' voice and instrument. The rigid schedule of performers on the stage debilitated the informality of the "rehearsal" stage and improvisation. Damian had only been to Nanook's Jam once because the bands played mostly reggae: "That is not what I'm accustomed to hearing. Especially for most of the night. I mean, when we have our events you would hear about half an hour of one style, then you would hear another half an hour of something different. Then it goes back to something similar to what they were playing before. They mix it up a little. But just from when I was here, for that event we had here that night, it just really seemed a little . . . I wouldn't say monotonous cuz I kinda enjoyed it, but it was kinda one-sided for me."[55] Rock scene members took issue with Nanook's playlist on Thursday nights.

FIGURE 10.2. Spontaneous capoeira breaks out during Jam at Tony's Bar. Photograph by author, December 2013

Individuals from other alternative scenes expressed some annoyance at the mainstream music featured; they would have preferred a more flexible interpretation of Jamaican tastes in music, which should have been seen in the variations in the stage performances. In effect, they missed the improvisation and attributed it to Nanook's overriding commitment to reggae. As such, it could not match the Jam at Tony's Bar, which was "a utopia of good vibes."

Nation Music

Reggae and dancehall are deemed core artefacts of the Jamaican national identity.[56] The analysis of the data collected during my fieldwork indicated that the Jamaican taste for dancehall and reggae connoted "natural," "right," and "authentic" preferences while the "unnatural" and "inauthentic" were local styles that merged with foreign sounds like rock music. In understanding distinction making in the production and consumption of Jamaican music, authenticity should not be understood as simply the fetishization of dancehall and reggae. The historical maturation of indigenized sounds to represent Blackness as well as other Jamaican realities are important in producing local music as well. Despite this, there has been considerable financial and cultural value endowed on sounds deemed nation music, which does not include local rock music.

Still, dancehall and reggae, despite their humble beginnings and symbolism of resistance, have matured into tools of social constraint. Hypernationalism enacted through censorious discourse and the stereotyping of alternative music styles were the nation's response to rock music. The nation stymied local rock music's expression much in the same way middle-class values sidelined dancehall's slack lyrics in the 1980s and reggae's Black-conscious motifs in the late 1960s. Now, dancehall and reggae are considered expressive forms that extend the definition of the Jamaican politic and are fully supported by the formal business economy in Jamaica.

Authenticity through syncretism and transformation from an oppositional status into the mainstream are major characteristics of nation music. The history of Western sounds that merged with local music has been ignored by the louder voices that highlight the Afro-Caribbean traditions that have shaped reggae and dancehall. For instance, the syncretism between reggae, rock, and rap is ignored in the present-day reggae revival.

Euro-American music represented imperialistic strategies to reinstate the mental, political, and economic bonds of slavery on the corporeal and psychological domains of the nation. Local rock music signified a return to colonialism, the subjection to a modern-day slavery where Euro-American tastes debilitated the potential of Jamaican music. As a result of the negative capital assigned to alternative sounds, not all proponents of the alternative scene stuck to their oppositional and ambiguous tastes as many became frustrated by their lack of success and entered the reggae industry like the reggae band Rootz Underground. Yet in an unlikely paradox, both mainstream and alternative sensibilities were used by reggae revivalists as they brought a foreign syncretized meter, performance style, and voice to the execution of reggae, which is reflected in the performances of Kabaka Pyramid. Though rap and rock influenced their work, "reggae" was the chosen moniker used to identify the music.

As a potential candidate to become nation music, rock may come to represent the authentic-syncretic parameters of Jamaica's social, cultural, and political artefacts. Or rock or rap music may simply be recruited into the exertions of the reggae revival and reaffirm reggae's importance to the Jamaican identity by privileging Afro-Caribbean discourses. There may be another option for the future of alternative music in the local sphere: it may be that the music never gets accepted into the popular domain and continues its existence within the alternative community. Reggae and dancehall had the advantage of representing the experiences of the masses (Black urban poor), which facilitated their acceptance into the mainstream. However, rock music projects the lifestyles and tastes of the advantaged few, as members of the rock scene were perceived as belonging to the upper economic and racial classes. The inability of rock music to authentically embody Jamaica's symbolic capital of Blackness may be the feature that forever alienates its reception into the mainstream.

Furthermore, dancehall and reggae have been naturalized as the authentic sounds of Jamaica by scholars like Rex Nettleford, Carolyn Cooper, Norman Stolzoff, and Donna Hope. Yet despite the lingering tension between these musics and middle-class morality, dancehall and reggae are never positioned in academic works as outside the popular. This consensus, aside from leaving glaring gaps in the analysis of how other types of music can express Jamaican narratives on race, color, class, and nation building, ignores how varying notions of locality, authenticity, and nationalism are performed and the politics of difference embedded in Jamaican music.

NOTES

1. Sonjah Stanley Niaah, *Dancehall: From Slave Ship to Ghetto* (Ottawa: University of Ottawa Press, 2010); Norman Stolzoff, *Wake the Town and Tell the People: Dancehall Culture in Jamaica* (Durham, N.C.: Duke University Press, 2000).

2. Keith Nurse, "Popular Culture and the Cultural Industry: Identity and Commodification in Caribbean Popular Music," in *Globalisation, Diaspora and Caribbean Popular Culture*, ed. Christine Ho and Keith Nurse (Kingston: Ian Randle, 2005).

3. Paul Gilroy, "'Jewels Brought from Bondage': Black Music and the Politics of Authenticity," in *Performance Studies*, ed. Erin Striff (New York: Palgrave, 2003).

4. Supriya Nair, "Creolisation, Orality and Nation Language in the Caribbean," in *A Companion to Postcolonial Studies*, ed. Henry Schwartz and Sangeeta Ray (Oxford: Blackwell, 2005), 238–40.

5. In using the term "nation music," I have in mind Kamau Brathwaite's ideas about "nation language." Brathwaite argues there are unique meanings and tones inflected in standard English to produce the Creole language of the Anglophone Caribbean. These meanings and tones are inherited from the creolized mixing during colonialism, from the languages of the enslaved and indentured laborers, from colonial masters and the Amerindians. But where Brathwaite emphasizes the "African aspect of our New World/Caribbean heritage," I do not because it is too narrow and foregrounds a conception of Caribbean identities. Kamau Brathwaite, *History of the Voice: The Development of Nation Language on Anglophone Caribbean Poetry* (London: New Beacon, 1984), 13, 17–19.

6. Victor Turner, *The Ritual Process: Structure and Anti-structure* (New York: Cornell University Press, 1977).

7. Mark Cieslik and Donald Simpson, *Key Concepts in Youth Studies* (Los Angeles: Sage, 2013), 122–23; Andy Furlong, *Youth Studies: A Global Introduction* (London: Routledge, 2012), 153–54.

8. Mathew Collin, *Altered State: The Story of Ecstasy Culture and Acid House* (London: Serpent's Tail, 2009), 7; Emma Baulch, *Making Scenes: Reggae, Punk, and Death Metal in 1990s Bali* (Durham, N.C.: Duke University Press, 2007), 3–5; Cieslik and Simpson, *Key Concepts in Youth Studies*, 124–25; Furlong, *Youth Studies*, 153.

9. Andy Bennett, "Consolidating the Music Scenes Perspectives," *Poetics* 32 (2004): 225, https://www.academia.edu/32658624/Consolidating_the_music_scenes_perspective.

10. David Hesmondhalgh, "Subcultures, Scenes or Tribes? None of the Above," *Journal of Youth Studies* 8, no. 1 (2005): 24, https://doi.org/10.1080/13676260500063652.

11. Chris Jenks, *Subculture: The Fragmentation of the Social* (London: Sage, 2005), 4.

12. Cookie, interview with author, April 4, 2014.

13. Don Letts with David Nobakht, *Culture Clash: Dread Meets Punk Rockers* (London: SAF, 2008).

14. "The Rolling Stones Recording in Jamaica," *Rolling Stone*, January 18, 1973, http://www.rollingstone.com/music/news/the-rolling-stones-recording-in-jamaica-19730118, accessed August 18, 2017.

15. "Chris Blackwell," Rock and Roll Hall of Fame, 2001, https://www.rockhall.com/inductees/chris-blackwell, accessed August 29, 2017.

16. Robert Palmer, "Bob Marley's Reggae Legacy: Sect, Drugs and Rock & Roll," *Rolling Stone*, February 24, 1994, http://www.rollingstone.com/music/news/bob-marleys-reggae-legacy-sects-drugs-and-rock-roll-19940224/, accessed August 19, 2017.

17. Kevin O'Brien Chang and Wayne Chen, *Reggae Routes: The Story of Jamaican Music* (Philadelphia: Temple University Press, 1998), 3.

18. "Demons & Sparta: The Tommy Lee Curse," Grassroots Jamaica, August 31, 2012, https://constructedthoughts.wordpress.com/2012/08/31/demons-sparta-thetommy-lee-curse/, accessed August 28, 2017.

19. Curwen Best, *The Popular Music and Entertainment Culture of Barbados: Pathways to Digital Culture* (Toronto: Scarecrow Press, 2012), 37, 109.

20. Tracy Assing, "Keep on Rocking," *Caribbean Beat*, March/April 2005.

21. Robin Balliger, "Popular Music and the Cultural Politics of Globalisation among the Post–Oil Boom Generation in Trinidad," in *Identity, Ethnicity and the Culture in the Caribbean*, ed. Ralph Premdas (St. Augustine: University of the West Indies Press, 1999), 72.

22. Best, *Popular Music and Entertainment Culture*, 158–66.

23. Ibo Cooper, interview with author, September 15, 2013. In Cooper's view, the cultural practices found in higher socioeconomic strata do not represent typical Jamaican cultural life, which he presents as closer to that of urban Black youth. "Jack" refers to a guitar's jack, which is present at the end of the instrument's cable and allows for the connection to audio devices.

24. Kwame Dawes, *Natural Mysticism: Towards a New Reggae Aesthetic* (Leeds: Peepal Tree Press, 1999); Jocelyn Guilbault and Timothy Rommen, "The Political Economy of Music and Sound: Case Studies in the Caribbean Tourism Industry," in *Sounds of Vacation: Political Economies of Caribbean Tourism* (Durham, N.C.: Duke University Press, 2019), 9–40.

25. Neil Lazarus, *Nationalism and Cultural Practice in the Postcolonial World* (Cambridge: Cambridge University Press, 1999); Stephanie Sadre-Orafai, "Hypernationalist Discourse in the Rapso Movement of Trinidad and Tobago," in Ho and Nurse, *Globali-*

sation, Diaspora and Caribbean Popular Culture, 215–41; Rex Nettleford, *Inward Stretch, Outward Reach: A Voice from the Caribbean* (London: Macmillan, 1993), 120–21.

26. Pierre Bourdieu, "The Forms of Capital," in *Handbook of Theory and Research for the Sociology of Education*, ed. John Richardson (New York: Greenwood, 1986).

27. Pierre Bourdieu, *Distinction: A Social Critique of the Judgement of Taste* (Cambridge, Mass.: Harvard University Press, 1984), 260–65.

28. Carolyn Cooper, Sound Clash: Jamaican Dancehall Culture at Large (New York: Palgrave Macmillan, 2004), 235–37; Larry Starr and Christopher Waterman, *American Popular Music: From Minstrelsy to MTV* (New York: Oxford University Press, 2003), 408–9.

29. Vernon Da Costa, interview with author, September 27, 2013.

30. As background, JaRIA was given an official mandate by the government to plan Reggae Month in 2009. Reggae Month is celebrated in February, which coincides with the country's Black History Month. Kamau Brathwaite, *The Development of Creole Society in Jamaica, 1770–1820* (Kingston: Ian Randle, 2005), 176–79; Stolzoff, *Wake the Town*, 33–34; Donna Hope, *Inna di Dancehall: Popular Culture and the Politics of Identity in Jamaica* (Kingston: University of the West Indies Press, 2006), 40–41.

31. Joan Webley, interview with author, March 25, 2015.

32. Rex Nettleford, *Mirror Mirror: Identity, Race and Protest in Jamaica* (Kingston: William Collins and Sangster, 1970), 17–27; Brian Moore and Michelle Johnson, *Neither Led nor Driven: Contesting British Cultural Imperialism in Jamaica* (Mona: UWI Press, 2004), 315–19.

33. Nettleford, *Mirror Mirror*, xxix–xxxi; Rex Nettleford, *Caribbean Cultural Identity: The Case of Jamaica: An Essay in Cultural Dynamics* (Los Angeles: UCLA Latin American Center, 1979), 4–5; Moore and Johnson, *Neither Led nor Driven*, xv–xix; Verene Shepherd, *I Want to Disturb My Neighbor: Lectures on Slavery, Emancipation and Postcolonial Jamaica* (Kingston: Ian Randle, 2007), 5.

34. Paul Love, interview with author, October 2, 2013.

35. Crystal, interview with author, September 8, 2013.

36. Ibo Cooper, interview with author, September 15, 2013.

37. Bourdieu, *Distinction*, 165.

38. Steven Grosby, *Nationalism: A Very Short Introduction* (Oxford: Oxford University Press, 2005), 5.

39. Grosby, *Nationalism*, 5, 98; Ernest Gellner, *Nations and Nationalism* (Oxford: Blackwell, 2006), 1, 47; James Kellas, *The Politics of Nationalism and Ethnicity* (Hong Kong: Macmillan, 1991), 20–22; Craig Calhoun, *Nations Matter: Culture, History and the Cosmopolitan Dream* (New York: Routledge, 2007), 114–15.

40. Neil Lazarus, *Nationalism and Cultural Practice in the Postcolonial World* (Cambridge: Cambridge University Press, 1999), 197.

41. Lazarus, *Nationalism and Cultural Practice*, 200–212.

42. Bourdieu, *Distinction*, 235.

43. Paul Love, interview with author, October 2, 2013.

44. Chang and Chen, *Reggae Routes*, 2–3; Stolzoff, *Wake the Town*, 227–28; Nettleford, *Mirror Mirror*, 39–57.

45. Nettleford, *Caribbean Cultural Identity*, 35.

46. Calhoun, *Nations Matter*, 152–54.

47. Vernon DaCosta, WhatsApp group chat, June 29, 2015.
48. Hope, *Inna di Dancehall*, 36, 79–82.
49. Allain, interview with author, September 8, 2013.
50. Crystal, interview with author, September 8, 2013.
51. Richard Schechner, *Between Theatre and Anthropology* (Philadelphia: University of Pennsylvania Press, 1985), 15.
52. Cookie, interview with author, April 4, 2014.
53. Spyda, interview with author, April 11, 2014.
54. Dominique Brown, interview with author, April 11, 2014.
55. Damian, interview with author, April 9, 2014.
56. Cooper, *Sound Clash*, 248–49; Hope, *Inna di Dancehall*, 3–9; Donna Hope, *Man Vibes: Masculinities in the Jamaican Dancehall* (Kingston: Ian Randle, 2010), xiii.

CHAPTER 11

The Problem of Race and Nation in Dominican Studies

BRENDAN JAMAL THORNTON AND DIEGO I. UBIERA

The time is ripe for a review of Dominican studies and to take account of current trends and directions in the interdisciplinary study of the Dominican Republic. In this chapter we identify the broad-reaching effect of several gatekeeping concepts on the production of academic conventions that have heretofore shaped scholarly discourse about the country. Academic writing on the Dominican Republic, particularly of late, has been dominated by several prevailing themes especially influential within the North American academy. These overriding themes are race and nation—theoretical metonyms for Dominican racial and national identity and Dominican/Haitian relations. We examine the historical origination of these themes and their frequent application to Dominican materials, speculate as to how they both shape and are shaped by conventional ideas about Dominican society, review several implications that follow from these trends, and consider how these approaches have come to characterize the field of Dominican studies today. We argue for deeper engagement with homegrown Dominican scholarship and voices on the ground and conclude with suggestions on growing the field.

Arjun Appadurai, in an essay reviewing the development of anthropological theory, has drawn attention to the tendency for places or regions to become showcases for specific issues over time. He cites analytical paradigms such as *hierarchy* in India, *filial piety* in China, and *honor and shame* in the circum-Mediterranean as classic examples of what he calls "gatekeeping concepts" or ideas that define the quintessential and dominant questions of interest in a region and thus limit theorizing about a place in question.[1] Several dominant tropes have framed social analysis in Caribbean anthropology for some time now, perhaps prime among them the concept of creolization.[2] It has become clear in recent years that in interdisciplinary scholarship on the Dominican Republic, powerful gatekeeping concepts like race and nation have established the country's ostensible defining characteristics and delineate the predominant idioms governing social scientific, not to mention historical and literary renderings of Dominican social and cultural realities.

The risk in overreliance on a limited range of conceptual perspectives should be clear. Gatekeeping concepts can lead to the overdetermination of certain social and cultural realities more than others, obscuring or distorting the contingencies of local accounts, native viewpoints, and the nuances of social interaction and signification in a complex modern world.[3] Applied to historical materials, these same concepts can mask as much as they reveal. To date, the influence of specific conceptual models on the imaginative and intellectual horizons of Dominican studies has gone unremarked. The sources and implications of the tendency to privilege some overarching themes over others are poorly understood despite exercising great authority over academic interpretation and description. The question we wish to ask below considering recent scholarship is why scholars continue to return to several well-worn topics. Do these gatekeeping concepts reflect something inherent or unique about the country itself, or are they merely indicative of scholarly trends and the interests of scholars who follow them?[4] How does the promotion of a narrow catalog of themes and perspectives constrain the potential of Dominican studies as an interdisciplinary project? The stakes, it seems, are clear: the definition of Dominican society, not only in academic discourse but also more broadly in how the country is conceived in both local and global contexts.

Dominican Studies Comes of Age

To the extent that Dominican studies constitutes a coherent interdisciplinary field of study, it remains relatively small.[5] It claimed even less space in North American academic circles in the 1980s and 1990s when it was largely ignored by the broader fields of Latin American and Caribbean studies, areas of budding social scientific and humanities concern that otherwise saw booming growth during this period.[6] By the 1990s a nascent field of Dominican studies in the United States gained important traction and a measure of institutional legitimacy with the founding of the City University of New York Dominican Studies Institute in 1992, establishing the nation's first university-based research institute devoted to the study of Dominicans, whose stated mission is to produce and disseminate research and scholarship about Dominicans and about the Dominican Republic. The institute houses the Dominican Archives and the Dominican Library dedicated to collecting primary and secondary source material about people of Dominican descent. However, it was not until the 2000s that the North American academy saw signs of the viable consolidation of an emerging Dominican studies paradigm following the publication of several higher-profile books on the region; an increase in publications dealing with Dominican materials; a growing academic interest in the country at graduate, undergraduate, and professional levels (likely due, at least in part, to the greater representation of Dominicans and Dominican Americans in U.S. institutions of higher education); and an increased number of scholars of the Dominican Republic holding positions at premier universities. Equally important developments were occurring simultaneously in popular culture. The burgeoning recognition during this time of Dominican American novelists like Julia Alvarez and Junot Díaz played a decisive role in bringing the Dominican Republic into national and international consciousness; this, along with the internationalization and popularization of bachata music beginning in the 2000s and the ascendant dominance of Dominican baseball players in the major leagues, coalesced to mainstream Dominican culture for U.S. audiences as never before.

Attending this increasing visibility of the Dominican Republic in scholarship and in popular media has been a conspicuous emphasis on research and publications focused on the comprehensive themes of race and nation and their various conceptual iterations. With little doubt these foci have been the richest source of new material on the country, not only in the form of scholarly publications but also in panel and conference themes, editorials, seminars and academic talks, calls for papers, and recent dissertation and master's theses.[7] Attention to these topics has increased with growing academic interest in the critical situation of Dominicans of Haitian descent, and urgent public debates about citizenship in the Dominican Republic.[8] In 2016 alone, at least three books were published on the explicit topic of race and nation in the Dominican Republic.[9]

Although picking up steam in the past couple of decades, academic interest in the subjects of race and nation in the Dominican Republic is not new and began much earlier. One early text in particular that set the tone for current research in this regard is Franklin Franco's *Los negros, los mulatos, y la nación dominicana* (1969), which inaugurated attempts by academics to acknowledge the "presence of the African-descended . . . as a legitimate component of the

Dominican nation, with a recognition of the marginalization of the Black experience in the discourse of the country's heritage."[10] In his introduction to the English translation, Silvio Torres-Saillant declares Franco's work a "classic if there ever was one," a text so seminal to Dominican studies he compares it to Herodotus and the invention of the field of historical study! According to Torres-Saillant, following Franco's classic work, at least eighty-six books have been published between 1970 and 2014 (not including countless articles and several titles since) on Blackness, ethnic identity, and race relations in the Dominican Republic.[11] Furthermore, Carlos Esteban Deive has recently published a 152-page bibliography of more than 790 sources on the subject of Dominican/Haitian relations and race in Hispaniola.[12]

In the North American and European academies, the topics of Dominican racial and national identity and Dominican/Haitian relations have been especially productive since the mid-1990s.[13] Studies on the national border and the Dominican Republic's antagonistic relationship with Haiti as well as studies on so-called Dominicanness constitute undeniable segments of this literature.[14] These studies have established nationality and national identity alongside race studies as dominant concerns of English-language scholarship on the country over the past several decades. This production has been impressive given the relative size of and interest in Dominican studies up to this point.

Scholarship in the areas of race and nation in the Dominican Republic is not entirely uniform; scholars hail from a variety of disciplines that employ differing modes of inquiry and explanation. Nonetheless, whether the study is historical or contemporary, about Blackness or nationhood, racism or Dominicanness, Afro-Dominican culture or anti-Haitianism, or the gradations of calculi therein, the expository possibilities of work in these areas are contingent on race and nation as conceptual vectors for analysis. The fact that scholars from across the disciplinary spectrum have found this particular lens similarly productive only highlights the overwhelming influence these gatekeeping concepts exercise on the imaginative horizons of Dominican studies. Obviously, exceptional work continues outside of this trend; it is unlikely, however, that any other topic has garnered as much sustained attention by humanities and social science writers. As scholars of the Dominican Republic based in the United States, we routinely face the vexing fact that what others know about the Dominican Republic is too often limited to some vague notion of Dominican racial exceptionalism and the country's strained relationship with Haiti. Those of us who are asked to serve as peer reviewers for journals and other publications, or who are regularly solicited to review applications for grants and fellowships, can attest to the frequency of the themes discussed here as they are routinely applied to the country time and again. If the Dominican Republic has become a showcase for specific issues, themes, and concepts over time, it must be conceded that it is here in the broad areas of race and nation that Dominican studies in the United States has made its most indelible mark.[15]

Race and Nation in the Dominican Republic

Scholars interested in studying and writing about the Dominican Republic are frequently drawn to seek answers to the oft-repeated observation that Dominicans, in general, rarely acknowledge their African ancestry with pride and are unlikely to self-identify as Black, despite their categorization as such by U.S. racial logics. Dominican Black denial is a commonplace refrain encountered in U.S. academic scholarship on the region and a familiar premise of popular media coverage of Dominican racial identity—like, for example, Henry Louis Gates's PBS series *Black in Latin America*—providing much grist for the race-conscious scholar's mill.[16] The social construction of race in the Dominican Republic, because it differs from that of the United States, is frequently viewed as an aberration, an anomaly to be explained. Why an apparently Black country refuses to see itself as such is viewed as an unusual delusion that must be accounted for, and Black denial consistently but misleadingly read as a special kind of self-hatred. Indeed, for quite a few scholars and, increasingly, for the larger public drawn to Dominican studies, the troubling question since the 1990s has been: how did Dominicans, obvious descendants of enslaved Africans, come to regard themselves as anything but Black?[17]

Dominicans, on the whole, have never been as conflicted about nor as enchanted by their own ethnic or racial identities as the scholars who write about them. Dominicans are, clearly, more than simple racial miscreants or blind custodians of a reviled false consciousness; they are, in the main, no more confused about their supposed racial or ethnic origins than anyone else. National identity is neither static nor agreed upon, and several competing discourses of identity circulate that articulate different ways of being Dominican that challenge any singular interpretation of *dominicanidad* as one way or another.[18] The meaning of racial categories is neither shared nor fixed, having been embraced and/or contested across the wide spectrum of Dominican experience since the very first colonial governors took office in Santo Domingo. It cannot be stressed enough that there is nothing inherently exceptional about Dominican racial logics, other than the simple fact that the racial categories themselves, and those who are assigned to them, differ from those in the United States and elsewhere, proving what most of us already accept to be true: that race is a social construct, that is to say, a function of context and perspective. In the Dominican Republic, who counts as white or Black (or *indio/a* as the case may be) may vary considerably from who gets assigned to those very same categories in the United States, all while invoking different meanings due to the country's unique colonial history, its protracted struggle for independence, its position within global and regional power structures, its contested cultural and political history, and its record of international and regional migration.[19]

In addition to a pervasive aesthetic preference for lighter skin (evidenced in local beauty pageants and dominant representations of beauty in local television and advertising), to be counted as *blanco/a* (white) in the Dominican Republic comes with significant social advantages while those stigmatized as *negro/a* (Black) face discrimination and other social obstacles. Indeed, as of yet, there is little in Dominican popular culture that would incentivize public affirmation of Black identity akin to the Afrocentric and Black Power movements of yesteryear observed in the United States, especially as Black ethnic identity is most often associated with the much-maligned Haiti and Haitianness. The predominant national mythologies that obscure if not outright deny ancestral origins in Africa are the handmaiden of cultural and political elites who are invested in a national image that deemphasizes foreign Black culture and Black African heritage and who sponsor in its place the promotion of Hispanic descent, Euro-Christian values, and (increasingly) white North American cultural ideals. Anti-Haitianism, a racist discourse of exclusion, works in tandem with this worldview to reinforce national narratives of Dominican *mestizaje* or "mixed" identity (some vague combination of Spanish, Indigenous, and African ancestry), in an operation that occludes Black origins, rendering Dominicanness not as white but as *not Black*.[20]

As an antidote to elite renderings of the country as mixed-white, or at least "not Black," scholars have looked to recover Black identity at the margins, to account for alternative imaginings of Dominican identity that are instead diverse and inclusive, and that positively identify Black African heritage and culture and contest any monolithic view of Dominican identity as stable, uniform, finished, or unchanging. Calling attention to the top-down erasure of Black identity from the cultural landscape, some of this literature looks to resuscitate what was always there but has been muted by power and the interests of a racist elite intent on whitewashing the country's image, especially in relation to Haiti.[21]

Within the Dominican Republic, scholarly attempts to recover the African heritage of Dominican culture are not scarce but have tended to consign Black traditions to the domain of folklore—that is, conspicuous cultural forms regarded as relics to be celebrated at specific times and in specific places. Here, Black or Afro-Dominican culture can be found in magical religious beliefs (e.g., Dominican *vodú*), in carnival and festival traditions (e.g., *el gagá*), or in folktales, dance, and traditional music (e.g., *palo*), but not usually in everyday social and cultural life, conceding, however erroneously, that ordinary Dominican culture is inherently non-Black since Black culture, to be present and operative, must be distinct or distinguishable from it (hyphenates like Afro-Dominican imply that Dominicanness on its own is absent of Black cultural attributes and therefore requires a modifier).[22] To the contrary, others have shown convincingly that Black and African cultural influences are in fact expressed in everyday life, particularly embedded in family dynamics, language, value orientations, culinary conventions, expressive culture, and elsewhere, making Black heritage a significant, inextricable property of contemporary Dominican society, and the country itself an important site of transnational Black cultural production and exchange.[23]

Establishing Race and Nation as Analytic Paradigms

Race and nation in the Dominican scholarly literature are constitutive categories that just as often recall one another whenever they are invoked. Almost predictably the themes of race and nation converge on the question of Dominicanness; at one time an interest of state builders and the intellectual elite, the idea of Dominicanness has piqued the interests of U.S.-based scholars, many of whom grew up in the context of U.S. multiculturalism and contentious identity politics and who find in the topic fertile material for historical and literary analysis. The topic itself is not new. What constitutes "true *dominicanidad*" has been a contentious subject on the island for some time, eliciting strident polemics from across the ideological spectrum. Issues of identity are always high stakes—the politics of belonging always concern access to material resources—and important debates over *identidad* play out all over Latin America in both scholarly and public forums.[24] However, even while Latin Americanist scholarship continues to address issues of identity in terms of race and nation, nowhere else does it appear to represent the dominant analytic paradigm to the exclusion of all others.[25] Dominican studies stands out from the crowd in its almost singular focus on issues of racial and national identity.

It must be affirmed that there is nothing inherently more or less racial or nationalistic about the Dominican Republic, and yet these themes endure as seemingly the most obvious and worthwhile areas of inquiry and analysis. We might ask why Dominicanness has become a preoccupation of contemporary Dominican studies while Haitianness or Jamaicanness seem far removed from dominating their respective area studies catalogs. Even as ideas about nationhood and belonging are ever evolving and regularly disputed, they are by no means new to the vast majority of citizens or unique to the Dominican Republic, belying the idea that nationality or cultural identity is of particular relevance or special concern to Dominicans above and beyond any other nation in today's globalized world.[26] Dominicans are not exceptional in this regard, and so it is curious that Dominicanness would claim such a prominent place in English-language scholarship on the Dominican Republic.

The Caribbean's distinctive history of colonialism, transatlantic slavery, transnational migration, variously successful independence movements, and its central role in the making of the modern world have made the region an especially apposite locale for the study of race and identity, as well as modern nationalisms. The anthropology and sociology of the region, influenced by the likes of Melville Herskovits, M. G. Smith, and Sidney Mintz, have been dominated by studies focused on the legacy and effects of New World slavery, African cultural retentions, forced and voluntary migration, and themes of cultural diversity, conflict, and transformation enlivened by the varied encounters of Europe, Africa, and the Americas. Historically, however, the Dominican Republic has not been a major focus of scholarly interest when compared with other West Indian locales, despite its notable status as the first colony in the Americas and its standing as the second largest country in the Caribbean.

The indifference to Dominican materials in Caribbean studies, while lamentable, is not entirely surprising. The Dominican Republic has never been a comfortable fit in the "savage slot" envisioned for it in the scholarly imagination of the American academy.[27] Dominican culture and society have consistently been viewed, however erroneously, as too ordinary, too Christian, and much too conventional to constitute an interesting Caribbean subject for North American scholars, especially for those seeking a tantalizing foreign Other to discover, celebrate, and/or liberate. The Dominican Republic has never been sufficiently exotic, alien, or *alter* enough to elicit the same kind of interest as, for example, Haiti (perhaps the quintessential exotic Black Other), or as politically captivating a place as Cuba (an alluring communist exception), or as religiously compelling a locale as Jamaica (birthplace of charismatic Rastafarians, who inspired a global music genre and international subculture).

Many scholars of late, influenced by postcolonial social theory, have sought out resistance in the "Third World," looking to highlight acts of opposition and defiance from below and uncover the hidden transcripts of the weak and powerless (à la James Scott); to lay bare the roots of cultural hegemony and its undoing in Latin America (following Antonio Gramsci); and to identify the machinery and malcontents of discourse and power wherever they may be encountered (in the spirit of Michel Foucault). Scholars inspired by this theoretical turn in area studies are stirred to find resistance to power but are often loath to find accommodation with it. From the outside, the Dominican Republic appears to evince the latter: a country that endured authoritarian rule for thirty years; a society intent on persecuting its Black immigrant neighbors; a country where skin-lightening creams are a ubiquitous feature wherever beauty products are sold and hair-straightening customs perfunctory for many if not most Dominican women. The Dominican Republic does not appear to be the ideal subject of cultural resistance and is, therefore, an imperfect subaltern subject, especially for ethnic and postcolonial studies.

Dominican refusals to be Black strike a chord with many scholars and observers alike; after all, the thought goes, if Dominicans are not Black, who on earth is? Whether exploring, complicating, debating, affirming, or refuting this claim, the outcome has been a prolific wave of publications aimed at understanding Dominicans as racial/racialized subjects.[28] Needless to say, it poses a problem for Pan-African, Black diasporic solidarity for the descendants of New World slavery to deny kinship with other Black populations. This and the very real effects of anti-Black racism have led some work to endeavor to "convince" or educate Dominicans about their racial origins, African ancestry, and debt to Blackness.[29] Others have proffered scholarly narratives that seek to highlight oppositional discourses to racial domination by outlining spaces of resistance to cultural hegemony and Black erasure.[30]

Whether or not, why, to what degree, under what circumstances, and how Dominicans consider themselves to be Black, mixed, white, Hispanic, *indio*, or whatever is one (albeit multifaceted) question, though not a particularly urgent one, despite its frequent invocation in the literature. For one thing, versions of this question have been asked for several decades, and the proposed answers seem always to return to familiar conclusions: identity is fluid, political, culturally and historically constituted, discursively constructed, and always contested. Despite the prospect of novel interventions, work on Dominican identity continues to unfold within the familiar conceptual limits of race and nation that routinely take Dominicanness (at home and abroad) to be a racial problem that needs repeated disambiguation. It remains unclear, however, why the question of *identidad*, per se, continues to be such a priority for Dominican studies when Dominicans themselves are so ambivalent about their own racial and national identity, and a preponderance of publications already exists expounding in great detail the tribulations of race in the Dominican Republic.[31]

The Problem of Representation

It is necessary to critically evaluate the pervasiveness of these themes in Dominican studies, not as an obvious reflection of an essential Dominican problem or issue unique to the Dominican experience, as we have questioned above, but possibly instead as a product of those who wish to write about them, revealing as much or more about the individual interests of scholars as it does about the country itself. Thus far, the field of Dominican studies, such that it is, lacks critical reflexivity and has not asked why we as scholars choose to take up some themes and concepts over any number of others. The regrettably narrow conceptual range of contemporary Dominican studies is not without consequences. Overemphasis on race, for instance, leads to the tacit conclusion that the country is somehow exceptional in this regard—it has been treated as such for years. It would seem that for many scholars, the Dominican Republic is racially pathological (or racist, or racially abused) or simply not interesting. But what exactly does it mean to conceptualize a place as a racial problem? Studies abound on Dominican racial formation, identity, and reckoning, not because the country challenges the almost universally accepted fact that race is a social construct but perhaps because by defining the Dominican Republic as a racial exception, the country better fits a deep-seated preoccupation in American scholarship—regardless of a scholar's political affiliation or ideology—with tropes of racial alterity when it comes to writing about Caribbean societies. Consider, for example, early interest in the Caribbean region represented by sensational accounts like William Seabrook's *The Magic Island* (1929), Hesketh Pritchard's *Where Black Rules White* (1900), and Faustin Wirkus and Taney Dudley's *The White King of La Gonave* (1931), as well as the contemporary overemphasis on metaphors of conflict, development, and heterogeneity that dominate the social science of the Caribbean today. Looking to the Dominican Republic, "Blacks who hate Blacks" or "Blacks who don't know they're Black" appear to be especially provocative formulations in the postmodern moment. From this perspective, the Dominican Republic is rendered an anomaly, an aberration that must be explained and ultimately righted.

Aside from the gatekeeping concepts of race and nation, it is worth mentioning that English language scholarship on the Dominican Republic has, though to a lesser degree, also found novelty in the study of dictatorship and sex tourism. Considering the scope of these additional themes alongside the dominant issues of race and nation, Dominican studies has time and again framed the study of Dominicans in terms of political, social, and sexual deviance in ways that position the Dominican Republic firmly within the exotic, rendering it a more familiar, perhaps more "proper," Caribbean subject for analysis. The considerable reluctance of scholars to pursue research questions outside of this frame (or at least the failure of such research to find widespread acceptance beyond it) cannot be explained without acknowledging what appears to be a compelling scholarly proclivity for ascertaining difference over sameness and a stubborn insistence on viewing the Caribbean as *alter*/other in order to theorize the Dominican Republic as a racial exception.

Scholarly representations of Dominican alterity are markedly noticeable of late in the form of "the suffering subject" or "the subject living in pain, in poverty, or under conditions of violence or oppression."[32] Revitalized academic interest in the concepts of race and nation have followed from *la sentencia* in 2013, a court order that stripped Dominicans of Haitian descent of their citizenship in the Dominican Republic, effectively leaving an estimated two hundred thousand people stateless. Some have pointed to the recent passing of *la sentencia* as an obvious impetus for new and continued studies in the areas of race and nation. However, the critical situation of Dominicans of Haitian descent is not new. It did not begin with *la sentencia*; rather, it came to a head, the culmination of decades of state antagonism toward Haitian immigrants and their children. Local writers, activists, NGOs, and religious organizations, as well as several international foundations and global organizations (the United Nations among them), had for years invested time and money into this issue long before recent scholars took notice. The legalized victimization of Dominicans of Haitian descent seems to have consolidated an already strong disciplinary interest in race and nation and the Dominican/Haitian divide and collapsed them together into an especially alluring scholarly narrative of Black suffering subjects of the state. Even as much of this work presumably proceeds from a genuine concern for the rights of the oppressed, it no less coincides with a long tradition in North American scholarship of portraying countries of the Caribbean as simultaneously Black, troubled, and in need of liberation.[33]

Prioritizing Dominican Voices

One way we as Dominicanists might avoid the problems of representation observed above is to be careful not to sideline or dismiss native voices, scholarly or otherwise. Serious engagement with local Dominican scholars should be a priority; it is essential that their work not be neglected.[34] Sincere attention to local scholarship will likely unsettle the conspicuous repetition of publications on Dominican identity as well as inspire original interventions reflective of native concerns. Rigorous and purposeful engagement with the local canon invites dialogue with homegrown expertise and nurtures conversation with domestic knowledge in ways that are vital to appreciating context-based specificities with regard to race and nation, and necessary to framing relevant reconstructions of Dominican political and social realities. To this point, we frequently hear complaints from Dominican academics that U.S. scholars are only interested in the country's pathologizing of race, a particularly ironic state of affairs, from their standpoint, considering the United States' own issues with racism. That being said, some Dominican scholarship has attempted to prop up the ideological interests of the ruling elite by advancing a racist narrative of Dominican exceptionalism;[35] yet today there are probably just as many or more who, rather than reproduce discourses that support racial oppression, are committed to alternatives that go against the grain of this particular brand of nationalist sentiment and look to rewrite a more polyvocal national narrative.[36] Local sources and experts must be consulted and their work taken seriously, or we have little more than foreign fantasies about the Dominican Republic that reify foreign categories of analysis and may very well tread dangerously close to trafficking in exoticism.

As a related priority, it is equally important to give ordinary Dominicans a voice in the scholarly literature. Specifically, there is a desperate need for comprehensive ethnographic research rooted in local experiences that give a voice to and therefore render audible the perspective of Dominicans on the ground. This approach is crucial to uncovering meaningful insight into the salience of social categories like race and the complexity of *identidad* to Dominicans themselves (the people for whom these categories have immediate material relevance) and not just the scholars who study them. We would submit that it is preferable to critique exclusionary racial and ethnic discourses by advancing the voices and experiences of those most negatively affected, putting a face on oppression and outlining the material and psychological wages of racism in local terms. This will necessitate thorough, sustained research that is sensitive to the concerns of context, native viewpoints, community dynamics, and individual interests, and therefore attuned to the nuances of lived experience and expression. Dominicanness, then, may be revealed to be as much about language use and ideology, gender and sexuality, religious commitments and convictions, value orientations and ethical alignments, performance genres and expressive culture, aesthetic elections and consumption practices, as it is about racial or ethnic identity alone.

Although questions about race and nation are important, they do not always reflect or even approximate the primary interests or motivations of local actors. Two of the most significant Dominican social movements over the past several years (notably, in 2012 and 2017) were inspired by government corruption, poverty, and resistance to the abuses of political authority following widespread dissatisfaction with incumbent politicians and broad disparities in wealth, power, and flourishing between political elites and the general populace. In 2012 thousands of Dominicans staged massive demonstrations against fiscal reform (President Danilo Medina's *paquetazo*) that sought to cut an enormous deficit by raising taxes on average Dominican citizens. More recently, beginning in 2017, tens of thousands of Dominicans took to the streets of Santo Domingo and elsewhere to protest wide-ranging political corruption at the hands of the state. The Odebrecht scandal served as the catalyst for these initial demonstrations; *el movimiento marcha verde*, or the Green March movement, as it has come to be called, is the outcome, decades in the making, of increased anger and frustration over government abuses and the impunity of state officials. The extant literature on race and nation presently dominating Dominican studies simply does not account for the context and meaning of this social upheaval and fails to provide, on the whole, a conceptual language for understanding political unrest of this kind.

More than another account that attempts to demystify issues of race in the Dominican Republic, more than another reproach of Black denial, more than another treatise on race and nation, we need more practical work that seeks out active solutions to anti-Black racism (and its ally, anti-Haitianism), now more than ever. This way the problem of race in the Dominican Republic would be more appropriately centered on material realities (how people identified as Black are treated) rather than on ideological propositions (Dominicans are or are not Black). Too much scholarship on race and nation in the Dominican Republic turns on nuanced variants of the latter, a position that risks creating new problems even as it looks to solve old ones (by trading one essentialism for another), while the former position speaks to the relative material conditions of everyday life and could be used to identify concrete areas for ameliorative action. The current danger, as we see it, is the potential for more publications that identify a familiar problem and its origins without articulating a proactive solution. More and more it seems race and nation represent prestige commodities for exchange in the academic marketplace—something to write a book about—and not critical analytic categories that might be used to unveil hegemony and dismantle oppression. Too often losing sight of the situated and constructed nature of both race and nation belies their imaginary or invented ontological status as real. Race is a social fiction, racism its material effects; any socially engaged scholarship would do well to heed the difference.

Orienting Dominican Studies

It is important to underscore the fact that Dominican studies is by no means limited to these gatekeeping concepts or dominant themes but is greatly influenced by them as a result of their persistent application to Dominican materials and recurrent evocation in academic conversations about the country. Of course, research publications outside of these frames do make an appearance from time to time and do have an impact. Yet when scant research dollars, fellowships, and conference space are allocated regularly to studies in only a select few areas, the state of the field suffers, hindering opportunities for advancing Dominican studies as a broad-reaching interdisciplinary project and putting limits on expanding our knowledge of all things Dominican in ways that would otherwise plainly benefit the field as a whole.

So much of the Dominican studies literature available to U.S.-based scholars today is work in the familiar areas of race and nation. It is scarcely possible in the current moment not to engage with it. Many of us (the authors included) are indebted to the contributions made by this scholarship, which today continues to inspire intellectual interest in the country. The canon informs our work to one degree or another, and it can be argued that advancements in the field follow as a result of this work, not in spite of it. It is imperative, however, that future scholarship not be limited by the dominant categories that have heretofore defined the field or be constrained by the narrow scope of theorizing envisioned by the available corpus.

A focus on Dominicanness as understood primarily through the lens of race and nation creates a blind spot over other potentially illuminating categories of analysis like social class, ethics, family and kinship, aesthetics, performance and creative art, gender and sexuality, sports and recreation, religion, and other important articulations of state, identity, society, and culture in the country. More than that, constantly invoking race and nation has a dulling effect and tends to oversimplify and render monolithic the otherwise complex diversity of Dominican social realities that animate racial and national consciousness. Persistent and exclusive reference to these categories to the exclusion of others creates a specter of race and nation that becomes determinative in its own right. The Dominican Republic of scholarly literature becomes only about ubiquitous racial logics, Dominicans only subjects or sovereigns of racial domination. By reading the Dominican situation in the exclusive terms of race and nation, however complex and nuanced, we concretize a mistaken belief about so-called nonwhite peoples: namely, that their ideas, dreams, desires, and motivations are never agential or creative but always a reaction to the dictates of racial structures or antagonisms, implicitly repeating the pernicious fallacy that race explains nonwhites and nonwhites only. Whiteness studies alongside critical race theory inform us that it is precisely these imaginaries that function to reproduce racial hierarchies by ranking and ordering alterity and normalizing whiteness as nonraced and unmarked.

The limitations do not stop there; the reliance on an abbreviated catalog of themes, no matter what they may be, alienates a potentially broader academic audience since research on race and nation in the Dominican Republic, for instance, often relies on esoteric or expert Dominican material, drawing on local histories and experiences that are difficult to put into conversation with academic discussions occurring elsewhere. For example, some of the work that has come out on Dominican racial identity fails to contribute meaningfully to contemporary theorizing about race, leaving us to wonder: what do we learn from more and more nuanced analyses of Dominican racial imaginaries, or yet another genealogy of Dominican Blackness? Dominican studies likely continues to be peripheral in both Latin American and Caribbean studies because too often it fails to engage with comparative material. Topics like *dominicanidad* have narrow relevance outside of the country itself. Failure to orient research questions within prominent regional discussions and themes, such as, say, clientelism or neoliberalism in Latin America, or creolization or development in the Caribbean, has alienated Dominican studies from broader area studies. It is incumbent on us as Dominicanists to foster dialogue and create intellectual lines of communication that connect with scholarly communities in places other than the Dominican Republic.

Dominican studies would profit from a reorientation toward a breadth of approaches that move beyond the restricted themes of race and nation and push the field past chiefly provincial concerns about identity that limit its comparative utility and cross-cultural appeal. One way is methodological; the other way is theoretical. Dominican studies is desperately thin when it comes to ethnography; to correct this lacuna, a more comprehensive pursuit of emic and prosaic perspectives on the island is needed.[37] Lack of ethnographic insight means that scholars too often speak *for* rather than *through* or *with* the subjects they discuss. For all the work done on Dominicanness, very little of it has the support of deep, long-term local involvement with folk, the everyday participants who actively shape, advance, and challenge the propositions of *dominicanidad*. More critical engagement with explanatory models that build on theoretical developments in conversation with local data would enrich Dominican studies immeasurably and likely lead away from exclusive concerns with race and nation into other areas of importance to Dominicans by decentering the analytic interests of the outsider and situating those interests more squarely with the concerns of subjects, insiders themselves. Thornton's own ethnographic work with Pentecostal Christian converts in Villa Altagracia, for example, demonstrates that for many Dominicans, ethnic/racial and national identity are subordinated to religious, social class, and other affiliations they deem to be more salient to their everyday lives.[38] Looking to new conceptual orientations that build on ethnographic knowledge and respect native viewpoints, however challenging, is a necessary counterweight to the prescriptive bias of gatekeeping concepts and a vital corrective to the analytic blind spots they create. Earnest consideration of contemporary local experience will go a long way to help explain emergent political movements like *marcha verde* and contextualize prospects for future social mobilizations (be they religious, moral, artistic, sexual, or racial), if we only make a better effort to prioritize Dominican voices on the ground.

There are, of course, alternative themes that we feel could push Dominican studies in fertile new directions, namely, research agendas with an eye on women and gender, neoliberalism, political economy, sexuality, clientelism, queer theory, historical memory, labor studies, globalization, economic development, feminist theory, and religion, all historically productive conceptual frameworks that cut across disciplines and would add to and even enhance existing and ongoing research in the more familiar areas of racial and cultural identity, nationality, and Dominican/Haitian relations, while bringing Dominican studies more in line with topics of enduring interest to Caribbean and Latin American studies. We might also think of creative new areas of inquiry and analysis that have yet to be developed or applied to Dominican materials. This does not mean abandoning the themes of race and nation—these issues are not trivial. Rather, we should regard them as valuable interpretive tools among many others in our ever-expanding analytic toolkit, at the same time taking stock of what has been done by others before us in order to move forward in novel directions. Moreover, it is crucial that we not ignore the broader political economy in which race and nation are important, but not singular, and seek to carve out imaginative space for social analysis that accounts for the contemporary Dominican experience in all of its complexity.

To this end we might take a cue from research being published elsewhere and compare Dominican studies to other regional or area studies. Dominican studies could draw more deliberately from the wider Caribbean literature for theory or conceptual breadth and would certainly benefit from work coming out of the Francophone and Anglophone Caribbean, not to mention research programs anchored in Cuba or Puerto Rico. One illustration of this could be employing Fernando Ortiz's transculturation, an underappreciated analytic in the Dominican Republic but one that has enjoyed considerable application throughout the Caribbean. It could also be something timelier like narco-economics, given the country's evolving relationship to the international drug trade, or maybe clientelism, a popular lens for examining political authority in Latin America. Studies of gender have been able to gain some traction of late, as have studies on neoliberalism, corruption, and political authoritarianism.[39] Alternatives abound.

Another example of this extension might be seen in recent work taking up a transnational perspective on Hispaniola, broadening Dominican studies to include Haiti and Haitian studies.[40] Although new scholars to the region should be wary of reproducing well-worn tropes linking Haiti and the Dominican Republic to race, racial formation, ethnicity, Blackness, and, of course, nation, this new orientation comes with the promise of deeper engagements with shared histories, cultures, and peoples whose similarities and reciprocal influences are more often overlooked than not.[41] Likewise, *The Dominican Republic Reader* is a well-considered collection that looks to light a broad, relatively interdisciplinary path for Dominican studies moving forward through a more comprehensive and diverse view of history, culture, and politics in terms other than simply race and nation.[42] Ideally, new research directions together with innovative conceptual approaches will lead to novel theorizing that affords robust new insights on which future research might profitably develop.

Possibilities for a vibrant and more influential field of Dominican studies will be contingent on diversifying scholarly approaches to Dominican subjects with a commitment to viewing them not as racial problems but as sociological ones in the broadest sense. It is imperative that we as scholars become critically conscious of our role as gatekeepers in defining for academic audiences the dominant and quintessential questions of interest as they apply to the Dominican Republic and actively work against the arbitrary foreclosure of alternative themes and perspectives that might invite richer analyses and greater scholarly dialogue with intellectual communities beyond the island.

The analytic paradigms of race and nation have dominated scholarship on the Dominican Republic by framing social and cultural analysis in ways that have limited the theorizing of Dominican materials to a narrow focus on identity. It is a challenge to think beyond these gatekeeping concepts and to imagine the Dominican Republic as something more than a racial problem. At the very least, the current moment begs for self-reflection, for these trends are not without consequences. A decentering of, rather than a departure from, race and nation as dominant modes of inquiry has the potential to generate new insight into the diverse and meaningful areas of meaning making that shape Dominican life. The second largest country in the Caribbean is an interesting case study for more than just a select few issues—this much is obvious—and it is up to all of us to push Dominican studies into new and productive directions even as we do not abandon important discussions of identity, violence, and exclusion, which are central to contemporary debates on race and nation in the Dominican Republic, as elsewhere.

NOTES

1. Arjun Appadurai, "Theory in Anthropology: Center and Periphery," *Comparative Studies in Society and History* 28, no. 2 (1986): 356–61, esp. 357.

2. Also reputation and respectability, colonialism, globalization, and transnational migration. Compare with Michel-Rolph Trouillot, who has argued instead that the Caribbean's heterogeneity and unique colonial history have precluded the formation of dominant tropes or gatekeeping concepts. Michel-Rolph Trouillot, "The Caribbean Region: An Open Frontier in Anthropological Theory," *Annual Review of Anthropology* 21 (1992): 19–42; Aisha Khan, "Journey to the Center of the Earth: The Caribbean as Master Symbol," *Cultural Anthropology* 16, no. 3 (2001): 271–302.

3. Khan, "Journey to the Center of the Earth," 294.

4. Cf. Appadurai, "Theory in Anthropology," 358.

5. Dominican studies, as it is currently constituted, is a loosely connected network of interdisciplinary scholarship across the humanities and social sciences addressing Dominicans and the Dominican Republic. Scholars writing from a variety of perspectives and disciplines have advanced Dominican studies by working on Dominican materials, not by explicitly locating their work within an area studies paradigm per se. In this chapter we confine our discussion of Dominican studies to scholarship written in English about the Dominican Republic published in books and journals chiefly oriented toward the English-speaking academies of North America and Europe.

6. One example of this is Doris Sommer's *One Master for Another*, one of the first monographs written in the United States to take Dominican literature and culture as its primary focus and an early intervention in the field of literary criticism, but which failed to make any kind of significant splash on Latin American studies generally. Doris Sommer, *One Master for Another: Populism as Patriarchal Rhetoric in Dominican Novels* (Lanham, Md.: University Press of America, 1983).

7. For example, see Pamela Cappas-Toro, "Race under Dictatorship: The Political Articulation of Blackness in the Dominican Republic and Brazil" (PhD diss., University of

Illinois, 2013); Daly Guilamo, "Fear of a Black Country: Dominican Anti-Haitianism, the Denial of Racism, and Contradictions in the Aftermath of the 2010 Earthquake" (PhD diss., Temple University, 2013); Saha Miranda, "Citizens without a Nation: The Construction of Haitian Illegality and Deportability in the Dominican Republic" (PhD diss., Illinois State University, 2014); Danilo Antonio Contreras, "Exit over Voice in Dominican Ethnoracial Politics" (PhD diss., University of Texas, 2015); Angelina Tallaj-Garcia, "Performing Blackness in a Mulatto Society: Negotiating Racial Identity through Music in the Dominican Republic" (PhD diss., City University of New York, 2015); Amelia Hintzen, "Cultivating Resistance: Haitian-Dominican Communities and the Dominican Sugar Industry, 1915–1990" (PhD diss., University of Miami, 2016); Jheison Romain, "The Dialectic of Blackness and Full Citizenship: A Case Study of Haitian Migration to the Dominican Republic" (PhD diss., University of Texas, 2016).

8. See Rachel Nolan, "Displaced in the DR: A Country Strips 210,000 of Citizenship," *Harper's*, May 15, 2015.

9. Lorgia García-Peña, *The Borders of Dominicanidad: Race, Nation, and Archives of Contradiction* (Durham, N.C.: Duke University Press, 2016); Edward Paulino, *Dividing Hispaniola: The Dominican Republic's Border Campaign against Haiti, 1930–1961* (Pittsburgh: University of Pittsburgh Press, 2016); Milagros Ricourt, *The Dominican Racial Imaginary: Surveying the Landscape of Race and Nation in Hispaniola* (New Brunswick, N.J.: Rutgers University Press, 2016).

10. Silvio Torres-Saillant, "A Dominican Classic of Caribbean Thought: Introduction to Franklin Franco's *Blacks, Mulattos, and the Dominican Nation*," in *Blacks, Mulattos and the Dominican Nation*, ed. Franklin Franco (New York: Routledge, 2015), 1–21.

11. Torres-Saillant, "A Dominican Classic of Caribbean Thought"; see, for example, Emilio Cordero Michel, *La revolución haitiana y Santo Domingo* (Santo Domingo: Editora Nacional, 1968); Pedro Mir, *Tres leyendas de colores* (Santo Domingo: Editora Nacional, 1969); Harry Hoetink, "Dominican Republic in the Nineteenth Century: Some Notes on Stratification, Immigration, and Race," in *Race and Class in Latin America*, ed. Magnus Morner (New York: Columbia University Press, 1970), 96–121; Hugo Tolentino, *Raza e historia en Santo Domingo* (Santo Domingo: Editora de la Universidad Autónoma de Santo Domingo, 1974); Carlos Esteban Deive, *Vodú y magia en Santo Domingo* (Santo Domingo: Museo del Hombre Dominicano, 1975); Fradique Lizardo, *Cultura africana en Santo Domingo* (Santo Domingo: Editora Taller, 1979); Martha Ellen Davis, *La otra ciencia: El vodú dominicano como religión y medicina* (Santo Domingo: Editora Universitaria, 1987); Meinert Fennema and Troetje Loewenthal, *La construcción de raza y nación en la República Dominicana* (Santo Domingo: Editora Universitaria, 1987); Celsa Batista, *Los africanos y nuestra isla* (Santo Domingo: Ediciones Cedee, 1989); Carlos Andújar Persinal, *La presencia negra en Santo Domingo: Un enfoque etnohistórico* (Santo Domingo: Impresora Buho, 1997); Franklin José Franco, *Sobre racismo y antihaitianismo (y otros ensayos)* (Santo Domingo: Impresora Librería Vidal, 1997); Juan José Ayuso, *En busca del pueblo dominicano* (Santo Domingo: La Trinitaria, 2003); and Natasha Despotovic, ed., *Presencia de África en el Caribe las Antillas y Estados Unidos* (Santo Domingo: FUNGLODE-GFDD, 2012), to name just a few in a long tradition of work in Spanish produced largely, though not exclusively, by Dominican Republic scholars.

12. Carlos Esteban Deive, *Bibliografía afrodomínico-haitiana 1763–2015* (Santo Domingo: Archivo General de la Nación, 2016); some of the sources Deive includes are Pablo Maríñez, *Relaciones domínico-haitianas y raíces histórico-culturales africanas en la República Dominicana: Bibliografía básica* (Santo Domingo: Editora Universitaria UASD, 1986); Frank Báez Evertsz, *Braceros haitianos en la República Dominicana* (Santo Domingo: Instituto Dominicano de Investigaciones Sociales, 1986); Wilfredo Lozano, ed., *La cuestión haitiana en Santo Domingo: Migración internacional, desarrollo y relaciones inter-estatales entre Haití y República Dominicana* (Santo Domingo: FLACSO, 1993); José Chez Checo, *La República Dominicana y Haití: Síntesis histórica de su problema fronterizo* (Santo Domingo: Editora Amigo del Hogar, 1997); Rubén Silié and Carlos Segura, eds., *Una isla para dos* (Santo Domingo: FLACSO, 2002); Aida Heredia, *La representación del haitiano en las letras dominicanas* (University, Miss.: Romance Monographs, 2003); Diógenes Abréu, *Sin haitianidad no hay dominicanidad* (Santo Domingo: Editora Nacional, 2014); Irene Hernández, ed., *República Dominicana y Haití: El derecho a vivir* (Santo Domingo: Fundación Juan Bosch, 2014).

13. Notable publications include Samuel Martínez, *Peripheral Migrants: Haitians and Dominican Republic Plantations* (Knoxville: University of Tennessee Press, 1995); Michiel Baud, "Constitutionally White: The Forging of a National Identity in the Dominican Republic," in *Ethnicity in the Caribbean: Essays in Honor of Harry Hoetink*, ed. Gert Oostindie (London: Macmillan, 1996), 121–51; Paul Austerlitz, *Merengue: Dominican Music and Dominican Identity* (Philadelphia: Temple University Press, 1997); Silvio Torres-Saillant, "The Tribulations of Blackness: Stages in Dominican Racial Identity," *Latin American Perspectives* 25, no. 3 (1998): 126–46; Silvio Torres-Saillant, "Introduction to Dominican Blackness," *Working Papers Series 1* (New York: City University of New York, 1999); Ernesto Sagás, *Race and Politics in the Dominican Republic* (Gainesville: University Press of Florida, 2000); Pedro San Miguel, *La isla imaginada: Historia, identidad y utopía en La Española* (Santo Domingo: La Trinitaria, 1997); David Howard, *Coloring the Nation: Race and Ethnicity in the Dominican Republic* (Boulder, Colo.: Lynne Rienner, 2001); Eugenio Matibag, *Haitian-Dominican Counterpoint: Nation, State, and Race on Hispaniola* (New York: Palgrave Macmillan, 2003); Jorge Duany, "Racializing Ethnicity in the Spanish-Speaking Caribbean," *Latin American and Caribbean Ethnic Studies* 1, no. 2 (2006): 231–48; Ginetta Candelario, *Black behind the Ears: Dominican Racial Identity from Museums to Beauty Shops* (Durham, N.C.: Duke University Press, 2007); Kimberly Eison Simmons, *Reconstructing Racial Identity and the African Past in the Dominican Republic* (Gainesville: University Press of Florida, 2009); Néstor Rodríguez, *Divergent Dictions: Contemporary Dominican Literature* (Coconut Creek, Fla.: Caribbean Studies Press, 2011); Ramón Antonio Victoriano-Martínez, *Rayanos y Dominicanyorks: La dominicanidad del siglo XXI* (Pittsburgh: Instituto Internacional de Literatura Iberoamericana, 2014); April Mayes, *The Mulatto Republic: Class, Race, and Dominican National Identity* (Gainesville: University Press of Florida, 2014); Alaí Reyes-Santos, *Our Caribbean Kin: Race and Nation in the Neoliberal Antilles* (New Brunswick, N.J.: Rutgers University Press, 2015), among others.

14. See Ernesto Sagás, "A Case of Mistaken Identity: Antihaitianismo in Dominican Culture," *Latin Americanist* 29, no. 1 (1993): 1–5; Richard Lee Turits, "A World Destroyed, a Nation Imposed: The 1937 Haitian Massacre in the Dominican Republic," *Hispanic*

American Historical Review 82, no. 3 (2002): 589–636; Sara Johnson, "The Integration of Hispaniola: A Reappraisal of Haitian-Dominican Relations in the 19th and 20th Centuries," *Journal of Haitian Studies* 8, no. 2 (2002): 4–29; Teresita Martínez-Vergne, *Nation and Citizen in the Dominican Republic, 1880–1916* (Chapel Hill: University of North Carolina Press, 2005); Samuel Martínez, "Not a Cockfight: Rethinking Haitian-Dominican Relations," *Latin American Perspectives* 30, no. 3 (2003): 80–101. For studies on the national border, see Lauren Derby, "Haitians, Magic, and Money: Raza and Society in the Haitian-Dominican Borderlands, 1900 to 1937," *Comparative Studies in Society and History* 36 (1994): 488–526; Robert Adams, "History at the Crossroads: Vodú and the Modernization of the Dominican Borderlands," in *Globalization and Race: Transformations in the Cultural Production of Blackness*, ed. Kamari Maxine Clarke and Deborah A. Thomas (Durham, N.C.: Duke University Press, 2006), 55–72; Maria Fumagalli, *On the Edge: Writing the Border between Haiti and the Dominican Republic* (Liverpool: Liverpool University Press, 2015). For studies on national identity, see José del Castillo and Martin Murphy, "Migration, National Identity and Cultural Policy in the Dominican Republic," *Journal of Ethnic Studies* 15, no. 3 (1987): 49–69; Ninna Nyberg Sørensen, "Creole Culture, Dominican Identity," *Folk* 35, no. 1 (1993): 17–35; Ninna Nyberg Sørensen, "There Are No Indians in the Dominican Republic: The Cultural Construction of Dominican Identities," in *Siting Culture: The Shifting Anthropological Object*, ed. Karen Fog Olwig and Kirsten Hastrup (London: Routledge, 1997), 292–310; Samuel Martínez, "The Masking of History: Popular Images of the Nation on a Dominican Sugar Plantation," *New West Indian Guide* 71, nos. 3/4 (1997): 227–48.

15. Not to be ignored, Junot Díaz's rise to prominence and vocal criticism of the Dominican Republic has also brought renewed interest in the country by foreign scholars. His literary output alone has provided a notably productive archive for literary scholars, inspiring a glut of publications in literary criticism over the past several years. Díaz's very public criticisms of Dominican racism, especially as it has been realized in the stripping of citizenship from Dominicans of Haitian descent, have drawn more attention to the issues of race and nation in the country. See Junot Díaz, Edwidge Danticat, Mark Kurlansky, and Julia Alvarez, "Two Versions of a Dominican Tale," *New York Times*, October 13, 2013; Zach Hindin and Mario Ariza, "When Nativism Becomes Normal," *Atlantic*, May 16, 2016; Christopher González, *Reading Junot Díaz* (Pittsburgh: University of Pittsburgh Press, 2015); Ellen McCracken, *Paratexts and Performance in the Novels of Junot Díaz and Sandra Cisneros* (New York: Palgrave Macmillan, 2016); Monica Hanna, Jennifer Vargas, and José Saldívar, eds., *Junot Díaz and the Decolonial Imagination* (Durham, N.C.: Duke University Press, 2016); Heather Ostman, *The Fiction of Junot Díaz: Reframing the Lens* (Lanham, Md.: Rowman & Littlefield, 2017); Mark Padilla, *Caribbean Pleasure Industry: Tourism, Sexuality, and AIDS in the Dominican Republic* (Chicago: University of Chicago Press, 2017).

16. Raj Chetty and Amaury Rodríguez, "Introduction: The Challenge and Promise of Dominican Black Studies," *Black Scholar* 45, no. 2 (2015): 1–9, esp. 2.

17. More recently, some scholars have written against this trend, highlighting evidence counter to the Black denial narrative from a variety of angles. See, for example, Ricourt, *Dominican Racial Imaginary*. For a call to move beyond the theme of Black denial, see Chetty and Rodríguez, "Introduction."

18. See Sørensen, "There Are No Indians," 297.

19. See Simmons, *Reconstructing Racial Identity*.

20. See Sagás, "Case of Mistaken Identity." According to Samuel Martínez, the official ideology of the nation equates racial distinction between Black and non-Black with the political and cultural boundary that defines Dominican and Haitian people. Dominicans, he argues, may be said to conflate race and nation by identifying Haitians as Black and themselves not as white but as non-Black. Official history and national identity thus dovetail with anti-Black/anti-indigene racial conventions, to place darker citizens not just disproportionally at the bottom of the social ladder but at the margins of constructs of cultural citizenship that give pride of place to lighter-skinned citizens. The local color term *indio/a* gestures toward this mixed, neither-white-nor-Black identity that Dominicans presumably share and which functions as a native category of Dominican creole identity. Martínez, "Masking of History." Also see Sørensen, "Creole Culture"; Torres-Saillant, *Tribulations of Blackness*.

21. See, for example, Silvio Torres-Saillant, "The Tribulations of Blackness: Stages in Dominican Racial Identity," *Latin American Perspectives* 25, no. 3 (1998): 126–46; Torres-Saillant, "Introduction to Dominican Blackness"; Dawn Stinchcomb, *The Development of Literary Blackness in the Dominican Republic* (Gainesville: University Press of Florida, 2004); Simmons, *Reconstructing Racial Identity*; Ricourt, *Dominican Racial Imaginary*.

22. See Andújar, *La presencia negra en Santo Domingo*; Dagoberto Tejeda Ortiz, *Cultura popular e identidad nacional* (Santo Domingo: Consejo Presidencial de Cultura, 1998); Soraya Aracena, *Apuntes sobre la negritud en República Dominicana* (Santo Domingo: Helvetas, 1999).

23. See Carlos Esteban Deive, *¿Y tu abuela dónde está? El negro en la historia y la cultura dominicanas* (Santo Domingo: Editora Nacional, 2013); Blas Jiménez, *Afrodominicano por elección, negro por nacimiento* (Santo Domingo: Editora Manatí, 2008); Blas Jiménez, *Caribbean African upon Awakening* (London: Mango, 2010); Brendan Jamal Thornton, *Negotiating Respect: Pentecostalism, Masculinity, and the Politics of Spiritual Authority in the Dominican Republic* (Gainesville: University Press of Florida, 2016).

24. For example, see Elizabeth Jacobs, *Mexican American Literature: The Politics of Identity* (New York: Routledge, 2006); Laura Gutierrez, *Performing Mexicanidad: Vendidas y Cabareteras on a Transnational Stage* (Austin: University of Texas Press, 2010).

25. For example, see Nancy Appelbaum, Anne Macpherson, and Karin Alejandra Rosemblatt, eds., *Race and Nation in Modern Latin America* (Chapel Hill: University of North Carolina Press, 2003).

26. This is not to say that questions of nationality are not urgent or even, for some, matters of life and death; to be sure, for many Black Dominicans and Dominicans of Haitian descent it is exactly that. Questions of citizenship and belonging are always contentious as citizenship is a discourse of exclusion as much as it is a prescription of rights and duties. These questions become all the more pressing in the neocolonial context of places like Puerto Rico and Martinique, where constructions of nationhood and nationality bump up against the precarity of statehood and eroding geopolitical boundaries.

27. Cf. Michel-Rolph Trouillot, *Global Transformations: Anthropology and the Modern World* (New York: Palgrave Macmillan, 2003).

28. For example, see Torres-Saillant, "Tribulations of Blackness"; Howard, *Coloring*

the Nation; Candelario, *Black behind the Ears*; Simmons, *Reconstructing Racial Identity*; Mayes, *Mulatto Republic*; García-Peña, *Borders of Dominicanidad*; and the recent call for a "Dominican Black studies" by Raj Chetty and Amaury Rodríguez, editors' introduction to "Dominican Black Studies," special issue, *Black Scholar* 45, no. 2 (2015): 4–5.

29. For example, Torres-Saillant, "Introduction to Dominican Blackness"; Stinchcomb, *Development of Literary Blackness*; Abréu, *Sin haitianidad no hay dominicanidad*; Jiménez, *Afrodominicano por elección*; Celsa Batista, *República Dominicana: Primer pueblo afrodescendiente de América* (Santo Domingo: Editora Búho, 2014). Raj Chetty and Amaury Rodríguez rightly caution scholars not to essentialize Black origins and to be wary of narrow conceptions of Black racial consciousness when critiquing Dominican racial attitudes that do not necessarily accord with familiar forms of Black identity politics. Chetty and Rodriguez, introduction to "Dominican Black Studies," 4–5.

30. For example, see García-Peña, *Borders of Dominicanidad*; Rodríguez, *Divergent Dictions*.

31. Eva Michelle Wheeler, "Race, Legacy, and Lineage in the Dominican Republic," *Black Scholar* 45, no. 2 (2015): 34–44.

32. Joel Robbins, in an incisive article considering changes in the primary object of attention in anthropology since the 1980s, argues that the "suffering subject" has replaced the "radical other" of anthropological imagination, a shift occurring in the analytic interests and perspectives of the field, not rooted in any particular historical event or changes in any human capacity or inclination. Analogously, our argument here is that the focus on race and nation in Dominican studies is not a natural reflection of some fundamental Dominican reality but an arbitrary construct of scholars who study the country. Joel Robbins, "Beyond the Suffering Subject: Toward an Anthropology of the Good," *Journal of the Royal Anthropological Institute* 19 (2013): 447–62.

33. In this way even the most avowed anti-racists can fall into the trap of promoting an image that shares a dangerous affinity with early twentieth-century neocolonial narratives used to justify imperialist military interventions.

34. Chetty and Rodríguez note the tendency of some U.S.-based scholars writing in English about Dominican race relations to overlook the work of Dominican scholars in this area. Introduction to "Dominican Black Studies," 3.

35. For example, see Manuel Núñez, *El ocaso de la nación dominicana* (Santo Domingo: Editorial Letra Gráfica, 2001); Joaquín Balaguer, *La isla al revés: Haití y el destino dominicano* (Santo Domingo: Fundación José Antonio Caro, 1983).

36. For example, see Raymundo González, ed., *Política, identidad y pensamiento social en la República Dominicana, siglos XIX y XX* (Santo Domingo: Academia de Ciencias de Dominicana, 1999); Quisqueya Lora, *Transición de la esclavitud al trabajo libre en Santo Domingo: El caso de Higüey (1822–1827)* (Santo Domingo: Academia Dominicana de la Historia, 2012); Celsa Batista, *Mujer y esclavitud en Santo Domingo* (Santo Domingo: Instituto Dominicano de Estudios Africanos y Asiáticos Sebastián Lemba-INDAASEL, 2013); Pablo Mella, *Los espejos de Duarte* (Santo Domingo: Instituto Filosófico Pedro Fco, 2013). Important work in this regard is also being done by scholars of Dominican descent in the United States, e.g., García-Peña, *Borders of Dominicanidad*; Paulino, *Dividing Hispaniola*; Ricourt, *Dominican Racial Imaginary*.

37. For good examples, see Barbara Finlay, *The Women of Azua: Work and Family in*

the Rural Dominican Republic (New York: Praeger, 1989); Tahira Vargas, *De la casa a la calle: Estudio de la familia y la vecindad en un barrio de Santo Domingo* (Santo Domingo: Centro de Estudios Sociales P. Juan Montalvo, 1998); Samuel Martínez, *Decency and Excess: Global Aspirations and Material Deprivation on a Caribbean Sugar Plantation* (London: Routledge, 2007); Candelario, *Black behind the Ears*; Padilla, *Caribbean Pleasure Industry*; Thornton, *Negotiating Respect*; Marion Werner, *Global Displacements: The Making of Uneven Development in the Caribbean* (Oxford: Wiley Blackwell, 2016). Also see Carlos Ulises Decena, *Tacit Subjects: Belonging and Same-Sex Desire among Dominican Immigrant Men* (Durham, N.C.: Duke University Press, 2011).

38. See Thornton, *Negotiating Respect.*

39. For example, see Maja Horn, *Masculinity after Trujillo: The Politics of Gender in Dominican Literature* (Gainesville: University Press of Florida, 2014); Sydney Hutchinson, *Tigers of a Different Stripe: Performing Gender in Dominican Music* (Chicago: University of Chicago Press, 2016); Thornton, *Negotiating Respect*; Lauren Derby, *The Dictator's Seduction: Politics and the Popular Imagination in the Era of Trujillo* (Durham, N.C.: Duke University Press, 2009); Christian Krohn-Hansen, *Political Authoritarianism in the Dominican Republic* (New York: Palgrave Macmillan, 2009).

40. Recently pioneering this effort is the Transnational Hispaniola working group. See April Mayes, Yveline Alexis, Ulices Decena, Kiran Jayaram, and Yolanda Martin, "Transnational Hispaniola: Toward New Paradigms in Haitian and Dominican Studies," *Radical History Review* 115 (2013): 26–32.

41. For recent examples, see Lucía Suárez, *The Tears of Hispaniola: Haitian and Dominican Diaspora Memories* (Gainesville: University Press of Florida, 2006); Sara Johnson, *The Fear of French Negroes: Transcolonial Collaboration in the Revolutionary Americas* (Berkeley: University of California Press, 2012); Anne Eller, *We Dream Together: Dominican Independence, Haiti, and the Fight for Caribbean Freedom* (Durham, N.C.: Duke University Press, 2016); Graham Nessler, *An Islandwide Struggle for Freedom: Revolution, Emancipation and Re-enslavement in Hispaniola, 1789–1809* (Chapel Hill: University of North Carolina Press, 2016).

42. Eric Roorda, Lauren Derby, and Raymundo González, eds., *The Dominican Republic Reader* (Durham, N.C.: Duke University Press, 2014).

CHAPTER 12

Moving beyond Narrow Nationalist Historiography

JEROME TEELUCKSINGH

> An obscure part of the New World is momentarily touched by history; the darkness closes up again; the Chaguanes disappear in silence. The disappearance is unimportant; it is part of nobody's story.
> —V. S. Naipaul, *The Loss of El Dorado*

There is a calculus of presences and absences in Caribbean history that produce a "mythologization of the Caribbean."[1] Although with different goals, techniques, and ethics, mythologization is nevertheless a feature shared by both the colonial and postcolonial West Indies; through seeking a kind of emotional and moral simplification, the process is conducive to legitimating the prevailing ruling relations.[2] To discuss the operation of these ruling relations in the twenty-first century, my focus is on the treatment of racial and religious minorities in West Indian historiography, broaching whether nationalism drives a form of intellectual discrimination that relegates minorities to attachments to society rather than allowing them to be actors in their own right.

There have been many valuable discussions and critiques of creolization, Creole societies and Creole nationalism, as well as the particular meanings and projects associated with that term in the English, Dutch, French, and Spanish Caribbean and the wider Americas.[3] As part of the intellectual project of trying to make sense of whether this line of conceptualization has utility, in her grand review of the historiography of the eastern and southern Anglo-Caribbean, Bridget Brereton notes that in the first few years of independence, professional and amateur historians spent considerable energy documenting the various "contributions" each social group made to Caribbean societies.[4] Now certainly there are many valid critiques of this intellectual nation-building project, but from the present perspective its efforts at mass inclusion are redeemable, if only because in the interim a calcified narrow version of this

251

historiography has become canonized. Philip Sherlock, an eminent Jamaican of the post–World War II era, wrote that "West Indian history begins with the folk who came in these ships."[5] But Caribbean history is more than enslavement and indentureship. To overlook the genocide of Indigenous peoples is to be complicit in perpetuating a silencing and disappearing that is ultimately to the detriment of producing a democratic image of the Anglo-Caribbean in which all can see themselves.

At risk of being greatly misunderstood, in the mature postcolonial era most of the public history of the Anglo-Caribbean has been rewritten and reshaped to reflect the contributions and struggles of African-descended persons. This is the "presumed fulcrum" of Caribbean history. Despite this portrayal of the Caribbean marginalizing the significant Indo-Caribbean population and other ethnic minorities including persons of Jewish, Syrian, Chinese, Lebanese, and Portuguese descent, it has remained relatively unchallenged outside of niche academic circles. Indeed, attempts to compile a critical total history have at times been met with ridicule or deliberately misconstrued as solely invested in promoting ethnic particularity. To wit, racial flattening and exclusion occur to the detriment of the minorities who have also been subject to the same logic of oppression that stems from racial capitalism.

A portion of this friction can be attributable to intraclass contests as the Caribbean class structure, or more precisely its self-comprehension, evolved in the latter part of the twentieth century. Another portion is attributable to the naturalization of the "Christian gaze." As the chapter proceeds, I explain how these factors coarticulate with one another to set the template for lay explanations about the desirability of a "narrow creolization" predicated on an Afrocentric fulcrum. Still, and I think it is important to be explicit on this point, the purpose of this chapter is not to relitigate debates about creolization. Nor is it to validate Indo-Caribbean "grievance politics." Rather, my aim is to point to the negative consequences for working-class solidarity when nationalist narratives of essentialism take root in Caribbean social life.

Among other things, this chapter examines how these legacies of middle-class mythologization hinder broad-based cross-racial solidarity. In practice this means that unproductive racial frictions remain unchanged. The pervasive dichotomy existing within the Caribbean is not an anomaly found in one or two spaces. Exclusion is widespread, and unfortunately many are either oblivious or deliberately ignore the ramifications of this discriminatory practice. And even when intense fractures are acknowledged, typically these are attributed to the brutal colonial past, as if there have not been more than sixty years to make amends. Solidarity is hard work, and many would rather play the "blame game" of believing the past is exclusively responsible for the terrible socioeconomic conditions and incompetent governance. The stark reality is that few persons are willing to point fingers at the modern society for its failure to improve and implement reforms. Redress is long overdue, because at stake is that in the twenty-first century Caribbean societies need to adopt a different mode of self-comprehension if they wish to thrive in a fiercely contested globalized world. Mass symbolic and material inclusion is central to this project.

How Politics Silences; How Ideology Disappears

Since the 1960s an explicitly Afrocentric discourse has increasingly become an acceptable replacement for the outdated colonial and imperial narratives. Yet, as Gerad Tikasingh provoked, "Did not indentureship have a greater impact on the nature and history of Trinidad?" Tikasingh's point is less about ethnic contributions or "ranking horrors" but more about drawing attention to the historical processes that shape and reshape the politics of that country. The failure to appreciate this scholarly questioning of historiography on its own terms, Tikasingh believes, is because "this aspect of Trinidad's history been overshadowed by a pervasive Black bias."[6] This Afrocentric discourse is not confined to the writing and interpretation of Caribbean history. It is also present in the effort to understand party politics. Discussing the recent history of British Guiana, for example, Percy Hintzen argues, "It was precisely Jagan's East Indian background and roots that led him on a political path that diverged significantly from the Afro-creole leadership in the rest of the English-speaking Caribbean."[7] Similarly, Trevor Sudama sought to explain the "predicament" in Guyana that involved "establishing the supremacy of a race which was in a numerical minority."[8] While race is an important category of analysis, and racial experience does inform political projects, these kinds of explanations are illustrative of historiographies where Indo-Caribbeans are almost always primarily driven by matters of identity and perceived social slights. And again, there are elements of truth here. But these kinds of explanations relegate matters of class, factionalism, ideology, and the politics around material culture to secondary effects.

Consider, for instance, how in compounding the "threat" of the Indo-Caribbean person as being adjacent (and hence less amenable) to the project of Western liberal capitalism, British Guiana was a subject of red scare politics. Tropes about the red scare were frequently reported in the newspapers of Trinidad and Tobago, a country that embraced American hegemony.[9] One *Trinidad Guardian* editorial in 1953 argued that "Britain has been perfectly right to take decisive action to keep British Guiana out of the grip of the communist octopus, which has been known for some time to be reaching out to the Caribbean."[10] Indeed, anticapitalism ideologies threatened the colonial bedrock, which required inequalities, injustices, racism, and religious discrimination in order to "successfully" function. The rumors of communism "infecting" other Caribbean countries through disloyal minorities provided the social license to view minorities with suspicion, always suspending the question of whether they could be deemed authentic national subjects, let alone representatives of it.

Racial and political prejudice are easily detectable in how regional leaders treated the overthrow of Jagan in 1953. Arguably this prejudice continued when under Forbes Burnham and later Desmond Hoyte, the election outcomes in 1968, 1973, 1980, and 1985 were attributed to election manipulation. Failure to do anything about the lack of free and fair election meant that the supporters of Jagan, especially the Indo-Guyanese, were disenfranchised.[11] This is not to suggest that regional leaders had decisive power, but rather that they decided to not use what clout they possessed.

Under the tyrannical rule of President Burnham, there were innumerable accusations of discrimination emanating from the Indo-Guyanese, many of whom received low wages in the sugar industry and few incentives in the rice industry during the 1960s.[12] This prejudice coupled with the Afrocentric ideology promoted by Burnham forced thousands of Indo-Guyanese into exile in Canada. Social conditions worsened in the early 1980s as food shortages coincided with a rapid deterioration of social and public services. The political solution was repression. For example, the assassination of Walter Rodney in 1980 demonstrated the horrific victimization endured by political opponents.

As a brief tangent, the supposed Afro-right-to-govern was repeated in 2020 when President David Granger falsely claimed victory in Guyana's national elections, which was associated with violence against Indo-Guyanese.[13] Granger was head of A Partnership for National Unity (APNU) and formed a coalition with the Alliance for Change (AFC), largely comprising Afro-Guyanese. He had been forced, due to international pressure, to concede victory to the opposition party comprising mostly persons of Indian descent.

The Limit of Public Representation

Suspicion does not only manifest during elections and other "big political contests." There is also a quotidian component to nationalism. Due to their ethnicity, religion, or race, portions of the Caribbean population are treated as second class citizens. These features become liabilities for Indo-Caribbeans and other minorities as they seek to attain recognition for their accomplishments. For example, in the postcolonial era, Afrocentric nationalists in the Caribbean have (selectively) sought to remove physical reminders of colonialism and imperialism. The change in the names of streets, highways, buildings, and parks were cosmetic efforts to establish a Caribbean identity. For instance, in 2017 Queen Street in the capital of Trinidad and Tobago was changed to Queen Janelle Commissiong Street to honor a former Miss Universe who is an Afro-Trinidadian.[14] In 2020 the "Park Street Extension" at Skinner's Park in South Trinidad was renamed the Dennis "Sprangalang" Hall Street.[15] This was to honor a comedian who is of African descent.

However, those who adhere to the goal of replacement of names and monuments too often overlook that identity is inherently social. They are not, and cannot be, created in isolation. So while decisions to change a national award from the Trinity Cross to Order of Trinidad and Tobago and the ongoing debate over removing the Christopher Columbus statue in Port-of-Spain might be important for citizens, if this is all there is to the recent debates about identity, then these debates are about appearances, not the substantive content of identity.[16] To put it more provocatively, how can changing a national award create a more materially inclusive society? Can the removal of a statue decrease levels of poverty and unemployment?

Interlocuters might respond and say this framing is unfair, that these projects have different aims. But that is precisely my point. These aims are adjacent to a politics first and foremost interested in a massive material reconfiguration of relations of power, a politics less interested in removing statues and more interested in removing the present hierarchies that presently marginalize people of working-class origin in a way that all but ensures that their interpretation of social life is excluded from official public history.

Consider Ali Mazrui's remarks that "Eric Williams believed in the unity of the two parts of Trinidad's ethnic dualism: the Afro and Indo components."[17] But this hagiography exaggerates Williams's inclusive embrace of Indo-Trinbagonians. The silencing of minorities was most evident during the 1960s when the Indo-Trinidadians endured significant institutional and interpersonal racism.[18] It is not uncommon to find memories like those of Ramnarine Binda, a working-class Indo-Trinidadian of central Trinidad. He recalled the remarks of a People's National Movement (PNM) government minister, an Afro-Trinbagonian, who attended a cultural reception held at Caroni County Council. On viewing the cultural performance the government minister said, "I see you have an Indian orchestra on here. Where do you think you are[,] India?"[19] Another illustration of inequity is Trevor Sudama, a former politician, who has been pilloried for highlighting the institutionalized discrimination against Indo-Trinbagonians in public service, access to funding, and allocation of funding for culture.[20] Sudama was part of a multiracial political party, the National Alliance of Reconstruction, that formed the government of Trinidad and Tobago in 1986, but soon the majority of Indo-Trinidadians comprising the cabinet experienced discrimination in appointments and treatment. They departed the cabinet to form another party. Such actions reinforce the view of scholars like Ralph Premdas who identified the "deep ethnically rooted sectionalism" that was prevalent in Trinidad.[21] Altogether this kind of discrimination seems to contradict the view of Orlando Patterson, a Jamaican scholar, who maintains that "West Indian nationhood has been a political failure, but it is not a cultural failure."[22] There is certainly a politics to culture, and this politics tends to exclude minority cultures, suggesting that their beliefs, values, and traditions have little place in modern Caribbean societies.

There are looping effects to the interplay of Afrocentric ideology like an entrenchment into ethnic particularity. This double movement has found a fertile political environment in Trinidad and Tobago. In 1993 Basdeo Panday, former opposition leader in the Parliament and trade unionist, in an address to a conference on the East Indians, contended: "Generally speaking, the Indian has been so cowed that the African feels no sense of shame or double standards in condemning white racism in South Africa with all his might while in the same breath calling the Indian a racist for daring to raise the question of African racism against Indians. In the past the Indian has always been on the defensive on the issue of racism against him in Trinidad and Tobago. There were many who felt inferior, physically, if not mentally."[23]

Less than a year later, in April 1994, Panday candidly confessed, "You know there is a strong perception in the society that you cannot trust an Indian to run the country. You cannot allow him to become Prime Minister."[24] Prem Misir sought to explain the rationale of this racism: "The African elite's technique was to create a mass hysteria among Africans on the possibility of a loss of political patronage to the average African, should Trinidad and Tobago fall into the hands of an East Indian prime minister."[25] Not surprisingly, public shaming of persons who highlight racism is an effort to humiliate and maintains an atmosphere of overt racism. Winston Dookeran, another Indo-Trinidadian, made a similar observation that the Indian segment of the population in Trinidad and Tobago are "relegated to the periphery of cultural and political developments."[26] In 2005 Kamla Persad-Bissessar, then leader of the opposition in the Parliament of Trinidad and Tobago, publicly expressed disapproval that the Caribbean Court of Justice lacked any judges of Indian descent. For many Indo-Caribbean persons it was unacceptable, but there was no viable means to air their grievances. Even if some protested over this discrimination, their actions and comments would be ignored. It is this distorted psyche that desperately clings to colonial vestiges and views the Privy Council in the United Kingdom as being able to provide the best forum for fairness and justice.

As I have alluded to, my central point is that most of the recent history of the Caribbean has been rewritten and reshaped to largely reflect the contributions and struggles of Afro-Caribbean persons. Two illustrations include popular textbooks such as *Caribbean Slavery in the Atlantic World* and *Caribbean Freedom: Economy and Society from Emancipation to the Present*.[27] Even positive, uplifting songs such as "Caribbean Man," sung by Black Stalin in 1979, were aimed at men of African descent.[28] This partial portrayal of the Caribbean leaves little space for minorities, let alone how majorities and minorities work to cocreate a polity where equality is prioritized above all else. Without a larger inclusive project where the Afro-Caribbean majority does not set the terms of inclusion, where the barometer of fair change is how minorities get to alter the society to such a degree that it cannot be described as Afrocentric in any respect, it is little wonder that portions of the Indo-Caribbean communities themselves have been swayed by the Hindutva that has emanated from India.[29] Granted, considerable funds have been put at the disposal of people who promulgate Hindutva—this ideology has transnational ambitions—and most certainly Indo-Caribbean people have agency about their beliefs, but there are also social forces that explain why these people might make for a ready audience. Culture can be harnessed for solidarity, or it can be used as a wedge issue.

Race as a Wedge Issue

As the postcolonial era matured, the intensification of racial, ethnic, and cultural politics eroded the progress that these three writers reference. The reasons for these changes are many and multifaceted, but one contributing factor is the broad retreat into essentialist racial ideologies, ideologies that political actors managed to harness to great effect. The result is that the current West Indian political class shares many of the same attitudes and beliefs as officials from the colonial era. This is a heavy charge, but one that can be evidenced when examining how the political and economic elites attempt to permanently improve the living conditions of the poorest Caribbean people. Instead politics is treated as a venue for self-aggrandizement and self-enrichment. C. L. R. James identified such people as "political fast talkers" and "turncoats," stressing the need for "rapid evaluation and expulsion of old fakers and new ones."[30] While there are crucial differences between James's time and ours, political fast talkers remain practiced at stoking racial divisions for their own ends.

Much of what I am alluding to can be described as the decline in the quality of party politics in the Caribbean. Still, there would be little utility in stoking racial resentments if it did not appeal to constituents. Additionally, given the general conditions of precarity of the West Indies, politics tends to be about capturing the government to distribute state tenders, housing, and targeting financial assistance programs to supporters. So even if portions of the electorate are not deeply invested in racial antagonisms, affiliating with a party that has a racial agenda is another way to potentially improve a situation if that party is successful at the polls. Perhaps to push the argument a bit more, even more so than when James was writing his polemics, the agenda of party politics has narrowed and become ever more about petty squabbles, all financed by "big men" who would gain much if their party gained power. In short, racial antagonisms are amplified precisely because these wedges are proven pathways for success at the ballot box.

Another set of wedge issues involves religion. In most Caribbean countries there is the unchallenged belief that it is the prerogative of Christians to shape moral, ethnic, and social values. To be blunt, there is little tradition of secularism in the Anglo-Caribbean. The result of the Christian imprint through colonialism has undeniably meant that religious minorities face inequalities, with their religion reasonings sidelined in government decision-making. The normalization of the Christian gaze may not be directly causally related to acts of religious bigotry, but it certainly does not speak to a social climate in which minority religions are not deemed of equal status to Christianity.

As there are few empirical studies on the matter, it is hard to track whether bigotry is advancing relative to other periods; still, there have been recent notable instances where religious iconography has been destroyed. For instance, in 2018 temples were vandalized in central Trinidad.[31] Additionally, in 2022 another Hindu space was desecrated.[32] These attacks are a disturbing phenomenon that displays much more than a lack of tolerance.[33]

Much like race shapes political affiliation, so does bigotry influence voting patterns. Returning to Trinidad and Tobago, it is a common enough belief that Christians were reticent to support the United National Congress when Basdeo Panday, a Hindu, led the party. The same sentiment exists at the moment for Kamal Persad-Bissessar, also a Hindu, as she occupies the leader's position. Altogether adherents to Rastafarianism, Hinduism, Orisha, Shango, Obeah, and Vodun have been stereotyped by the Christian gaze; herein their rituals or religious practices by these minorities are typically framed as "backward" and "primitive." Certainly there are activists who are making the public case that Obeah and Vodun were used by the enslaved and thus form part of the region's history culture.[34] But with all these kinds of laudable efforts, there are still enduring press reports of students with dreadlocks being denied entry to primary and secondary schools in Jamaica and Trinidad and Tobago.[35]

Islam has also been subject to prejudice. Following the 1990 attempted coup in Trinidad and Tobago, there has been a Christian moral panic about the "spread of radical Islam." Indeed, Islamic religious leaders are frequently spoken of as being the root cause of narco-capitalism. Unevidenced claims like this make it easier for the Christian public to believe outlandish reports, like that in 2017 Trinidad and Tobago had "the greatest number of foreign terrorist fighters in the region to Iraq and Syria on a per capita basis."[36] Sadly these ridiculous claims have real consequences. For example, in 2018 a Muslim teacher wearing a hijab was barred from teaching at a Hindu school in Trinidad.[37]

To draw all these points together, while these dynamics are not confined to countries like Guyana and Trinidad and Tobago, the general result is that parties tend to lack an explicit political-economic agenda; or to put it differently, parties have been able to naturalize a merger between race-based nationalism and southern neoliberalism in which the latter component is overshadowed by the former. The degree to which this is true can be seen in states like Saint Lucia and Saint Vincent and the Grenadines. Here the party politics are "contested within the context of variations of the traditional ideologies inherited from the Eurocentric models."[38] In summary, charismatic leaders deploy brute versions of nationalism because of the broader agreement in the political class about the general desirably of southern neoliberalism. Returning to the theme about the continuities between James's era and ours, the emergence in the postwar era of charismatic politics remains a central feature of Caribbean societies and their political culture.[39]

Class Structure and Revolt

In *Beyond a Boundary* C. L. R. James contended, "I haven't the slightest doubt that the clash of race, caste and class did not retard but stimulated West Indian cricket."[40] Likewise, Clem Seecharan noted that cricket during the colonial era served "to shape the rudiments of a national consciousness."[41] Sport was also important among the Indo-Caribbean population. Indo-Guyanese cricketer Rohan Kanhai played a pivotal role in shaping the ethnic consciousness of many Indians, the same with Sonny Ramadhin, an Indo-Trinbagonian who was a renowned spin bowler of the West Indian cricket team. Seecharan captured the feeling in the early 1960s: "Little boys would crudely extract pictures of Kanhai from the *Argosy*, the *Chronicle* or the *Graphic* and casually paste them amidst the pictures of Hindu deities on the walls of their homes," while Claudius Fergus maintains that "Ramadhin was symbolic of a new cultural visibility for Indians as part of the wider Caribbean society on equal terms with other ethnic groups."[42] James, Seecharan, and Fergus have good cause to credit these conditions for a particular kind of cultural dynamism, as evident in sport and some other practices. However, if they were writing today, would they reach the same conclusion?

The Anglo-Caribbean has a peculiar history that "has been traditionally ruled by white oligarchies who distributed power, privilege, and prestige on the basis of gradations in skin colour."[43] David Baronov and Kevin Yelvington contended, "The lasting legacy of colonialism, the plantation system, and slavery has been the European fixation on race and the notion of *whiteness*."[44] In this racial ordering, lighter-skinned people are deemed more attractive, treated with more respect, and entitled to social credence. The benefits of whitening yield such advantages to employment prospects and promotion that skin bleaching in Jamaica is a large industry.[45]

It is this racial ordering, and the capitalist political economy from which it emerged, that were the central targets of decolonization in the British West Indies. This is not to deny that this process was easy—far from that. At the end of the nineteenth century and in the first half of the twentieth, the Black intelligentsia and the educated French Creole were among the leading protagonists in the movement for West Indian self-determination, a phenomenon Dylan Kerrigan addresses in his chapter in this collection. They denounced Crown Colony government and campaigned for constitutional reform. Among these colored and Black reformers were lawyers who were educated at British institutions and returned to lead the Caribbean's reform initiatives.

The composition of the Caribbean class structure has altered since independence. In the post–World War II era, the term "working class" was synonymous with trade unions and those involved in manual and lowly paid mental labor, while the upper and middle classes were defined by their wealth and occupational status. Rodney sought to explain the economic transition that unfolded in the Anglophone Caribbean: "The pattern is that a predominantly African (and mulatto) professional, bureaucratic and careerist political element has strategic control over the state. They can thus raise their own level relative to the better established sectors of the West Indian petty bourgeoisie, such as the Syrian, Jewish, Chinese or Indian merchants and the French Creole or Indian landed proprietors." Rodney further identified their inadequacy, which influenced the desire for political power: "the new petty bourgeoisie have no immediate base in production and hence their need to maintain political hegemony."[46] Yet from the 1970s onward, riding the oil boom and the rise of neoliberalism, some workers in Trinidad and Tobago and other Caribbean countries were redescribed as having and given some semblance of middle-class status. Yet the change in status did little to offset inflation and other more fundamental economic problems, which have made it harder to sustain that moniker. Presently there is much talk about middle-class decomposition, but in practice this is little more than reality asserting itself—that in a capitalist political economy most people are forced to sell their labor to reproduce themselves. Concurrently, small business owners and well-paid professionals are quickly retreating to gated communities, a telling development about the anticipated fallout from a capitalist political economy that immiserates many.

The effects of Anglo-Caribbean class structure once again became obvious during the COVID-19 pandemic, especially when it came to "essential workers." Typically, lighter-skinned and wealthier persons were able to weather lockdowns in their gated communities and continue their work remotely.[47] Conversely, darker-skinned and poorer persons had to subject themselves to the risk of infection on public transport to even arrive at work—that is, unless they were laid off because the kinds of work they did could not be done remotely. These differences also manifested in one's relative position within the "vaccine hierarchy": wealthier persons with connections were able to get vaccinated fairly early when AstraZeneca and Pfizer vaccines became available. However, when mass public vaccination programs were rolled out, it was suggested that workers accept the Sinopharm vaccines, which were coded as being of inferior quality.

My goal here is to not adjudicate the efficacy of any one vaccine regimen. Rather, the point is to highlight how workers felt aggravated that the wealthy received preferential treatment.[48] These perceptions were reinforced when press reports circulated in Trinidad and Tobago that in June 2021, four hundred two-dose vaccines from the United States were secretly sent as a small gift to the Ministry of National Security.[49] The subsequent exposure of this "gift" resulted in a public scandal of favoritism and again revealed that some privileged persons would have access to Pfizer's vaccines. These types of inequities mirror a society with inequities and an absence of social justice. Granted, by August 2021 some of these specific inequalities became somewhat moot as the United States donated thousands of Pfizer vaccines to the Caribbean.[50] However, working-class memories are long, especially when everyday treatment reminds workers that they cannot practice their rights in the same way as the wealthy.

Conclusion

The Caribbean has been described as a "collection of satellites" linked to foreign spheres of power like the United States, Spain, and the Netherlands.[51] Certainly these foreign powers maintain mechanisms of control, most visibly in places like Aruba, Bermuda, Puerto Rico, and the Turks and Caicos.[52] Yet the Caribbean's social structure is neither fixed nor permanent. But remaking this social structure and the social relations to and around it requires an inclusive radical critique attentive to local circumstances. For instance, the labor movement in the Caribbean has experimented with Fabianism, socialism, and communism and dabbled with Black Power, but the unions have never developed a unique, comprehensive ideology tailored to the region. This is not to claim that other experiences cannot help inform strategy and tactics, but rather that these need to complement local conditions. Similarly, whether in the United Kingdom, the United States, or Canada, a highly selective diasporic romanticism perpetuates soft-nationalist narratives that blunt the cross-racial solidarities required to generate a politics that assist West Indians in remaking their societies such that there is less pressure to migrate.

Returning to the central theme of this chapter, in the early twenty-first century a narrow nationalist historiography is more likely to exacerbate already existing social divisions than to be a source of deep and meaningful solidarity. Sadly, the culture and art forms of ethnic minorities in the Caribbean are given token appreciation as their culture is celebrated and showcased in special events or for entertainment purposes. Their culture is only valued when adhering to Afrocentric first principles. The source of this politics of history reflects ethnic entrepreneurialism with its promise of scaling the existing commanding heights, not the promise to build a progressive civilization.

While there are many other factors that can and do help explain why radical structural critiques of capitalism tend not to have public purchase, the dominance of a narrow historiography that gives little space to the work of non-Black, non-Anglo-White groups hinders the development of histories in which all people in the Caribbean can see themselves. For Caribbean history to be everyone's story, we must work to ensure that everyone is given their place. This is the basic orientation for a historiography of solidarity that Scott Timcke discusses in the introduction to this collection.

NOTES

The author would like to thank Scott Timcke for his advice and input on this chapter.

1. See Catherine Brown, "Myth, History, and the Idea of the Nation in Derek Walcott and V. S. Naipaul," *Studies in Ethnicity and Nationalism* 20 (2020): 267–86.

2. See Stanley Griffin and Scott Timcke, "Re-framing Archival Thought in Jamaica and South Africa: Challenging Racist Structures, Generating New Narratives," *Archives and Records* 43, no. 1 (2022): 1–17.

3. See O. Nigel Bollard, "Creolisation and Creole Societies: A Cultural Nationalist View of Caribbean Social History," *Caribbean Quarterly* 44, nos. 1–2 (1998): 1–32.

4. See Woodville Marshall and Bridget Brereton, "Historiography of Barbados, the Windward Islands, Trinidad and Tobago, and Guyana," in *General History of the Caribbean*, ed. B. W. Higman (New York: Palgrave Macmillan, 2003), 544–603.

5. Philip Sherlock, "Reflections on Changing Perspectives of the West Indian Past," in *Face of Man: The Dr. Eric Williams Memorial Lectures, 1983–1992* (Port-of-Spain: Central Bank of Trinidad and Tobago, 1994), 76.

6. Gerad Tikasingh, *Trinidad during the 19th Century: The Indian Experience* (La Romaine: RPL, 2013), ix.

7. Percy Hintzen, "Cheddi Jagan (1918–97): Charisma and Guyana's Challenge to Western Capitalism," in *Caribbean Charisma: Reflections on Leadership, Legitimacy and Populist Politics*, ed. Anton Allahar (Kingston: Ian Randle, 2001), 125.

8. Trevor Sudama, *The Political Uses of Myth or Discrimination Rationalized: A Collection of Articles* (San Fernando: Battlefront, 1993), 70.

9. See editorials: "Red Intrigue in B.G.," *Trinidad Guardian*, October 7, 1953, 6; "Wanted—A Dash of Caution," *Trinidad Guardian*, October 13, 1953, 6.

10. "Editorial," *Trinidad Guardian*, October 9, 1953.

11. Clem Seecharan, "The Anatomy of Cheddi Jagan's Marxism," in *Calcutta to Caroni and the Indian Diaspora*, ed. John La Guerre and Ann Marie Bissessar (Saint Augustine: School of Continuing Studies, 2005), 424. See also Ralph Premdas, "Ethnic Conflict in the Caribbean: The Case of Guyana," in *The Enigma of Ethnicity: An Analysis of Race in the Caribbean and the World*, ed. Ralph Premdas (Saint Augustine: School of Continuing Studies, 1993), 155–79.

12. See Patrick Dial, "History of Indians in Guyana since 1945," in *Global Indian Diaspora: Yesterday, Today and Tomorrow*, ed. Jagat Motwani, Mahin Gosine, and Jyoti Barot-Motwani (New York: Global Organization of Peoples of Indian Origin, 1993).

13. Editorial, "Guyana: Granger Re-Elected amidst Voter Fraud Charges," *St. Kitts and Nevis Observer*, March 6, 2020, https://www.thestkittsnevisobserver.com/guyana-granger-re-elected-amidst-widespread-voter-fraud-charges/, accessed June 28, 2021.

14. Marlene Augustine, "Queen Street to Be Renamed on September 22," *Newsday*, September 1, 2017, https://newsday.co.tt/2017/09/01/queen-street-to-be-renamed-on-september-22/.

15. Stacy Moore, "'Sprang' Immortalised with Street Sign," *Newsday*, November 19, 2020, https://newsday.co.tt/2020/11/19/sprang-immortalised-with-street-sign/.

16. Michelle Loubon, "Calls for Removal of Columbus Statue," *Trinidad Express*, June 16, 2020, https://trinidadexpress.com/news/local/calls-for-removal-of-columbus-statue/article_2785e2b8-b039-11ea-b1fe-cf0de0c7a273.html, accessed July 10, 2021.

17. Ali Mazrui, "On the Eve of the New Millennium—Challenges Ahead for Dual Societies: From Cyprus to Trinidad and Tobago," in *Face of Man*, 63.

18. See H. P. Singh, *The Indian Struggle for Justice and Equality against Black Racism in Trinidad and Tobago (1956–1962)* (Couva: Indian Review Press, 1993).

19. Ramnarine Binda, *Courage in Caroni: The Autobiography of Ramnarine Binda* (Arima: Saffire, 2008), 122.

20. Trevor Sudama, "Ferdie's Blessed PNM," *Trinidad Guardian*, June 26, 2020, 18.

21. Ralph Premdas, "Elections, Identity and Ethnic Conflict in the Caribbean: The Trinidad Case," *Pouvoirs dans la Caraïbe* (2004): 17.

22. Orlando Patterson, "Ethnicity and Change in the Commonwealth Caribbean," in *Face of Man*, 15.

23. Basdeo Panday, "Address on the Occasion of the Publication of the Proceedings of the Conference of the East Indian Diaspora Committee: On Saturday, October 2, 1993," in *Race Relations in Trinbago: Afro and Indo-Trinbagonians, and Basdeo Panday*, ed. Frankie B. Ramadar (New York: Caribbean Diaspora Press, 1997), 76.

24. Interview with Basdeo Panday, April 7, 1994, at Rienzi Complex, Couva, cited in Samaroo Siewah, *Lotus and the Dagger: The Capildeo Speeches (1957–1994)* (San Juan: Chakra, 1994).

25. Prem Misir, "Basdeo Panday: His Struggle against East Indians as Inverted Racists," in Ramadar, *Race Relations in Trinbago*, 86.

26. Winston Dookeran, "East Indians and the Economy of Trinidad and Tobago," in La Guerre and Bissessar, *Calcutta to Caroni*, 91.

27. Verene Shepherd and Hilary McD. Beckles, eds., *Caribbean Slavery in the Atlantic World: A Student Reader* (Kingston: Ian Randle, 2000); Hilary Beckles and Verene Shepherd, eds., *Caribbean Freedom: Economy and Society from Emancipation to the Present* (Kingston: Ian Randle, 1996).

28. Ramesh Deosaran, "The 'Caribbean Man': A Study in the Psychology of Perception and the Media," *Caribbean Quarterly* 27, nos. 2/3 (1981): 60–95. See also images in Paul A. Davis, "The Black Man and the Caribbean as seen by Nicolas Guillen and Luis Pales Matos," *Caribbean Quarterly* 25, nos. 1/2 (1979): 72–79.

29. Tina Ramnarine, *Creating Their Own Space: The Development of an Indian-Caribbean Musical Tradition* (Kingston: University of the West Indies Press, 2001).

30. C. L. R. James, "Tomorrow and Today: A Vision," n.d., box 1, folder 11, Darcus Howe Papers, Columbia University, 86.

31. Seeta Persad, "Temple Vandalized," *Newsday*, July 9, 2018, https://newsday.co.tt/2018/07/09/temple-vandalized/; "Temple in the Sea Targeted by Vandals," *Loop*, April 19, 2017, https://tt.loopnews.com/content/temple-sea-targeted-vandals.

32. Raphael John Lall, "Thieves Desecrate Carapo Temple, Cook Corned Beef in Their Pot," *Trinidad Guardian*, May 7, 2022.

33. Susan Mohammed, "'We Will Cut Off Your Feet'—Catholic Priest Attacked, Robbed," *Trinidad Express*, September 3, 2018; Gyasi Gonzales, "Suspect Sent to St Ann's," *Trinidad Express*, April 26, 2022.

34. Corey Connelly, "Obeah, They Wukking Obeah!" *Newsday*, October 14, 2018, https://newsday.co.tt/2018/10/14/obeah-they-wukking-obeah/, accessed July 13, 2021.

35. Claude Mills, "Dreadlocked Child's Father Bemoans 'Backward Step' after Court

Ruling," *Loop*, August 1, 2020, https://jamaica.loopnews.com/content/dreadlocked-childs-father-chides-backward-step-after-court-ruling, accessed July 11, 2021.

36. Evan Ellis, "Drugs, Gangs and Radical Islam in a Caribbean Paradise," *Crime Report*, September 12, 2017, https://thecrimereport.org/2017/09/12/drugs-gangs-radical-islam-in-a-caribbean-paradise/.

37. Janelle de Souza, "Faith vs School Rules," *Newsday*, June 2, 2018, https://newsday.co.tt/2018/06/02/faith-vs-school-rules/, accessed July 9, 2021.

38. Kerry Sumesar-Rai, "Crisis of Governance in Small States: Leadership and Ideology in the Anglophone Caribbean," in *Regional Discourses on Society and History: Shaping the Caribbean*, ed. Jerome Teelucksingh and Shane Pantin (New York: Peter Lang, 2020), 133.

39. See Anton Allahar, *Caribbean Charisma: Legitimacy and Political Leadership in the Era of Independence* (Kingston: Ian Randle, 2001).

40. C. L. R. James, *Beyond a Boundary* (London: Stanley Paul, 1990), 72.

41. Clem Seecharan, *Muscular Learning: Cricket and Education in the Making of the British West Indies at the End of the 19th Century* (Kingston: Ian Randle, 2006), 16.

42. Clem Seecharan, *From Ranji to Rohan: Cricket and Indian Identity in Colonial Guyana, 1890s–1960s* (Hertford, U.K.: Hansib, 2009), 178; Claudius Fergus, "The Contribution of Calypso in Transforming Race Relations in Trinidad and the Wider Caribbean through the Subject of Cricket," in Teelucksingh and Pantin, *Regional Discourses*, 99.

43. Anthony Layne, "Race, Class, and Development in Barbados," *Caribbean Quarterly* 25, nos. 1/2 (1979): 40. See also Joseph Ragatz, *The Fall of the Planter Class in the British Caribbean, 1763–1833* (New York: Octagon, 1963), 3.

44. David Baronov and Kevin Yelvington, "Ethnicity, Race, Class and Nationality," in *Understanding the Contemporary Caribbean*, ed. Richard S. Hillman and Thomas J. D'Agostino (Kingston: Ian Randle, 2003), 213.

45. Christopher Charles, "Skin Bleaching, Self-Hate, and Black Identity in Jamaica," *Journal of Black Studies* 33, no. 6 (2003): 711–28.

46. Walter Rodney, "Contemporary Political Trends in the English-Speaking Caribbean," *Black Scholar* 7, no. 1 (September 1975): 17. For the linkages among ethnicity, class, and nationhood, see Jean Grugel, *Politics and Development in the Caribbean Basin* (London: Palgrave, 1995), 61–93.

47. Scott Timcke and Shelene Gomes, "Essentially Disposable," *Exertions: The Magazine of the Society for the Anthropology of Work*, November 2020, https://saw.americananthro.org/pub/essentially-disposable/release/1.

48. Donstan Bonn, "Vaccination Stress: Senior Citizens Caught in the Rain," *Trinidad Express*, June 16, 2021, https://trinidadexpress.com/news/local/vaccination-stress-senior-citizens-caught-in-the-rain/article_d61e4a2c-cf05-11eb-9e33-3b301567b505.html, accessed July 13, 2021.

49. Renuka Singh, "Hinds Gets 400 Pfizer Doses for His Ministry from U.S.," CNC3, June 13, 2021, https://www.cnc3.co.tt/hinds-gets-400-pfizer-doses-for-his-ministry-from-us/, accessed July 11, 2021.

50. "U.S. to Deliver Nearly 837K Pfizer Vaccines to Caribbean," *U.S. News and World Report*, August 11, 2021, https://www.usnews.com/news/us/articles/2021-08-11/us-to-deliver-nearly-837k-pfizer-vaccines-to-caribbean, accessed August 19, 2021.

51. Kirk Meighoo, "Organic Theorising in Inorganic Societies, or the Need for Epistemic Sovereignty beyond Radicalism and Rebellion," in *The Thought of New World: The Quest for Decolonisation*, ed. Brian Meeks and Norman Girvan (Kingston: Ian Randle, 2010), 128.

52. See Guy Lasserre and Albert Mabileau, "The French Antilles and Their Status as Overseas Departments," in *Patterns of Foreign Influence in the Caribbean*, ed. Emanuel De Kadt (New York: Oxford University Press), 82–102; Harry Hoetink, "The Dutch Caribbean and Its Metropolis," in De Kadt, *Patterns of Foreign Influence*, 103–20.

PART FOUR

LOCAL POLITICS AND INTERNATIONAL PRESSURES

CHAPTER 13

The Background of Guyana's 2020 Election Impasse

DUANE EDWARDS

On March 2, 2020, Guyana held what many expected to be the most significant election in the postindependent period. The election would decide which of the two ethnic-based parties would govern the country in the context of new oil wealth. Even without a history of continual low-intensity ethnic conflicts and intermittent high-intensity upsurges, such an election would have been significant in any country transitioning to a new economic phase which many experts predicted would see tremendous positive increases in GDP.[1] The event took on added significance in Guyana, however, because there was an expectation that with the stakes so high, the losing party would find it difficult to concede defeat, and this would push the country into open conflict.[2]

When the elections were called on March 2, 2020, everything went well. Domestic and international observers published statements in support of the free and fair nature of the election up to a certain point.[3] That point was four days after the elections on March 6, when the statements of poll (SOPs) of the largest region were being tallied. By that time, the People's Progressive Party/Civic (PPP/C) was leading the incumbent, A Partnership for National Unity and Alliance for Change (APNU+AFC), by over fifty thousand votes. The general view was that although the last region traditionally went to the People's National Congress (PNC) now part of the APNU+AFC coalition, it was impossible for that gap to be bridged resulting in a victory for the APNU+AFC. While tallying the SOPs for the last region, a string of suspicious events unfolded. These include the Returning Officer for Region Four falling ill on March 4, the insistence on using spreadsheets as opposed to statements of polls for the tallying and corroboration process, and the presentation of numbers via the spreadsheet that deviated from what were printed on the SOPs in the presence of political parties and domestic and external observers.

It became obvious by then that attempts at rigging the elections were underway and that interventions would have to be made to interrupt this process. Interventions took the form of court injunctions, strongly worded warnings from the ABC-EU countries (America, Britain, Canada, and the European Union), and street protests by supporters of the opposition. In a joint statement on March 5, 2020, heads of the U.S. Embassy, the Canadian High Commission, and the British High Commission in Guyana remarked: "Based on our observation of today's GECOM proceedings at their Region 4 office, and the fact that the full count was not completed, we question the credibility of the Region 4 results published by GECOM today. . . . We urge the Guyana Elections Commission, and all relevant actors, to expeditiously complete the tabulation on the basis of the statement of polls."[4] The Private Sector Commission which was accorded domestic observer status expressed similar sentiments: "The Private Sector Commission urges the Chairman, Chief Elections Officer, and the Returning Officer of Region Four to conclude the process in a transparent manner as quickly as possible to enable Guyanese as individuals and the economy to return to normalcy."[5] Under pressure from the International Community, the President invited the Caribbean Community (CARICOM) to supervise a recount of the votes in the presence of all stakeholders. CARICOM, headed by Mia Motley, Prime Minister of Barbados, quickly acquiesced to the request and dispatched a team of scholars and experts to oversee the recount. The process was initially aborted because of a court injunction filed by a supporter of the incumbent, acting in the capacity of a private citizen. The Court of Appeal decided that the Guyana Elections Commission (GECOM) was the only constitutional authority to supervise an election recount.[6] Any role being played by CARICOM would have to be limited to observing rather than supervising the recount. CARICOM was forced to leave while the case was before the court. After the conclusion of the matter in the Court of Appeal, CARICOM, tasked with a new mandate, returned on May 1, 2020, to observe the recount.[7] The recount revealed that barring some irregularities the PPP/C won the elections by approximately ten thousand votes, equivalent to a one-seat majority in the national assembly. Although all parties agreed to the recount, the incumbent challenged the legitimacy of the recount in court. The legitimacy was, however, upheld by the court. After exhausting all means to remain in power, the incumbent was forced to relinquish power on August 2, 2020, exactly five months after the elections on March 2, 2020.

It is important to note that while these electoral and constitutional matters were being played out at the highest levels, the citizens were divided in their support for the two major parties. Preliminary observation showed that with some differences, most Afro-Guyanese organizations and individuals supported the government in various ways. They either accepted and promoted the narrative of rigged elections by the PPP/C by means of multiple voting, favoritism by the international community towards the PPP/C, or they called for some form of power sharing which would see the incumbent not totally losing power.[8] On the other side, most Indo-Guyanese institutions and individuals called for the strict adherence to the "rules of the game" which would have clearly seen the new government coming to power.[9] It is important to note that the point about the split in opinion mostly along ethnic lines depends only on casual observation of opinions being expressed in the public sphere. The accuracy of this observation will have to be tested by a systematic sentiment analysis of opinions in the public sphere during the period in question.

The differences of opinion, though largely played out via the press and the digital social media, erupted in violence in one instance in which a predominantly Indo-Guyanese community protested the attempt to rig the elections in favor of a predominantly Afro-Guyanese party.[10] That one instance of violence notwithstanding, the high-intensity conflict which was expected, as mentioned above, was averted by the use of the judicial system as the main institutional mechanism to settle disputes.[11]

The conflict which arose postelection and which was brewing since the no-confidence motion in December 2018 has two dimensions: a political dimension and an ethnic dimension. The current study focuses on the ethnic dimension by highlighting the social and structural forces which provided the support systems for the two factions in the conflict. It is my opinion that without this social/structural support system, the behavior of the political factions would have been different even with looming oil wealth. The support system serves as a necessary condition for social conflict. It is essential, therefore, to subject this support system to sociological analysis.

The purpose of this chapter is to offer a sociological explanation of the election crisis and the tendency for the society to swing from low- to high-intensity conflict every electoral cycle. I put forward two main postulates. The first is that the social "substructure" of the society predisposes the society to conflicts along ethnic lines. By social substructure, I mean the specific way various modes of division are stacked upon each other more or less coincidingly.

This postulate goes a little further than general claims about ethnic diversity and conflicts. The claim being made here is that it is not ethnic diversity itself which predisposes societies to ethnic conflicts, but the degree to which ethnicity coincides with other modes of division in society. The novelty of this postulate is that it goes beyond the assumption that the very existence of different groups in the society predisposes the society to conflict. The problematic factor is the way the groups are arranged with respect to other critical social divisions. Stressing this point in the context of Guyana is important to policy conceptualization. The policy implication of this postulate shifts the focus from elite-based solutions to mass-oriented solutions as will be expounded on in the final section of the chapter. Secondly, I argue that the institutional domains (namely economy and polity) are incongruous with solidarity-building outcomes. They therefore exacerbate rather than ameliorate conflicts. Lastly, I argue that based on the two postulates above, the most sustainable approach to mitigating ethnic conflicts lies in social structural transformation.

After a brief review of the ethnic conflict literature I provide a descriptive analysis of the social structure of the Guyanese society using data from the most recent 2012 National Census. The extent to which ethnicity coincides, stacks upon, or is overdetermined by other modes of differentiation in the society is demonstrated by a brief vignette. Next I argue that the two main institutional domains—namely the economy and polity—exacerbate rather than ameliorate the existing social conflict. The chapter concludes with a discussion on how Guyana could transition from being characterized by a conflict-generating social system to a solidarity-building system.

Ethnic Conflict and Its Causes

The literature on ethnic conflict and its causes is a very rich one. The richness of the literature is justified by the fact that many modern societies are ethnically plural and experience some measure of ethnic conflict ranging from low-intensity, nonviolent conflicts to high-intensity, very violent conflicts. In attempting to arrive at an understanding of the essential causes of ethnic conflicts, scholars have come up with various hypotheses and theories. The most popular of these will be engaged with in this section of the chapter.

Writings on ethnic conflict in Guyana take various forms in terms of the factors used to explain conflict. There are about four main factors identified as critical in explaining ethnic conflicts in plural societies. These are resource competition, social segmentation, outside intervention, and political institutions.

The resource competition hypothesis is among the dominant hypotheses used to explain ethnic conflicts. The argument provided is that when a country is beset by scarcity of resources, groups in the society tend to mobilize along ethnic lines with the intent of securing their economic fortunes. Ethnic identity is instrumentally invoked in pursuit of collective action because of the competitive advantages attached to this collective action solution. The literature suggests that ethnic elites use the state and other political machines to direct resources to their own ethnic constituency. The economic competition perspective seems to be the dominant perspective in Guyana, which suggests that better economic circumstances will inevitably breed better ethnic relations.[12]

Quite related to the resource competition hypothesis is the external intervention hypothesis. While the former focuses on the internal dynamics of the various ethnic groups competing for economic resources through the capture of the state, another focuses on the role international capitalist organizations play in influencing the nature of these conflicts.[13] Percy Hintzen has argued that international capitalist firms either directly or indirectly influence ethnic conflicts in developing countries through preferential relations with select groups or with the state captured and controlled by select groups within a country, thus enhancing the relative position of that group to other groups and increasing the potential for ethnic conflict and communal confrontation. Working within the theoretical framework of world systems theory, Perry Mars explains how ethnic conflict is related to and accentuated by poverty and the immiseration of the state whose legitimacy is undermined because of its inability to respond to the material and security needs of the population.[14] For Mars, conflict arises out of the tension between the demands of global capitalism on one hand and the demands of the local state and other important domestic groups on the other hand. Though Mars recognizes the centrality of class-related issues in generating ethnic conflicts, he concedes that the ethnic manifestation of such conflict could only be possible in societies with preexisting segmentation.

This preexisting segmentation is problematized by the social segmentation scholarship. As an alternative to the resource hypothesis, these scholars have broadened their analysis to ascribe equal weight to noneconomic factors as explanatory variables.[15] They argue that ethnic affiliation and conflict are driven by claims of a more collective nature rather than the individualistic nature implied by the resource competition hypothesis. Marko Klašnja and Natalija Novta draw attention to how ethnic segregation fuels ethnic conflict.[16] Robert Milne argues that in socially segmented or bicommunal societies some semblance of stability could be maintained through the hegemonic rule of one section over the other.[17] The presence and absence of conflict need not be a result of the distribution of economic resources. He highlights other factors which lead to conflict in ethnically segmented societies. Among these are external intervention, geographic concentration of ethnic groups, and the potential for secessionist calls and activities.

In addition to the postulates above, there is the institutionalist hypothesis which emphasizes the role the absence of critical institutions plays in engendering ethnic conflicts. Institutions develop as a prescriptive system of sanctions. They specify acceptable forms of behavior and provide rewards and punishments as ways of reinforcing conformist behavior. Whether ethnic differences result in ethnic conflicts depends on the extent to which a country's institutions prescribe and reward cooperation as opposed to conflicts or whether institutional channels are available for the sublimation of conflicts.[18] In line with this hypothesis, various political institutional solutions have been posited for countries beset by ethnic conflicts. These include federation, consociational democracy, alternative vote, among other such interventions. Scholars reacting to this perspective, however, argue that many of the institutional solutions proposed further ethnicize the social and political systems while trying to prevent conflicts in the short term.[19] This leads to more conflict in the long term.

The situation in Guyana is a complex one that exhibits elements from all the above as is with many cases of ethnic conflict.[20] However, without the social substructure characterized by sharp, coinciding borders, the opportunity for ethnic conflict would be slim thus rendering the other contributing factors to ethnic conflict as ineffective. Therefore, the substructure of social segmentation enjoys theoretic priority. This adds to the social segmentation hypothesis by postulating that it is not merely the presence of different social (ethnic, racial) segments that predisposes ethnically plural societies to ethnic conflicts, but how those social segments are organized. It is how they are arranged with respect to other social divisions and differentiations in the society. If they are stacked, more or less coincidingly, on these other divisions the society becomes more prone to conflicts than if they are significant overlaps and intersections. The argument being proffered here, therefore, is that the social substructure in Guyana is characterized by sharp, coinciding borders and as such the country is more predisposed to ethnic conflicts than countries without this coincidence of ethnicity and other modes of social differentiation. Any of the aforementioned factors, namely external intervention, scarcity of resources, religion, could aggravate ethnic conflicts at any time with the least of efforts. The history of the country is replete with examples of the country being pushed to the brink of ethnic conflict by the least prodding by politicians, external interest, and religious leaders. The next section will focus on giving a descriptive analysis of Guyana's social structure with the intent of substantiating the claim that it predisposes the country to ethnic conflicts.

Description of Guyana's Social Structure

Using data from the 2012 National Census, this section describes Guyana's social structure. The census provides data related to the ethnic/racial breakdown in the society, the geographic settlement, and the religious distribution of the various ethnic groups. The conceptual framework provided by Michael Smith which breaks down plural systems into segmental plurality and hierarchical plurality will be adopted here.[21] Under segmental plurality it will be demonstrated that the various ethnic groups are by and large inhabitants of distinct communities and subscribe to distinct systems of social action. The description will focus on how structural factors such as residential, occupational, religious, and political differences coincide with claims of ethnicity. It will go further to highlight how channels of social action such as religion, civil society organization, and political parties are by and large coinciding with claims of ethnicity. This stacked system, with increasing though not sufficient degrees of overlap notwithstanding, creates a social substructure which predisposes the country towards conflicts along ethnic lines. The three main ethnic groups in Guyana are divided geographically, while two of them, namely Africans and East Indians, are also divided largely along political, occupational, and other institutional differences thus resulting in structural plurality.[22]

Segmental Plurality

According to the 2012 National Census, there are seven main ethnic/racial groups in Guyana along with a catch-all category labeled "Other" that captures all other numerically insignificant groups (see table 1). The four numerically significant groups are the Africans, East Indians, Indigenous Peoples, and the Mixed groups. The association of the four groups with various geographic locations could be assessed on various spatial levels and dimensions. One could either use the administrative delineation which is officially used to demarcate the country into ten administrative regions, the hinterland/coastland, rural/urban, or the villages demarcation, or all together.

In prior work I used ethnolinguistic fractionalization index (ELF) to ana-

TABLE 13.1. Distribution of the Population by Ethnicity

Ethnicity	African/Black	Amerindian	Chinese	East Indian	Mixed	Portuguese	White	Other
Number	218,483	78,492	1,377	297,493	148,532	1,910	415	253
Percentage	29.25	10.51	0.18	39.83	19.88	0.26	0.06	0.03

SOURCE: 2012 Population and Housing Census, Guyana

lyze how ethnically homogenous or heterogenous are the various levels of geographic separations. I found that the hinterland areas are dominated primarily by the Indigenous Peoples, and the coastland by Afro-Guyanese and Indo-Guyanese. With respect to the urban/rural divide, I found that both Indo-Guyanese and Afro-Guyanese reside in urban and rural areas although there might be a greater presence of Indo-Guyanese in rural and Afro-Guyanese in urban areas. What is important to note, however, is that the East Indian population makes up 69 percent of the urban population in Region Two and 62 percent of Region Three while the African population accounts for 61 percent of the urban population in Region Ten. The urban population of Region Four which is the numerically largest region is relatively diverse with Afro-Guyanese accounting for a tad over 50 percent of the population. When assessed at the level of the Administrative regions, the results showed that apart from regions 1, 8, 9 which are hinterland regions dominated almost exclusively by Indigenous Peoples, all the other regions are diverse. This regional diversity, however, masks the mono-ethnic nature of the thousands of villages that are scattered across the country. Of the 2,177 villages assessed, approximately two-thirds (1,417) were ethnically homogenous, while one-third were ethnically diverse. This broad association between ethnicity and geographic location predisposes the country to ethnic conflict in two ways. In the first instance it decreases the opportunity for social contact among the various groups. As such, groups hardly share the same primary institutions such as kinship, religion, and culture. Secondly, as found by Elif Koromaz in the case of Istanbul, different residential areas differ in their environmental qualities, development potential, and access to social goods such as education and employment.[23] Ethnic groups living in these areas will therefore be differentially impacted. Negative environmental impact on specific ethnic groups could easily be translated into the language of political discrimination and be used as fodder for ethnic contestation.

Along with this general association between race/ethnicity and geographic settlement specifically at the village level and in some cases at the other levels, there is a similar association between race/ethnicity and religion. Africans subscribe primarily to some version of Christianity, while East Indians subscribe primarily to Hinduism and Islam. Eighty-seven percent of Africans subscribe to one of the many Christian denominations, while 60 percent of East Indians subscribe to Hinduism and 15 percent to Islam. This means that approximately 80 percent of both major groups subscribe to religions that they do not hold in common. Moreover, while 80 percent of Africans share Christianity with sizable cross sections of the other groups, Hinduism and Islam are almost exclusively subscribed to by East Indians. It must be emphasized, however, that because Christianity is multidenominational, sharing the same Christian religion does not necessarily translate into a high probability of common congregation. For the 80 percent of Africans that share Christianity with the 22 percent of East Indians and the over 80 percent of Indigenous Peoples, most Africans are Pentecostals, while Indigenous Peoples are Roman Catholic and East Indians subscribe to a Christian denomination captured by the label "Others." So, while the main groups share Christianity as a common religion, they do not congregate regularly because they subscribe to different Christian denominations.

The breakdown between race/ethnicity and geography and race/ethnicity and religion is important for an assessment of race/ethnicity and kinship. It is through the institution of kinship that racial borders become most blurred by the forging of a physical connection between racial groups through intermarriages and sexual relations.[24] But the probability of this happening depends in no insignificant way on the opportunity for meeting and mixing provided by the other two structural variables highlighted above, namely geographic location and religious denominations. While, as demonstrated above, there is a significant association between race/ethnicity and geography on one hand and race/ethnicity and religion on the other hand which lessens the probability of the racial/ethnic groups interacting with each other outside the marketplace, there are still sizable overlaps that provide opportunities, though limited, for intermixing sexually and maritally.

The census data shows a sizable and growing mixed population in Guyana. There has been a 3 percentage point increase in the mixed race/ethnicity group from the 2002 Census to the most recent 2012 Census. This increase could be the result of two factors. The first is the direct sexual relationships between various ethnic groups. The second is most likely a result of more persons beginning to identify themselves as Mixed as opposed to one of the other racial/ethnic groups. An analysis of the mixed group has revealed that areas with larger percentages of Africans and Indigenous Peoples, irrespective of the makeup of the smaller population in those areas, are more likely to have larger percentages of mixed population as opposed to areas with larger percentages of East Indians. Interethnic kinship relations seem to be more likely in these areas. This could be a result of two factors. The first relates to the urbanity of the areas dominated by Africans particularly but to a lesser extent, Indigenous People. The second factor could be the opportunity of interaction that having common religion affords.

This brief descriptive analysis is sufficient to demonstrate the extent to which the main racial/ethnic groups are not only ethnically divided, but that their ethnic differences are reinforced by structural differences such as geographic location, religion, and kinship. Because of the stacking of these various modes of differentiation, the opportunity for shared experiences, interest, welfare are lower than if these differences intersected. The groups are likely therefore to interpret and react to negative environmental, economic, social, and political experiences through a racial/ethnic lens. If the government of the day reflects a different ethnic makeup from the affected group, this could easily erupt into ethnopolitical conflicts.

Incongruity of the Institutional Domain

The analysis above demonstrates the extent to which the society is an ethnically diverse society. The structural dimension of this diversity results from the organization of the society during the colonial era. Since independence, little changes have been made to the social substructure of the society to the extent that after fifty years of independence, the society's substructure resembles its pre-independence pattern.

In societies that could be labeled complex pluralities according to the characteristics of a complex plurality given by Michael Smith in which structural plurality accords with cultural plurality, leaders, policymakers, and thinkers are faced with various challenges with regards to preventing conflicts and ultimately promoting solidarity and cohesion among the disparate groups.[25] The popular response is to design and implement institutions which would mitigate the tendency towards disintegration. Political scientists proffer such solutions as consociational democracy, federalism, among other political institutional changes.[26] Economists on the other hand call for a more equitable distribution of wealth and the blurring of the lines between race and class. Unfortunately, Guyana remains a complex plurality with political and economic institutions which are inimitable to solidarity across race and ethnicity. In fact, the main economic and political institutions in Guyana exacerbate rather than ameliorate conflicts. The rest of this article seeks to demonstrate this claim.

Comprador Capitalism in a Plural Society

This section of the chapter puts forth two descriptive facts. The first is that the economy is based on resource extraction, primary commodity production, and peripheral service provision. The second is that similar to the social structure, the economic structure is also ethnicized, that is to say, ethnic groups are associated with various occupations and economic activities to the extent government policy which targets a particular sector has direct benefit for a particular ethnic group. These descriptive facts are used as the basis to put forward my main postulate. That is, the institutional domain of the economy exacerbates rather than ameliorates ethnic conflicts. The structure of the economy itself contributes to social volatility in two critical ways. First, the concentration of economic activities in the services sector privileges extractive, appropriative economic behavior as opposed to productive behavior. Secondly, the lack of economic differentiation means that the basis upon which social differentiation is most achievable is lacking. This means that groups are concentrated in a small set of economic sectors rather than dispersed (both vertically and horizontally) across a large set of sectors. Concentration in a small set of sectors translates into identity of economic interests, stakes, and welfare. When these sectors are, by and large, ethnicized, that is to say, associated with identifiable ethnic groups, the social situation becomes more volatile.

Most studies of the relationship between ethnicity and economy focus on the adverse effect ethnic fractionalization has on economic growth and level of income.[27] A subset of this literature establishes a link between the level of ethnic diversity in a society and the nature of economic behavior in the society. More diverse societies lead to higher probability of appropriative and extractive economic behavior, while less diversity leads to higher likelihood of productive economic activities.[28] There is a paucity of literature on the opposite effect, that is, how the structure of the economy affects ethnic conflict. With respect to Guyana, however, DaCosta (2007) demonstrates how the structure of the economy affects the development of institutions and ethnic conflicts. Similarly, Tarron Khemraj demonstrates that the social structure of the economy, that is, how economic agents are spread across a large geographic coastline, negatively affects economic growth and by extension fuels the competition for the scarce resources in the country.[29] Khemraj's study is important as it shows the inverse of the normal relationship posited between society and economy by the earlier theorists cited above. His contribution is important as it demonstrates the extent to which a country could be caught in an underdevelopment trap by the interaction of economy and society. While

Mark DaCosta and Khemraj highlight how the social and geographic structuring of the economy affects growth and how the lack of growth affects ethnic relations, other scholars are teasing out the extent to which the very structure of an economy, irrespective of the level of economic growth, could affect human development and social conflicts.[30]

The resources competition scholarship, as highlighted above, emphasizes the importance of economic growth not only to development but also to social stability. If social conflicts are essentially about the scarcity of resources, then economic growth makes resources available to distribute and stave off social conflicts. Although alternative theories of ethnic conflicts shift focus from purely economic factors, there is no doubt that economic factors play key though not exclusive or ultimate parts in influencing ethnic conflicts. Economically struggling societies hardly have the resources to fund the kinds of high-priced institutions recommended for resolving conflicts. Moreover, if wealth is not created then there is hardly anything available to appease ethnic entrepreneurs who capitalize on the misfortunes of their own group for social and economic rewards. Economic growth is therefore important. Growth without structural differentiation in the economy along the lines argued by Collin Constantine, Tarron Khemraj, Dani Rodrik, and Dominik Hartmann is not sufficient to help resolve conflicts.[31] Because growth without economic structural transformation could lead to a concentration of activities in the appropriative/extractive sectors thus engendering more rather than less ethnic conflicts since, as argued by Osbourne (2000), high productivity in the appropriative sector induces more of it hence the concentration of wealth among the dominant players in that sector.

Quite in the relation to this postulate, there is an emerging literature in development economics which emphasizes the importance of economic complexity to economic and human development. The literature argues that in addition to horizontal diversification, development also calls for vertical sophistication, backward and forward linkages in the productive sector.[32] Dominik Hartmann goes further by positing the positive benefits that economic complexity can have for networking among various groups.[33] Highly complex economies are more likely to effectuate the interaction of various social groups with each other. On the other hand less complex economies will result in identifiable groups being concentrated in particular sectors creating the conditions for favoritism and discrimination.

Economic Structure and Social Transformation

The structure of an economy is revealed in the relationship between three main industrial sectors, namely agriculture, services, and manufacturing. Of the three sectors, as argued above, the manufacturing sector has greater potential of structurally transforming a society as it is the sector most likely to enable a transition from primary commodity production associated with agriculture and peripheral service provision associated with the services sector.[34] Currently, however, the largest sector in the Guyanese economy is the services sector. This sector contributes as much as 70 percent of GDP, while agriculture and industry account for approximately 15 percent each. Services could be broken down into public- and private-sector services. In the private sector, services are by and large characterized by the wholesale and retail of imported goods from advanced capitalist societies. This is followed by the transportation and storage, construction, and financial subsectors.[35] The differential strength of these sectors determines whether groups act "productively" with each other or "appropriatively" against each other (Osbourne 2000). A comparatively larger manufacturing sector creates the environment for intergroup productive relations and activity, while a comparatively larger services sector creates the environment for rent-seeking and appropriative activities. Moreover, the manufacturing sector calls for a wider range of skills and education along a vertical continuum than the services sector. Of the services subsectors highlighted, only the financial services subsector requires a high degree of knowledge and skills. The other sectors are low-skills sectors that employ a larger percentage of their workforce only completing primary and secondary education.[36] This has implications for the degree to which groups are susceptible to political mobilization and manipulation.

While the structure of the economy predisposes the society to ethnic conflicts, this is compounded by the distribution of the ethnic groups throughout certain economic sectors. Although it is generally claimed that Afro-Guyanese dominate the public sector, the data from the most recent census does not confirm this claim. The data shows that Afro-Guyanese are a little overrepresented in the sector, while Indigenous Peoples are underrepresented, and the Indo-Guyanese are consistent with their percentage in the larger society. A similar trend is seen with regards to employment in the private sector. On the other hand, when it comes to business ownership Afro-Guyanese and Indigenous Peoples are generally underrepresented while Indo-Guyanese and Portuguese are overrepresented.[37] The distribution of Indigenous Peoples is roughly in keeping with their percentage in the larger society.

It is the overrepresentation of Afro-Guyanese in the public sector employment and the corresponding overrepresentation of Indo-Guyanese and Portuguese in ownership in the private sector that these sectors come to be associated with the groups in the popular mind. When looked at in terms of industry rather than sectors, a closer association between race/ethnicity and sector/occupation reveals itself. Agriculture is by and large the economic domain of Indo-Guyanese. The same goes for wholesale and retail trade. Afro-Guyanese on the other hand are usually associated with public administration and defense.

This association has influence on government policies at the national level. A recent example is provided by the change of regime in 2015. The PPP/C government had a lackluster approach to the public sector. Wages were largely stagnant, and the minimum wage was $39,570 GYD (equivalent of approximately $200 USD). When the APNU+AFC government took up power in 2015, the approach to the public sector had changed dramatically. Public sector wages had increased an overall 70 percent during the five-year period, the minimum wage was changed from $39,570 in 2015 to $70,000 GYD ($350 USD) in 2019, and a public sector institute was established for the professional training of future public servants.[38] The behavior of the two regimes were different when it came to the private sector. Under the pre-2015 PPP/C government, it is argued that government was used as a means of transferring wealth to what was called a newly emerging private sector, a lackluster attitude towards taxation, and import duties.[39] After 2015 when the government changed, the relationship between the government and the private sector became very strained. There was a vast reduction in the implementation of the Public Sector Investment Programme which focused on public infrastructure and the awarding of contracts to established private firms mostly owned and operated by Indo-Guyanese.[40] What this vignette suggests is that whenever ethnicity is associated with economic sectors and occupations, ruling elites representing one ethnic section attempt to mask ethnic patronage under broad sectoral policies as in the case of the newly elected president signaling his intent to shift economic policy towards strengthening the private sector while deemphasizing the public sector.[41] The concurrent restricting of opportunities for the other ethnic groups in sectors associated with those groups creates incentives for the political representatives of those groups to mobilize their support base through public discourse, street protest, and other types of contestations.

Political System

The political system is another area of ethnic contestation. It is both an outcome of and a contributor to the nature and intensity of ethnic conflicts in Guyana. There are various features of the political system which exacerbate rather than ameliorate conflicts in Guyana.[42] Three that are important to this analysis are the winner-takes-all characteristic of the system, the executive presidency, and the list system. Each of these will be discussed in this section.

WINNER-TAKE-ALL

There is almost a consensus among scholars and researchers that ethnic conflict in ethnically plural societies could be best ameliorated with some form of devolution of power away from the center or power sharing at the center. Whether the form of shared governance takes the form of federalism where each region, province, canton, state enjoy some level of autonomy, Madisonian democracy in which power is decentralized through a separation of power mechanism or executive power sharing, or consociational democracy in which executive power is shared with representatives of minority groups, depends on the particularity of the country or society in question. What is generally accepted, however, is that centralized systems of governance in which one party dominates power spell disaster for societies with ethnic conflict.

Despite this consensus, Guyana's governance system is what is generally described as a winner-take-all system. Many scholars and social commentators pinpoint this political reality as being a main contributor to ethnic conflicts.[43] Whenever a party wins the presidency either by a plurality or majority of the popular votes that party forms the new government. The President of the winning party has the authority to form a cabinet and appoint ministers to the various ministries, albeit from a list voted on by the electorate. S/he has the power to appoint permanent secretaries to the various ministries and commissioners to the various commissions. Jobs in the upper echelon of the public sector fall directly under the control of the executive. Moreover, the awarding of contracts at all levels is either directly or indirectly under the control of the executive. By indirectly, we mean that even when systems are in place to decentralize power, the executive always finds ways to subvert those systems with impunity. The executive therefore exercises tremendous control over the mechanisms through which resources are distributed to the population. It also controls indirectly the said institutions which are expected to check its power and safeguard the rights of the citizenry.[44] This provides a readily available, formal patronage network which is supplemented with less obvious and less official networks of patronage. The subservience of other institutions, agencies, and individuals which result from this patronage system provides an ideal opportunity for ethnic clientelism and consequently ethnic tensions and conflicts.[45] Winner-take-all creates both political and economic losers. Because of the convergence of interest among political elites and losers in the larger society, mainly ethnic elites and masses in this case, political elites are incentivized to engage in the kinds of political rhetoric which paints the government as discriminating to mobilize its own support base. Mobilized by such rhetoric, the ethnic groups which are locked out from the rewards distributed through this system resort to both formal and informal means to contest the skewed distribution of social goods. Evidence of this is provided when there is a change of regime, and the "ethnic cleansing" in the public service accusations and counteraccusations are expressed in the public sphere.[46]

EXECUTIVE PRESIDENCY AND LIST SYSTEM

Related to the winner-take-all characteristic of the system that gives tremendous power to the winning party, Guyana has an executive presidency which is given tremendous power by the constitution of Guyana. This leads to a centralization of power in the hands of one person who enjoys a fair amount of immunity. By itself, "presidentialism implies a single powerful office that tends to generate a strong likelihood of winner-take-all competition between rival ethnies."[47] When this is combined with a system in which persons selected as part of the government (both the executive and legislature) are selected by a list system, it becomes clear why an elected government tends to behave oligarchic and dictatorial further inflaming tensions in the society.[48]

Guyana has a hybrid presidential system and a parliamentary system of governance if one uses the classification provided by Cheibub.[49] As part of the presidential system, the President is elected directly by the electorate by means of a plurality of the popular vote. The President contests the elections as head of his party's list of candidates. The electorate votes for the President and the list *en masse* as opposed to individuals on the list. It is from this list that members are selected to sit in the National Assembly. The elections are therefore simultaneously for the President and for Members of Parliament. At the conclusion of the election, the leader of the list has the power and privilege to decide which of those on the list will represent the party in the Cabinet, in case of a win, and/or in the House. The elected President enjoys a fair amount of power and immunity once elected.

As executive president, the president acts as the head of government and state and commander-in-chief of the army. As head of government, s/he delegates her/his powers to ministers drawn from the list voted on by the electorate. These serve as cabinet members and are answerable directly to the president. The executive president has been bestowed tremendous powers in the 1980 constitution.[50] Subsequent efforts to reform the constitution have marginally affected those powers.[51]

Notwithstanding the extent of executive power, the constitution reposes significant power also in the legislature. The legislature has the power to remove the government if it finds that the government is acting *ultra vires*. This is more likely, however, in cases in which the government does not enjoy a significant majority in the legislature. In cases where the government is a minority, the fact that a parliament could end the constitutional term of a president and government elected by popular votes only introduces more instability to an already volatile system. The checks therefore are as much conflict generating as the problem they intend to constrain. Hamid Ghany draws attention to this area of instability in our political system.[52] This area of instability has been responsible for a yearlong political and constitutional crisis in Guyana starting from December 2018 with the no-confidence motion. This instability could definitely play itself out ethnically as was demonstrated in the post no-confidence motion period and as I will demonstrate in the hypothetical situation below. Moreover, the fact that no-confidence motions were used in the last two parliaments suggests that it will be a normal feature since the parliamentary gap between the government and opposition has closed significantly owing to demographic changes and migration. This could either contribute to political impasse or to political compromises in the future. Let's say that in the next election, the support of the Liberty and Justice Party (LJP) increases based on the Indigenous Peoples' votes giving the party two seats in the National Assembly. The other sixty-three seats are shared between APNU and PPP with a combination which gives one of the parties thirty-two seats and the other thirty-one. This would mean that the Presidency goes to the party with the thirty-two seats which does not enjoy a parliamentary majority. For the slightest of reasons, the other two groups (either the LJP and APNU+AFC or the LJP and the PPP depending on who wins the plurality) could call a no-confidence motion and remove the government. This could spill over into the society with claims of ethnic groups "banking up" on each other. This has been the story of Guyana quite saliently since 2018 and there is no doubt it would continue under any future minority governments. Donald Horowitz had drawn attention to the likelihood of this parliamentary power causing political crises even in parliamentary systems in which the government serves at the behest of parliament, let alone in presidential systems in which the government serves at the behest of the popular mandate.[53]

Based on studies which highlight this combination, that is presidential systems and list systems, as being more prone to corruption and ethnic violence, many social and political commentators are calling for us to revert to the constituency-based system.[54] This is in spite of the fact that political scientists in Trinidad, a plural society with a different governance system, were highlighting the failures of the constituency system there. The system produced the same results, that is, consolidation of support behind a party, characteristic of the list system. So, while the combination of executive presidency and a list system produces oligarchic and dictatorial tendencies, it is not clear that the solution lies in the institutional changes to a constituency-based system as in Trinidad and Tobago.

The Proportional Representation Electoral System

Another area of instability is the proportional representation (PR) voting system. This system has been recommended by Donald Horowitz for plural societies.[55] The logic behind Horowitz's recommendation is that if seats are distributed proportionate to votes garnered in an election, there is a high likelihood of ethnic or other groups galvanizing political support around the parties which represent their particular interest in the public sphere. This could lead to a proliferation of parties being represented in the legislature occasioning coalitions between and among various groups. This is exactly what obtains in systems with PR according to recent research.[56] This still provides an incentive for mobilization to be carried out along ethnic lines in societies characterized by ethnic differences. This keeps ethnopolitics alive although it provides for cross-ethnic coalitions as with the case of APNU+AFC in 2015. It is important to note that where the PR system exists parties are initially formed along the lines of the most salient group boundaries in the society. After some time, aspiring elites seek out other opportunities for political participation and form parties along the lines of less salient group boundaries such as economic interest, industries, ideologies, religion, profession, etc.

Guyana transitioned from a constituency system to a PR system in 1964 after it was seen by the opposition that seats in the legislature are disproportionate to the percentage of the popular votes gained in the election.[57] This transition led to a more accurate distribution of seats in the legislature, but it also led to the consolidation of ethnic voting.[58] Situated geographically in South America, Guyana's electoral system is similar to other countries in South America.

Most countries in South America have electoral systems that incorporate some variant of presidentialism and proportional representation. As a result, in line with the analysis by Donald Horowitz, the legislatures in these countries comprise more than two parties with no party having an absolute majority.[59] However, the outcome of that system is different in Guyana. The dominance of two main parties in the legislature resembles what transpires in the Commonwealth Caribbean which is characterized by the Parliamentary systems. The Legislatures in most Commonwealth Caribbean countries are dominated by two parties with one party enjoying an absolute majority. There has been no academic inquiry into this anomaly. However, this anomaly results from the absence of any provision for a postelection coalition in Guyana. The political system, as is, therefore, encourages the consolidation of votes so as to win an outright majority.

The descriptive analysis above shows that both at the level of social structure and social institutions, Guyana is predisposed to ethnic conflicts or other conflicts playing themselves out ethnically. In such a situation the least tension in the society could spiral out of control with identifiable groups targeting each other. While this is quite acknowledged by social scientists over the decades since independence, the focus of these social scientists has been on providing policy solutions which favor the political elites. The dominant solution proffered is executive power sharing. Apart from or along with this, there have been calls for constitutional reforms to limit executive power, change the voting system, and activate various rights commissions. Most solutions targeted the institutional structure. There has been no solution which targets the social or relational structure. The focus therefore seems to be on solidarity imposed from above by either satisfying the thirst for power by the political elite in the losing party (executive power sharing) or on the proliferation of constitutional and institutional reforms which have repeatedly proven ineffectual. There seems to be no focus on how organic solidarity could naturally emerge from below based on the frequent interactions and convergence of interest of the various ethnic groups. In line with Peter Siavelis, I argue that while institutional solutions are necessary they are not sufficient to curtail ethnic tensions and conflicts.[60]

Transitioning from a Conflict-Generating to Solidarity-Building Social System

Having established that Guyana's social substructure sets the condition for ethnic tension and conflict and that the institutional structure is more conflict generating than solidarity building, it is easy to see why elections are almost always attended by political protests and the unwillingness of the losing side to concede defeat. Losing an election in Guyana is not simply losing the mandate to govern the country; it is also losing streams of income and the opportunity to economically empower and politically protect ethnic communities from intentional and unintentional discriminatory practices of the group in power. As such the need to retain power by ethnic elites finds support among the ethnic masses who interpret their livelihood as being intrinsically wrapped up with the political fortunes of its own political elites. The high-stakes nature of the 2020 elections merely enhanced the social dynamic described above.

The policy question that besets us then is: being cognizant of this predisposition to ethnic tensions and conflicts, how do we transition from a conflict-generating to a solidarity-building system? The general approach to this question is to call for more solidarity-building or rights-reinforcing institutions such as executive power sharing, rights commissions, and constitutional reforms.[61] These solutions remind one of what Acemoglu and Robinson refer to as "Doppelganger solutions and checks and balances [that] don't solve the Gilgamesh problem because without society's vigilance constitutions and guarantees are not worth much more than the parchment they are written on."[62] Society's vigilance could only come about as a result of a fair amount of cohesion among its disparate parts which in part depends on the extent to which these various parts share similar or intersecting interests, welfare, primary institutions, cultures, and networks. Real, sustainable change should, therefore, affect the social substructure or the relational structure, and solidarity-building institutions will emerge naturally from organic solidarity among peoples. They also fail to consider the "paradox of representation" thesis proposed by David Lublin and Scott Mainwaring.[63] Both authors show that changes in the social substructure, that is to say, how specific groups are dispersed throughout rather than concentrated within other social divisions, tend to produce more sustainable political solutions.

By contrast I argue for a bottom-up (organic) approach to social solidarity that complements the top-down (mechanical) approach emphasized by the political institutions' literature. There is much evidence of the effectiveness of this bottom-up approach. In Guyana, demographic changes which brought about population shifts and blends and which came about independent of political or other interventions have had the most significant impact on the political system than all the institutional interventions since independence in 1966. For instance, the weakening of the People's Progressive Party in 2011, a party which held power from 1992 to 2015 with a significant majority, has been occasioned by demographic changes which result in a higher decline of its traditional support base with respect to the support base of its main competitor and a larger Mixed and Indigenous population. It is this population change that was critical for a minority government in 2011 and regime change in 2015 and 2020. The Mixed group, especially those that reside in the urban areas, are more likely to switch electoral support than the other groups. The larger the Mixed group grows, the less any one ethnic group commands an electoral majority. Taking a cue from this, intervention should aim, therefore, at creating opportunities for intersecting of interests in the economy and in communities by a dispersion of the various groups throughout various occupational categories and economic classes and various communities. The latter is already being done by means of housing policy that distributes house lots on a lottery basis. Because of the random nature of the distribution, the new communities are highly likely to become multiethnic as opposed to the mono-ethnic communities of the past. The positive outcome of the lottery system is however blunted by the stratification of the house lots into low-, medium-, and high-income lots. In a society already affected by horizontal inequality, a situation could arise in which the higher the strata, the more mono-ethnic the new communities become. If this aspect of the housing distribution initiative is corrected, then this intervention could carry the society a long way towards the convergence of interest at the level of communities. It also removes one of the bases upon which political players could distribute social goods in a discriminatory manner. With respect to the intersection of economic interest, there needs to be deliberate policies to encourage underrepresented groups such as Indigenous Peoples and Afro-Guyanese to achieve ownership in the upper strata of the private economy, and fair representation of Indo-Guyanese and Indigenous Guyanese in all levels of the public sector. The former could be accomplished by a combination of strategies. In the first instance, the government has the responsibility to ensure that wealth distributed by means of state contracts does not overly favor any particular racial/ethnic group thus contributing to ethnic inequality. Data regarding public procurement should be collected and assessed at intervals to get a sense of how government contracts are contributing to the economic empowerment of one group in relation to other groups in the society. When that is ascertained, procurement criteria should be established to raise the numbers of underrepresented groups doing business with the state at all levels. These policies aimed at building solidarity at the bottom through the convergence of interests and welfare of the masses could work in tandem with policies aimed at equality of representation at the top through power sharing. This combination of intervention strategies will bring about more sustainable solutions to the problems of ethnic conflict.

Conclusion

The social substructure and the institutional domain of the Guyanese society predispose the society to conflicts along ethnic lines. The main ethnic groups in the society are largely separated by structural barriers such as geography, religion, occupation, and kinship. These structural barriers reduce opportunities for interaction and the convergence of identity and interest while they provide the basis for political mobilization along ethnic lines. Along with these, the economic and political institutions incentivize the promotion of conflict rather than social solidarity among the masses. It is against this background that the 2020 National and Regional Elections should be viewed. As such, the five-month-long impasse that attended the 2020 elections in Guyana should not be seen as a pathological occurrence. It should be assessed within the particular structural and institutional context in which it occurred. This suggests that if the players are changed and the context remains, the behavioral outcome is highly likely to be the same. It also suggests that even without oil production, other social, economic, or political incidents could have triggered the same behavior among political elites and their ethnic support base. It might be important to note here that the 2015 elections were also attended by claims of rigging and the labeling of the government as illegitimate. Similar claims attended most elections since 1964. The promise of oil wealth therefore merely enhanced the social dynamics which already existed in the society. The fact that Guyana's social system is conflict-generating has long been established by scholarship on Guyana. The scholarship, however, focuses on the institutional, as opposed to the structural, side of the conflict-generating system. Logically, therefore, it privileges an institutional solution that shares political power among ethnic elites or that offers checks and balances to the use of power. This article draws attention to the structural side of the system while still recognizing the role played by institutional incentives. Quite logically, therefore, it puts forward a solution that shifts some attention away from the pursuit of solidarity among ethnopolitical elites to building solidarity among the masses. It argues that while it might be necessary to bring about some measure of elite accommodation at the level of government, a more sustainable approach to solidarity lies in building solidarity among the masses by removing the structural barriers which militate against the convergence of interests and welfare at the level of the people in all aspects of social, political, and economic life.

NOTES

1. Elections in Guyana have been historically accompanied by social unrest, looting, and violence perpetrated by one political community towards the other. Outside of this cycle of violence and social unrest following each election, there have been some periods in which violence erupted beyond the low-intensity violence at each election. A few of these occurred in the 1960s and between 2002 and 2008.

2. See Evan Ellis, "Guyana at Risk: Ethnic Politics, Oil, Venezuelan Opportunism and Why It Should Matter to Washington," Center for Strategic and International Studies, January 8, 2019, https://www.csis.org/analysis/guyana-risk-ethnic-politics-oil-venezuelan-opportunism-and-why-it-should-matter-washington.

3. See joint statement by foreign diplomats, U.S. Embassy in Guyana, March 3, 2020, https://gy.usembassy.gov/joint-statement-on-guyanese-elections/.

4. See joint statement by foreign diplomats, U.S. Embassy in Guyana, March 5, 2020, https://gy.usembassy.gov/joint-statement/.

5. See full news article "PSC Boss Urges GECOM to Act Transparently in Releasing Elections Results," *iNews Guyana*, March 13, 2020, https://www.inewsguyana.com/psc-boss-urges-gecom-to-act-transparently-in-releasing-elections-results/.

6. See news reports: "Court of Appeal Rules CARICOM's Supervision of Recount Is Unconstitutional," Department of Public Information, April 5, 2020, https://dpi.gov.gy/court-of-appeal-rules-caricoms-supervision-of-recount-is-unconstitutional/; "Guyana Court of Appeal Rules That CARICOM-Supervised Recount Is Illegal," *Barbados Today*, April 5, 2020, https://barbadostoday.bb/2020/04/05/guyana-court-of-appeal-rules-that-caricom-supervised-recount-is-illegal/.

7. See CARICOM news report, "CARICOM Observer Team for Guyana Elections Recount Arrives," CARICOM, May 1, 2020, https://caricom.org/caricom-observer-team-for-guyana-elections-recount-arrives/.

8. Political commentators, namely David Hinds, Henry Jeffrey, and Lincoln Lewis, had made calls for some form of power sharing before the 2020 elections; they all used the opportunity provided by the impasse generated by claims of fraud and rigging during the 2020 elections to renew those calls. See link for the views expressed by David Hinds, "Scrap the Election and Install an Interim Government," *Kaieteur News*, April 5, 2020, https://www.kaieteurnewsonline.com/2020/04/05/scrap-the-election-and-install-an-interim-government/; Henry Jeffrey, "For a Government of National Unity," *Stabroek News*, March 11, 2020, https://www.stabroeknews.com/2020/03/11/features/future-notes/for-a-government-of-national-unity/.

9. See news items and statements at the following webpages: "Joe Singh Calls on President to Ensure Recount of Ballots," *Stabroek News*, March 19, 2020, https://www.stabroeknews.com/2020/03/19/news/guyana/joe-singh-calls-on-president-to-ensure-recount-of-ballots/; "Yesu Persaud Urges President Granger to Take Steps to Preserve Democracy," *Stabroek News*, March 24, 2020, https://www.stabroeknews.com/2020/03/24/news/guyana/yesu-persaud-urges-president-granger-to-take-steps-to-preserve

-democracy/; statement by C. N. Sharma in "JFAP Stands by Call for Coalition to Concede," *Stabroek News*, July 19, 2020, https://www.stabroeknews.com/2020/07/19/news/guyana/jfap-stands-by-call-for-coalition-to-concede/.

10. The protest resulted in damage to property including a school bus transporting schoolchildren. It is important to note that the school bus was part of the President's initiative to provide transportation for schoolchildren. The bus had the name of the President blazoned across the side and front and painted in party colors. The protest also saw the death of a protestor who was killed by the police after allegedly confronting the police. See news report "Protestor Shot Dead by Police in Cotton Tree," *iNewsGuyana*, March 6, 2020, https://www.inewsguyana.com/protestor-shot-dead-by-police-in-cotton-tree/.

11. Cynthia Barrow-Giles and Ronnie Yearwood, "CARICOM and the 2020 Unsettled Elections in Guyana: A Failed Political (Legal) Solution?," *Commonwealth Journal of International Affairs* 109, no. 5 (2020): 506–25.

12. Stacey-Ann Wilson, *Politics of Identity in Small Plural Societies: Guyana, the Fiji Islands and Trinidad and Tobago* (New York: Palgrave Macmillan, 2014); Tarron Khemraj, "The Colonial Origins of Guyana's Underdevelopment," *Social and Economic Studies* 64, nos. 3/4 (2015): 49–83; Tarron Khemraj, "Two Ethnic Security Dilemmas and Their Economic Origin," 2019, Research Gate DOI: 10.13140/RG.2.2.34742.96326.

13. Percy C. Hintzen, "Ethnicity, Class, and International Capitalist Penetration in Guyana and Trinidad," *Social and Economic Studies* 34, no. 3 (1985): 107–63; David Carment, "The International Dimensions of Ethnic Conflict: Concepts, Indicators, and Theory," *Journal of Peace Research* 30, no. 2 (1993): 137–50; Perry Mars, "Ethnic Politics, Mediation, and Conflict Resolution: The Guyana Experience," *Journal of Peace Research* 38, no. 3 (2001): 353–72.

14. Mars, "Ethnic Politics."

15. Michael G. Smith, *The Plural Society in the British West Indies* (Los Angeles: University of California Press, 1974), 6; John S. Furnivall, *Colonial Policy and Practice: A Comparative Study of Burma and Netherlands* (Cambridge: Cambridge University Press, 1984), 304; Marko Klašnja and Natalija Novta, "Segregation, Polarization, and Ethnic Conflict," *Journal of Conflict Resolution* 60, no. 5 (2016): 927–55, https://doi.org/10.1177/0022002714550084.

16. Klašnja and Novta, "Segregation."

17. Robert S. Milne, "Bicommunal Systems: Guyana, Malaysia, Fiji," *Journal of Federalism* 18 (1988): 101–13.

18. Beverly Crawford, "The Causes of Cultural Conflict: An Institutional Approach," in *The Myth of "Ethnic Conflict,"* ed. Beverly Crawford and Ronnie D. Lipschutz (Berkeley: University of California Press, 1998), 17.

19. Cynthia Enloe, "The Growth of the State and Ethnic Mobilization: The American Experience," *Ethnic and Racial Studies* (1981): 123–36; Joane Nagel, "The Political Construction of Ethnicity," in *Competitive Ethnic Relations*, ed. Susan Olzak and Joane Nagel (Boston: Academic Press, 1986), 93–112.

20. Bojana Blagojevic, "Causes of Ethnic Conflict: A Conceptual Framework," *Journal of Global Change and Governance* 3, no. 1 (2009): 1–25.

21. Michael G. Smith, *Plural Society*; Michael G. Smith, *Culture, Race and Class in the*

Commonwealth Caribbean (Kingston: Department of Extra-Mural Studies, University of the West Indies, 1984).

22. Michael G. Smith, *Pluralism, Politics and Ideology in the Creole Caribbean* (New York: Research Institute for the Study of Man, 1991).

23. Elif Kisar Koromaz, "The Spatial Context of Social Integration," *Social Indicators Research* 19, no. 1 (2014): 49–71.

24. Christiaan W. S. Monden and Jeroen Smits, "Ethnic Intermarriage in Times of Social Change: The Case of Latvia," *Demography* 42, no. 2 (2005): 323–45; Jeroen Smits, "Ethnic Intermarriage and Social Cohesion: What Can We Learn from Yugoslavia?," *Social Indicators Research* 96, no. 3 (2010): 417–32.

25. Michael G. Smith, *Pluralism, Politics and Ideology*, 7.

26. William Easterly, "Can Institutions Resolve Ethnic Conflicts?," *Policy Research Working Paper* 2482 (World Bank Development Research Group, 2000).

27. Pooja Karnane and Michael A. Quinn, "Political Instability, Ethnic Fractionalization and Economic Growth," *International Economics and Economic Policy* 16 (2017): 435–61; Elissaios Papyrakis and Pak Hung Mo, "Fractionalization, Polarization, and Economic Growth: Identifying the Transmission Channels," *Economic Inquiry* 52, no. 3 (2014): 1204–18; William Easterly and Ross Levine, "Africa's Growth Tragedy: Policies and Ethnic Divisions," *Quarterly Journal of Economics* 112, no. 4 (1997); Stephen Knack and Philip Keefer, "Does Social Capital Have an Economic Payoff? A Cross-Country Investigation," *Quarterly Journal of Economics* 112, no. 4 (1997): 1251–88; Erkan Gören, "How Ethnic Diversity Affects Economic Growth," *World Development* 59 (2014): 275–97; Dani Rodrik, "Where Did All the Growth Go? External Shocks, Social Conflict, and Growth Collapses," *Journal of Economic Growth* 4, no. 4 (1999): 385–412.

28. Evan Osborne, "Diversity, Multiculturalism, and Ethnic Conflict: A Rent-Seeking Perspective," *Kyklos* 53 (2000): 509–26.

29. Khemraj, "Colonial Origins of Guyana's Underdevelopment."

30. Mark DaCosta, "Colonial Origins, Institutions and Economic Performance in the Caribbean: Guyana and Barbados," *IMF Working Paper WP107143*, International Monetary Fund, 2007.

31. Dominik Hartmann, *Economic Complexity and Human Development: How Economic Diversification and Social Networks Affect Human Agency and Welfare* (London: Routledge, 2014); Dani Rodrik, "Premature Deindustrialization," *Journal of Economic Growth* 21, no. 1 (2016): 1–33; Collin Constantine, "Economic Structures, Institutions and Economic Performance," *Journal of Economic Structures* 6, no. 2 (2017): 1–18; Collin Constantine and Tarron Khemraj, "Geography, Economic Structures and Institutions: A Synthesis," *Structural Change and Economic Dynamics* 51 (2019): 371–79.

32. Dominik Hartmann, Miguel R. Guevara, Cristian Jara-Figueroa, Manuel Aristarán, and Cesar A. Hidalgo, "Linking Economic Complexity, Institutions, and Income Inequality," *World Development* 93 (2017): 75–93; Constantine, "Economic Structures."

33. Hartmann, *Economic Complexity and Human Development*.

34. Rodrik, *Premature Deindustrialization*.

35. Inter-American Development Bank, Private Sector Assessment of Guyana, 2014, https://competecaribbean.org/wp-content/uploads/2015/02/2014-Guyana-Private-Sector-Assessment-Report.pdf.

36. See the Guyana Labour Force Survey for reports about education.

37. Collin Constantine, "The Rise of Income Inequality in Guyana," *Social and Economic Studies* 66, nos. 3/4 (2017): 65–95.

38. Paul McAdam, "$70,000—New Minimum Wage," Department of Public Information (DPI), November 13, 2019, https://dpi.gov.gy/70000-new-minimum-wage/.

39. See "PPP/C Does Not Believe in Excessive Taxation—Jagdeo," *Guyana Times*, September 19, 2020, https://guyanatimesgy.com/ppp-c-does-not-believe-in-excessive-taxation-jagdeo/; "PPP/C Elected Councils Will Not Support Rates and Taxes Hike—Jagdeo," *Stabroek News*, November 8, 2018, https://www.stabroeknews.com/2018/11/08/news/guyana/ppp-c-elected-councils-will-not-support-rates-and-taxes-hike-jagdeo/; Janette Bulkan and John Palmer, "Rentier Nation: Landlordism, Patronage and Power in Guyana's Gold Mining Sector," *Extractive Industries and Society* 3, no. 3 (2016): 676–89.

40. The implementation rate of the Public Sector Investment Programme fell from 80 percent to 20 percent under the Granger-led regime. See Denis Chabrol, "Public Sector Investment Implementation Down to 20 Percent; Rescue Plan on the Cards," *Demerara Waves*, May 11, 2017, https://demerarawaves.com/2017/05/11/public-sector-investment-implementation-down-to-20-percent-rescue-plan-on-the-cards/.

41. "Gov't to Announce Range of Incentives for Private Sector—Looking to Reduce Energy Cost by 60% over Three Years," *Newsroom*, August 31, 2020, https://newsroom.gy/2020/08/31/govt-to-announce-range-of-incentives-for-private-sector/, accessed September 2, 2020.

42. Ralph Premdas, "Elections and Political Campaigns in a Racially Bifurcated State: The Case of Guyana," *Journal of Interamerican Studies and World Affairs* 5, no. 3 (1972): 271–96; Ralph Premdas, "Competitive Party Organization and Political Integration in a Racially Fragmented State: The Case of Guyana," *Caribbean Studies* 12, no. 6 (1973): 5–35.

43. David Hinds, "Beyond Formal Democracy: The Discourse on Democracy and Governance in the Anglophone Caribbean," *Commonwealth and Comparative Politics* 46, no. 3 (2008): 388–406; Ralph Premdas, "Ethnic Conflict and Modes of Accommodation: Problems and Opportunities in Multi-ethnic States," Working Paper, Department of Behavioural Sciences, University of the West Indies, Saint Augustine, 1997; Alissa Trotz and Arif Bulkan, "Guyana's Political Tragedy," *Stabroek News*, June 30, 2020, https://www.stabroeknews.com/2020/06/30/features/in-the-diaspora/guyanas-political-tragedy/.

44. Janette Bulkan, "REDD Letter Days: Entrenching Political Racialization and State Patronage through the Norway-Guyana REDD-plus Agreement," *Social and Economic Studies* 63, no. 3 (2014): 249–79.

45. Osborne, "Diversity."

46. David Hinds, "Hinds' Sight: Putting the Aggressive Charges of 'Ethnic Cleansing' in Context," *Guyana Chronicle*, September 6, 2015; Ivelaw Griffith, "Political Change, Democracy, and Human Rights in Guyana," *Third World Quarterly* 18, no. 2 (1997): 267–85; Deryck R. Brown, "Ethnic Politics and Public Sector Management in Trinidad and Guyana," *Public Administration and Development* 19 (1999): 367–79.

47. Bernard Grofman and Robert Stockwell, "Institutional Design in Plural Societies: Mitigating Ethnic Conflict and Fostering Stable Democracy," UC Urvine Center for the Development of Democracy Working Papers (2001), 13, https://escholarship.org/uc/item/16s1comt.

48. Tarron Khemraj and Diana Hinova, "Elected Oligarchy and Economic UnderDevelopment: The Case of Guyana," MPRA 31387, 2011; Freddie Kissoon, "Elected Dictatorship in Guyana and Its Apologists," *Kaieteur News*, July 6, 2010, http://www.kaieteur newsonline.com/2010/07/06/elected-dictatorship-in-guyana-and-its-apologists/.

49. Jose A. Cheibub, *Presidentialism, Parliamentarism, and Democracy* (Cambridge: Cambridge University Press, 2007).

50. Kate Quinn, "Colonial Legacies and Postcolonial Conflicts in Guyana," in *Postcolonial Trajectories in the Caribbean: The Three Guianas*, ed. Rosemarijn Hoefte, Matthew L. Bishop, and Peter Clegg (London: Routledge, 2017).

51. Arif Bulkan, "Democracy in Disguise: Assessing the Reforms to the Fundamental Rights Provisions in Guyana," *Georgia Journal of International and Comparative Law* 32 (2004): 613–55.

52. Hamid Ghany, "Correcting Arend Lijphart's Hybrid VI: The Case of Guyana," *Journal of Legislative Studies* 26, no. 2 (2000): 314–27.

53. Donald L. Horowitz, "Comparing Democratic Systems," *Journal of Democracy* 1, no. 4 (1990): 73–79.

54. Jana Kunicova and Susan Rose-Ackerman, "Electoral Rules and Constitutional Structures as Constraints on Corruption," *British Journal of Political Science* 35, no. 4 (2005): 573–606; Ulrike G. Theuerkauf, "Presidentialism and the Risk of Ethnic Violence," *Ethnopolitics* 12, no. 1 (2012): 72–81.

55. Donald L. Horowitz, *Ethnic Groups in Conflict* (Berkeley: University of California Press, 1985); Donald L. Horowitz, *A Democratic South Africa? Constitutional Engineering in a Divided Society* (Berkeley: University of California Press, 1991).

56. Duane Edwards, "Institutional Reform for the Maximisation of the Benefits of Oil Revenues in Guyana," Policy Brief no. 1, Department of Government, Sociology, Social Work and Psychology, University of the West Indies, Cave Hill, 2019.

57. Duane Edwards, "The Constituency System Will Entrench the Rule of One Party," *Stabroek News*, August 11, 2014, https://www.stabroeknews.com/2014/08/11/opinion/letters/constituency-system-will-entrench-rule-one-party/.

58. Chaitram Singh, "Ethnicity and Democracy in Guyana," *Journal of Third World Studies* 11, no. 1 (1994): 405–22.

59. Horowitz, *Ethnic Groups in Conflict*.

60. Peter M. Siavelis, "Crisis of Representation in Chile? The Institutional Connection," *Journal of Politics in Latin America* 8, no. 3 (2016): 61–93, https://doi.org/10.1177/1866802X1600800303.

61. Arend Lijphart, "Constitutional Design for Divided Societies," *Journal of Democracy* 15, no. 2 (2004): 96–109.

62. Darron Acemoglu and James A. Robinson, *The Narrow Corridor: States, Societies and the Fate of Liberty* (New York: Penguin Press, 2019), xvi.

63. David Lublin, *The Paradox of Representation: Racial Gerrymandering and Minority Interests in Congress* (Princeton, N.J.: Princeton University Press, 1997); Scott Mainwaring, "The Crisis of Representation in the Andes," *Journal of Democracy* 17, no. 3 (2006): 13–27.

CHAPTER 14

Global Capitalism and Regime Volatility in Suriname

JACK MENKE

The 1980s transition to a global neoliberal and free-market capitalism in various South American nations was accompanied by expanding resource-seeking extractive capital. While in this new phase of capitalism in some countries various economic services became dominant, in Suriname natural resource extraction remained the pillar of the economy. In this country the transition to gold mining in the 1980s gave raw material extraction precedence over industrial processing, just like the bauxite-alumina sector that dominated the Surinamese economy from 1916 to 2016. Veltmeyer and Petras observe that in Latin America, in addition to natural resource extraction capitalism, a form of narco-capitalism evolved, based on the accumulation of capital through the production and/or trafficking of illegal drugs.[1] This has been the case in Suriname, where local people employed in natural resource extraction (e.g., gold and lumber) and the export of primary commodities became involved in narco-capitalism and national politics. This chapter addresses the impact of changes in global capitalism on the shifting modes of governmentalized power in Suriname. The aim is to assess the way national modes of power, as employed in Suriname by different regimes—consociational, autocratic (military), and leftist populist—responded to the transition of global capitalism to its neoliberal form.[2] Next the nature of consociationalism and leftist populism are addressed, with focus on how the political leadership justifies each of these systems.

Nature of Consociationalism and Populism

Consociationalism is a majority party system based on a proportionate principle in the electoral system and coalition formation, and power sharing between the elites of the parties based on ethnic, religious, or other affiliation.[3] Suriname's consociational politics goes back to the 1950s when the country went through a monocultural resource extraction economy in the context of global free-market capitalism. Some political scientists considered Suriname's twentieth-century consociationalism the ideal solution to the assumed political tension and conflict arising from the country's ethnic diversity.[4] The form of "false consciousness" is framed in the necessity of cooperation between the elites of ethnic parties, which is justified to prevent assumed conflicts between ethnic groups. In reality, however, this elite perspective of a multiethnic society underlies the political practice that justifies the delegation of power from the people to the elites of the different ethnic groups. The elites thus "empower themselves" on behalf of their followers to negotiate on power sharing in politics and positions within the state. This elite negotiation includes the distribution of departments as well as key posts within state enterprises and government, such as ministers and ambassadors. While the consociational leadership preaches peace and harmony between political leaders and believes that through them harmony between (ethnic) groups is maintained, there are serious limitations to this system. A critical analysis brings up a major issue: the strong emphasis on ethnicity and potential explosive situation for ethnic conflict is often a diversionary tactic to deny inequalities at the national level and within the various ethnic groups. As such this serves a false consciousness.

Historically, the NPS (Creole), VHP (East Indian), and KTPI (Javanese) were in the forefront of the first general elections and consociational regimes in the twentieth century. The fact that none of the major ethnic groups had a demographic majority influenced the emergence of consociationalism with ethnic parties representing the interests of their ethnic rank and file.

In the heyday of consociationalism the foundations were laid for an "ethnic state" in which certain departments and state-owned enterprises are allocated to certain political parties and their related (ethnic) constituency.[5] The "ethnic state" was also reflected in the distribution of government funds and Dutch aid to various economic sectors. In this way, in addition to being an instrument for exercising political power, the state became a source for the economic and social mobility of the various ethnic groups. Due to shifts in the global modes of capitalism and the rise of leftist populism, the practices of consociationalism changed into what Edward Dew conceptualized as "partnerships [that] are essentially little time bombs waiting to explode."[6]

Populism

Conceptualizations of populism have changed over time, depending on the global and national context. Illustrative is the conceptualization of populism by Peter Worsley in the 1960s, who from an anticolonial Third World perspective stresses the contradiction between local people and foreign capitalists.[7] Contemporary populism is a two-edged sword: "on the one side is the voice of the people, on the other edge voices of fear, anger, hatred, and revenge."[8] The voice of the people points to a high esteem for the virtues of common persons, while the voices of anger and hatred are framed to indicate the elite. Populism is a way of gaining and exercising government power whereby the populist leader identifies with the "common people" to then construct an antagonistic relationship between "the people" and "the elite." Leftist populism in Suriname finds its origin in the 1980s when an autocratic military regime was in the power center and responded to the global shifts of capitalism toward a neoliberal form.

It is important to note that consociationalism and populism do not refer to political systems, like fascism and socialism, but rather ways of mobilizing followers and exercising government power. However, this does not take away that both systems operate in a specific mode of power and political-economic context, which will be dealt with next.

Global Capitalism and Emergent Regimes

Since the first general and free election in Suriname in 1949, three regime types have emerged: consociational,[9] autocratic military, and leftist populist regimes (table 14.1). From 1949 to 1980 global capitalism dominated Suriname's political economy through the dependence on bauxite extraction and Dutch development aid. In this political-economic context consociationalism emerged with a power-sharing tradition between ethnic and religious parties that by and large represented the major groups of Creole, East Indian, and Javanese.[10] In addition to Dutch aid, the consociational regimes relied heavily on global capital investments in bauxite mining according to the Puerto Rican development strategy that invites foreign capital under attractive fiscal and economic conditions.[11] Thus Suriname's state structure displayed characteristics of an allocation state where commodity exports guaranteed a significant

TABLE 14.1. Political Regimes in Suriname, 1949–2020

Period	Regimes
1949–1980	Consociational regimes
1980–1987	First autocratic military regime
1987	Elections under new constitution during redemocratization
1987–1990	First consociational regime after first military regime
1990–1991	Second autocratic military regime
1991–2020	Volatility of consociational and leftist populist regimes

portion of the state income.[12] In the 1950s the bauxite sector provided more than 80 percent of the total export value. The high point of consociationalism was reached from 1958 to 1973. This period coincided with investments in the Brokopondo project, a mega bauxite mining and hydroelectricity project, driven by a U.S.-based transnational enterprise. After a military coup by noncommissioned officers in 1980, Suriname went through two autocratic regimes in 1980–87 and 1990–91. These regimes relied heavily on new economic opportunities as the traditional revenues from global capitalist resource extraction (bauxite mining) declined and Dutch aid was suspended.

From 1991 to 2020 the political landscape showed a volatility of consociational and leftist populist regimes. During the autocratic military regimes the seeds were laid for leftist populism, which was further extended when the National Democratic Party (NDP)—an offspring of the military regime—took office from 1996 to 2000 and 2010–20. But the NDP, amid a severe financial crisis and rampant corruption, was defeated in the 2020 election. The Verenigde Hervormings Partij (VHP), a political party with a major East Indian constituency, won this election with twenty of the fifty-one parliamentary seats and formed a power-sharing coalition government with three other parties.[13]

Next the regime volatility is explained in the context of the changing modes of global capitalism in the 1980–2020 period. The focus is on how local modes of power have been linked to global transitions of neoliberal capitalism.

Explaining Local Power Shifts and Regime Volatility

This section elaborates on how during the military regime and postmilitary period capital groups and the major political parties made cross-ethnic alliances that favored new modes of capitalism. It explains the attraction of the National Democratic Party of which the populist leadership became involved in local modes of capitalism that were strongly related to shifting modes of global capitalism.

In the 1980s global capitalism shifted to a neoliberal and free-market capitalism. This created new opportunities for expanding resource-seeking extractive capital and provided the environment for the transition from bauxite mining toward gold mining and small-scale onshore oil production in Suriname. Like in many Latin American nations, narco-capitalism evolved next to natural resource extraction capitalism in this country, with direct links to particularly exponents of the military regime and new political parties that entered the political arena. During this transition the economic power base of the older ethnic parties, the NPS and the VHP, declined in two ways.[14] First, the traditional power formation of these parties, which was historically linked to the monocultural bauxite industry and the Dutch aid, weakened. Second, major financial groups turned their support from the traditional ethnic parties to the NDP in particular.

How to explain the political survival of the military leadership and its continued political involvement in the NDP and related and economic circles? The military leaders responded in various ways to their eroded legitimacy—due to the 1982 murders of political opponents, the suspension of the Dutch aid, and reduced revenues from the bauxite industry. First, in the sphere of the political economy the autocratic regime responded to shifts in the global modes of capitalism. Following the suspension of Dutch aid and the decline of the international bauxite industry in the 1980s, the military initiated new economic initiatives in gold mining and linked with regional and international narco-capitalism. These economic opportunities were elaborated in the context of extended populism by the National Democratic Party (NDP), a political party that emerged from the military leadership. During the three civilian governments led by the NDP (1996–2000 and 2010–20), leftist populism became institutionalized in Suriname, especially from 2015 to 2020. Contrary to the social contracts and the promised foundations for sustainability in the economy, ecology, and education as well as land rights for Indigenous and tribal people, the credibility of the NDP government was undermined by rampant corruption and state bankruptcy. This contributed to the outcome of the 2020 election as voters sought to replace leftist populism with a consociational coalition headed by Chan Santokhi.

A second response of the military leadership was to initiate a dialogue with leaders of the old ethnic parties to open the door for redemocratization. This dialogue was considered necessary for a balanced withdrawal of the military while guaranteeing the reservation of state power in the aftermath of the 1987 elections. The reservation of state power in defense and national security was also meant to guarantee incremental changes and secure that the power should remain in the hands of the military.[15] These issues were included in the military decrees prior to the elections of 1987. They also conform to James Petras's observation that military regimes generally opt for dialogues with civilians who prefer juridical-political changes to socioeconomic changes.[16] In the case of Suriname, the military leaders opted for civilian dialogue partners who were willing to prioritize juridical-political issues, such as new decrees and a new constitution. With this strategy the military leadership was able to reserve state power through the decrees "National Army" and "Charter for Military Officers" to guarantee their own security and the continuation of revolutionary ideals.

In addition to formally reserving state power, the military leaders (who became the political leaders of the NDP) reserved state power outside the elections and the state. They were actively involved in the formation of a new economic elite, which became apparent on the eve of the 1987 elections. The leader of the military regime proclaimed the "economic revolution" and connected with new and existing capital groups of the old ethnic groups and political parties, including the VHP. In this process, which continued into the 1990s, the economic base of the NDP was strengthened. The 1996 election marked a turning point for the marriage between the new economic and political power, while the basis was laid for strengthening leftist populism.

Turning Point

Ever since the first military regime (1980–87), there has been an urge to unite the temporarily separated economic and political power, which was achieved around the 1996 elections. This was expressed by the political splits in two ways: the split of existing ethnic political parties or political combinations, and the representation of each ethnic group by more than one party in the National Assembly. A historically remarkable fragmentation of existing political blocs or parties occurred after the elections. The incumbent consociational Nieuw Front Government (VHP, NPS, KTPI, and SPA) won twenty-four of the fifty-one seats in Parliament but failed to reach consensus with other political organizations to extend the existing coalition for acquiring a parliamentary majority.[17] The NDP maneuvered itself in a position to elect the president and vice president with the support of the members who withdrew from other political blocs.[18]

Why can the emergence of a nontraditional coalition in 1996 be qualified as a turning point in the national political relations and mode of governmentalized power? The first explanation is the urge to unite economic and political power. This stems from the military coup in 1980 when state power was seized by the military and temporarily separated from the existing economic power groups. To reunite economic and political power, new economic groups emerging across ethnicities during the military regime searched for alliances with the new political leaders and vice versa. Consequently, after the 1996 elections important capital groups moved away from the major traditional ethnic parties and joined the new populist NDP government. During the military regimes and through its offspring, the National Democratic Party (NDP), the military leadership gradually transferred state power into political power that further facilitated economic opportunities emerging from shifts in global capitalism.[19]

The second explanation for the turning point in national political relations in 1996 is the urge for completing the emancipation of socially and economically disadvantaged ethnic groups. This is accompanied by nontraditional voting across ethnicity, which is demonstrated by parliamentary members of a particular ethnicity who do not represent a party linked to their own ethnic group.[20] Illustrative is the composition of the 1996–2000 Parliament, where representatives of East Indian, Creole, Javanese, and Maroon ethnicities are found across political parties. This is characteristic for "ethnic delinking" and emancipation, a process that has a certain sequence. By ethnic delinking I mean the transition of traditional mono-ethnic parties to include and attract voters of other ethnic groups. Ethnic delinking occurred first among the Creole and Mixed group in the early 1950s. The East Indians followed in the 1960s, with a climax reached in 1996.[21] Non-Javanese parties have not succeeded yet in attracting significant portions of Javanese voters, which indicates that ethnic delinking of this group is far from being completed.[22]

The third explanation for considering the emergence of a nontraditional coalition in 1996 as a turning point relates to the shift in the interaction of three forms of capitalism: capitalism as usual, extractive capitalism, and narco-capitalism.[23] Suriname's post–World War II political economy with its dependence on bauxite extraction and Dutch development aid was being replaced by extractive capitalism in gold mining in interaction with narco-capitalism unfolding on a Latin American and global landscape.

Gold, Drugs, and the New Power Elites

While the economic power base of the traditional ethnic parties, representing the Creole and the East Indian, respectively, eroded after the 1987 election, the political leaders of the NDP, who gained state power through elections in 1996, evolved toward a new economic elite in Suriname.

TABLE 14.2. Export Value of Mineral Products in Suriname, 2006–2020 (millions USD)

Product	2006 Absolute	2006 Percent %	2010 Absolute	2010 Percent %	2015 Absolute	2015 Percent %	2020 Absolute	2020 Percent %
Alumina	559.3	54	427	23	232.7	18	0	0
Oil	57.2	6	267.2	14	156.4	12	154.4	7
Gold*	410.1	40	1175	63	916.2	70	1959.5	93
Total	1026.6	100	1869	100	1305.3	100	2113.9	100

SOURCE: Stichting Planbureau Suriname.
*Nonmonetary gold.

Since the 1980s the transition of Suriname's economic base occurred through natural resource extraction in gold mining and narco-capitalism, based on the trafficking of illegal drugs.[24] A narco line between Suriname and Colombia was set up to finance the revolution of the Surinamese military, who had seized power through a coup with involvement of the National Military Council. After the U.S. and Dutch intelligence agencies obtained sufficient information about the drug activities in Suriname, important leaders of the military and political world in Suriname were convicted in the United States and the Netherlands.[25]

The available data on the increasing production and export of gold also show a growing involvement of exponents of the military and political leadership. In the twenty-first century gold has overshadowed bauxite as the stronghold of the economy.[26] Gold production peaked in the 2015–20 period and reached a historical high export value of almost USD $2 billion in 2020, representing 93 percent of the total export of the most important mineral goods (table 14.2).

The question is how the new political elites took advantage of the growing production and export of gold, and how political and economic power were being connected. During the Bouterse regimes (2010–15 and 2015–20) the economic power base of the Surinamese gold elites was expanded amid a favorable global financial environment for gold. The new Surinamese power elite took advantage in two ways. First, by granting gold concessions in gold-rich areas to the ruling political party elites of nontraditional parties—particularly the NDP and the ABOP—they became involved in medium- and small-scale mining.[27] The official medium- and small-scale gold production represents an important share of the total gold production and in 2015—with 63 percent of total production—a higher share than the foreign-owned large-scale gold production (table 14.3).

Additionally, the new political elites took advantage of the growing gold production by striking deals with large gold multinationals. In the context of

TABLE 14.3. Gold Production and Processing (1,000 kilogram)

Production type	2015 Absolute	2015 Percent %	2016 Absolute	2016 Percent %	2017 Absolute	2017 Percent %	2018 Absolute	2018 Percent %	2019 Absolute	2019 Percent %
Large scale	9.39	35.4	12.93	46.1	25.85	62.4	25.97	62.2	25.69	61.8
Small/medium scale	17.10	64.6	15.12	53.9	15.55	37	15.77	37.8	15.91	38.2
Total gold production	26.49	100	28.05	100	41.40	100	41.74	100	41.60	100

SOURCE: Stichting Planbureau Suriname.

an international gold price of over USD $1,700 per ounce, an agreement was reached in 2012 between the Canadian IAMGOLD Corporation and the government of Suriname, which was approved in 2013 by the National Assembly.[28] The questioned agreement was signed amid fierce parliamentary and public debates whereby the government was accused of corruption, clientelism, and selling out the country's gold resources.[29]

Since the 1990s a strong relationship has been developing between politics and the gold economy. A public sector database of owners and management of gold companies combined with data from the Chamber of Commerce in 2011 provides some insight in the power elite in the gold sector. Within the top ten positions are the politicians Desi Bouterse and Ronnie Brunswijk, leaders of the NDP and the ABOP, respectively, two new political parties founded in the 1980s and 1990s. Of the total official gold export in 2011 with a world market value of over USD $1.5 billion, the Surinamese government received 12 percent in tax, royalties, and consent law from the gold sector.[30] While gold has evolved into the public sector's main source of income, a large share of this precious metal is produced by the informal sector. It is estimated that there are thirty thousand small producers. Their contribution to government revenues is poor because most informal small gold miners evade fiscal regulations, while the uncontrolled use of mercury and other pollutants are causing serious damage to the environment. Finally, the political impact should not be underestimated, for many Surinamese gold miners are voters in interior electoral districts of Brokopondo, Marowijne, and Sipaliwini, where the NDP and the ABOP have a political stronghold. So the political and economic interests of the small goldminers are linked. They may flourish by skirting governmental environmental regulations and evading fiscal regulations, which is tolerated by the leadership of political parties with their vested interests in the interior electoral districts.

A Critique of Consociational and Leftist Populist Ideologies

Though the ideologies of the consociational and populist regimes in Suriname show striking differences, there are similarities in the development strategies. This section critiques the ideologies and policies pursued by both regimes.

The system of consociationalism is justified with the argument that the power-sharing principle corresponds with the expectations of the respective party electorates and that this is necessary to guarantee the political and social peace in a divided society. In the case of Suriname, the first precondition for the existence of consociationalism is that the political elites of the different ethnic groups are aware of the possible explosive situation that could lead to an ethnic conflict. It is believed that only then will these elites be willing to cooperate politically. Unlike most other countries, the backbone of the Surinamese consociationalism in the 1950s and 1960s was the informal relations between the leaders of the most important elites, particularly the Creole and East Indians. This characteristic is considered one of the causes of political instability in Suriname's politics, which is referred to as anti-consociationalism.[31]

Despite observed limitations of consociationalism, some scholars justify this system to prevent interethnic conflicts, while other scholars additionally emphasize the positive characteristic of a means for political mobilization and for the emancipation of ethnic elites.[32] My first critique is that consociational regimes seem to be primarily concerned with the pacification of supporters within the traditional power-sharing lines based on ethnicity. As such, consociationalism is an elitist political agenda, through which the delegation of power from the people to the elites of the different ethnic groups is legitimized. The elites, on behalf of the ethnic groups, authorize themselves to negotiate on the sharing of appropriated power.[33] The focus on consensus among leaders and allocation of key posts within the state apparatus encourages accommodation of often incompetent party loyalists and opportunists, which cripples innovation and a coherent development strategy.

Another critique of consociational theory points to overlooking the relationship between political and economic power, and processes concerning authoritarian regimes and political party fragmentation. In this regard, the state can be temporarily disconnected from its social class and economic base. This was evident during the military regime (1980–87) in Suriname—particularly when Dutch development aid was suspended—and the economic spinoff of the bauxite industry declined. The leaders of the military regime were involved in shifting the economic base in the context of global capitalist opportunities toward gold and narco-capitalism. Furthermore, they gradually transferred state power into political power and created conditions for future economic opportunities by founding a civilian political party, the NDP. For segments of the new and old economic elites these opportunities have been an important pull factor toward a preference for alliances with the NDP over the traditional ethnic parties.

Leftist Populist Ideology

In Suriname leftist populism plays a significant role in postmilitary Suriname as it challenges consociationalism politics based on power-sharing coalitions

TABLE 14.4. Common Values of Leftist Populism in Suriname

Negative values	Positive values
Antielitism	National capitalism
Antiparliamentary	National culture oriented
Anticolonial nationalism	Appreciation of Indigenous culture
Anti–rule of law	Appreciation of Suriname's bromki jari ("flower garden")

led by traditional ethnic parties. The relatively successful mobilization of the NDP—apart from creating an economic power base for their politics—is due to the way populism-related values are translated in easy-to-understand narratives like "bakra basi keba" (an anticolonial nationalism saying that Dutch colonialism is over) and "Neks no fout" (anti–rule of law) (table 14.4).

The threat of populism for the wider society is not in the populist leader as such, but in the normalization of antidemocratic values such as antiparliamentary values and anti–rule of law as illustrated in table 14.5. This corresponds with Antonio Gramsci's concept of "hegemony," indicating that ideological control harbors the key for dominance.[34] The expressions used by the leaders have been constructed through social interactions in the course of the history of the society concerned and are shaped by the dominant ideology. The framing of these expressions with a certain cultural meaning conditions followers to think in the constructed frames of the given time and circumstances.

Electoral Defeat of Leftist Populism

To accommodate followers the leftist populist NDP implemented short-term and ad hoc policies from 1996 to 2000 and from 2010 to 2020 in the absence of a clear development strategy. They opted to combine "development by national financial resources" and "high-interest foreign loans," which resulted in huge internal and external debts. This partially explains why the leftist populist NDP lost the 2020 elections. The seeds for the electoral defeat of the NDP were laid in macroeconomic policies pursued during the first Bouterse government (2010–15). The victory of the NDP in the 2015 election occurred amid an economic downturn that began in 2013. As the price of global commodities like gold and oil fell, government revenues fell sharply. Notwithstanding the negative macroeconomic environment, social benefits were significantly increased prior to the elections, contributing to the NDP's historic electoral victory in 2015 with 45.5 percent of the national votes, versus 37.3 percent for the oppositional V7, a combination of mostly mono-ethnic parties.[35] At the same time, an important element of the leftist populist policies, a "social contract," was concluded. This policy targeted the poorer strata and was accompanied by excessive social expenditures, resulting in a scarcity of foreign currencies and high inflation.

A second reason why the NDP lost the 2020 elections relates to widespread corruption, the undermining and breakdown of key institutions, and the frequent replacement of ministers. The undermining of core institutions across vital sectors and resources is reflected in the frequent firing of professional experts who are wrongfully criminalized, with the aim of replacing them with persons serving the interests of the party.[36]

A third factor that led to the electoral decline of the leftist populist NDP is the undermining of the rule of law. The many attacks on the rule of law, such as the adoption of the amnesty law by the second Bouterse government (2015–20), were also seeds for its own downfall. This controversial occasional law that indemnifies suspects of the 1982 December murders from criminal charges was passed in Parliament in 2012 and has been characterized as a dark era in Suriname's parliamentary history. The silent march held by civil society and church organizations on April 10, 2012, was the first widespread protest against the controversial amnesty law by civil society and authoritarian institutions expressing concern about attacks on the rule of law.

Discussion and Conclusion

The volatility of political regimes in Suriname from 1980 to 2020 is to a certain extent related to the shifting modes of global capitalism. This means that the way national modes of power, as employed in Suriname by consociational, autocratic (military), and leftist populist regimes, responded differently to the transition of global capitalism to its neoliberal form.

At the same time Suriname's frequent regime shifts must be understood in the context of a politics of redemocratization during which military leaders sought to secure incremental changes and guarantee their own security and revolutionary ideals. In the redemocratization process the military leaders who became the political leaders of the NDP reserved state power within and outside the state and were central in the formation of a new economic elite.

The changing economic basis since the late 1980s, from bauxite and Dutch aid toward the production and export of gold, coincided with a growing economic involvement of exponents of the NDP. Effectively, the export and mining of gold and involvement in global narco-capitalism became the economic pillars of the autocratic military and leftist populist regimes. In this way they responded to the transition of global capitalism to its neoliberal form and brought about changes in governmentalized power in Suriname.

Turning to political analysis, there are two shortcomings in consociational theory and practice when it comes to explaining the dynamics of politics in Surinamese society. First, consociationalism is concerned primarily with the pacification of supporters along ethnic lines. This points to an elite agenda that presumes that the delegation of power from the people to the elites of the different ethnic groups can be legitimated. Second, consociational theory overlooks the relationship between political and economic power, and processes concerning autocratic regimes and political party fragmentation. This is precisely where leftist populism created opportunities for regime changes and reconnecting political power, economic power, and the state under novel conditions.

Leftist populism was shaped as a way of exercising political power, in which the opposition between "the people" and "the elite" is stressed and translated in easy-to-understand narratives representing anti-elitist and antidemocratic values. The ideological control is sustained through the framing of such expressions, which conditions followers to think and act according to these frameworks, even when democratic institutions are being eroded.

Despite ideological and policy differences between consociational and leftist populist regimes in Suriname, both have features in common with the new developmentalist regimes in Latin America regarding policies based on alliances with global and national mineral elites. They aim at maximizing investment and economic growth, even if it comes at the expense of genuine sustainability, redistributive policies, and changes in property ownership. This is also evident for Suriname's left-wing populist and consociational regimes that forged alliances with global and national gold mining elites. Despite differences in strategic policy issues and codes of behavior, the consociational and leftist populist regimes have in common that they presently do not provide sustainable responses to the twenty-first-century development challenges of the Surinamese allocation state, which through commodity exports guarantees a significant portion of the state's income to be redistributed by the centralist government.[37] The Surinamese allocation state facilitated and provided previously almost all of the state's income, mainly through the export of bauxite. Since the 1980s gold and narco-capitalism increasingly has taken over from bauxite in terms of state and foreign exchange revenues. Thus the Surinamese allocation state has continued to rely on the export of mining products across consensus, military, and populist regimes. Despite the frequent shifts of consociational and populist regimes in the postmilitary era, the structural foundations of the neoliberal political economy did not change.

The Surinamese case demonstrates that both populist and consociational regimes have been using the state for narrow party interests. Clientelism and corruption have had a detrimental impact on the economy and society. Both forms of governance contradict liberal economic efficiency as top jobs or positions tend to be allocated on the basis of ethnic preference. It demonstrates how—due to its fragile political and economic base—the state continues to degenerate into a central source for political power and short-term acquisition of economic wealth by the ethnically diverse and poorly developed entrepreneurial groups. In the end, both the power-sharing and populist regimes have maintained an inefficient and ineffective public sector along ethnic lines, requiring many loss-making state-owned companies to secure their political power base. In the end, autocratic, leftist populist, and consociational regimes all failed to structurally enhance development and reduce poverty and inequalities in a sustainable way.

NOTES

1. Henry Veltmeyer and James Petras, *Latin America in the Vortex of Social Change Development and Resistance Dynamics* (London: Routledge, 2019).

2. Broadly, a regime refers to the system of government that covers relations with power, the legal scope, the level of democracy, and the rights of its citizens.

3. Arend Lijphart, *Democracies: Patterns of Majoritarian and Consensus Governments in Twenty-One Countries* (New Haven, Conn.: Yale University Press, 1984).

4. Arend Lijphart, *Thinking about Democracy: Power Sharing and Majority Rule in Theory and Practice* (London: Routledge, 2008); Edward Dew, *The Difficult Flowering of Suriname: Ethnicity and Politics in a Plural Society* (The Hague: Martinus Nijhoff, 1978).

5. Jack Menke, "The State in the Development Process of Suriname," in *Problem of Development of the Guianas*, ed. Henry Jeffrey and Jack Menke (Paramaribo: Anton de Kom University of Suriname, 1991), 59.

6. The American political scientist Edward Dew initially praised the Surinamese consensus coalition model but reevaluated his conclusion in 2001: "Although the multiplicity of ethnic groups makes consociational coalition democracy possible, it also tends to block development initiatives, undermine nation-building and invite regime collapse.... The partnerships are essentially little time bombs waiting to explode." It is these time bombs that invite populism. Edward Dew, "Can Nation-Building Be Achieved through Consociationalism in Suriname?," in *Identity, Ethnicity and Culture in the Caribbean*, ed. Ralph R. Premdas (Saint Augustine: University of the West Indies, School of Continuing Studies, 2001).

7. Worsley stresses the ideological aspect of populism and counters the Marxist notion of "false consciousness." Populism constitutes an ideology insofar as class divisions exist in the Third World. But in many of these countries, classes are not distinct, and the major antagonism is between the local people and foreign capitalists. Peter Worsley, *The Third World* (Chicago: University of Chicago Press, 1964).

8. Anthony R. Brunello, "The Madisonian Republic and Modern Nationalist Populism: Democracy and the Rule of Law," *World Affairs* 181, no. 2 (2018): 110–11.

9. I use the concept "consociationalism" interchangeably with "power sharing" as conceptualized by Arend Lijphart. Historically many political parties in Suriname have been affiliated with one ethnic group. This means that ethnicity has played a major role in politics. However, in the postmilitary period some political parties have been evolving toward multiethnic organizations. See Lijphart, *Thinking about Democracy*.

10. Suriname has a remarkable ethnic diversity with four major groups in the 2012 census: East Indians (27 percent) and Javanese (14 percent), descendants of indentured workers from India and Indonesia, respectively; Creoles (16 percent), the descendants of African slaves; and Maroons, composed of six tribal peoples. Maroons are demographically the fastest-growing group and represented 22 percent of the total population in the 2012 census. Suriname's cultural richness is also reflected in the country's linguistic and religious diversity. There are more than twenty languages spoken. Of the approximately 0.6 million inhabitants, 48 percent practice Christianity, 22 percent Hinduism, 14 percent Islam, and the remainder Afro-American and other religions.

11. Jack Menke, "The State in the Development Process of Suriname," in *Problems of Development of the Guianas*, ed. Henry Jeffrey and Jack Menke (Paramaribo: Anton de Kom universiteit van Suriname, 1991).

12. Giacomo Luciani, "Allocation vs. Production States: A Theoretical Framework" (Graduate Institute of International and Development Studies, Anton de Kom University, 1987).

13. In 2020 established power-sharing coalition government consisted of the following parties: the VHP, twenty seats; the Algemene Bevrijdings en Ontwikkelings Partij (ABOP), eight seats; the Nationale Partij Suriname (NPS), three seats; and the Pertjaja Luhur (PL), two seats.

14. Jack Menke, "Democracy and Governance in Multi-ethnic Societies: The Case of Suriname," *Caribbean Dialogue* 6, nos. 3/4 (2000): 67–88.

15. Jack Menke, *Restructuring Urban Employment and Poverty* (Paramaribo: Stichting Wetenschappelijke Informatie, 1998).

16. James Petras, "The Redemocratization Process," *Contemporary Marxism* 14 (1986): 1–15.

17. Two months after the election, the Nieuw Front consociational coalition lost ten seats due to party fragmentation. The VHP lost five elected seats to members who founded a new party. The Javanese-related KTPI withdrew its five seats from the Nieuw Front and, like the VHP dissidents, joined the opposition NDP. In addition, two other parties—Alliance and DA91—lost seats as some elected members also joined the new coalition of the NDP, which won sixteen parliamentary seats. See Jerome Egger, "Chronologisch overzicht 23 mei–14 september 1996," in *Politiek in Suriname, Politieke ontwikkelingen en verkiezingen voor en na 23 mei 1996*, SWI Forum voor Wetenschap en Cultuur, vol. 12/2–13/1 (Paramaribo: Stichting Wetenschappelijke Informatie, 2016).

18. The resulting coalition in 1996 was made up of the NDP (leftist populist), PVF (left-wing farmworkers), HPP (center-left), and center or center-right parties BVD, KTPI, and OPDA.

19. Menke, "State in the Development Process."

20. Marten Schalkwijk, "De etnische stem in de Surinaamse politiek," in *Politiek in Suriname*.

21. The 2000 elections show a further fragmentation in terms of splitting of existing political parties. The difference from 1996 was that the fragmentation in 2000 occurred before the elections, resulting in five new political parties.

22. Schalkwijk, "De etnische stem in de Surinaamse politiek."

23. Henry Veltmeyer and James Petras, *Latin America in the Vortex of Social Change Development and Resistance Dynamics* (London: Routledge, 2019).

24. Armand Snijders, "Suriname en de cocaïnehandel" (1), *De Ware Tijd*, July 15, 2022.

25. Armand Snijders, "Suriname en de cocaïnehandel" (1); Armand Snijders, "Suriname en de cocaïnehandel" (2), *De Ware Tijd*, July 18, 2022.

26. In January 2017 Alcoa announced the permanent closing of the Suralco alumina industry and bauxite mines in Suriname, which had been curtailed since November 2015. The bauxite industry, which started in 1916, had a very low export value of USD $7.1 million in 2016 (Central Bank Suriname).

27. The ABOP (Algemene Bevrijdings- en Ontwikkelingspartij, or General Liberation and Development Party) is a party with many Maroon followers. It was founded in 1990 and chaired by Ronnie Brunswijk.

28. According to the 2013 agreement, IAMGOLD will maintain all its existing entitlements in the Rosebel operations and in the Gross Rosebel exploitation concession and will extend the term of its existing mineral agreement by fifteen years to 2042. The agreement will further establish a new joint venture growth vehicle (the JV) under which Rosebel would hold a 70 percent participating interest, and the government will acquire a 30 percent participating interest on a fully paid basis. The source of the official list of concessionaires and maps of the concessions issued in the "area of Interest Surgold" is the letter of June 7, 2013, addressed by the president of Suriname to the president of the National Assembly. The JV area has been defined as a circular area extending 45 km from the Rosebel mill but excluding the Gross Rosebel concession, for a net JV area of approximately 6,190 km².

29. Prior to the National Assembly's approval of the final agreement in 2013, the incumbent government issued many concessions in the so-called area of interest of the Newmont gold company, while the Geological Mining Service (GMD) was bypassed (*Starnieuws*, June 17, 2013). The official list with names of concessionaires and maps of issued concessions in the "area of Interest Surgold," according to registration of the Geological Mining Service, contained seventy-seven issued concessions ranging from 200 to 28,174 hectares. Among the names on the list were the president's attorney and the chair of the political party ABOP, which was part of the 2010–15 government. The opposition raised a few other objections against the area of interest. First, this term does not occur in Surinamese mining law. This law is the basis for issuing mining concessions to national, international, and multilateral companies where "area of interest" of Iamgold and Surgold (joint venture between Suralco and Newmont) was introduced by the Bouterse government. Another concern was raised regarding the fact that many habitats of traditional peoples are located in the area of interest. The forest management law of 1992, the L-decree of 1982, and the nature conservation law of 1982 state explicitly that residences and habitats of the traditional peoples' areas may not be allocated to third parties. Mem-

bers of the political opposition in the National Assembly named eight companies and individuals who had received concessions but were not on the list of concessions issued, and thus questioned the completeness of this list.

30. Parbode, "De 10 golden boys van Suriname," *Parbode*, September 1, 2012, https://www.parbode.com/de-10-golden-boys-van-suriname/, accessed October 3, 2021.

31. Dew, *Difficult Flowering of Suriname*.

32. R. Hoppe, "Het politieke systeem van Suriname; Elite-kartel democratie," *Acta Politica* 11, no. 2 (1976): 145–77; Dew, *Difficult Flowering of Suriname*.

33. Jack Menke, "Laudatio Eward Dew," *Academic Journal of Suriname* 6, no. 1 (2015).

34. Antonio Gramsci, *Selections from the Prison Notebooks of Antonio Gramsci*, ed. and trans. Quintin Hoare and Geoffrey Nowell Smith (London: Lawrence & Wishart, 1971).

35. Jack Menke, "Elections in Suriname: A Historical Power Shift," in Olhares Amazônicos, *Revista científica do núcleo de pesquisas eleitorais e políticas da Amazônia* 3, no. 2 (2015).

36. An example is the Gold Sector Regulation Committee, which was established in 2011 but has been undermined by the conflict of interest of high-ranking politicians and business persons involved in the gold business.

37. Giacomo Luciani, "Allocation vs. Production States: A Theoretical Framework," in *The Rentier State*, ed. Hazem Beblawi and Giacomo Luciani (London: Routledge, 1987), 63–84.

CHAPTER 15

Antisystem Politics in the Postcolonial Predicament

SCOTT TIMCKE

The year 2022 marked sixty years since Jamaica and Trinidad and Tobago attained independence and began their respective journeys to democratic freedom. There is much worth celebrating. Institutionalized prejudice has waned with political rights supported by free and fair elections, periods of economic growth, and a relatively free media, and an active civil society has meant there has been little protracted civil strife. These multiracial societies have had several multiparty elections governed by the rule of law to elect representatives. This is a commendable achievement, especially considering the varied trajectories of other members of the second wave of democratization.

There is, however, much that dampens the mood too. The state coffers are empty. Service delivery is weakening. Prolonged oil extraction has caused untold environmental disaster in Trinidad while interpersonal violent crime is escalating in both countries and their murder rates are among the worst in the world. There is considerable sexual and gender-based violence with rights around sexuality still to be consolidated. By international benchmarks these countries' poverty and unemployment outcomes rank poorly. Illicit narco-capitalism fuels mafias. State officials pursue private rent-seeking strategies. Between these two forces corruption has been normalized while the poor are at best an afterthought. But scapegoats must be found. Growing nativist sentiment licenses open xenophobia in Trinidad toward Guyanese migrants and Venezuelan refugees. On the economic front, there have been downgrades from rating agencies due to worries about sovereign debt. One way or another this is at the expense of citizens. Collective bargaining membership is in retrograde while successive governments have done little to boost the protective role of trade unions. These are all major problems that hinder the belief in democratic governance. The result is that all too frequently when walking on the streets of Kingston and Port of Spain one hears passionate arguments for a strongman to "jump up and fix it." And one must remember that the discourse in the boardrooms a few stories above is similar, albeit more polished.

The inauspicious events listed above have several specific and generic explanations, but they are united by being a consequence of a deep political and economic estrangement that can be explained best by decisions to retreat from egalitarian politics in the late twentieth century. Arguably there has been no further substantive democratization since. This is important to remember because freedom is not equivalent to liberation from colonial rule. To believe otherwise is to confuse the formal polity with everyday realities. Nor can freedom be satisfactorily found with minor modification of pre-reform nineteenth-century British protoliberalism, its norms, institutions, and civic relations. Moreover, the nature and maintenance of democratic freedom has tended to slip from public discourse; instead, the interests of capital predominate. In summary, both Jamaica and Trinidad and Tobago are now neoliberal market economies whose governments typically promote uncomplicated pro-market visions that expose their citizens to regular trying social upheavals.

Extending concepts and analysis developed by Jonathan Hopkin and Orlando Patterson, respectively, in this chapter I aim to showcase the "antisystem politics" that characterize the "postcolonial predicament." Whereas Hopkin examines how permutations of electoral systems and creditor-debtor relations shape the character of popularist responses to rising social inequality in rich countries in the Global North, I aim to extend his thesis to poorer societies in the Caribbean.[1] To assist in this exercise, I draw on Orlando Patterson's analysis of cartel politics in the Caribbean to undertake a comparative analysis of contemporary popular politics in Jamaica and Trinidad and Tobago.[2] Doing so can add another data point in the debate on the rise of populism.

The argumentation in this chapter is organized in the following way. The second section elaborates on Jonathan Hopkin's and Orlando Patterson's ideas. The third section shows how a synthesis of these two arguments can be applied to deeply felt grievances and dissatisfactions that currently circulate in Jamaica and Trinidad and Tobago. The fourth section deals with issues of inequality in Trinidad and Tobago, while the fifth section turns to austerity in Jamaica. In different ways these sections show how movements in these two countries have drawn on protectionist ideas to advance their politics, at times pressuring the prevailing social pacts to accommodate soft-protectionist rhetoric to ward off being completely outflanked on this issue. In addition to offering a conclusion, the final section outlines a series of strategic responses to address social inequality, which, if carried out rigorously and on a sufficient scale, would do much to overcome the deep mistrust that effectively blocks egalitarian social development and inclusive economic activity in Jamaica and Trinidad and Tobago.

Finally, this is a chapter about the shifting boundaries of politics. By necessity it covers the history of political parties in these two countries, their formation, and their governmentality during their time in office. But it is also a chapter that goes beyond this activity to focus on *le politique*. This French term translates poorly as "the political" but signifies the meta-exercise—the work—undertaken to create the elements like the state, the nation, citizenship, and so on that come to be employed in the activity of politics.[3] As I use it, "the political" denotes the Foucauldian "regulatory power" over what Marx called the "basic forms" of a society, the commodity form and the money form being among the most well known. It is from this perspective that this chapter assesses whether the politics in Jamaica and Trinidad and Tobago can generate social and economic progress, whether predicaments may once again become prospects.

Patterson and Hopkin

As mentioned, this chapter draws on Jonathan Hopkin's and Orlando Patterson's respective concepts to theorize how social inequality constrains freedom. *The Confounding Island* is capstone to Patterson's long career charting the material reverberations of enslavement through the totality of Jamaican life. For example, in his first major work, *The Sociology of Slavery*, Patterson shows how enslavement and colonization produced societies rife with disintegration.[4] Dispensing with the legal definition of property and exploitation, he deems enslavement to be an institution dedicated to "the permanent, violent domination of natally alienated and generally dishonored persons," which leaves behind discontinuity and destruction. This is "social death" due to a "conditional commutation" of death.[5] These are the preconditions for what Patterson calls the "postcolonial predicament," an exploration of the promise of socialist decolonization and how it became an unfulfilled aspiration to conceptualize and realize new forms of freedom.[6] For Patterson democratic independence involves not only vital constitutional elements, like rights, elections, and the transfer of power, but also the formation of a civic culture, responsive institutions, public engagement, social data, and an epistemology that shows regard for the people previously exploited and oppressed. In this radical social and economic transformation, the hierarchies built on natal alienation were to be replaced by egalitarianism; development pathways could be built with the existing modes of trade and commerce rather than hastily imported industrial policies while empowered communities did not require huge state bureaucracies for governance. But this aspiration never came about.

Through an embrace of neo-institutionalism for his comparative historical sociological analysis of Jamaica and Barbados, Patterson seeks to account for the divergent developmental outcomes between the two countries.[7] Although they share "the English language, Westminster parliamentary democracy, constitutional protection of private property, English common law, and the Anglican Church," Patterson contends that white and Black Barbadians were better able to adopt and appropriate these institutions for their needs. Patterson arrives at this conclusion by undertaking a broad social history, inclusion of settlement patterns relative to geology, the nature of firms, attributes of the tradable commodities, and colonial governance. For example, the Jamaican topography lent itself to a series of rebellions by the enslaved and Maroon communities. The major consequence of the 1865 Morant Bay rebellion was the disbandment of the local assembly suspending self-rule. By contrast Barbados had fewer absentee plantation owners, meaning there was more investment in stable self-government. So while not without racist institutions and class oppression, Barbados was sufficiently stable that "a single cultural system emerged," according to Patterson. Come independence, "the crucial difference" for Barbados was "that now the electorate was expanded to the entire adult population and its leaders derived from the formerly excluded classes." This helped form a peaceful transition to self-rule and an acceptance and comprehension of the inherited political institutions. Together this led to Barbadian political parties being better able to adhere to "disciplined policy choices."[8]

By contrast, Jonathan Hopkin focuses on how economic distress shapes ideology and politics. Drawing on the intellectual categories and motifs of Karl Polanyi to look at the transformation of institutions as they drive or react to material developments, Hopkin's chief case study is the fallout from the 2008 Great Recession. The main outcome was that rich democracies prioritized safeguarding the wealth of shareholders over the general interests of citizens. Actions like these provoked great anger, and justifiably so.[9] "Banking bailouts and austerity were political choices, and citizens could not be expected to be indifferent to their consequences," Hopkin writes.[10] This decision was consistent with The Great Commodification that occurred in the late twentieth century. This development saw the creep of market logics into all areas of social life; it swept away the post–World War II social pact that had established institutions geared toward welfare and redistribution. The periodic and broad social upheavals to places and communities resulted in the loss of confidence in the capitalist political economy in European neoliberal democracies. Perhaps predictably, the leadership of neoliberal democratic parties was no longer seen as credible. In this gap antisystem politics mobilize a rhetoric of elite betrayal to foreground a structural critique, ultimately advocating for what they deem to be more democratic control of the market.

When rising inequality meets a financial shock it creates conditions ripe for a political backlash, a condition Hopkin describes as antisystem politics. Although there are both left and right expressions of antisystem politics, what unites them is the pursuit of limited decommodification of social goods like health, housing, and income protection, as was the case with Western democracies. While taking various organizational forms and advancing different ideological rhetoric, the various branches of antisystem politics distrust the organized consensus of mainstream neoliberal governance predominant in Western democracies that tacitly accepts social harms. Antisystem politics rejects the current social pact over the appropriate hands-off role of the market and government. It rejects the "cartel politics" of the neoliberal type of democratic governance model, which regularly downplays the contradictions between capitalism and democracy.[11] Instead there is a demand that governments act quickly to address the sources of economic distress and social inequality.

In a context in which parties delegated the management of the market to experts while competing on administrative competency or mythologized cultural distinctions, these "scientifically grounded technical fixes" hardly addressed redistribution politics. There was a vast silence on class decomposition, precariatization, stalled wages, and other predictable and known outcomes of the ordinary operation of markets. At its most crisp, antisystem politics seeks to reassert the power of politics over markets and money; the demand for social protections against the ordinary operation of the market is an organic and organized response to capitalist development producing wealth and fragile societies concurrently. For this domestication to be successful they must be "meaningful mass participation in political decision-making over whatever matters society thinks are important."[12]

The character of antisystem politics in different countries can be explained by "the nature of party politics and the development of economic and social policies" that are also the key "variables [that] explain why some countries have been far better equipped to survive globalization and its attendant economic shocks than others."[13] Put differently, antisystem politics tends to emerge where trade deficits exist, welfare systems are in retrograde, and election laws artificially limit representation, like in the Westminster parliamentary system. Nationalist expressions tend to appear in creditor countries when weak welfare systems are eroded further and migrants take advantage of labor mobility rules. Progressive expressions tend to appear in debtor countries where young populations may likely not inherit the same welfare as prior generations.

Hopkin is adamant that "rather than dismissing anti-system politics as 'populism,' driven by racial hatred, nebulous foreign conspiracies, or an irrational belief in 'fake news,' we need to start by understanding what has gone wrong in the rich democracies to alienate so many citizens from those who govern them."[14] Certainly, nationalists do marshal racist grievances, but progressives seek to expand democratization through providing protection from market rule. And so there is wisdom in Thomas Piketty's observation that "in practice, the term 'populism' has become the ultimate weapon in the hands of the objectively privileged social class, a means to dismiss out of hand any criticism of their preferred political choices and policies."[15] Accordingly, antisystem politics is not inherently antidemocratic, but through dismissal it underscores how elite neoliberals skirt democratic accountability for "the upheavals of the second decade of the twenty-first century."[16]

Through looking more deeply at aspects of political economy, can these two explanatory frameworks be applied to the contemporary West Indies? I believe so, especially when comparing the various popularist responses to "Caribbean neoliberal democracy" as shaped by experience of enslavement and legacy of colonialism as well as the policy choices by political parties. Indeed, doing so can help flesh out what is at stake in the "postcolonial predicament."

Party, State, and Society in Postcolonial Plantation and Enclave Economies

The skeletal picture of Jamaican and Trinbagonian economy and society is that of the result of British colonial rule overseeing plantations stocked with bonded labor, a system mostly unaltered for roughly two centuries aside from minor relaxation with apprenticeship and indentureship following abolition in 1833. To supplement the suppressed plantation contract wages, Black household production and cultivation formed a "slave proto peasantry" complemented with remittances from migrated workers.[17] The rise of industrialism brought enclave extractivism of minerals like bauxite, recourses like oil, and more recently the experience of international tourism, much more so in the case of Jamaica.

While an *oikouménē* is clearly identifiable, the maturing musculature reveals two different developmental paths.[18] So while Jamaica and Trinidad and Tobago were both subject to "the British system," the regime change instituted by independence nevertheless led to different experiences of transitional democratization.[19] These experiences were especially dissimilar in the closing decades of the twentieth century, in part due to the particularities of their economic base formed decades prior. Indeed, as it came to the future of politics, different material consolidations led to different formulations of the question of reform, revolution, or revanche as well as different modes of attendant reasoning. The legacies of the internally contested questioning of the consolidation provide the contextual frame for the governing circumstances in the first two decades of the twenty-first century.

To begin with Jamaica, due to foreign capital injection in the early twentieth century to modernize the plantation system through introducing the internal combustion engine and new cane strains as well as consolidating agribusiness through fewer but more productive factories, both of which generated a degree of subsequent inertia, Jamaican economic performance was passable up until the mid-1960s.[20] But this superficial prosperity camouflaged structural weaknesses like accumulating technological deficiencies in small and medium enterprises, the intensification of antagonistic resentments between workers and capitalists, and the conflict between foreign capital and the local elites' conception of the national interest. The sugar industry was then Jamaica's single largest employer and second leading foreign exchange earner. It declined due to monocultural production and inefficient land use exacerbated by stringent prices on the world market and the aggressive repatriation of surpluses to the metropole. The late 1960s were characterized by the onset of an organic crisis with its attendant social instability. Responding to secular stagnation, the agro-proletariat channeled their grievances into class struggles; meanwhile due to racial exclusivity the lack of management opportunities for locals meant these antagonisms were not attenuated. As Carl Feuer summarizes, "Ten years after political decolonization it was clear that the process of national liberation and development was moving in reverse."[21]

The contradictions of underdevelopment brought the People's National Party (PNP) to power. Under Michael Manley the party won the 1972 election with an implicit democratic socialist platform predicated on pursuing growth through redistribution and nationalization policies to provide relief.[22] This program was funded via domestic and external borrowing causing net external debt to rise from JMD $352.8 million in 1975 to JMD $1.328 billion in 1979. Subsequently from 1974 to 1980, Jamaica experienced an average decline of -2.8 percent to its GDP.[23] Unemployment skyrocketed. Skilled labor migrated. Rural depopulation drove massive urbanization. Certainly, the PNP made errors. But regardless of any academic assessment of this policy course, the material conditions in the preceding paragraph constrained the possible solutions. Same, too, with the 1973 oil crisis.

Given its democratic socialist agenda, the PNP's policy course alienated the U.S. government and the local lumpen bourgeoisie. This dissatisfaction was personified by targeting Manley for his cooperative conduct toward Cuba, his support for the MPLA in Angola, and his advocacy for Puerto Rican self-determination. Accordingly, U.S. bilateral assistance nearly halved, falling from USD $32.2 million in 1977 to USD $14.6 million in 1980. This signal was clearly designed to precipitate a change in Jamaican government.[24] This happened when the Jamaica Labour Party (JLP) won the 1980 election in a landslide over the PNP, fifty-one seats to nine.

Under Edward Seaga the JLP government aggressively pivoted the state toward U.S. economic policy preferences. The abrupt conservative policy course has been accurately described as a "return to dependent capitalism" with the JLP hoping that by hitching a wagon to the locomotive power of the First World, benefits would trickle down.[25] Shamelessly Jamaica became a full-fledged client state; the reality of the subordinate relationship interdicted through excessive consumption by inflating a mythologized Jamaican cultural distinctiveness, attributes that would later be commodified when adhering to U.S. neoliberalization. But sporadic growth in the early 1980s showed that allegiance does not always bring growth, and by 1984 the economy fell into a recession. Fast forward a couple of years and the JLP government's "pragmatic" monetarism was unable to turn the economy around. While the International Monetary Fund (IMF) had sniffed around in the late 1970s, what followed was a series of IMF stabilization programs and World Bank structural adjustment loans to enforce strict fiscal discipline and harsh constraints on public spending on social protection.[26] A massive privatization campaign in the 1980s and 1990s is indicative of this pivot. In this period there was full or partial disinvestment from sixty-seven state-owned enterprises that spanned the finance, insurance, manufacturing, minerals, and tourism sectors. These entities were either asset stripped, leased, or listed.[27]

Bound by cross-conditionality, successive Jamaican governments had few

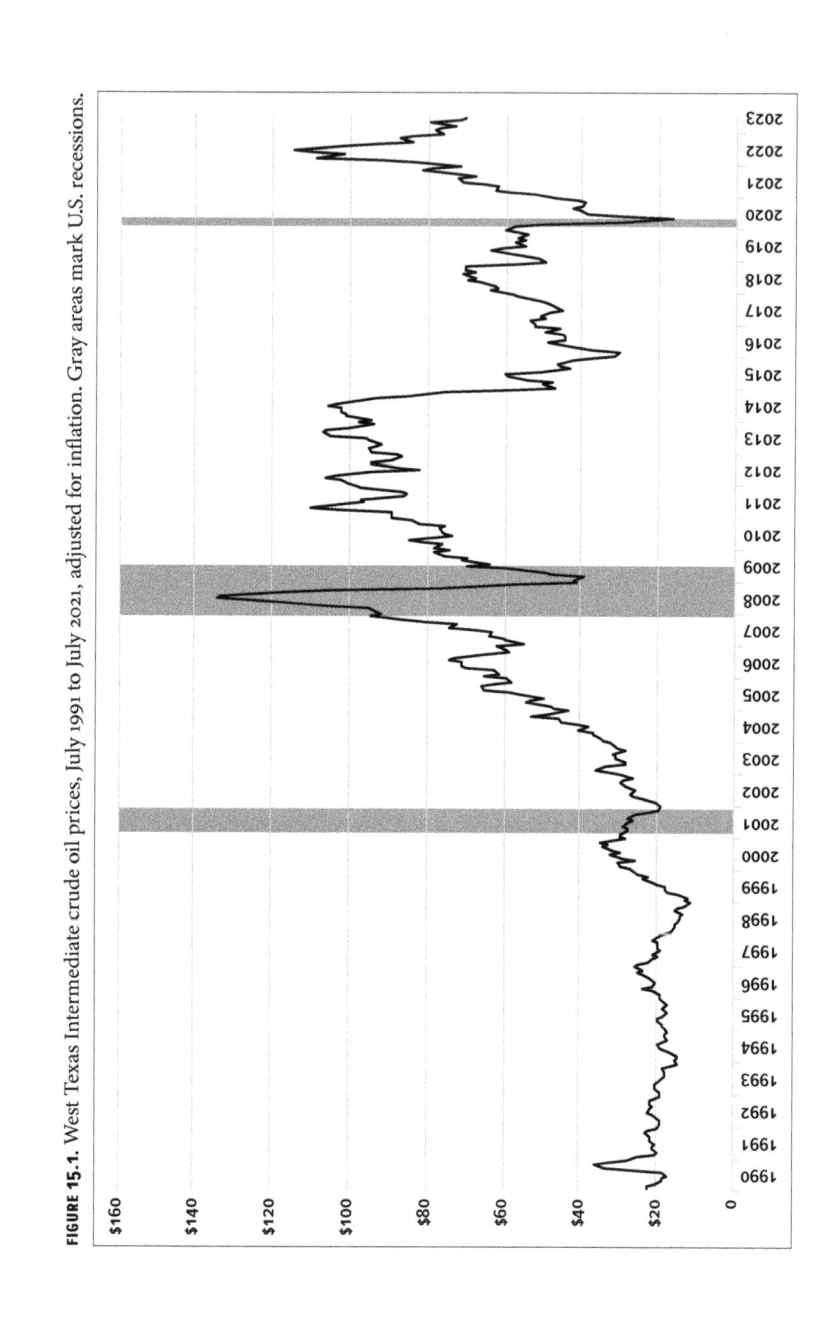

FIGURE 15.1. West Texas Intermediate crude oil prices, July 1991 to July 2021, adjusted for inflation. Gray areas mark U.S. recessions.

TABLE 15.1. Crude Oil Price Supercycles, 1982–2012

Crude oil prices	1892–1947	1947–1973	1973–1998	1998–2012
Peak year	1920	1958	1980	2008
Percent rise in prices during upswing (%)	402.8	27.4	363.2	466.5
Percent fall in prices during downswing (%)	-65.2	-23.1	-69.9	—
Length of the cycle (years)	55	26	25	—
Upswing	28	11	7	10
Downswing	27	15	18	—

SOURCE: Bilge Erten and José Antonio Ocamp, "Super-cycles of Commodity Prices since the Mid-Nineteenth Century," DESA Working Paper no. 110, February 2012, p. 13, https://www.un.org/esa/desa/papers/2012/wp110_2012.pdf.

tools to attend to the negative social effects of austerity, of which there were many and which still haunt the country to this day.[28] While poverty was reduced from 44.8 percent of the population in 1991 to 16.7 percent in 2001, this was achieved at the cost of increasing foreign currency reserves through acquiring debt. The result has meant that when events like the global coronavirus pandemic occurred, Jamaica did not have the fiscal means and monetary policy tools to adequately intervene and reshape the economy. This is partly why the country's GDP decreased by 9 percent in 2020 and why at least 50,000 people directly lost employment within the tourism sector alone.[29]

Comparatively, the postindependence experience of Trinidad and Tobago is simpler to convey, if only because it orbits the combustible politics of petrocapitalism. Key to this social contract was that governments prioritized the fiscal management of natural resource revenues to periodically fund welfare programs that sought to justify and legitimate extractivism. This politics solidified the ties between the exploitation of nature and nationalism.[30] Following the postwar boom in oil and the "democracy dividend" from independence, enterprise burgeoned in Trinidad and Tobago. While the 1973 oil crisis proved difficult for other Caribbean counties, it ushered in nearly a decade of prosperity for Trinbagonians due to high oil prices. From 1983 to 1993, while there was a negative real growth—a factor in the 1990 attempted coup—the subsequent quarter century of high oil prices generated considerable growth (see figure 15.1). Still, these periods of growth and decline point to how volatility arising from the ending of commodity supercycles in the international political economy deeply shapes everyday life in the country (see table 15.1) like the rise in intense anti-incumbency sentiment expressed in the 1986, 1991, 1995, and 2015 national elections. Throughout, from 1970 to 1995, Trinidad and Tobago grew at 2 percent annually.

Turning to party politics, the People's National Movement (PNM) dominated the early period of postindependence. This dominance led to perceptions that Afro-Trinbagonians dominated the public realm and Indo-Trinbagonians dominated the private realm. With such a sharp divide between politics and the market, racial resentments generated unhealthy stereotypes that limited the formation of ideologically oriented parties.[31] Given its extended time in office, the PNM's postindependence government at times faced economic volatility, stagnation, and extraparliamentary opposition from the Black Power movement.

Economic woes and a harsh structural adjustment program caused a catastrophic electoral defeat for the PNM in 1986; the National Alliance for Reconstruction (NAR) formed a government with Arthur N. R. Robinson as prime minister.[32] This election was won through assembling a coalition from all racial groups. The NAR sought to reach an internal postracial settlement in the hopes of attaining a long occupation of power. Yet despite a multiracial membership, the NAR faced persistent charges of an Afro-Trinbagonian leadership catering to special pleading from that constituency.[33] Excommunication of key Indo-Caribbean cabinet officials reinforced this perception. When combined with weakening economic conditions due to declining oil prices—with these costs disproportionally carried by the poor—the coalition lost legitimacy, culminating in an attempted coup in 1990.

The mismanagement of the NAR coalition generated the conditions for the political rise of Basdeo Panday's United National Congress (UNC) during the 1990s. Between 1995 and 2001 the UNC formed a government. It signaled a shift in the site and sources of power, from urban northern Trinidad to rural southern Trinidad. Through pursuing Indo-populism and an expansive legislative agenda, the UNC government sought to remake national institutions. Meanwhile a generational shift in leadership and more political work to make Tobago a stronghold returned the PNM to relevance in the last decade of the twentieth century. Their policy agenda was predicated on the rollout of the neoliberalization of governance.

Class and Sectorial Inequalities

Several explanations are typically given to account for the poor economic performance in the wider Anglo-Caribbean. These range from weak demand, inefficient institutions, and the lack of formal entrepreneurship to low education levels and hence poor workforce development policies. Other explanations focus on the skills deficiencies in the public sector that traverse and cut across the managerial, administrative, and technical layers of bureaucracy. This hampers individual departments from meeting their strategic objectives. There are spillover effects too, like being unable to maintain the market, through, for instance, consistency issuing business licenses in a timely manner. Finally, there is the path dependency set by British colonialism. To a greater or lesser extent all these factors apply to Jamaica and Trinidad and Tobago. But from my perspective they are downstream from more fundamental issues like the composition of—and relationship between—these countries' economies and classes. To move toward that point, there is value in looking at how wealth distribution and living standards are broadly shaped by the organization of infrastructure and institutions. To recall Hopkin's model, these kinds of divisions may suggest some important answers to questions about the rise of antisystem politics.

Despite the rhetoric of economic diversification by a variety of actors in Trinidad and Tobago, the country's exposure to risk has only increased as the energy sector has increased its share of the economy. Where once the energy sector comprised a quarter of the GDP in 1985, presently it accounts for upwards of 40 percent of GDP, 80 percent of exports, and 5 percent of employment. The dependency on energy extraction is underscored by the fact that since 1991, about 90 percent of capital has been directed to oil and gas. Rather than diversifying the economy away from oil, successive Trinidad and Tobago governments have permitted, even encouraged, concentration. This has made the small economy even more vulnerable to external energy price shocks. Therefore, the pursuit of extracting the recently discovered liquefied natural gas reserves has been at the expense of investment into other sectors like tourism, services, and nonchemical manufacturing, the types of industries that could provide a buffer to downturns in specific commodity prices. It is for this reason that Trinidad and Tobago has been characterized as a "dual economy," one booming, the other sluggish, but both exposed to the changing composition of energy sources across the globe.[34]

Trinidad and Tobago greatly benefited from the most recent commodity supercycle that began in 1999. This cycle was sustained by both China's rapid industrialization following membership in the World Trade Organization in 2001 and the subsequent removal of commercial barriers as well as the U.S. invasion of Iraq. Strong demand and stagnating world production eventually led to the oil shock of 2007–8.[35] Initially the Great Recession curtailed the demand for industrial commodities, meaning the price of oil dropped from USD $134 per barrel in June 2008 to USD $39 in February 2009, whereupon the Obama administration shepherded the American Recovery and Reinvestment

Act of 2009 into law. Without the imminent collapse of the global financial system, the price of oil stabilized in the range of USD $100 to USD $120 per barrel until 2015.[36] The result for Trinidad and Tobago was improvement in several key socioeconomic indicators. But these improvements are fragile given they came through exposure to macro-volatility, which in turn led to underinvestment in infrastructure, which compounds the underdevelopment of nonenergy sectors. In summary, successive governments did not use the country's resource endowments to produce a more diverse and inclusive economy.

The conclusion is clear. The more any Trinidad and Tobago government invests in oil and gas, the more it traps citizens with the underdevelopment of other sectors, forcing them to become more productive to compete, but facing systematic constraints like "poor management, low profitability, lack of human capital, poor access to foreign markets" and limited infrastructure when it comes to roads, ports, water, and telecommunications.[37] These constraints are compounded by mediocre state administration. For example, recent ease of doing business surveys place the country in the sixth decile of the 190 economies ranked.[38] Although not perfect, this metric can be used as a proxy indicator for responsiveness of the state in meeting everyday needs. The problems are so acute that it is not a matter of "fine tuning." Rather, it demands a holistic and structural rearrangement of the axioms of local political-economic planning. Without this change in preconceptions, existing efforts are likely to be so piecemeal as to be practically meaningless.

Altogether growth is not the main problem in Trinidad and Tobago. Rather, it is that the livelihoods of Trinbagonians are subject to the overdetermined whims of international market forces as they meet a one-dimensional economy. Furthermore, the governing class lacks the political vision to intervene in the market to ensure that the dividends of growth are first and foremost channeled to develop a wider array of nonenergy sectors to buffer against these whims. Doing so would have meant that the country was less vulnerable to the volatility in the energy market. The urgency of implementing this vision has become even more acute in the past three years as there is evidence that the proverbial "fat years" may be at an end. Undoubtedly Trinidad and Tobago was fortunate to benefit from "a commodity price boom that was unprecedented in its magnitude and duration."[39] As this supercycle has ended, it may well be indicative of the politics to come that during the 2017–18 local recession the government has implemented an aggressive austerity program including privatizing several state-owned enterprises and eroding state welfare programs with the express aim of repairing the damage to Trinidad and Tobago's public finance. Certainly, the impact of coronavirus has been terrible as recent state budgets attest, but it has also accelerated the fundamental unsound socioeconomic conditions.

The changing nature of class relations can help explain sectorial inequalities too. To elaborate, the profits from oil extraction that come from the extraction of surplus value are themselves predicated on significant drainage at the level of social reproduction. When examined at the granular level, effectively Trinidad and Tobago's nonenergy sector subsidizes the energy sector. Consider Rhoda Reddock's argument around the role of gender in class formation focused on the consequences arising from the transition from the plantation system to industrialization in Trinidad.[40] Whereas women labored during slavery and indentureship, Reddock examines how women were expelled from the emerging industrial labor market regime, confined to the domestic realm through naturalized expectation that they reflexively undertake undervalued—and often unpaid—socially reproductive roles with cheer.

Concurrent to proletarianization, this patriarchal revanche generated an ideological superstructure that found coarticulation in all the major societal institutions thereby reinforcing a gendered subjective comprehension of duty and diligence. Certainly, there was resistance, some of it organized, but Reddock notes that conditions meant they were generally auxiliaries. Indeed, women themselves failed to generate binding solidarity because they were crosscut by affiliations, class positions, and racial identities. This made it harder to sustain momentum for a unified anticolonial stance. Through providing a near complete account for why Trinidad and Tobago has had difficulties forming a multiracial anticapitalist movement, Reddock affirms the cautionary insights provided by Marx and Engels in *The German Ideology* that actually existing consciousness is entangled with the interests, assumptions, and norms of bourgeois ideology. So aside from there being little value in romanticizing the worker as a revolutionary actor, doing so will likely lead to intense disappointment.

The effects of class can be found in the stark differences in household incomes, asset ownership (either in business ownership or stock), access to quality education, and uneven municipal infrastructure, imbalances that leave many people lagging behind the wealthy in these countries. An examination into the local stock market can give some indication of the narrowness and interrelatedness of the Trinidad and Tobago's ruling class. Of the nearly twenty-nine thousand operating in the country, only twenty-eight firms were listed in 2005. As of 2024 there are now thirty-five. Whereas nearly 15 percent of British firms are listed, about 0.1 percent of Trinbagonian ones are. Reasons provided for the lack of listing include the legacy private ownership as well as existing listed firms controlled by interlocking directors who comprise "a few major market actors."[41]

Poor working-class Afro-Trinidadians have a sociopolitical restlessness that has expressed itself in labor unrest in the interwar years of 1934–39 and the Black Power revolt in the early 1970s, which sought to destabilize a PNM government whom they saw as governing for the Afro-Trinbagonian middle class. It goes to an interesting question of which class within an Afro-Trinbagonian bloc has a near monopoly on professional historiography and the production of popular culture as well as who financially benefits from the commercialization of Afro-Caribbean working-class culture, or who gets to validate the history of Black working-class protest movements.

The change in class structure and composition to which Reddock alludes created other means for political distinction-making practices and expressions of critique of the existing power structure. Furthermore, another consequence of the absence of class solidarity is that petty bourgeoisie class habitus is taken as the social fulcrum. Upward mobility and aspirational working class must enact the habitus of bourgeoisie mores, embody these traits, and safeguard and revere them as routes to respectability. But tacit acceptance does not mean that class cleavages do not exist. Indeed, given the fragility, coalitions cannot be mentioned lest it fracture fickle reifications of differences that have only relatively recently become politically meaningful. For example, within the Indo-Trinbagonian community, class differences split the UNC in the first decade of the 2000s, with the formation of the Congress of the People. The split was seen as urban, upwardly mobile Indo-Trinbagonians abandoning their rural roots, becoming "knife and fork Indians," as Basdeo Panday demeaned the breakaway faction.[42]

So whereas Selwyn Ryan puts great emphasis on ethnicity to explain postindependence Trinidadian politics, Kirk Meighoo believes this thesis is empirically threadbare.[43] Meighoo grants that ethnicity is a factor, but hardly an overdetermining one; instead, political alliances, pacts, and class interests are not bound by the dynamics of racialization. That said, racial divisions in Trinidad and Tobago do matter, as the resurgence of Indo-Trinbagonian nationalism, assertion of cultural pride, and racial mobilization in recent decades attests. Plus, there have been simmering pockets of Afro- and Indo-superiority as formal politics had been used to stave off Indo-Trinbagonians from using their market power to subordinate Afro-Trinbagonians. Though coded in racial terms, electoral politics is seen to counterbalance the power of the market, not for wider democratic ends but narrow nationalistic ones.[44]

While religious affiliation is strong, it especially factors into political life for

Muslim and Hindu Trinidadians, serving typically to articulate grievances, thereby becoming a glue for existing racialized coalitions. For example, since September 11, 2001, Muslim Trinbagonians testify that they believe they are victims of state surveillance. Hindu fundamentalists say that religion is a protective harbor against an Afro-Creolized agenda, which they view as trying to culturally erase the Indo-Caribbean person and practices from the conception of the ideal national subject.

Concurrently Trinidad is gentrifying. Formerly rural areas like Chaguanas are being suburbanized, with big box stores, strip malls, and large housing developments being constructed. So the "distance" in worldview that existed between peasant Indo-Trinbagonians and the working class, professionals, and petty bourgeoisie in the urban areas is narrowing. That distance typically meant that urban classes, Afro- and Indo- alike, had more political touchpoints and incentives and interests in coalitions for a share of economic growth—some of the things that gave the NAR its electoral victory. But this has waned as the Indo-peasantry has been converted into workers of all kinds, making racial fixing a more prominent feature of politics and requiring the Indian party to tolerate and tacitly court the fundamentalists. It is for this reason that Anton Allahar's arguments about ethnic entrepreneurs have such purchase. He writes, "Though having great differences between them, Afrocentrism and Hindu nationalism are political appeals made by ethnic entrepreneurs. Such entrepreneurs have very clear and narrow class and power interests at heart, but to realise those interests, they will mask them by emotional appeals to race, hoping thus to gain the support of as broad a base as possible."[45] Effectively, ethno-religious-racial mobilization becomes a cynical means of attaining political power, which can only come about through downplaying or attempting to discredit class-based movements.

This kind of political entrepreneurship can also be seen in the demand that Venezuelan refugees and migrants be deported. Certainly this is xenophobic. But the sentiment can also be restated as a demand for labor protectionism through calling for the state to intervene in the price mechanism in the Trinbagonian labor market by restricting supply. This is in a context where successive Trinbagonian governments have made liberal use of work schemes to artificially lower the official unemployment rate.[46] The popular assumption here is that the presence of Venezuelans introduces higher risks of unemployment as well as a downward pressure on wages. Effectively organized Trinbagonian labor wishes for citizenship to protect against competition in the labor market. Not for the first time are migrants to Trinidad deemed a threat to employment, existing wages, and living standards.[47] These kinds of ideas are indicative of not only exploitative, oppressive, and alienating conditions that workers contend with but also how they are equally susceptible to bourgeois ideology with its tropes of individualism, materialism, and promised prosperity.[48]

Even before the COVID-19 pandemic, almost five decades of neoliberal oil policy created extreme income, wealth, and social inequalities, with a volatile business cycle and many people with few qualifications on low wages, low job security, and dependence on a retreating state welfare system. The rise in housing prices means few people can get onto the property system. A national survey in 2010 found that slightly more than half of the 1,503 respondents were dissatisfied with the practice of democracy in Trinidad and Tobago, with nearly a quarter believing that the country is "not very democratic." Twelve percent expressed a preference for an unelected authoritarian regime, provided there was a "strong leader."[49] Sentiments like this can partially explain the narrow but trenchant support for Gary Griffith, a politician who was selected as Trinidad and Tobago's national police commissioner in 2018. Griffith's frequent wearing of fatigues and sidearm, accompanying police raids, and repeated remarks about killing "cockroaches" with "one shot one kill" when speaking about impoverished petty thieves are serious concerns to civil-security relations,[50] let alone the lack of comprehension of criminogenic environments in a petro-state like Trinidad and Tobago.

Rather, the popularist paradigm advocates for violent repression of the racial poor through aggressive criminalization. "After all," Keston Perry notes, "black and brown bodies are merely commodities which the parasitic oligarchy use to extract wealth for themselves—and therefore [are] dispensable when it suits them." The result is "seething distrust in our governing arrangements and in the ability of politicians to serve us [which] has bred alienation, xenophobia, disdain, hyper-individualism and a lack of empathy."[51]

Electoral System and Debt Relations

The rules that govern political interaction, like regime type, characteristics of institutions, and election cycles, reinforce the influence of party structure—or temporarily mute it. This section focuses on how electoral systems can give rise to political expressions like antisystem politics. As a baseline C. L. R. James noted how like in other newly independent societies the cadre of leaders in these new parties in the Anglo-Caribbean were typically prepared and trained in the metropole, with colonizers hoping these leaders would sympathize with—and cater to—the interests of the imperial bourgeoisie and thus be suitably entrusted to run former colonies. James does not spare "the West

Indian middle classes" from this critique. He writes that their "ignorance and disregard of economic development is profound and deeply rooted in their past and present situation. They do not even seem to be aware of it. . . . I do not know of any social class which lives so completely without ideas of any kind."[52] According to Anton Allahar, writing shortly after the turn of the millennium, "not much has changed."[53]

Allahar's view is fair given the extent to which the PNP and the JLP engage in "tribal politics" over "scarce benefits and spoils." Rather than ideology or platform, these parties' reliance on political patronage for electoral turnout has left the larger Jamaican electorate estranged from politics. The result is that where voter turnout averaged 83 percent in the 1980s,[54] in the 2010s it averaged 45 percent. Given the normalization of cash-in-hand voter buying and "election hampers," especially in marginal constituencies, this situation greatly helps these two parties lower outlays and associated costs of election campaigns. Jamaicans who sell their votes rationalize their participation due to financial need, indistinguishable party platforms, and the attitude that "Jamaica is a 'big hustle.'"[55] On this topic, Patterson writes that "Jamaica's flawed democracy, especially its clientelistic, garrison-based politics has independently generated a great deal of violence and laid the foundation for the current high rate of urban gang violence."[56] To legitimate themselves, organized urban criminal syndicates have stepped in by taking up the slack from the state's lack of service delivery. Furthermore, key portfolios of government like housing, water, transportation, and infrastructure have been centralized in the office of the prime minister. These portfolios give enormous power to a handful of people, making the stakes of interparty and national electoral contests much greater.

While there are many reasons for vote buying and other de-democratizing practices in Jamaican electoral politics, one cannot discount how Seaga's JPL repeatedly conceptualized democracy in narrow terms, like majority rule, or on a good day the electoral procedures that produce majorities. Arguably this construction sought to discredit broader conceptions of democracy that draw from revolutionary tradition, as Manley did.[57] But even in Seaga's terms of reference there was a significant democratic deficit because entities like the IMF and World Bank had (and continue to have) greater sway in the future of the Jamaican economy than Jamaican citizens. With the democratic infrastructure and imagination in the Jamaican repository the politics of austerity was not as sharp. What I mean is that there were fewer mechanisms for state-backed collective insurance to guard against unemployment and homelessness. Instead, most Jamaicans dealt with economic insecurity in small units, either as individuals or as part of a family. Many simply exited the polity by moving to the United States, Canada, or the United Kingdom.

Throughout the 1990s unemployment was consistently around 15 percent, although the poverty rate dropped from around 44 percent to just under 17 percent in the same period.[58] Systemic corruption in the public sector festered. The case of the National Solid Waste Management Authority is a good example of this endemic. From what is publicly known, between 2002 and 2005 there was JMD $1.96 billion in irregular spending. The Integrity Commission concluded that irregular spending was indicative of "a breakdown of governance and a rejection of the principle of accountability."[59] In short, the Jamaican political class abuse their positions of authority, engage in rent-seeking behaviors, and use state capture to divert state resources for their own enrichment. If it is true that anticorruption exercises are first and foremost always a political struggle about the form of the state, then what might the state-owned enterprise Petrojam not being able to account for nearly USD $40 million in income between 2013 and 2018 tell us about the probable victors in this struggle?[60]

The Jamaican economy staggered along like this until the Great Recession curtailed remittances by USD $250 million in 2009.[61] The local impact was so considerable that by the early 2010s, real wages had declined by 17 percent. Winning the 2011 election, the PNP government prioritized debt restructuring and another IMF conditional loan for nearly USD $1 billion over four years.[62] The high debt burden (and interest payments) limited government investment and capital spending in the economy. Such decisions can partially explain why in 2014 Jamaica's economy was smaller than in 2008 while in the interim poverty had doubled. Due to the IMF agreement, in 2015 Jamaica ran "the most austere budget in the world" with a surplus of 7.5 percent. (By contrast, after Greece's negotiation with the European Union, it ran a surplus of 3 percent of GDP.)[63] As of 2020, the Jamaican state had USD $14.7 billion in debt (105.5 percent of GDP), down from a high point of USD $21.6 billion in 2012 (143.9 percent of GDP), but nearly twice the amount it entered the twenty-first century with (USD $8.4 billion and 91.8 percent of GDP). Presently Jamaica's credit rating is highly speculative.[64] In summary, "the island's economic stagnation at the middle level of development," Patterson writes, "has independently generated a great deal of violence resulting from over-urbanization and the massive spread of smoldering slums, poverty, youth unemployment, precarious adult employment and income, and poor education."[65] Moreover, there are questions about how class and racial inequalities shape the distribution of the burdens borne from this economic arrangement.

Still, Jamaica's saving grace has been investments from China and Venezuela. Together these states have loans or investments totaling USD $62 billion across the Caribbean. Since 2005 China has reportedly lent Jamaica USD $2.1 billion for infrastructure development as well as invested USD $3 billion into sugar and bauxite enclave extractivism.[66] Like with other countries, Jamaica entered Venezuela's PetroCaribe oil program loans with these deferred payments permitting foreign currency reserves to be spent on other goods.

One consequence of the various interventions by the IMF and World Bank in Jamaica was an exaltation of monetarist dogma complemented by a neo-modernization paradigm that rested on an incredibly flat and partial—nay, fully mythologized and historically illiterate—rendering of Western development. With budget surpluses prioritized over public investment being the prominent feature in Jamaica's story, is there any real surprise that Black nationalists have taken an antiliberal sentiment, one that expresses itself in antisystem rhetoric? The hostility to Europe has much to do with decolonization, but the tapestry of Eurosceptic thinking weaves together several different strands of critique. One of these is how Black nationalists marshal opposition to European inherited institutions for no other reason than being European, believing that the form of these institutions themselves overdetermines local institutional culture and sidelines Jamaican lay social epistemology. But they do downplay the personnel that staff these institutions, their capability, and their willingness to serve the public.

The populist Black nationalist Right in Jamaica articulates skepticism, if not downright hostility, to Europe and European-originating principles of economic governance or the critique thereof, regardless of the merit of the ideas themselves. Put simply, these nationalist groups pursue projects that pivot on decolonization, not decommodification. For example, despite being bitter rivals, the PNP and JLP have a détente around reparations. Indeed, both parties support the National Council on Reparation. To wit, Paul Gilroy's remarks about Afrocentrism identarian movements lacking "even the possibility of imagining an alternative to capitalism" remain relevant.[67] The Jamaican nationalist has accepted the locomotive power of capitalism and fully amplified the use of civic ascriptions to stave off a politics centered on working-class aspirations. Their main concern is redeeming the injustice of economic drainage, not ending the possibility of drainage altogether and forever more. By contrast, in Jamaica there are several popular movements like #GhettoLivesMatter that perceive they have been neglected by government policies that prioritize asset protection over community investment. The central target of this critique is the state security forces that joyfully staff a carceral state doling out punitive, and sometimes violent, punishments to people living in criminogenic social and economic conditions, conditions that have been created with the aid of the nationalists.[68] As with intellectual exercises to "start with Africa"[69] and other kinds of primordial investigations, this is a conservative retreat from freedom and embrace of nationalism. The recognition, the conservatism, common origins, distinctive cultural heritage, are fashioned to be closer to imagined African practices. Instead, Black people in the Americas should go "beyond 'blackness.'" In a passage from decades prior, but which could equally apply now, Patterson argued,

> The Blacks of the Americas now face a historic choice. To survive, they must abandon their search for a past, must indeed recognize that they lack all claims to a distinctive cultural heritage, and that the path ahead lies not in myth making and in historical reconstruction, which are always doomed to failure, but in accepting the epic challenge of their reality. Black Americans can be the first group in the history of mankind who transcend the confines and grip of a cultural heritage, and in so doing, they can become the most truly modern of all peoples—a people who feel no need for a nation, a past, or a particularistic culture, but whose style of life will be a rational and continually changing adaptation to the exigencies of survival, at the highest possible level of existence.[70]

Decolonization involves the claim that democratic freedom and self-rule are universal. Yet freedom remains elusive because of Black particularism and cultural nationalism, the gap between democratic expectations and experiences.

Where growth is anemic and sovereign debt is high, debates about poverty and social services fail to honestly convey that mass unemployment is here to stay. Prior to the COVID-19 pandemic Jamaica had an unemployment rate close to 10 percent. Similarly, at the height of the most recent commodities super cycle, Trinidad and Tobago had 4 percent unemployment, but typically it is closer to 6 percent and would be higher if not for an overstaffed public sector with many "make work" projects.[71] But with a significant economic contraction, how likely is it that these figures will be significantly lower? Only in fever dreams. The sooner politicians, policymakers, and citizens internalize this fact and stop perpetuating thought-terminating clichés over false binaries about state spending like austerity or investment, the sooner more creative efforts can be carried out with existing resources. If extensive social grants are unaffordable, what *is* affordable? Might progressive taxation, even a wealth tax, be necessary? Would regressive indirect taxes or user fees be fair? In effect, questions of redistribution become more important than questions of growth because growth has not been sufficiently inclusive for governments to fulfill the democratic duty to offer citizens meaningful lives. Still, one thing is clear: withdrawing social protections to the unemployed, as one example, implies that these people have no place in the future except to counter bargaining demands from labor; it implies that the social contract no longer includes them, that their views and thoughts do not count. How might they reply? How should they reply?

Conclusion

This chapter has argued for why parts of the Caribbean are developing an antisystem politics. In Jamaica this is a lagging consequence to how austerity policies have failed to create broad political economic inclusion. In Trinidad and Tobago antisystem politics is a reaction to the increasing impotence of established political parties to address the upheavals brought about by economic concentration during commodity supercycles in the global market. Though the differences are important, the common objection is that a coercive state apparatus maintains public and social order to safeguard a favorable investment climate before the life chances of locals. Although expressed in a variety of ways, antisystem actors appear to be the only grouping willing to present an alternative pathway for Jamaica and Trinidad and Tobago to leave their current postcolonial predicaments. By asserting the need to alter policy decisions imposed by supranational institutions and global markets, in their respective ways antisystem politics calls for reining in the political sphere to make it follow the "will of the people" and for a greater democratization of the economy. While these are laudable goals, details and policy prescriptions do matter. For example, nationalists in Trinidad and Tobago wish to use citizenship to deny goods and services to new migrants, regardless of whether this violates human rights. In Jamaica ideas orbiting reparations are less concerned with anticapitalist imperatives and more invested in acquiring a capital injection to subordinate the market to local social imaginaries. These groups may not be offering the best ideas, but they are the only ones offering any.

This development in the postcolonial predicament has arisen because the ideological spectrum of neoliberal political parties is so narrow that there is effectively no ideological contest, let alone any strong progressive argument, about addressing pressing social questions. The expansion of social democracy to curb the downsides of the market is simply not present within the

Overton window of either society. There may well be a good reason for this gap in representation. As acerbic as astute, James said that the Caribbean political class had little comprehension of their functional role. "Many of them have the illusion that they are taking part in the exercise of parliamentary democracy," he wrote. With little admiration of the rise of this cadre, he called the various parties "rival gangs for possession" who serve the "age-old West Indian function of representing absentee owners."[72] If politics in Jamaica and Trinidad and Tobago is first and foremost about asset protection, extraction, and inflation targeting, could it ever serve the needs, wants, and desires of citizens?

I want to underscore that regardless of shortfalls in attaining freedom, by no means do I consider Jamaica and Trinidad and Tobago to be authoritarian. Populist movements typically do not exist in authoritarian regimes because these regimes submerge divisions. Elections are postponed. The opposition becomes managed. Parliaments unanimously ratify legislation. Apparent unity is neatly choreographed because these kinds of governments have little interest in mobilizing the public lest they get carried away and chase the security forces back to the barracks. And that is altogether undesirable.

Rather, these two countries are democracies facing justifiable grievances from their citizens. There is little patience for long-term investments by incumbent governments, at least by their calculations. Instead, distributive expectations feature prominently in the foreground because the ring of elections, though faint, can be heard. Opposition parties too know this. But without any anticipation of reaping collective gains from today's investments, they agitate through claiming that their constituents are excluded from short-term disbursements. The problem with this political merry-go-round is that disbursements are typically evaporated by inflation, so transitional conditions become difficult to exit. No doubt this is why pleas arise for a popular leader to disrupt things and take the reins.

Absolute prediction about the relative likelihood of scenarios is impossible; that said, Jamaica's and Trinidad and Tobago's respective situations will depend on political organization as well as economic outcomes. The existing patterns of politics are not necessarily immutable either. But there are limits to change when any "fixed politics" creates "fixed identities."[73] These in turn limit the political learning required to encourage cooperative attempts to find policy alternatives to increase the chance of deep, broad, and meaningful human flourishing.

NOTES

1. Jonathan Hopkin, *Anti-System Politics* (Oxford: Oxford University Press, 2020).
2. Orlando Patterson, *The Confounding Island: Jamaica and the Postcolonial Predicament* (Cambridge, Mass.: Harvard University Press, 2019).
3. Pierre Rosanvallon, *Counter-Democracy: Politics in an Age of Distrust* (Cambridge: Cambridge University Press, 2008), 5–12.
4. Orlando Patterson, *The Sociology of Slavery* (Rutherford, N.J.: Fairleigh Dickinson University Press, 1969).
5. Orlando Patterson, *Slavery and Social Death: A Comparative Study* (Cambridge, Mass.: Harvard University Press, 1985), 13.
6. Patterson, *Confounding Island*.
7. There is qualified utility to neo-institutionalism, especially in the work of Daron Acemoglu and James Robinson. See Scott Timcke, "The One Dimensionality of Econometric Data," *Triple-C* 18, no. 1 (2020): 429–43.
8. Patterson, *The Confounding Island*, 28, 78, 83, 32.
9. Also see Eric Lonergan and Mark Blyth, *Angrynomics* (Newcastle upon Tyne: Agenda, 2020).
10. Hopkin, *Anti-System Politics*, 14.
11. Hopkin, 39.
12. Hopkin, 43, 257.
13. Hopkin, 14.
14. Hopkin, 3–4.
15. Thomas Piketty, *Capital and Ideology* (Cambridge, Mass.: Harvard University Press, 2020), 962.
16. Hopkin, *Anti-System Politics*, 250.
17. Sidney Mintz, *Caribbean Transformations* (Chicago: Aldine, 1974), 130–55.
18. Sidney Mintz, "Enduring Substances, Trying Theories: The Caribbean Region as Oikoumene," *Journal of the Royal Anthropological Institute* 2 (June 1996): 289–311; George Beckford, *Persistent Poverty: Underdevelopment in Plantation Economies of the Third World*, 2nd ed. (Kingston: University of the West Indies Press, 1999), appendix 2.
19. Along with other Anglo West Indian territories, there was an attempt to form a political union. While it is beyond the scope of this chapter to precisely discuss the reasons for its failure, the West Indies Federation was short lived, lasting from 1958 to early 1962.
20. Gisela Eisner, *Jamaica, 1830–1930* (Manchester: Manchester University Press, 1961), 289–317.
21. Carl Henry Feuer, "Better Must Come: Sugar and Jamaica in the 20th Century," *Social and Economic Studies* 33, no. 1 (1984): 1–49, quotation on 40.
22. See Evelyne Huber Stephens and John Stephens, *Democratic Socialism in Jamaica: The Political Movement and Social Transformation in Dependent Capitalism* (Basingstoke: Macmillan, 1986).
23. Holger Henke, "Foreign Policy and Dependency: The Case of Jamaica, 1972–89," *Social and Economic Studies* 43, no. 1 (1994): 181–223.
24. Henke, "Foreign Policy and Dependency."
25. Stephens and Stephens, *Democratic Socialism in Jamaica*, 251.
26. World Bank, "Structural Adjustment in Jamaica, 1981–85," July 1990, https://

documents1.worldbank.org/curated/en/720261468038699062/pdf/29191.pdf; Damien King, "The Evolution of Structural Adjustment and Stabilisation Policy in Jamaica," *Social and Economic Studies* 50, no. 1 (2001): 1–53.

27. Rosalea Hamilton and Ann-Marie Grant, "Update on the Economy of Jamaica," *Caribbean Dialogue: A Journal of Contemporary Caribbean Policy Issues* 9, no. 2 (2004): 27.

28. See Elsie Le Franc, ed., *Consequences of Structural Adjustment: A Review of the Jamaican Experience* (Kingston: Canoe Press, 1994).

29. Maria Emilia Cucagna and Suzette Johnson, "Return to Paradise: A Poverty Perspective on Jamaica's COVID-19 Recovery Response," November 17, 2020, https://blogs.worldbank.org/latinamerica/return-paradise-poverty-perspective-jamaicas-covid-19-recovery-response.

30. Scott Timcke, "There Are No Jobs on a Dead Planet: The Combustible Politics of Rentiership in Caribbean Carbon Capitalism," unpublished working paper.

31. Selwyn Ryan, "One Love Revisited: The Persistence of Race in the Politics of Trinidad and Tobago," *Caribbean Affairs* 1, no. 2 (1988): 67–127.

32. Kirk Peter Meighoo, *Politics in a Half-Made Society: Trinidad and Tobago, 1925–2001* (Oxford: James Currey, 2003).

33. Ryan, "One Love Revisited."

34. Daniel Artana, Sebastián Auguste, Ramiro Moya, Sandra Sookram, and Patrick Watson, "Trinidad and Tobago: Economic Growth in a Dual Economy," in *Growing Pains: Binding Constraints to Productive Investment in Latin America*, ed. Manuel Agosin, Eduardo Fernández-Arias, and Fidel Jaramillo (Washington, D.C.: Inter-American Development Bank, 2009).

35. James Hamilton, "Causes and Consequences of the Oil Shock of 2007–08," Brookings Papers on Economic Activity, no. 1, 2009, https://www.brookings.edu/bpea-articles/causes-and-consequences-of-the-oil-shock-of-2007-08/.

36. Christiane Baumeister and Lutz Kilian, "Forty Years of Oil Price Fluctuations: Why the Price of Oil May Still Surprise Us," *Journal of Economic Perspectives* 30, no. 1 (2016): 139–60.

37. Artana et al., "Trinidad and Tobago," 411.

38. World Bank, *Doing Business 2020* (Washington, D.C.: World Bank, 2020), 4.

39. Bilge Erten and José Antonio Ocamp, "Super-cycles of Commodity Prices since the Mid-nineteenth Century," DESA Working Paper no. 110, February 2012, https://www.un.org/esa/desa/papers/2012/wp110_2012.pdf, 13.

40. Rhoda Reddock, *Women, Labour and Politics in Trinidad and Tobago: A History* (London: Zed, 1994).

41. Artana et al., "Trinidad and Tobago," 382.

42. Dave Ramsaran and Linden Lewis, *Caribbean Masala: Indian Identity in Guyana and Trinidad* (Jackson: University Press of Mississippi, 2018), 57.

43. Meighoo, *Politics in a Half-Made Society*.

44. See Ufot Inamete, "Politics and Governance in Trinidad and Tobago: Major Issues and Developments," *Caribbean Studies* 25, nos. 3/4 (1992): 305–24.

45. Anton Allahar, "False Consciousness, Class Consciousness and Nationalism," *Social and Economic Studies* 53, no. 1 (2004): 120.

46. For a discussion of race and labor policy, see Ramsaran and Lewis, *Caribbean Masala*, 55–59.

47. See Jerome Teelucksingh, *Labour and the Decolonization Struggle in Trinidad and Tobago* (New York: Palgrave Macmillan, 2015).

48. On the topic of false consciousness in the Caribbean, see Allahar, "False Consciousness, Class Consciousness and Nationalism."

49. Raymond Mark Kirton, Marlon Anatol, and Niki Braithwaite, "The Political Culture of Democracy in Trinidad and Tobago: 2010," June 2010, https://www.vanderbilt.edu/lapop/trinidad-tobago/2010-political-culture.pdf, 26–30.

50. Griffith Jensen La Vende, "My Language Is to Protect My Officers," *Newsday*, July 3, 2020, https://newsday.co.tt/2020/07/03/griffith-my-language-is-to-protect-my-officers/.

51. Keston Perry, "Trinidad and Tobago's Populist Moment: We Need Structural Change; Not a Superman," *Wired868*, December 2, 2018, https://wired868.com/2018/12/02/trinidad-and-tobagos-populist-moment-we-need-structural-change-not-a-superman/.

52. The main aim of the West Indian middle class, James says, is to "find some communists against whom they can thunder." Given Seaga's subsequent conduct in office, these remarks were prescient. See C. L. R. James, *Spheres of Existence: Selected Writings* (London: Allison & Busby, 1980), 131–34.

53. Allahar, "False Consciousness, Class Consciousness and Nationalism," 115.

54. Hamilton and Grant, "Update on the Economy of Jamaica," 18.

55. Office of the Political Ombudsman, 2020 General Election Campaign Review Report, 2021, 17–18, https://opo.gov.jm/wp-content/uploads/2021/05/2020-General-Election-Campaign-Review-Report.pdf.

56. Patterson, *Confounding Island*, 144.

57. Henke, "Foreign Policy and Dependency."

58. Hamilton and Grant, "Update on the Economy of Jamaica," 15.

59. Integrity Commission, NSWMA Final Report, June 2005, 35, https://integrity.gov.jm/sites/default/files/nswma_final_report_22june05.pdf.

60. Auditor General of Jamaica, *A Review of Aspects of PCJ and a Comprehensive Audit of Petrojam Limited*, December 2018, https://auditorgeneral.gov.jm/wp-content/uploads/2018/12/AuGD_Compendium_Report_on_PCJ_and_Petrojam_Limited.pdf.

61. Eliud Georg Ramocan, *Remittances to Jamaica*, Bank of Jamaica, 2011, https://boj.org.jm/uploads/pdf/papers_pamphlets/papers_pamphlets_Remittances_to_Jamaica_-_Findings_from_a_National_Survey_of_Remittance_Recipients.pdf.

62. IMF, Press Release: IMF Executive Board Approves U.S.$932.3 Million Arrangement under the Extended Fund Facility for Jamaica, May 1, 2013, https://www.imf.org/en/News/Articles/2015/09/14/01/49/pr13150.

63. Jake Johnston, *Partners in Austerity: Jamaica, the United States and the International Monetary Fund*, Center for Economic and Policy Research, April 2015, https://cepr.net/documents/Jamaica_04-2015.pdf.

64. By contrast, Trinidad and Tobago's rating is deemed to be lower medium grade.

65. Patterson, *Confounding Island*, 144.

66. Kirk Semple, "China Extends Reach in the Caribbean, Unsettling the U.S.," *New York Times*, November 8, 2020, https://www.nytimes.com/2020/11/08/world/americas/china-caribbean.html.

67. Paul Gilroy, *Against Race: Imagining Political Culture beyond the Color Line* (Cambridge, Mass.: Harvard University Press, 2000), 210.

68. Anonymous, #GhettoLivesMatter, Mr Policeman, *The Gleaner*, July 18, 2016, https://jamaica-gleaner.com/article/letters/20160719/ghettolivesmatter-mr-policeman.

69. Jahlani A. H. Niaah and Erin C. MacLeod, eds., *Let Us Start with Africa: Foundations of Rastafari Scholarship* (Kingston: University of the West Indies Press, 2013).

70. Orlando Patterson, "Toward a Future That Has No Past—Reflections on the Fate of Blacks in the Americas," *Public Interest*, Spring 1973, 60–61, https://www.nationalaffairs.com/storage/app/uploads/public/58e/1a4/b4b/58e1a4b4b40e5097156427.pdf.

71. If one looks around the Caribbean there is much work to be done. The point is that no one wants to pay for it.

72. C. L. R. James, "Tomorrow and Today: A Vision," *New World* 2, no. 3 (1966): 86.

73. Shelene Gomes and Scott Timcke, "The Decolonial Ends of Caribbean Ethnography," in *Decolonial Perspectives on Entangled Inequalities: On Europe and the Caribbean*, ed. Rhoda Reddock and Encarnacion Gutierrez-Rodriguez (London: Anthem, 2021), 155–72.

CHAPTER 16

China and the Caribbean beyond South-South Relations

RUBEN GONZALEZ-VICENTE AND ANNITA MONTOUTE

Introduction

In barely two decades, the People's Republic of China (PRC) has become one of the Caribbean's major trade partners, foreign investors and international lenders. However, despite the vast and excellent tradition of Caribbean literature on developmental matters, analyses of China-Caribbean relations are mainly technical in nature, neglecting critical local perspectives. This chapter revisits the tradition of Critical Caribbean Development Thought (CCDT) to apply it to the study of China-Caribbean relations. By giving the main stage to theorists from the region, we hope not only to capture the nuance of Sino-Caribbean relations but also to restore the work and spirit of scholars who were committed to empowering the region's capacity for agency and independent critical thought. Critical Caribbean Development Thought offers a theoretically robust and politically empowering alternative to otherwise predominantly empirical accounts of the Caribbean's relationship with China, raising important questions about continuing epistemic dependency, structural impediments to development in small and highly open states, and a number of unresolved issues relating to the postcolonial condition in former plantation societies. Drawing upon these insights, we explain how the expectations placed on the emerging "South-South" link with China are easily overstated, given China's elitist business-centric approach to development, the eschewing of participatory approaches in Sino-Caribbean ventures, the "passive incorporation" of the Caribbean into China's global vision, and the competitive pressures inherent to a consolidated world market.

The chapter is organized as follows: The first section revisits the tradition of CCDT, with an explicit but not exclusive focus on the English-speaking Caribbean, and suggests updates that account for the transformation of the global economy since the 1980s. The second section introduces Sino-Caribbean relations. The remaining sections apply a series of theoretical and analytical CCDT insights into the analysis of Sino-Caribbean relations.

The Emergence, Decline, and Continued Relevance of Critical Caribbean Development Thought

The Caribbean's tradition of critical thinking on development emerged out of a broader effort to resist colonialism and racism—both understood as derivatives of capitalist exploitation.[1] Much of the progressive intellectual scholarship in the region was fueled by, and had a symbiotic relationship with radical projects in the 1960s and early 1970s, such as Rastafarianism, the Black Power Movement, socialism, and the Third World's quest for a New International Economic Order.[2] As such, CCDT was part of a wider intellectual endeavour about the kind of social, economic, and political order that should be pursued in the post-independence era.[3] Inspired by these multiple movements, many Caribbean intellectuals shared a diagnosis for the underdevelopment of the region, attributing Caribbean underdevelopment to the unequal relations emanating from the Caribbean's passive insertion in the global economy. However, a schism emerged between those who proposed a complete overhaul of the capitalist system and those who ideated solutions within it.[4]

Carl Stone, Walter Rodney, and C. Y. Thomas were among the former. Their emphasis on class struggle resonated in the highly stratified Caribbean societies of the time, and their analysis of the unequal international division of labor in the postcolonial world gained adepts in the region and beyond—see for example Rodney's *How Europe Underdeveloped Africa*.[5] Situated within the Marxist orthodoxy of the time—which identified imperialism as a high stage of capitalism[6]—these scholars understood that social development could only be realized if the existing economic system was replaced in its entirety.[7] Emerging in the 1960s, the Plantation Economy School—espoused by intellectuals of the New World Group—shared the crux of the analysis, but sought to provide solutions suited to the peculiarities of Caribbean economies within the existing capitalist framework. Its key proponents included Lloyd Best, George Beckford, Kari Levitt, Norman Girvan, and James Millette.

The Plantation School's position became more prominent as the region gradually gained political independence. These scholars reassessed Arthur Lewis' proposals to promote agricultural productivity as a stepping stone towards the development of a competitive manufacturing sector.[8] Contrary to Lewis, they maintained that the establishment of a free peasantry and the availability of surplus labor—which could facilitate diversification away from sugar production—was not enough to increase productive capacity and break the traditional mercantilist links.[9] Whereas Lewis maintained that international trade and investment could kickstart the development process, the Plantation School saw in these links the very roots of underdevelopment.

The continued dependence on the plantation sector and other similarly foreign-controlled, natural resource–based and export-oriented sectors provided a good explanation of the external underpinnings of postcolonial underdevelopment.[10] However, the Plantation Economy School also explored how the dependent and exploitative ties with the metropole had shaped internal social, economic, and political institutional arrangements that would persist after independence.[11] Some of the most distinct contributions of CCDT coalesce in the dialectical relation between internal and external processes. Here, the idea of "epistemic dependency" stands out. Epistemic dependency expands the analysis of dependency beyond the economic basis and espouses it also as a "syndrome in [the region's] psychological makeup."[12] Drawing from Fanon's[13] thinking, independence was interpreted as a mere takeover of (neo)colonial administration as well as merchant and professional roles by local elites—or, in other words, little more than "flag independence."[14] As such, it remained constrained both by international economic hierarchies and by the region's postcolonial inability to reimagine development independently.

Therefore, the first step towards an alternative regional vision was the development of independent Caribbean political thought.[15] The peculiar challenges of the region needed to be addressed, in particular, its dependence due to its small size, high degree of openness, and ties to former colonial powers. This dependence was seen to pervade various sectors of the economy. These included the monetary system, public financing, and the extractive industries, which were at the mercy of multinational corporations.[16] In the immediate post–World War II period (1940s and 1950s), the Anglophone Caribbean followed Lewis's proposals for industrialization via foreign investment. This strategy yielded positive outcomes in growth and living standards, but failed to emerge as a self-sustaining formula for growth and socio-economic development.[17]

The Caribbean turned to import substitution industrialization strategies in the 1960s and 1970s, developing manufacturing bases in Trinidad and Tobago, Jamaica, and Barbados. However, local manufacturing was unable to tackle unemployment or to truly substitute imports.[18] Jamaica, under the leadership of Michael Manley, implemented a program of democratic socialism in 1974, nationalizing the bauxite sector and strengthening trade unions and worker rights.[19] However, low economic productivity, external pressures (e.g., a CIA-led destabilization campaign), and the debt crisis of the 1980s would bring the experiment to a halt. "Cooperative socialism" in Guyana under Forbes Burnham had a similarly redistributive rhetoric. However, the model displayed more elements of economic nationalism than of actual socialism.[20] The Grenada model of 1979–1983 demonstrated a more substantive socialist commitment, as it included full worker participation in the management and profits of state and parastatal enterprises.[21]

Some of the historical shocks sketched above—debt crisis, U.S. interventions—would precipitate the decline of CCDT. Other dynamics were internal. Around the early 1970s, the New World Group split, and its members left in different directions.[22] The schism between Marxist socialists and Plantation School scholars remains unresolved, with each group accusing the other of dependence on external influences, theoretical and methodological errors, and unrealistic expectations. The rise of nationalism and the growing intolerance of some Caribbean governments also contributed to the New World group's demise. Increasingly, nationalist leaders and university managers became wary of the group's interference in national affairs, and promoted the "nationalisation" of the staff of the individual campuses of the University of the West Indies. The latter gave rise to "new educated elites with a vested interest in insular nationhood."[23] The neoliberal turn in the global economy also adversely impacted the study of development economics in the region.[24] As state-driven development approaches declined in popularity, a new paradigm emerged in which the market became pre-eminent. Academia, business, and government shifted to survival mode. Training in political economy became subordinated to management education with a business-oriented mindset.[25] Indeed, some authors within the region have carried the torch of critical scholarship to our days, for example Violet Eudine Barriteau, Anthony Bogues, Tennyson Joseph, Don Marshall, Patricia Northover, and Rhoda Reddock. However, their most critical insights have often been sidelined in regional policy debates.

Despite its relative contemporary ostracism, CCDT remains relevant for a number of reasons. The Caribbean's increased participation in a globalized economy only emphasises Girvan's note of caution about "the consequences of passive incorporation into the world economy."[26] As noted above, such a mode of incorporation is both ideational and structural, and has as one of its corollaries the enduring hegemony of merchant capital over production.[27] The structure of underdevelopment has, however, transformed. Hierarchies that were once international are today global, with states increasingly catering to transnational capital.[28] The Caribbean participates today in a global economy that is more integrated than it was in the 1960s and 1970s.[29] National development strategies are aligned to both World Trade Organization obligations and bilateral partnerships, limiting the maneuvering space. Therefore, while the underlying philosophy and general principles of CCDT continue to be relevant, references to these frameworks in discussing the Caribbean's development challenges must necessarily take account of the new global environment. Here, without a doubt, the emergence of China as a key trade and investment partner, as well as a "development finance" powerhouse, is of critical importance.

The Sino-Caribbean Development Nexus

The Caribbean, like most developing regions, felt the first shockwaves of China's economic ascendance in indirect ways. Acutely decimated by two decades of neoliberal austerity, countries within the region that aspired to develop globally competitive manufacturing bases saw those aspirations thwarted by China's growing competitiveness since the 1990s—while consumers in the region benefitted from access to cheap products imported from China. Additionally, economies with an abundance of natural resources found in China a market and a driver for high commodity prices during the 2003–2013 resource boom. With the exception of Cuba, which had developed important trade and investment relations with China following the collapse of the USSR in the early 1990s,[30] most Caribbean economies started to develop more solid economic ties with the Asian country towards the late 2000s. Bilateral trade between the CARICOM and China was USD 3.4 billion in 2018,[31] out of USD 46 billion of total CARICOM trade.[32] Today, investment (over USD 9 billion in CARICOM) and finance (around USD 8.9 billion in loans to CARICOM countries) are the two most prominent vectors through which the PRC shapes the trajectory of Caribbean development.[33]

We observe three types of Chinese investments in the Caribbean region, which may be accompanied by varying degrees of state financing. In the first group are companies that have a cumulative impact in the region's economy. These companies invest in consolidated sectors such as tourism in Bahamas and Barbados, and in rising sectors such as the oil industry in Guyana. Their impact is cumulative in that they join other transnational investors and add on to existing trends within the region—although the initial investment may benefit from access to cheap credit from Chinese policy banks. In the second group are a number of Chinese businesses that invest in sunset industries. These companies have been able to cut managerial salaries and other production costs.[34] In Jamaica, for example, Chinese investments of over USD 260 million helped to keep the country's decaying sugar sector afloat for a number of years (more on this below). Similarly, the Jiuquan Iron and Steel Company (JISCO) was able to bring Jamaica's ALPART alumina processing plant back into businesses after it had lain abandoned for nine years. Jiuquan Iron and Steel Company's strategy included a reduction of costs in managerial salaries, the use of Chinese labor with different levels of qualification, and the increased casualization of local labor, now hired under shorter term contracts with salaries that are lower than those received in 2009.

The third type of Chinese investment involves a tandem of Chinese state finance and construction companies, and it is perhaps the most prominent in regional debates. Chinese construction companies made their first inroads in the region with the 2007 Cricket World Cup, when they helped to finance and construct or upgrade stadiums in Antigua and Barbuda, Jamaica, and Grenada (the latter amid diplomatic disputes with Taiwan). Chinese contractors have evolved from this niche and are now involved in expanding ports and airports (e.g., Antigua and Barbuda, Guyana), building roads (e.g., Bahamas, Jamaica), constructing and rehabilitating hotels and resorts (e.g., Bahamas, Barbados, Guyana), developing government buildings and hospitals (e.g., Antigua and Barbuda, Trinidad and Tobago), erecting convention centers and auditoriums (e.g., Antigua and Barbuda, Guyana, Jamaica, Trinidad and Tobago), and planning industrial parks (e.g., Antigua, Jamaica, and Trinidad). While a few companies have transited into private procurement, most of them operate within government-to-government frameworks. These arrangements are characterized by close negotiations between the Chinese and local governments, and involve a loan from a Chinese policy bank[35] to purchase the services of a Chinese state-owned contractor. Local governments provide sovereign guarantees for repayment, which reduces risks on the bank's investment. In some cases, the loans can be paid for with commodities or public assets. This has been the case for Jamaica's North–South highway, where a USD 457 million loan from the China Development Bank (CDB) was paid for with a 1200-acre land concession.[36]

These arrangements introduce a new "mechanism of accumulation" in the region, dependent not on global firms devoted to financial markets and shareholder value, but on the Chinese entrepreneurial state apparatus.[37] This mechanism has reactivated government spending in a region where many economies are crippled by high levels of public debt.[38] In turn, it has also opened debates about debt sustainability, and raised questions about the prices paid for projects that are not subject to open tenders. Moreover, while Chinese-financed infrastructures do not require wholesale macroeconomic reform, as traditional multilateral lending does, they necessitate spaces of exception.[39] Throughout the region, governments have waived labor regulations and taxes in Chinese construction sites.[40] In these spaces of exception, Chinese contractors are often exempted from custom duties on machinery and operate with large contingents of Chinese workers who are paid lower salaries than is customary in the Caribbean and who cannot join local independent unions.

Overall, while some of these trends may seem transformative, it is important to note that Chinese enterprises have readily engaged the region's liberal regimes. At the same time, they have also deployed innovative mechanisms that expand markets and with them, inevitably, processes of uneven development. In what follows, we address four themes prevalent in CCDT in order to explain and theorize the underlying dynamics of Chinese capitalism in the region.

EPISTEMIC DEPENDENCY

From Fanon to Beckford, or Garvey to Best, Caribbean thinkers placed emancipated political thought at the center of the struggle for postcolonial freedom. The question of epistemic dependency continues to burden regional politics—whether this is in the form of elevation of European cultural practices, or Washington's tutelage over regional development policy.[41] Within this context, the PRC's engagement in the region has paradoxically restored political leeway to central government leaders while simultaneously contributing to undermine emancipatory development approaches. We identify three emerging trends associated with China's engagement in the region: increased political maneuvering space away from U.S. and EU guidance, reinforcement of a narrow developmental trajectory, and weakening of social participation and subsequent consolidation of elite development thought.[42]

Regarding the first of these trends, the introduction of Chinese finance in the region has allowed regional leaders to triangulate in search of better credit terms.[43] The lack of macroeconomic conditionalities has turned many governments in the region towards Chinese banks, which have signed loans to CARICOM countries totalling around USD 8.9 billion since 2000.[44] Regional politicians frequently contrast the flexible Chinese approach with the rigidity of International Monetary Fund (IMF) lending.[45] Whereas Chinese banks also offer a fixed lending template, this is a model that in certain junctures suits the interests of regional economies better. Caribbean countries can now seek external finance without needing to embrace the wholesale neoliberalization of their economies. This is not merely a minor victory, as conditional lending has been a major source of discontent in the region since the debt crisis of the early 1980s.[46] Moreover, contrary to some commentary on China's "debt trap diplomacy," actual data suggests that Chinese policy banks are relatively open to renegotiating lending terms in favor of the borrowing country—particularly when other sources of finance are available.[47] Therefore, loans that are part of broader infrastructure deals are now popular across the region—while also heatedly debated after leading to seven cancelled or stalled projects at a value of USD 4.2 billion.[48]

There are, however, limits to the flexibility of Chinese loans, and indeed to their role as catalysts for emancipatory development models. The region experiences already high degrees of liberalization—particularly in terms of marketization and openness to trade and investment. In this context, Chinese loans have not been used to roll back neoliberal reform but to honor existing debts and increase public spending on infrastructure. Infrastructural loans are destined for culture and leisure (e.g. cricket stadiums and convention centers), government buildings, a small number of medical facilities, or, more often, a wide array of projects that seek to enhance comparative advantages within a liberal market order. In general, Chinese finance has allowed some regional economies to circumvent the liberalization and "good governance" agendas promoted by the IMF, World Bank, or Inter-American Development Bank. However, countries in the region have fallen short of completing a post-liberal turn. This stands in relative contrast to countries such as Ecuador under Rafael Correa's presidency, which galvanized Chinese finance to default on sovereign bonds in 2008 and embraced elements of an indigenous-inspired development agenda—even if failing to resolve key postcolonial and market inequalities.[49]

Chinese investments and finance are also limited in terms of content, and as such, they foment a narrow developmental template. Here, it is important to note that the current wave of Chinese investments as part of the Belt and Road Initiative responds not to benevolent goals but to a crisis of overaccumulation in China's construction sector.[50] Therefore, these investments are constrained to a limited number of sectors, and tend to emphasize infrastructural growth and natural resource exploitation. For example, in 2017 news emerged that the China Development Bank was helping the government of Grenada draft a national development strategy that involved the construction of a highway, a railway, a deep-water port, a wind farm, and the modernization of the Maurice Bishop International Airport—as well as a call to take strong measures to protect foreign investors.[51] While Grenada's Prime Minister would clarify that the plan would need to be ratified by the citizens of the country, the case highlighted China's infrastructural focus and Grenada's enduring dependence on external models of development.

China's engagement in the region has also narrowed the scope of social participation. Infrastructural agreements are reached in government-to-government negotiations and bypass open tenders. This has consolidated a model of top-down elite-led governance that eschews transparency and participation in terms of decision-making and scrutiny.[52] Projects are approved without standing the test of public deliberation, and as such they cannot serve as the basis for a truly emancipatory developmental paradigm. Some of the more recent plans to develop special economic zones with Chinese capital, such as the Phoenix Park in southern Trinidad, could indicate a resurgence of state economic planning. However, expectations still need to be matched by results, and there are major structural constraints that suggest success in these areas is unlikely (see below). Moreover, such success under the current socioeconomic circumstances would produce very uneven forms of development that would chiefly benefit transnational investors and local merchant capitalist elites.

In sum, a narrow developmental imaginary seems to coalesce when the capabilities and interests of Chinese investors are brought together with the constraints that local political and business elites face in envisioning long-term development goals. Girvan traced these constraints in Jamaica to the fact that the decades-long IMF control over economic policy had severely decimated the government's capacity for autonomous planning.[53] Other explanations can also be sought in the austerity measures that neoliberalized academia and pushed scholars and pundits to fund their research through consultancies to the World Bank, European Union, and other agencies;[54] in the immediate urgency for jobs and investment that tends to invite improvisation and hamper forward-looking strategies; or the prevalence of merchant capital and "conservative enterprise culture" among local bourgeoisies.[55]

PASSIVE INCORPORATION

Critical Caribbean Development Thought scholars have often remarked how the region was "passively incorporated" into the international economy, a trend that is not divorced from the question of epistemic dependency.[56] Passive incorporation entailed a structurally subservient economic role during the colonial years, persisting economic dependency in the immediate postcolonial period, and extreme vulnerability in the world market amid high levels of liberalization since the 1980s. Like other small states, Caribbean states share a series of characteristics that exacerbate their vulnerability: small populations, limited human and natural resources, small physical and economic size, distance from international markets, and a high level of openness. As a result, Caribbean economies find it difficult to cushion exogenous shocks, such as external economic crises, natural disasters, and climate change.[57] Whereas the nascent relation with China holds significant potential, several constraints block the region's ability to fully harness these opportunities. In what follows we highlight three of these constraints: the exacerbation of production hierarchies and trade imbalances, the structural limitations associated to the types of Chinese investment available in the region, and the ways in which low transparency impedes an effective regulation of investment flows.

Within a global liberal economic order, economic development in China has tended to exacerbate international hierarchies of production and trade imbalances. This is due first of all to the gradual relocation of value chains to Asia, and secondly to the ways in which urban and industrial growth in Asia has increased the pressure on commodity consumption. In this context, trade between China and the Caribbean has risen exponentially. Commodity exporters have enjoyed a growing demand for their products (Jamaica—aluminium oxide; Trinidad and Tobago—oil and gas; Suriname and Guyana—minerals and timber). Conversely, all Caribbean economies import finished manufactured goods from China, which has resulted in negative trade balances.[58] However, China cannot be seen as a buoyant "metropole" in the classical dependency theory sense. Rather than unilaterally concentrating financial and industrial capacity, China has emerged instead a hub for transnationalized production,[59] where a majority of the population endures, in fact, lower living standards than the citizens of many Caribbean countries. And yet, China's key economic features—a huge low-wage labor force and a high demand for commodities for urbanization and globalized production—have tended to crowd other developing economies out of manufacturing sectors and push them further into a commodity-producing role (while some low-cost manufacturing has in recent years moved from China into South and Southeast Asia).

Under late capitalism, dependency is not international towards a defined set of countries, but global towards mobile flows of transnational capital. Nonetheless, under these new conditions, the structural burdens of the Caribbean remain disturbingly similar to those discussed by classical CCDT authors. The region faces high current account trade imbalances, resulting from a low level of diversification of markets and products,[60] an erosion of preferences for agricultural commodities and garment exports,[61] and some of the highest debt burdens in the world relative to economic size.[62] As Caribbean states have been categorized as middle-income economies (and above), some have graduated from bilateral and multilateral grants and other forms of concessional funding. High levels of poverty and income inequality persist despite good progress on human development.[63] This situation is compounded by the burdensome conditions for the repayment of international loans. More recently, the region has faced the threat of termination or restriction of correspondent banking services and their participation in the global banking system because of the perception of high risk associated with doing business there.[64]

The focus of Chinese investments on infrastructures or consolidated sectors (natural resources or tourism) adds on to these trends. This was most acute in tourism-dependent countries in the aftermath of the 2007/2008 Global Financial Crisis, whereas waning resource prices at the end of the 2003–2013 resource boom took a dent on commodity exporters.[65] Chinese investments and loans in infrastructure surpass other areas of development, with 18 out of 23 loans of China's policy banks in the region concentrated in this sector.[66] Without careful planning, large infrastructural projects will struggle to generate sufficient economic capacity to make up for a rising debt burden. With the possible exception of a number of yet-to-be realized industrial parks, Chinese infrastructural projects have not been focused on the region's key economic constraints, such as promoting production or integrating the region into economies of scale.

The questions of labor opportunities and technology transfer have also been points of contention. Traditional sectors such as natural resource extraction and tourism are renowned for creating a limited number of jobs or placing locals in low-skilled service roles, while the control of these industries is typically in the hands of foreign investors.[67] Adding to these trends is the fact that many Chinese construction projects rely on contingents of Chinese labor, limiting local employment opportunities. This has been deemed inimical for development, even if the ratio of Chinese and local labor is subject to negotiations, with those projects employing a higher percentage of local workers resulting in higher costs.[68]

Overall, there are serious concerns that Chinese firms may be undercutting national contractors thanks to a series of privileges, rather than to their inherent competitiveness.[69] These include access to inexpensive credit, tax breaks, and duty-free concessions on equipment and materials, and exclusive access to cheap Chinese labor. The counterarguments here would be that infrastructures can improve productive capacity, and that the Chinese state has provided a number of scholarships for Caribbean citizens to pursue an education in the PRC. Yet, while improvements in logistics or skills training can indeed result in positive outcomes, the questions of foreign capital control and passive incorporation remain, while the Caribbean continues to endure one of the world's highest levels of youth unemployment and emigration of tertiary-educated and skilled individuals.[70]

THE (STILL) ELUSIVE QUEST FOR REGIONAL INTEGRATION

The small size of Caribbean economies and the fragmentation of their approach to global challenges have traditionally worked to reinforce some of the trends described above. In particular, the challenges to act as a market or institutional block weaken the region's negotiating capacity, impedes the development of economies of scale, and creates redundancies in the public sector. Thereby, regional integration and cross-regional solidarity have been central to emancipatory agendas. However, Girvan's[71] concern about the subordination of regional interests to national priorities is evident in the CARICOM-China relationship, and particularly given China's general avoidance of substantial regional agreements, preference for bilateral relations, and eschewing of civil society participation.

The project of regional integration (among largely the Anglophone Caribbean) faced challenges prior to China's rise as a significant economic force in the region. The CARICOM engages in a minimalist approach to integration and functions as a community of sovereign states based on a model of intergovernmentalism in which member states retain their sovereignty in cooperation arrangements.[72] The Caribbean Community also adopts a top-down approach to decision-making to the near exclusion of civil society and private sector engagement.[73] Moreover, the economic divergences and varying or competing interests between member states also cause problems for foreign policy coordination.[74]

China's mode of engagement has further fractured the regional project. The PRC has promoted a number of forums with diverse regional foci, but these exclude some CARICOM members. Caribbean leaders have participated in some of these, such as the Belt and Road Forum for International Cooperation, the CELAC-China Summit, and the China/Caribbean Economic and Trade Cooperation Forum. Excluding the latter, the role reserved for Caribbean states is nominal. Also, despite facilitating socialization, these forums are invariably focused on "generating good will and prestige for Beijing, despite the fact that the overwhelming content of relations [...] still flow through bilateral channels."[75] There is, in short, little substance beyond vague pledges towards the broader region that only materialize in bilateral negotiations. The forums are also notorious for their exclusion of civil society. The Caribbean Community should remain in this sense the prime forum for regional cooperation in the relation with China. However, CARICOM's interests are often "compromised as it attempts to coordinate and leverage such a large number of players with competing interests," something that has been exacerbated by the One China Policy.[76] Given that a number of members (Belize, Haiti, Saint Kitts and Nevis, Saint Lucia and Saint Vincent, and the Grenadines) do not hold formal diplomatic relations with the PRC, China's diplomacy bypasses CARICOM.

China's preference for bilateral engagement has also encouraged competition rather than collaboration for Chinese development cooperation.[77] In this regard, the prospect of CARICOM's leveraging the Belt and Road Initiative for regional connectivity looks dim, and it has instead fomented race-to-the-bottom competition among member countries to host some of China's projected infrastructures. These include, for example, a much-debated deep-water port to facilitate the distribution of container cargo throughout the region. Thus, China's approach has empowered central government elites through bilateral dealings while closing off spaces for supranational regulation and bottom-up civil society participation.[78] Combined with CARICOM's own shortcomings, China's growing role in the region is bound to make the possibility for effective regional cooperation an even more distant prospect.

THE POSTCOLONIAL CONDITION

So far, we have used the three broad themes above to unpack perennial questions in the relation between the Caribbean and the global economy, and to offer analytical insights into the region's contemporary relations with China. In this last section, we use the broad theme of the "postcolonial condition" to address the internal sociological makeup of the Caribbean region as evolved from former plantation economies and into their current hybrid selves. In particular, we want to clarify that the Caribbean is not only "impacted" by China, but that there exists a dialectical tension between the Caribbean's pre-existing social configurations and its shifting international linkages, particularly regarding questions of class relations, racial and gender dynamics, state configuration, and the co-constitution of national identities and modernity imaginaries. Therefore, Chinese businesses in the region are not only external vectors of change, but become local actors subject to transformation in the context of Caribbean social relations and agency. A first example can be found in the ill-fated investments of Complant International in the sugar sector in Jamaica. Complant arrived in Jamaica in 2010, acquiring three factories and leasing around 18,000 hectares in the south of the island for a period of 49 years. The ambitious plan to reduce operation costs by 30% and boost productivity did not yield the expected outcomes despite drastic cuts in the labor force.[79] Chinese entrepreneurs have blamed their poor performance on questions of low productivity and cultural barriers for communication.[80] However, what is missing in this analysis is an in-depth understanding of the socio-political complexity of the sector in its Jamaican context. The decline of productivity in the sugar sector following independence was met by Prime Minister Michael Manley's commitment to full employment as a form of social justice.[81] Building on this sensibility and electoral politics, the sector developed, orientated towards livelihood provision through political party–centred clientelistic networks with weak regulations and incentives, rather than towards global competitiveness.[82] Sugar, of course, also occupies a complex position in the region's historical memory, being at the same time central to its culture and economic organization and symbolic of severe labor exploitation in the plantation economies. In such a context, attempts to boost productivity such as the Chinese-led ones were necessarily in tension with local models of subsistence and sociocultural expectations.

However, pre-existing social structures do not necessarily act so as to block the advance of Chinese capital. In certain situations, they can actually facilitate it. Our second example is one of electoral politics. In Trinidad and Tobago, very much like Guyana, racial divisions translate into ethnic voting patterns. While the exact definition of, and attitudes towards ethnic difference have shifted through time,[83] today, there are in Trinidad and Tobago two major parties, one of them (the People's National Movement—PNM) having a majority Afro-Trinidadian electorate, and the other (the United National Congress—UNC) supported mostly by Indo-Trinidadians. In this context, the National Academy of Performing Arts was inaugurated in 2009 as the flagship project of Prime Minister Patrick Manning's (PNM) dealings with China. The project, constructed by the Shanghai Construction Group (SCG), was not exempt from controversies, on issues such as flaws in its original design, significant cost overruns, potential embezzlement, and the need to close down the building six years after its inauguration for major repairs.[84] Despite delivering severe critiques while in the opposition, Kamla Persad-Bissessar's administration (UNC, 2010–2015) would continue with the construction of a similar facility, the Southern Academy of Performing Arts (SAPA), also built by the SCG and completed in 2012. SAPA is located in the city of San Fernando, and the priority given by the UNC to this facility during their years in power has been associated with the complex geographical voting and ethnic patterns in Trinidad, with many UNC votes concentrated in the central plains since the 1960s.[85]

In sum, electoral politics pushed both major parties to rely on Chinese loans and corporations to augment their infrastructural legacies. Meanwhile, the Artists Coalition of Trinidad and Tobago protested the failure to consult local artists. Fundamentally challenging the Chinese infrastructure-based development approach, they reminded their country's leaders that "development is not about buildings. It is about people; the energy of the people."[86]

Conclusion

Critical Caribbean Development Thought offers invaluable insights into the analysis and theorization of Chinese capital in the Caribbean. Decades ago, regional scholars developed theories and analytical insights on epistemic dependency, passive incorporation, regional integration, and postcolonial development that are still relevant today, and which remain pertinent for understanding the region's contemporary relationship with China. Perhaps less evident is the fact that at least two aspects of these theories—epistemic dependency and passive incorporation—can also shed light on the dynamics of China's Belt and Road Initiative beyond the Caribbean. As the Chinese government invites its counterparts to join the Belt and Road Initiative and Chinese capital penetrates new markets, large swaths of the developing world are being passively integrated into the Chinese government's global vision and into the world market, often exacerbating structural constraints and epistemic dependency, and in the process hindering bottom-up processes of emancipatory development.

Decades ago, Latin American and Caribbean theories of dependency made the leap to become central to many debates on development and IR. The key in these theories was not that they were "Latin" or "Caribbean," but that they spoke to a universal experience of postcolonial capitalism in the Third World. In a similar vein, we hope to have demonstrated here that CCDT can help to analyze the many challenges and opportunities that the region faces in its relationship with China, and indeed to more broadly theorize the Belt and Road Initiative as a new mechanism of capitalist accumulation that remains, for the time being, unable to provide satisfactory answers to the emancipatory aspirations of the Third World.

NOTES

1. Paget Henry, "Caribbean Marxism: After the Neo Liberal and Linguistic Turns," in *New Caribbean Thought: A Reader*, ed. B. Meeks and F. Lindahl (Kingston: University of the West Indies Press, 2001), 325–354.
2. Norman Girvan, "New World and Its Critics," in *The Thought of New World: The Quest for Decolonisation*, ed. B. Meeks and N. Girvan (Kingston: Ian Randle Publishers, 2010), 3–29.
3. Norman Girvan, "Introduction to the New World," *New World Journal* (2020), https://newworldjournal.org/independence/introduction/.
4. Lloyd Best and Kari P. Levitt, *Essays on the Theory of Plantation Economy: A Historical and Institutional Approach to Caribbean Economic Development* (Jamaica, Barbados, and Trinidad and Tobago: The University of the West Indies Press, 2009).
5. Walter Rodney, "Contemporary Political Trends in the English-Speaking Caribbean," *The Black Scholar* 7, no. 1 (1975): 15–21; Walter Rodney, *How Europe Underdeveloped Africa* (London: Verso, 2018); Carl Stone, "Patterns of Insertion into the World Economy: Historical Profile and Contemporary Options," *Social and Economic Studies* 32, no. 3 (1983): 1–34; Carl Stone, "Prospects for Socialist Transformation: Reflections on Jamaica, Guyana and Grenada," in *A Caribbean Reader on Development*, ed. Judith Wedderburn (Kingston: Friedrich Ebert Stiftung, 1986), 20–48; Clive Y. Thomas, "The Caribbean State as Agent of Social Change," in *A Caribbean Reader on Development*, ed. Judith Wedderburn (Kingston: Friedrich Ebert Stiftung, 1986), 177–194.
6. Vladimir Lenin, *Imperialism, the Highest Stage of Capitalism* (Moscow: Progress, 1970).
7. Matthew Louis Bishop, *The Political Economy of Caribbean Development* (Basingstoke: Palgrave Macmillan, 2013); Stone, "Prospects for Socialist Transformation"; Thomas, "The Caribbean State."
8. W. Arthur Lewis, "Economic Development with Unlimited Supplies of Labour," *The Manchester School* 22, no. 2 (1954): 139–191.
9. Best and Levitt, *Essays on the Theory*, 196.
10. Norman Girvan, "Plantation Economy in an Age of Globalization (Foreword)," in *Essays on the Theory of Plantation Economy: A Historical and Institutional Approach to Caribbean Economic Development*, ed. Lloyd Best and Kari P. Levitt (Jamaica, Barbados, and Trinidad and Tobago: The University of the West Indies Press, 2009), xvii–xxii.
11. George L. Beckford, *Persistent Poverty: Underdevelopment in Plantation Economies of the Third World* (New York: Oxford University Press, 1972).
12. Beckford, *Persistent Poverty*, 234–35.
13. Frantz Fanon, *The Wretched of the Earth* (London: Penguin Books, 2001).
14. V. Eudine Barriteau, "The Relevance of Black Feminist Scholarship: A Caribbean Perspective," *Feminist Africa* 7 (2007): 9–31.
15. Lloyd Best, "Independent Thought and Caribbean Freedom," *New World Quarterly* 3, no. 4 (1967): 16–24; Patricia Northover and Micheline Crichlow, "Beyond Survival: Rethinking Strategies for 'Sustainable Economic Growth' in the Caribbean," *Social and Economic Studies* 54, no. 3 (2005): 247–274.
16. Girvan, "New World."

17. Nelson W. Keith and Novella Z. Keith, *The Social Origins of Democratic Socialism in Jamaica* (Philadelphia: Temple University Press, 1992).

18. Caribbean Development and Cooperation Committee (Economic Commission for Latin America and the Caribbean), *The Caribbean in the Decade of the 90s: Summary* (Port of Spain: ECLAC Sub-Regional Headquarters for the Caribbean, 2000).

19. Evelyne H. Stephens and John D. Stephens, *Democratic Socialism in Jamaica: The Political Movement and Social Transformation in Dependent Capitalism* (Princeton: Princeton University Press, 2017).

20. Stone, "Prospects for Socialist Transformation."

21. Stone, "Prospects for Socialist Transformation."

22. Brian Meeks, "Introduction: Remembering the New World," in *The Thought of New World: The Quest for Decolonisation,* ed. Brian Meeks and Norman Girvan (Kingston: Ian Randle Publishers, 2014).

23. Girvan, "New World," 11.

24. Girvan, "Plantation Economy"; Girvan, "New World"; Levitt, "In Search of Model IV," in *Essays on the Theory of Plantation Economy: A Historical and Institutional Approach to Caribbean Economic Development,* ed. Lloyd Best and Kari P. Levitt (Jamaica, Barbados, and Trinidad and Tobago: The University of the West Indies Press, 2009), 189–196; Brian Meeks, "Introduction: On the Bump of a Revival," in *New Caribbean Thought: A Reader,* ed. Brian Meeks and Folke Lindahl (Kingston: University of the West Indies Press, 2001), viii–xix; Henry, "Caribbean Marxism."

25. Levitt, "In Search of Model IV."

26. Girvan, "Plantation Economy," xxii.

27. Don Marshall, "At Whose Service? Caribbean State Posture, Merchant Capital and the Export Services Option," *Third World Quarterly* 23, no. 4 (2002): 725–751.

28. Toby Carroll, Ruben Gonzalez-Vicente, and Darryl S. L. Jarvis, "Capital, Conflict and Convergence: A Political Understanding of Neoliberalism and Its Relationship to Capitalist Transformation," *Globalizations* 16, no. 6 (2019): 778–803.

29. See ECLAC, *The Caribbean in the Decade.*

30. Adrian H. Hearn, "China, Global Governance and the Future of Cuba," *Journal of Current Chinese Affairs* 41, no. 1 (2012): 155–179.

31. Sarah Baksh et al., "A Proposal for a Comprehensive Economic and Trade Agreement between CARICOM and China," Sir Shirdaph Ramphal Centre and TradeLab, 2020, https://www.tradelab.org/single-post/2020/07/01/A-Proposal-for-a-Comprehensive-Economic-and-Trade-Agreement-between-CARICOM-And-China.

32. UN Comtrade, "2018 International Trade Statistics Yearbook, Volume 1: Trade by Country," United Nations, 2019, https://comtrade.un.org/pb/downloads/2018/VolI2018.pdf.

33. The figure is likely higher, but there is an issue of data unavailability, inaccuracy, and inconsistency across databases, particularly when it comes to the smallest Caribbean countries: American Enterprise Institute, "China Global Investment Tracker," 2020, https://www.aei.org/china-global-investment-tracker/.; Red ALC-China, "Monitor de la OFDI China en ALC," *Red ALC-China,* 2017, https://www.redalc-china.org/monitor/.

34. See Ching Kwan Lee, *The Specter of Global China: Politics, Labor and Foreign In-*

vestment in Africa (Chicago: University of Chicago Press, 2017), on the austere "managerial ethos" at Chinese companies in Zambia.

35. Usually at market rate; see Deborah Bräutigam and Kevin P. Gallagher, "Bartering Globalization: China's Commodity-Backed Finance in Africa and Latin America," *Global Policy* 5, no. 3 (2014): 346–352.

36. Ruben Gonzalez-Vicente, "Varieties of Capital and Predistribution: The Foundations of Chinese Infrastructural Investment in the Caribbean," *Made in China Journal* 5, no. 1 (2020): 164–168.

37. Ruben Gonzalez-Vicente, "The Internationalization of the Chinese State," *Political Geography* 30, no. 7 (2011): 402–411; Gonzalez-Vicente, "Varieties of Capital."

38. Cyrus Rustomjee, "Pathways through the Silent Crisis: Innovations to Resolve Unsustainable Caribbean Public Debt," *Center for International Governance Innovation Papers*, no. 125 (2017).

39. Ruben Gonzalez-Vicente, "Make Development Great Again? Accumulation Regimes, Spaces of Sovereign Exception and the Elite Development Paradigm of China's Belt and Road Initiative," *Business and Politics* 21, no. 4 (2019): 487–513.

40. Theodor Tudoroiu and Amanda R. Ramlogan, *The Myth of China's No Strings Attached Development Assistance: A Caribbean Case Study* (London: Lexington Books, 2020).

41. Norman Girvan, "50 Years of in-Dependence in Jamaica: Reflections," delivered at the SALISES 50–50 Conference "Critical Reflections in a Time of Uncertainty," Kingston, August 22, 2012.

42. See Benjamin Selwyn, "Elite Development Theory: A Labor-Centred Critique," *Third World Quarterly* 37, no. 5 (2016): 781–799.

43. Richard Bernal, *Dragon in the Caribbean: China's Global Re-Dimensioning—Challenges and Opportunities for the Caribbean* (Kingston: Ian Randle Publishers, 2016).

44. Jevon Minto, "Examining the Lending Practices of Chinese Policy Banks in the Caribbean (2000–2018)," in *China's Financing in Latin America and the Caribbean*, ed. E. Dussel Peters (México, D.F.: Universidad Nacional Autónoma de México, 2019a), 153–176.

45. "PM Browne Castigates IMF in Vision Statement," *Daily Observer*, August 20, 2014, https://www.antiguaobserver.com/pm-browne-castigates-imf-in-vision-statement/.

46. Stephanie Black, *Life and Debt* (New York: New Yorker Films, 2001).

47. Agatha Kratz, Allen Feng, and Logan Wright, "New data on the 'debt trap' question," *Rhodium Group*, April 29, 2019, https://rhg.com/research/new-data-on-the-debt-trap-question/.

48. Minto, "Examining the Lending Practices," 153.

49. Ruben Gonzalez-Vicente, "South-South Relations under World Market Capitalism: The State and the Elusive Promise of National Development in the China-Ecuador Resource-Development Nexus," *Review of International Political Economy* 24, no. 5 (2017): 881–903.

50. Gonzalez-Vicente, "Make Development Great Again?"

51. Stephen Chen, "China set to move into United States' Backyard with National Development Plan for Grenada," *South China Morning Post*, December 19, 2017, https://www.scmp.com/news/china/diplomacy-defence/article/2124925/china-set-move-united-states-backyard-national.

52. A. Raymond, "G2G Policy," *Afraraymond.net*, April 30, 2014, https://afraraymond.net/2014/04/30/g2g-policy/.
53. Girvan, "50 Years of in-Dependence."
54. Tennyson Joseph, "The Intellectual under Neo-Liberal Hegemony in the English-Speaking Caribbean," *Social and Economic Studies* 66, no. 3–4 (2017): 97–122.
55. Marshall, "At Whose Service?" 747.
56. Girvan, "Plantation Economy."
57. International Monetary Fund (IMF), *Macroeconomic Issues in Small States and Implications for Fund Engagement* (Washington, D.C.: IMF, 2013).
58. Raymer Díaz, "La Nueva Relación de América Latina y el Caribe Con China: ¿Integración o Desintegración Regional? El Caso de la CARICOM," in *La Nueva Relación Comercial de America Latina y el Caribe Con China: ¿Integración o Desintegración Regional?* ed. E. Dussel Peters (México, D.F.: Unión de Universidades de América Latina y el Caribe, 2016), 141–194; Mark D. Wenner and Dillon Clarke, *Chinese Rise in the Caribbean: What Does It Mean for Caribbean Stakeholders?* (Washington, D.C.: Inter-American Development Bank, 2016).
59. Ruben Gonzalez-Vicente, "The Political Economy of Sino-Peruvian Relations: A New Dependency?" *Journal of Current Chinese Affairs* 41, no. 1 (2012): 97–131.
60. ECLAC, *The Caribbean Outlook* (Santiago: ECLAC, 2018).
61. Matthew L. Bishop et al., *Caribbean Regional Integration: A Report by the UWI Institute of International Relations (IIR)* (Trinidad and Tobago: The Institute of International Relations, 2011), https://caricom.org/documents/9774-iirregionalintegrationreport final.pdf.
62. ECLAC, *The Caribbean Outlook*.
63. ECLAC, *The Caribbean Outlook*.
64. ECLAC, *The Caribbean Outlook*.
65. Inter-American Development Bank (IDB), "Development Challenges in the Caribbean," *Caribbean Region Quarterly Bulletin* 7, no. 3 (2018): 1–35; ECLAC, *The Caribbean Outlook*.
66. Kevin P. Gallagher and Margaret Myers, *China–Latin America Finance Database* (Washington, D.C.: Inter-American Dialogue, 2020).
67. Polly Pattullo, *Last Resorts: The Cost of Tourism in the Caribbean* (New York: Monthly Review Press, 2005).
68. Gonzalez-Vicente, "Make Development Great Again?"
69. Lenworth Kelly, "Level Construction Playing Field," *Jamaica Gleaner*, September 8, 2019, http://jamaica-gleaner.com/article/commentary/20190908/lenworth-kelly-level-construction-playing-field.
70. ECLAC, *The Caribbean Outlook*.
71. Norman Girvan, "CARICOM's Original Sin," paper presented at the CARICOM Regional Civil Society Consultation, Port of Spain, Trinidad and Tobago, February 10–11, 2011.
72. Wendy Grenade, "Regionalism and Sub-Regionalism in the Caribbean: Challenges and Prospects: Any Insights from Europe?" *Jean Monnet/Robert Schuman Paper Series* 11, no. 4 (2011): 2–25, http://aei.pitt.edu/33484/1/GrenadeCaribRegionalismLong 2011edi.pdf.
73. Bishop et al., *Caribbean Regional Integration*.

74. Girvan, "CARICOM's Original Sin"; Grenade, "Regionalism and Sub-Regionalism."

75. Chris Alden and Ana Cristina Alves, "China's Regional Forum Diplomacy in the Developing World: Socialisation and the 'Sinosphere,'" *Journal of Contemporary China* 26, no. 103 (2017): 151–165; see also T. Tudoroiu and A. Ramlogan, *China's International Socialization of Political Elites in the Belt and Road Initiative* (London: Routledge, 2002a).

76. Annita Montoute, *CARICOM's External Engagements: Prospects and Challenges for Caribbean Regional Integration and Development* (Brussels: German Marshall Fund and OCP Policy Centre, 2015), https://www.policycenter.ma/sites/default/files/OCPPC-GMF-1517v2.pdf.

77. Annita Montoute, "Caribbean-China Economic Relations: What Are the Implications?" *Caribbean Journal of International Relations and Diplomacy* 1, no. 1 (2013): 110–126.

78. Ruben Gonzalez-Vicente, "The Limits to China's Non-Interference Foreign Policy: Pro-State Interventionism and the Rescaling of Economic Governance," *Australian Journal of International Affairs* 69, no. 2 (2015): 205–233.

79. Jevon Minto, "The Impact of Chinese OFDI in Jamaica (2000–2017)," in *China's Foreign Investment in Latin America and the Caribbean: Conditions and Challenges*, ed. E. Dussel Peters (México, D.F.: Universidad Nacional Autónoma de México, 2019), 287–308.

80. Mark Titus, "Chinese Hit Hard by Realities in Local Sugar Industry," *Jamaica Gleaner*, November 21, 2017, http://jamaica-gleaner.com/article/lead-stories/20171121/chinese-hit-hard-realities-local-sugar-industry#.XVxzYcbz2Hw.email.

81. Michael Manley, *The Politics of Change: A Jamaican Testament* (London: Andre Deutsch, 1974), 90.

82. Israel Drori and Dennis J. Gayle, "Youth Employment Strategies in a Jamaican Sugar-Belt Area," *Human Organization* 49, no. 4 (1990): 364–372; Patricia Northover, "The Role of the State in Caribbean Agriculture in the New Liberal Trade Order," *Caribbean Dialogue* 7, no. 3/4 (2001): 73–98.

83. Sara Abraham, "The Shifting Sources of Racial Definition in Trinidad and Tobago, and Guyana: A Research Agenda," *Ethnic and Racial Studies* 24, no. 6 (2001): 979–997.

84. Willem Oosterveld, Eric Wilms, and Katarina Kertysova, *The Belt and Road Initiative Looks East: Political Implications of China's Economic Forays in the Caribbean and the South Pacific* (The Hague: The Hague Centre for Strategic Studies, 2018).

85. Ralph R. Premdas, "Elections, Identity and Ethnic Conflict in the Caribbean: The Trinidad Case," *Pouvoirs dans la Caraïbe Revue du Centre de Recherche sur les Pouvoirs Locaux dans la Caraïbe* 14, no. 14 (2004): 17–61.

86. Quoted in Andre Bagoo, "Stop the South Academy," *Newsday*, March 26, 2010, https://archives.newsday.co.tt/2010/03/26/stop-the-south-academy/.

ACKNOWLEDGMENTS

Like the Caribbean itself, this project was long in formation and dynamic, with meanings shifting as new points of emphasis were identified by our contributors. We first wish to thank our contributors for trusting us with their work, for seeing the larger vision of this project, and for being good interlocutors. Several contributors participated in a July 2022 symposium we organized and which was supported by H-Net's H-Empire, CLACSO's Crisis, Respuestas y Alternativas en el Gran Caribe Working Group, and the Lloyd Best Institute. Exercises like this helped initially constitute the lines of analysis in this collection.

The collection was conceived, drafted, edited, and reviewed during the global coronavirus pandemic. The wider conditions made things difficult for us as editors and for our contributors. An earlier version of the project had more attention to the politics of indigeneity while chapters on environmental matters were aggressively sought after. While practical matters intercede in all intellectual projects, no doubt this collection would be different if we faced "routine pressures" as opposed to the acute pressures of the last few years. Still, with the climate emergency hitting Caribbean shores, we hope for the return of "routine pressures."

And yet these same conditions pressed all of us to think in ways adjacent to relatively depoliticized language of "health and well-being" circulating in Caribbean states and international development circles. There is certainly a history, sociology, and politics to these categories. As each of our contributors show, Caribbean people are not "problems" to be "solved." Indeed, appreciating different interests is key for any agenda involving critical analysis. We wish to thank our contributors for repeatedly stressing that Caribbean people have politics.

Several people have helped support this project, chief among them Nate Holly, our editor at the University of Georgia Press. He deserves special mention for his support throughout the process, as does the team at the Press. The peer reviewers were excellent, and we greatly admired their knowledge of the Caribbean as well as their attentiveness to the argumentation in each chapter and the collection as a whole. We are humbled by the generous and patient guidance of Caribbeanists, and we wish to single out Jessica Byron, Maarit Forde, and Patricia Mohammed. Their friendship has greatly enriched our lives, and they have done scholarship worth emulating. All shortcomings and oversights are our own.

CONTRIBUTORS

Savrina Chinien is a lecturer in French, Francophone literatures, and film at the University of the West Indies, Trinidad and Tobago. She is an associate member of the CLARE/CELFA Research Group at Bordeaux University, France, and a member of the African Federation of Film Critics (AFFC), Dakar, Senegal. Her areas of research focus mainly on Francophone Caribbean and African literatures as well as Caribbean and African films.

Duane Edwards is a senior lecturer in the Department of Sociology at the University of Guyana where he teaches social theory and research. His research areas include ethnic dynamics in plural societies, the social implications of Caribbean philosophical and development thought, and sociocultural systems in developing societies. His substantive research explores the theoretical linkage between social differentiation and identity.

Maria Thérèse Gomes is a social worker. She holds an MSc. in social policy and planning from the London School of Economics and Political Science as well as a PhD and MSW from Howard University, where she previously taught. A proponent for social justice, Maria's research interests include elder caregiving, migration, and transnational social work.

Shelene Gomes is a lecturer of social anthropology and sociology at the University of the West Indies, Saint Augustine campus in Trinidad and Tobago. She is a 2023–24 visiting scholar-in-residence at the University of Cape Town and a member of the Globalization, Accessibility, Innovation and Care research network. Her monograph, *Cosmopolitanism from the Global South*, explores Caribbean migratory movements, specifically of Rastafari spiritual repatriation to Ethiopia, tracing the linkages between African diasporic imaginings and Caribbean cosmopolitan sensibilities.

Ruben Gonzalez-Vicente is associate professor in political economy at the University of Birmingham, where he chairs the Political Economy Research Group. His research interests include "South–South" relations, China's engagement in Latin America and the Caribbean, the role of natural resources in processes of development, and the transformation of politics and international relations under late capitalism. He is an editor at the People's Map of Global China and the Global China Pulse.

Contributors

Stanley H. Griffin is deputy dean, Undergraduate Matters, and senior lecturer based at the Department of Library and Information Studies at the University of the West Indies, Mona Jamaica Campus. His research interests include multiculturalism in Antigua and the Eastern Caribbean. His coedited books include *Decolonizing the Caribbean Record: An Archives Reader* and *Archiving Caribbean Identity: Records, Community, Memory*.

Julio César Guanche holds degrees from the University of Havana, the University of Valencia, and FLACSO-Ecuador. He has taught as an adjunct professor at the University of Havana and has published six books on Cuban politics and society. He has been a visiting scholar at Northwestern University, Harvard University, and the Max Planck Institute for European Legal History.

Juan Vicente Iborra Mallent is a PhD candidate in Latin American studies at National Autonomous University of Mexico (UNAM). His ongoing research focuses on the displacement of the Garifuna population from their lands on the island of Saint Vincent and their later deportation to the Bay of Honduras in 1797 during the Age of Revolutions.

Dylan Kerrigan is a Caribbeanist who has held positions at the University of the West Indies and the University of Leicester in anthropology, sociology, and criminology. Recently he has been working on a multidisciplinary team researching the definition, extent, experience, and treatment of mental health, neurological, and substance-use disorders in Guyana's jails, both among inmates and the people who work with them. He has coauthored three books and most recently published *Growing Up Woodbrook—A Tapestry of Then and Now: An Amazing Square Mile in History* in 2022.

Jack Menke is a social scientist whose work is focused on a pluralistic methodology and various academic innovations. He is professor of research methodology in multiethnic societies at the Anton de Kom University of Suriname. His book, *Sustainability at a Crossroads: Challenges and Opportunities of the Guiana Shield*, illustrates the positioning for action at a crossroads of an ongoing planetary degradation and the proposed path with novel solutions to enhance local, regional, and global development. His most recent book is *Suriname Land of Diversity: Balancing Nature and Culture for Development* (2024).

Annita Montoute is senior lecturer and interim director at the Institute of International Relations, the University of the West Indies, Saint Augustine Campus, Trinidad and Tobago. Her research interests are civil society and the Caribbean's external relations. She is the coauthor of *Changing Cuba-U.S. Relations: Implications for CARICOM States* and coeditor of *The ACP Group and the EU Development Partnership: Beyond the North-South Debate*. She was previously a research fellow at the European Centre for Development Policy Management in Maastricht, Netherlands. She holds a PhD in international relations from the University of the West Indies.

Antonia Mungal holds a BA in communication studies from the University of the West Indies, Saint Augustine campus, Trinidad and Tobago. She works as a creative copywriter with a focus on naturopathic care and practices.

Kimberly Palmer is from Saint Vincent and the Grenadines and holds a PhD in environmental studies from York University in Toronto, Canada. An interdisciplinary scholar, she examines the intersections of class, race, gender, space, and place in the circum-Caribbean. She has published articles on Garifuna social movements in *Caribbean Quarterly*, *Caribbean InTransit*, and *Nómadas*.

Maikel Pons-Giralt is a Black and migrant Cuban, anti-racist activist, and educator. He holds a PhD in education from the Federal University of Minas Gerais, Brazil. He is a visiting professor at the University of Santa Cruz do Sul and a research associate at CAPES Foundation, Brazil. He completed a postdoctorate at the University of São Paulo. He examines the intersection of race, class, education, and migration in Latin American and Caribbean contexts, particularly in contemporary Cuba.

Amílcar Peter Sanatan is an interdisciplinary Caribbean artist, educator, and activist. He is a PhD candidate in cultural studies at the University of the West Indies, Saint Augustine Campus. His research and social leadership promote the transformation of men and masculinities in the Caribbean and the Americas, gender justice, literary and performing arts, youth and student development, and human geography.

Gerald Stell worked at the University of the West Indies (Mona, Jamaica, and Saint Augustine, Trinidad and Tobago) between 2013 and 2017. He is currently an associate professor of sociolinguistics at the University of Lausanne. His area of specialization is language contact and the ways that languages and "ways of speaking" are perceptually associated with postcolonial ethnoracial constructs and creatively deployed to negotiate them.

Jerome Teelucksingh is a senior lecturer from the University of the West Indies in Trinidad and Tobago. His books include *Ideology, Politics, and Radicalism of the Afro-Caribbean*, *Civil Rights in America and the Caribbean, 1950s–2010s*, and *Labour and the Decolonization Struggle in Trinidad and Tobago*. He served as the deputy chair of the Board of Governors of Cipriani College of Labour and Co-operative Studies in Trinidad and Tobago and was a member of Leverhulme Project Advisory Board for the project Trade Unions and Spaces of Democratization in Britain, the Caribbean, and Greece.

Brendan Jamal Thornton is an anthropologist and associate professor of religious studies at the University of North Carolina at Chapel Hill. His scholarship on religion and culture in the Caribbean is interdisciplinary and has been published in *Anthropological Quarterly*, *Journal of the American Academy of Religion*, *Latin American Research Review*, and elsewhere. He is the author of the award-winning book *Negotiating Respect: Pentecostalism, Masculinity, and the Politics of Spiritual Authority in the Dominican Republic*.

Scott Timcke is a sociologist working on political economy, development, economic history, and imperialism. He is a research associate with the University of Johannesburg's Centre for Social Change and affiliated with the Center for Information, Technology, and Public Life at the University of North Carolina at Chapel Hill. His third book, *The Political Economy of Fortune and Misfortune*, was released in 2023.

Diego I. Ubiera is associate professor of Latin American and world literatures at Fitchburg State University. His research and teaching interests include Latin American and Caribbean literature, multiethnic American literature, critical pedagogy, and world literature.

Nadia Whiteman-Charles is an assistant professor in the Department of Africana Studies at the University of Arizona. She previously taught at the University of the West Indies for nine years. She has also worked as a research and brand insights specialist in the Caribbean's advertising sector. Her research interests include Black nationalism, Caribbean music scenes, and consumer practices.

INDEX

A Partnership for National Unity (APNU), 254, 269, 282, 285, 286; Guyana elections, 21, 254, 269–95
abjection, 2, 4, 131
accumulation of capital, 19, 35, 45, 296
Afro-Saxon, 27, 38, 39, 40, 42, 43, 44, 47, 48, 52; elitism, 30–32
aging populations, 100, 109, 110, 118
agriculture, 32, 70, 94, 97, 167, 196, 281, 282, 360; bauxite, 6, 296, 298, 299, 300, 303
alienation, 16, 89, 116, 189, 190, 210, 317, 330
Allahar, Anton, 2, 51, 263, 265, 329, 331, 338, 339
Alliance for Change (AFC), 254, 269; Guyana elections, 21, 254, 269–95
alterity, 236–37, 241
Amerindian/Indigenous, 275–78, 281–82; Black, 83; electorate, 285, 289; genocide, 59, 107; identity, 213, 232; *indio/a*, 232, 235, 248n20; Kalinago, 58, 81; lingua franca, 162; organizing, 83–84, 152; race/ethnicity, 163–64, 223n5; state conflict, 2, 6, 300; technologies, 94
androcentric, 144, 146, 152; scholarship, 143–60
Anglo-American Caribbean Commission, 38, 41
Anglo-Caribbean, 8, 12, 16, 21, 22, 251, 252, 260, 261, 324, 331
Anguilla, 54, 59, 66, 70, 71, 73
anthropology, 106, 228, 234, 249n32. *See also* West Indies
anticapitalism, 9, 15, 16, 22, 196, 327, 335
anticolonial nationalism ("bakra basi keba"), 307. *See also* Suriname

Antigua and Barbuda, 54–78
Antigua and Barbuda Bulletin, 63, 67, 74, 75
anti-system politics, 314–40
apprenticeship, 55, 319; indentureship, 28, 33, 107–8, 252–53; postemancipation, 107
Aucan, 165–77; Kwinti, 165. *See also* ethnicity
austerity, 315, 317, 323, 326, 331, 334, 335, 345, 349
authenticity, 4, 91, 201–26
autocratic military, leftist populist regimes, 298; Nieuw Front Government, 301

banana, 5, 79, 81, 82, 86, 91, 94. *See also* agriculture
Barbados, 13, 28, 149, 270; climate change in, 6; versus Jamaica, 317, 344; music in, 205; versus smaller colonies, 54, 58, 59; tourism in, 345, 346
Belize, 6, 81, 353
Belt and Road Initiative, 355
Beyond a Boundary (James), 259
Bhabha, Homi, 182, 190, 194, 197
Bhattacharya, Tithi, 9
Binda, Ramnarine, 255
Bird, Sir Vere Cornwall, 61–62
Black Jacobins, The (James), 1, 3
Black middle class, 36
Black nationalism, 2
Black Power movement, 43, 153, 232, 262, 324; Black Power revolt, 328
Blackness, 52n65, 56, 91
Bonilla, Manuel, 81
Bourdieu, Pierre, 185, 190–91, 207, 212–13
bourgeoisie, 331
Bouterse, Desi, 303, 305. *See also* Suriname

Brazil (Brazilians), 8, 122, 163
bribery, 13
British Labour Party (BLP), 36–37
British West Indies, 19, 33, 54, 58, 107, 260
Brown, Gaston, 68
Brunswijk, Ronnie, 305. *See also* Suriname
bureaucracy, 10, 43, 65, 260, 325
Burnham, Forbes, 64, 143, 149, 344; tyranny of, 254. *See also* Guyana
Burnham, Viola, 143. *See also* Guyana

Canada, 6, 19, 47, 106, 254, 262, 270, 332
capitalist logic of work and kinship, 20, 100, 116
care, 100–119, 149, 150, 151
Caribbean Community (CARICOM), 63, 270, 352–53
Caribbean Development Bank, 6
Caribbean Left, 143–60
Caribscape, 192, 194
Carnival, 13, 15, 39–40, 45, 64, 114–15, 233; Crop Over, 13. *See also* Barbados
cartel politics, 315, 318
Castro, Fidel, 123–25, 143
Cayman Islands, 6
census, 103, 122, 127; Guyana population and housing, 275–77, 281; Suriname's 2012 census, 311
Césaire, Aimé, 4, 181, 183, 184
Chile, 8
Chinese state: People's Republic of China, 333, 341–60; Uyghur, 7
Chlordecone, 6
Cipriani, Andrew Arthur, 27–53
citizenship (legal), 10, 47, 64, 69, 88, 237, 330, 335; cultural citizenship, 11, 195, 229, 316; gendered, 101; migration, 62; race, 96
citizenship by investment, 5
civic ascription, 4, 17, 49, 120, 333
civic life, 13
civic nationalism, 214
clientelism, 331
climate change, 6–7, 10, 350
coalition workers' unions, 147; political, 254, 269, 286–87, 297, 299–302, 329
cocoa industry, 29–30; cocoa estate, 30, 33; "golden years of cocoa in Trinidad," 29
collective memory, 183–84
colonial honorifics, 16
Colonial Office, 31, 33–34
coloniality of power, 20, 181–200
common civilization, 7; Black civilization, 184; colonized civilization, 183; progressive civilization, 262
communication accommodation theory (CAT), 162
Community of Morenos Naturales of Cristales and Río Negro (Trujillo), 81. *See also* Garifuna
comprador class, 8, 31
consociationalism, 297–99, 306, 310n6, 311n9; critique, 305; democracy, 274, 278, 283, 301; regimes, 296, 308; theory, 309–10
cooperative sector, 126
corruption, 79, 239, 243, 286, 299, 300, 305, 308, 310, 314, 332; anticorruption, 332
counterculture, 188; dread culture, 203; rude boy culture, 203. *See also* Jamaica
COVID-19, 94, 103, 104, 117n8, 330, 334; coronavirus, 323, 327, 330; lockdown, 95, 261
Craig, Susan, 36
Creft, Jacqueline, 1, 143, 149
creolization, 2, 210, 228, 241, 251; *Boslandscreool* ("Bushland Creole"), 169; creole language, 190–91; creole nationalism, 27, 30–32, 46–48, 251; creole white, 190; Créolité literary movement, 181; *Éloge de la Créolité*, 184–90; French Creole, 29–32, 34, 36, 49n6; narrow creolization, 136, 252
cricket, 66, 259, 260, 346, 348; Rohan Kanhai, 259–60; Sonny Ramadhin, 260
crime, 5, 183, 314; against humanity, 46
critical Caribbean development thought (CCDT), 341–60
cronyism, 44
Crown Colony, 60
Cuba, 7, 20, 58, 86, 120; Fidel Castro, 123–24, 143

debt, 330
decarbonization, 22
decolonization, 334; decolonial futures, 92
de-democratization, 11, 331
demobilization, 33
democracy, 15–18, 21, 130–31, 153, 274–83; Caribbean neoliberal democracy, 318–19; democracy dividend, 323–31; political democracy, 21; social democracy, 336
diaspora, 19, 86; diasporic communities, 13, 14, 121, 235, 262. *See* Garifuna
Discharged Soldiers Central Authority, 34

Index **369**

disinformation, 85. *See also* Honduras; property relations
displacement, 80–91, 96–97, 194
disposability, 4
diversality, 188, 192, 195–96
division of labor, 96, 100–101, 108, 115, 151–52, 182, 188, 193
DOM (*département d'outre-mer*), 182
Dominica, 61, 66–67, 69, 71, 149
Dominican Republic, 20, 55, 65, 86, 227–44
dominicanidad, 227–50. *See also* Dominican Republic
dual economy, 325
Dutch disease, 43
Duvalier, François, 1; Haiti, 227–50

East Indians, 180n31, 253, 256; in ethnic hierarchy, 38, 45, 60, 275–78; as plantation laborer, 28, 35, 66; in Suriname politics, 297–99, 302, 306, 311n10
Eastern Caribbean, 54–78, 81
elderly, 20, 154, 206, 300; care for, 101, 103, 107, 109, 111; COVID-19, 100; in Suriname, 171, 174, 175, 176, 178
Emancipation (from slavery), 13, 17, 28, 38, 55, 108, 130, 156, 302, 306; universal human emancipation, 3; Taubira law, 183
enclave economies, 319
energy sector, 325, 327, energy extraction, 325; hydroelectricity, 299; oil, 332; wind, 349. *See also* Suriname; Trinidad
enslavement, 12; colonialism, 21, 60, 181; indentureship, 252; as institution, legacy of, 316, 319; modes of domination, 7; sugar production, 122
epistemological project, 17, 129, 183; epistemology, 193, 317; social epistemology, 333
estate, 28; employment, 320; exports, 6, 122; historical memory, 354; labor, 66; sugar industry, 5, 29, 63, 254, 320, 333; sugar plantation, 86
ethnicity, 243, 254, 272, 275–76, 328; consociationalism, 297; ethnic entrepreneurship, 262, 280, 329; gender and, 166; language and, 20, 161–78; power-sharing, 306; race and, 121–23, 277, 279, 282; voting, 302
ethnography, 241
ethnolinguistic vitality, 163; ethnic autochthonous policies and groups, 83. *See also* diaspora; Garifuna

Eurocentric, 14
extraction, 320; mining, 303

family and kinship, 12, 20, 100, 107–15, 240, 276–78, 280; matrifocal, 107; race and ethnicity, 235
Fanon, Frantz, 1, 4, 55, 183, 343, 347
Federation of the West Indies, 42
feminism, 132, 148; antifeminism, 144; Caribbean, 100; Marxism and, 154–55; socialist, 144, 146, 148; second wave, 149
folklore, 64, 233; Institute of Ethnology and Folklore, 124. *See also* Cuba
food security, 94
Fort-de-France, Martinique, 183
freedom myth, 11; freedom of movement, 65, 69 (*see also* migration)); Bob Marley, 12, 203, 204; Songs of Freedom, 12 (*see also* Garifuna)
French Republic, 193
fungibility, 4. *See also* Marxism

Garifuna, 79–99; Bay of Trujillo, 79–99; Delcio, 87–89, 92, 97n1; dreadlocks, 89, 259; Gari Rastas, 80–95; Garinagu, 79–95; Julián, 89, 91, 92. *See also* Honduras
gatekeeping, 11, 16, 227, 228, 230, 236, 240, 242–44
GDP (gross domestic product), 6, 269, 281, 321, 323, 325, 332
gender equity, 10; gender oppression, 12
genocide, 2; Indigenous, 185, 252
gentrification, 27–53, 329
global capitalism, 8, 32, 111, 273, 296, 298–300, 302, 308, 309
global commodity chains, 29
Global North, 14, 111, 154, 315
Global South, 9, 102, 108, 117, 118, 153, 183
globalization, 9, 192, 194, 242, 244n2, 319
Gramsci, Antonio, 31, 36, 39, 235, 307; hegemony, 33, 39; historical bloc, 31, 32, 36, 39, 43
Granger, David, 254
grassroots, 72, 148, 153
Great Commodification, 317–18
Greater Antilles, 58
Grenada, 2, 66, 69, 71, 143–60, 344, 346, 348, 349; Grenada Revolution, 20, 143–60
Grenada Manual and Mental Workers Union, 146
Grenada Students' Association of Trinidad and Tobago, 154

Grenada United Labour Party (GULP), 147
Grenada Women's League, 147
Guadeloupe, 6, 58, 70, 182, 186
Guatemala, 81
Guyana, 2, 4, 6, 164; British Guiana, 66, 253–54; independence, 64; politics, 259; race, 253; 2020 elections, 21, 254, 269–95
Guyana Elections Commission (GECOM), 270

Hall, Stuart, 55–56
health care, 66, 89, 148. *See also* care
heritage languages, 20, 161–64, 170–78
Hintzen, Percy, 253, 273
Hispaniola, 58, 230, 243
historical materialism, 17–18
historiography, 11–12, 143, 251–68; feminist, 144, 145–56; gendered, 20; leftist, 145; social, 27, 47
Honduras, 79–99; Manuel Bonilla, 81; 2009 coup d'état, 19
Hopkin, Jonathan, 315–40
Hoyte, Desmond. *See* Guyana
Hudson, Peter, 9
Hurricane Mitch, 87. *See also* Honduras
hypernationalism, 214, 222

identidad, 233, 235, 238
ideology, 3, 32–35, 39, 116, 253, 317; bourgeois, 327–31; dominant, 144, 307; leftist populist, 306–8; masculinist, 155; national, 121, 130–31. *See also* Cuba; Gramsci, Antonio
imagined place, 42; place-making, 92, 94; post-plantation geographies, 91; Sylvia Wynter, 92
imperialism, 16, 18, 42, 93, 96, 187, 192, 255; anti-imperialism, 17; cultural, 20, 206, 210–14; economic, 194, 342; French, 191; military, 15
incarceration, 86; mass, 89; self-incarceration, 192
informal economy, 88–89
International Monetary Fund (IMF), 321, 331, 341–60

Jagan, Cheddi, 143, 253–54. *See also* Guyana
Jagan, Janet, 143. *See also* Guyana
Jamaica, 7, 15; Kingston, 202–3, 206–7, 315
Jamaica Labour Party (JLP), 321
Jamaica Reggae Industry Association (JaRIA), 206–7

James, C. L. R., 1–26, 43, 52, 257–58, 260, 330–31, 336; *Beyond a Boundary*, 259; *The Black Jacobins*, 1, 3
Jones, Claudia, 1, 146

Kamau Brathwaite, Edward, 90, 223n5
Kanhai, Rohan, 259–60
Kelley, Robin, 9
Kingston, Jamaica, 202–3, 206–7, 315
knowledge economy, 16

labor of love, 100, 113; reserve army of labor, 96, 110. *See also* Marxism
Lamming, George, 41, 153
Latin America and the Caribbean (LAC), 228, 241, 246, 355, 357, 358, 360
Law of Free Prior and Informed Consultation (FPIC), 83. *See also* Garifuna
Leeward Islands, 54, 58, 59, 65, 66, 54–78
Leeward Islands Act, 60
liberation, 4, 12, 148, 154, 155, 196, 237, 312n27; of enslaved, 130, 132; national, 151, 315, 320; racial, 12; women's, 151
Little Carib Theatre, 38. *See also* Trinidad

mainstream, 145, 201–26, 222, 223, 229, 318
Manley, Michael, 320–21. *See also* Jamaica
Manley, Norman, 320–21. *See also* Jamaica
Marley, Bob, 12, 203, 204
Maroon, 5, 96, 133, 161–80, 302, 311n10, 317; cimarrón, 132–33; maroonage, 132–34
Mars, Perry, 273. *See also* Guyana
Martinique, 6, 20, 58, 70, 181–88, 196; Fort-de-France, 183
Marxism: critique of capitalism, 9, 17, 146, 316, 327; limits of Marxism-Leninism, 146–48, 154
masculinism, 143–60
McBurnie, Beryl, 39, 40
media, 15, 44, 87, 131, 168, 206, 210, 215, 229, 231, 271, 314
medicinal herbs, 95
mestizo, 120, 126, 127, 136; class, 35–36, 137, 260; colored social mobility, 28–30, 33; colored/white binary, 34; "culture," 125–27, 137; mulatto race, 49n6, 55, 123; reformers, 260
methodology, 18, 105, 124, 145, 146, 165, 241, 344; critical reflexivity, 236; "friend of a friend," 165; interview, 102, 103, 106, 113, 165, 166, 189, 202, 212, 213;

method, 1, 17, 72, 80, 145; positionality, 105, 166; self-reflexivity, 107
migration (colonialism), 59, 107; care-motivated, 100–103; citizenship and policy, 62–67; *coyotaje* (migrant smuggling), 89; deportation, 80–97; forced, 19; transnational, 234–44
military, 31, 32, 135, 153, 311n9; National Security Doctrine, 82; U.S. imperialism, 15, 68, 82, 86. *See also* Honduras
military regime, 21, 296, 298–303, 306, 308, 309; military leadership, 300; postmilitary, 299, 306
miscegenation, 56, 121, 122, 125, 127–29
modernization, 12, 14, 349
Montserrat (Montserratians), 54, 58–59, 61, 66–69, 71
multiculturalism, 12, 39, 45, 73n1, 233
mystification, 17, 42, 43, 110; demystification, 239
mythologization, 251–52

National Agrarian Institute (INA), Santa Fe, 82. *See also* migration
National Theater of Cuba, 124
National Women's Organisation, 148, 155
nationness, 182, 194; Homi Bhabha, 182, 190, 194, 197
neocolonialism, 6, 27, 44, 45, 123, 148; neocolonial economic inequality, 42
neoliberal democracy, 18, 22, 319
neo-modernization, 333
Nettleford, Rex, 55, 65, 213, 223
New Jewel Movement, 2, 147, 153. *See also* Grenada
New World Group, 2, 341–44
Nicaragua, 81–82; revolution, 147

One China Policy, 353
Organization of Eastern Caribbean States (OECS), 57
other/alter, 236–37, 241

palo, 233. *See also* Dominican Republic
Pan Africanism, 196n3, 236; Négritude, 181–82, 184–85; Pan-African thought, 13
Panday, Basdeo, 256, 258, 324, 328. *See also* Trinidad and Tobago
Partnership for National Unity, A (APNU), 254, 269, 282, 285, 286; Guyana elections, 21, 254, 269–95
patriarchy, 327; misogyny, 153

Patterson, Orlando, 256, 315, 316
pauperization, 29, 31
peasantry, 147, 195, 329; free, 343; Indo-peasantry, 329; movements, 82; slave proto peasantry, 107, 319. *See also* plantation society
pension, 104, 110, 112
People's National Movement, 40, 255, 324, 354. *See also* Trinidad and Tobago
People's National Party, 320–21. *See also* Jamaica
People's Progressive Party/Civic (PPP), 269; Guyana elections, 21, 254, 269–95
People's Revolutionary Government, 146, 147, 149
Persad-Bissessar, Kamla, 256, 354. *See also* Trinidad and Tobago
Peru, 8, 58
petro-capitalism, 323
plantation society, 101–7; plantation economy, 96, 213, 342, 343
plantocracy, 30, 147, 210; British plantocracy, 29
platforms, 320, 331. *See also* politics
political economy, 314–40; passive incorporation, 344, 349, 352, 355
politics: of difference, 202, 223; of voice, 154, 182, 185, 222, 238, 298, 314–40
populism, 297, 319
poquiteros, 81
postcolonial predicament, 21, 314–40. *See also* Patterson, Orlando
postconsumerism, 22
postslavery, 184
precarity, 318
prison industrial complex, 88–89, 96
private/public sphere, 102
proletarianization, 327
property relations (neoliberalism), 8, 19, 30, 316–17, 330; ownership, 65–69, 83–85, 309, 233; property rights, 19, 195
protoliberalism, 315
public service, 168, 254, 256, 284
Puerto Rico, 5, 58, 86, 243, 262

racial capitalism, 9, 21, 252
Ramadhin, Sonny, 260
Ramphal, Sir Shridath, 56, 59–60. *See also* Barbados; Guyana
recession: Indo-Trinidadian, 43, 101, 148, 321–22, 326; of 2008, 325, 332
Regiment, 33; contemporary West Indies,

319; postcolonial West Indies, 251; West Indies Associated States Council of Ministers, 69; West Indies Associated States Supreme Court, 71; West Indies Federation, 61, 69, 72, 107, 337n19
religion, 240, 242, 272, 275; anti-secularism, 258; Christianity, 164, 277; Hinduism, 164; as institution, 278; Islam, 164; minority status, 258; politics, 207; race/ethnicity, 276–78
rent seeking, 6, 281, 314, 332
reparations, 6, 7, 18, 333, 335
republic, 130, 132
Returned Soldiers and Sailors Council, 33. *See also* Trinidad
revolution, 320; revolutionary politics, 12, 151; revolutionary strategy, 11; revolutionary tales, 20
Rodney, Walter, 342
roots, 56, 87, 91–93, 235, 328, 343; cultural, 45, 80, 81, 253; familial, 65, 67
ruling class, 2, 11, 22; Jamaica, 209; local, 40; metropolitan, 33; Trinidad and Tobago, 327

Saint Kitts, Saint Christopher, and Nevis, 5, 54, 58–59, 61, 66, 71, 353
Saint Lucia, 5, 69, 71, 205, 259, 353
Saint Vincent and the Grenadines, 69, 71, 81, 149, 259, 353; Yurumein, 81
Sankeralli, Burton, 43
Santokhi, Chan, 300. *See also* politics; Suriname
Second Carib War, 81
segregation (race), 123; ethnic segregation, 168, 274; segregationist heritage, 168
Selvon, Samuel, 60
social contract, 308
social history, 251–68
social movement, 93, 144, 239; #GhettoLivesMatter, 334. *See also* Jamaica
social progressivism, 11; social pact, 318
social sciences, 17, 116, 230, 236, 244
social services, 335
social structure, 19, 21, 31, 49n6, 123, 196, 262, 272, 275, 279, 287, 354
social transformation, 281
social wages, 11
socialism, 143–60, 341. *See also* Grenada
sociolinguistics, 161, 165; ethnolinguistic group, 162–63, 165, 167, 176; macrosociolinguistic, 166, 167;

sociolinguistic literature, 166; sociolinguistic studies, 162
Soldiers and Sailors Union, 32. *See also* Trinidad
spatial imaginaries, 14, 94
Special Development Economic Zones (ZEDE), 84, 96. *See also* Garifuna; Honduras
spectacles of accumulation, 14
state violence, 19, 27, 147; gender-based violence, 314
states, 5, 72, 143, 162–63; Afro-Saxon, 38; condition, 353–55; elite, 31; emigration, 107; era, 252, 255, 257; experience, 58; Grenada, 146; ideology, 32; society and economy, 44, 101, 147, 151, 153; theory, 16, 192, 194, 234–35; West Indies, 251
steel band, 39
stigma, 4, 11, 80, 89, 90, 94, 169, 171, 232
stratification (social), 27, 38, 48, 164; class, 162; economic, 29; inequality, 123; racial, 55
strike, 35–36, 82, 182, 186–87, 195; march, 83, 308; social protests, 120
subaltern, 187, 235
subculture, 202, 203, 234
substructure, 271–72, 274–75, 278, 288, 290
suburban, 67, 329
sugar production, 2, 30, 58–59, 63, 66, 186, 343, 346; declining production, 354
Suriname, 4–5, 296–313; Euro-Surinamese, 165, 167–68, 177; political economy, 21; Surinamese language practices, 165; Suriname-Guyana basin, 6
surveillance, 15, 183, 303, 329
symbolism: class, 10, 16, 30, 105; class decomposition, 46–47; history, 31; language, 161, 170; literary critique, 188; music, 206, 210, 211–13, 219; nation building, 14–15, 38–40, 45, 134, 253, 260; political organization, 35–36; of sugar, 354; symbolic capital, 183–85, 190, 213, 223, 233; symbolic violence, 191
taste, 4, 29, 121, 202; music tastes, 204–10, 212–13, 217–19, 221–23
tax, 334–35
Third World, 298, 341–60
tourism, 320, 323 351; drug trafficking, 296; narco-capitalism, 314
trade unions, 36, 41, 256, 260, 315, 344; collective bargaining, 314–15
Treaty of Basseterre, 69–70; Revised Treaty of Basseterre's Economic Union, 60

Trinidad, 19, 27–53, 72, 149, 154, 205, 206, 253, 255, 258; care in, 100–119; versus Jamaica, 21, 61; music in, 205, 206; versus smaller colonies, 54
Trinidad and Tobago, 256, 257, 251–68, 286, 314–40
Trinidad Workingmen's Association (TWA), 32

unemployment, 314, 332
University of the West Indies, 63, 154, 344; UWI Socialist Student Conference, 154
University of Woodford Square, 40. *See also* Trinidad
urbanization, 108, 164, 321, 332, 350; urban studies, 162

violence, 34, 44–45, 85, 124, 185; crime, 46; discourse, 237; gender-based, 314; migration, 96; racial/ethnic, 64, 128; state, 19, 27, 46, 64, 147, 254, 271, 286, 291n1, 331–32; symbolic, 191–94, 237
Virgin Islands, 54, 61, 66; British Virgin Islands, 70–71
Wani Lee land recuperation, 79. *See also* Honduras
West Indies, 40–42, 49n6, 54, 58, 61, 258; British West Indies, 19, 260

whiteness, 56, 169; blanco/a (white) 232; white supremacy, 2; whiteness studies, 241
Williams, Eric, 9, 12, 47, 255; Afro-Saxon, 43; Woodbrook, 30–32, 38–39, 41–42
Wilson Gilmore, Ruth, 9
Wynter, Sylvia, 92
Woodbrook, 27–53. *See also* Trinidad
Woodford Square, 40, 41
Working People's Alliance, 2, 151. *See also* Guyana
working-class aspiration, 333; consciousness, 33, 35; historiography, 255, 262; political class, 3, 22, 28–29, 36–38, 42, 52, 209, 329; race, 41, 206, 255, 328; solidarity, 31–33, 252, 206
World Bank, 331
World War I, 32
World War II, 68, 86, 157n21, 164, 252, 260, 302, 318, 343
world-system, 182, 184, 186, 193, 273

xenophobia, 329; anti-Haitianism, 230, 232, 239

Zapatista, 152